Contemporary Chinese Civil and Commercial Law

Loic Cadiet · Yulin Fu
Editors

On Judicial Management from Comparative Perspective

International Association of Procedural Law Conference (8–10 Nov. 2017, Tianjin, PRC)

Springer

Editors
Loic Cadiet
Sorbonne Law School
Université Paris 1 Panthéon-Sorbonne
Paris, France

Yulin Fu
Peking University Law School
Beijing, China

Executive Editor
Zhixun Cao
Peking University Law School
Beijing, China

ISSN 2524-6194 ISSN 2524-6208 (electronic)
Contemporary Chinese Civil and Commercial Law
ISBN 978-981-19-8672-7 ISBN 978-981-19-8673-4 (eBook)
https://doi.org/10.1007/978-981-19-8673-4

This Springer imprint is published by the registered company Springer Nature Singapore Pte Ltd.
The registered company address is: 152 Beach Road, #21-01/04 Gateway East, Singapore 189721, Singapore

Preface I

It is for me a great honor, a great privilege, and a great satisfaction to preface this book containing the contributions to the conference held in Tianjin on *Judicial Management from Comparative Perspective* (8–10 Nov. 2017). This book is a valuable source of information which allow to reflect further about the issues explored during the conference.

I would like to dedicate this preface to prominent colleagues, who passed away shortly before the conference or since the conference: Profs. Jose Barbosa Moreira and Ada Pellegrini Grinover, both honorary vice presidents of the IAPL; Prof. Myklos Kengyel, from Hungary, honorary member of the IAPL Council; and Prof. Marcel Storme, IAPL president between 1995 and 2007. They were very close members of the association; some of them organized memorable congresses or conferences of the association; Prof. Storme was an inspirational president. They will miss us.

The organization of an international conference is never a small business and this one, indeed, was not without its own challenges, regarding the dates of the conference, its venue, and the very possibility of organizing the event. But, finally, all is well that ends well. It is the one thing that matters. This happy result was made possible thanks to the understanding, the involvement, and the incessant efforts of our Chinese colleagues and the cooperation of the Chinese authorities. Let me please express to them my sincere gratitude on behalf of the International Association of Procedural Law.

The idea of organizing a conference in China was first suggested by Prof. Federico Carpi, during a meeting of the presidium and the council of the association on the occasion of our annual conference held in Buenos Aires in June 2012. Contacts were made with our Chinese colleagues, especially Prof. Zhang Weiping, president of the China Academy of Civil Procedural Law. I wish to thank here and now the role played in this mediation by our colleague Prof. Masahisa Deguchi, former IAPL vice president. Professor Zhang Weiping proposed to host and organize in China the 2017 IAPL Conference. The proposal was enthusiastically accepted by the presidium of the association which met in Cambridge in the Spring of 2013 and the process then began in which Prof. Fu Yulin was involved and progressively took the major part, for better or for worse, I would say for worse yesterday and for better today.

Since then, the exchanges between us did not stop. Much discussion occurred concerning the organization of this conference in Athens in 2013, Luxembourg and Seoul in 2014, Istanbul and Valencia in 2015, Luxembourg again and Bogota in 2016, and in Salamanca in February 2017. We exchanged a lot of emails and preparatory documents.

This event was prepared with great care as much in its scientific dimension as in its material aspects. I know how the organization of such a conference requires time and energy, often to the detriment of personal and family life. I sincerely thank Profs. Zhang Weiping, Fu Yulin, and all the members of the organizing committee for that.

This colloquium was indeed a very great event; no doubt it was a major landmark in the history of the Association.

It was the first time that a colloquium of the *International Association of Procedural Law* was held in China since the association was founded in Florence in 1950 in the aftermath of the Second World War, on the ruins of nazism and fascism.

Regarding the history of our Association, I would only like to draw the reader's attention to two things.

The first is that the history of our association is that of a collective challenge taken on by several generations of lawyers over sixty years under the inspirational leadership of successive presidents, Enrico Redenti, Niceto Alcalà-Zamora y Castillo, Mauro Cappelletti, Marcel Storme, Federico Carpi, and Peter Gottwald.

Thanks to them, the Association has been consolidated over the years, has spread throughout the world, and has increased its activities. Originally centered on Europe and America, mainly Latin America, our association has today nearly four hundred members worldwide, representing around fifty countries. In order to contribute, with modesty, as lawyers, to the building of a better world, our duty is to go further by welcoming legal experts from all parts of the world, especially Asia where China holds of course a very important place. I must add that the choice of Tianjin for hosting our conference is an excellent one when recollecting the special role played by Tianjin at the tormented end of the nineteenth century. Indeed, some experts in world history see in Tianjin the first laboratory of globalization to come.

The second thing I want to recall is that civil procedure is not only a question of legal technique since this technique is meant for a universal finality, which is justice. I know that universality is a controversial concept and it is not my role to contribute to this debate. I just want to say that justice does not consist only of giving each his due, the *suum cuique tribuere* of the Romans; it is also to ensure social peace with equal respect to personal rights. The right to a fair trial is the expression of a philosophy of justice enshrined in the *Universal Declaration for Human Rights* and other international conventions that followed. The technical rules for proceedings must respect the fundamental principles of procedure.

It is the responsibility of our association to help all proceduralists around the world to share the fire of solidarity and friendship in order to promote a justice with a human face, beyond their respectable mutual differences, which are numerous and cannot be denied. Differences are not a problem since there is no progress without debate and no debate without differences. Cooperation is the keyword that must prevail. In this respect, Prof. Marcel Storme who was not able to attend our conference, with big regret, taught me that the Chinese ministry of justice, Wei Wenbo, went to Gand, in Belgium, in 1980, in order to conclude the first international agreement on legal education with the faculty of law of Gand whose dean was at that time Prof. Storme, who became three years later Executive Secretary general of the IAPL, Mauro Cappelletti becoming simultaneously the new president of the Association.

We must remain ever vigilant in this matter because the quest for justice is not like a journey down a long and quiet river. It is a battle without end everywhere in the world, today no less than in the past, and this battle is not necessarily a political battle. For instance, the economic globalization, in which one sees easily a source of progress, and it is for one part, generates also the risk of reducing the guarantees of good justice when, in the name of an ever greater search for efficiency, it favors legal dumping and threatens social rights or environmental requirements. The logic of the global market and the logic of human rights do not easily co-exist.

In this respect, no doubt that judicial management is one of the main tendencies influencing the contemporary evolution of civil procedure in all countries, but it is an ambiguous trend, I would say a perverse trend. Management in the field of justice may be a good thing when it prevents the wasting of public money which is the money of the people. On the contrary, it is not a so good thing when the quest for efficiency becomes an end in itself to the detriment of what justice means. The first session of the conference, moderated by Prof. Oteiza (elected since IAPL president in Kobe, 2019), presented the general issue of the topic thanks to introductory reports related to the situation in China, Asia, North America, latin America and Europe. The second and the third sessions focused, respectively, on managing the litigation cases and on managing the justice system, before that the fourth session, in a synthetic way, addressed the framing of the structure of the court system from the perspective of case management. The fifth and final session was devoted to a separate topic with the call for papers on fact-finding and legal theory. Every session generated a large, dense, and stimulating debate.

We worked a lot.

These five work sessions meant twelve general reports supplied by ten national reports, twenty-three speakers from eleven countries of Asia, Europe, and the Americas, and more than two hundred participants, including forty-six attendees from nineteen foreign countries.

At the end of the conference, it became clear that the topic of judicial management from a comparative perspective was really a good choice.

The proceduralists cannot just deal with the procedure strictly speaking, the written or oral nature of the proceedings, the respective roles of the judge and the parties, the law of evidence, the *res judicata*, the means of recourse, and the enforcement of judgments. They have to consider the process more than the proceedings, I mean the proceedings with respect to the substance of litigation as well as the proceedings with respect to the administration of the justice system, without forgetting its economic, social, political, and cultural environment.

Judicial management is a good example of this opened conception of procedure, articulating court administration and proceedings in a global and plural system of justice where economy, sociology, and even psychology have also a role to play.

In some jurisdictions, the judicial management generates psychosocial risks for the judges and the clerks. It is not anecdote or *coquetterie*. When the quest for efficiency becomes an end in itself, the pressure is too important and the human machine breaks down. Justice done by a judge under pressure cannot be a good justice and I am not sure it is a good output for the whole system of justice itself with regard to the possible recourses against the judgments or to the onset of conflicts between the parties.

Our comparative journey was enriching and fascinating, from China to Latin America, from Latin America to Europe, from Europe to Asia, and from Asia to North America. Especially, we learnt a lot about China thanks to the impressive richness of the presentations made by our Chinese colleagues and, also, thanks to the discussion between them when the floor was opened.

At the end of the day, I shall make two comments.

First, I do not think that the reality can be summarized in an unequivocal and, therefore, simplistic choice between black or white; the world is gray and there are many nuances of gray. Everywhere the same problems arise; everywhere the same problems need efficient solutions for managing the cases and for managing the court; and everywhere these new managerial tools impact more or less but impact the structure of the court system.

Secondly, in this landscape, however, we may draw attention to the concept of management. We deal a lot with the scope of and with the tools of case and of court management; but what do we mean by management? What about the conception of management? The issue is addressed by some reports. I think that Margaret Woo was right when she wondered whether case management serves accuracy and justice or simply processing and diverting cases. That depends on the conception of the management we adopt and this is right for case management as well as for court management. What do we put into this concept? Management is like cholesterol : there is a bad one and there is a good one. Do we choose an authoritarian conception of management, a topdown model of management, vertical and quantitative, the result shall not be the same as adopting a concerted conception of management, circular and qualitative, based on consultation between all stakeholders. Cultivate consent of stakeholders—the parties in case management, their lawyers, the judges, and the clerks in court management—strengthens the legitimacy of the decision and therefore the efficiency of the whole system. This model of concerted management has clearly something to do with the development of a cooperative conception of the procedure, transcending the divide between adversarial and inquisitorial systems. Procedural protocols are part of this conception and there is not a problem with regard to public norms since the judge is involved in these protocols by controlling their validity or by conditioning their efficiency such as with the procedural timetable.

I must leave my assessment here and, in order not to unduly hold the reader's attention, I turn to the most important thing to do at the end, I mean expressing my warmest thanks to all who have contributed to the success of this meeting, in whatever way they did:

- To all the institutions and organizations who have brought financial or material support, mainly China Civil Procedural Law Society, China Law Society, Tianjin University, and the faculty of law and DESCI Asset management;
- To all the session moderators, general and national reporters, and all who participated during the course of our debates;
- To the technicians, public relations body, students, and, especially, the translators. We all know and we all appreciate the eminently difficult role they play in this domain of comparative procedural law where translation is as much linguistic and cultural;
- To the Supreme People's Court and the Chinese People's Political Consultative Conference;
- And, last but not the least, to our colleagues Profs. Zhang Weiping and Fu Yulin and their team, who worked tirelessly to prepare this conference in order to assure its success. Anyone who has ever organized a conference of this sort knows how much it can be a source of stress, in the months leading up. There are always obstacles to overcome, even at the very last minute and we must be grateful to them for their invaluable efforts in this matter. I thank them for making themselves available, for their efficiency, their constant attention, and the kindness of their hospitality. They have allowed a new page to be written in the great book of the International Association of Procedural Law. I hope that the Tianjin conference and this memorable book made possible by the powerful commitment of Prof. Fu Yulin will contribute to a deepening of the connection between our association and the lawyers of Asia.

感谢您的关注!

July 2020

Loic Cadiet
Former President of the International
Association of Procedural Law
Paris, France
Loic.Cadiet@univ-paris1.fr

Preface II

This book is based on the general reports of the international conference on Judicial Management from Comparative Perspective held in Tianjin in 2017, which have been revised and proofread repeatedly by the authors and the editors for five years since then. The conference was co-hosted by the International Association of Procedure Law (IAPL) and the China Law Society, and co-organized by China Civil Procedural Law Society (CCPLS) and Tianjin University. Scholars and judges approach 300, of whom 46 are top foreign scholars from 19 countries in Asia, Europe, North America, and Latin America; and 12 general reporters presented based on 60 national reports, with 23 participants from 11 countries who made comments. The conference convened in China for the first time is an important milestone in the history of IAPL, as the IAPL Chairman Prof. Loic Cadiet said at the opening ceremony; while, for the Chinese colleagues, the conference has strengthened contact and cooperation with the international counterparts and jointly contributed wisdom to the sound development of a community with a shared future for mankind.

After a short opening ceremony with the leaders' brief speeches (see the attached agenda), the introductory session focus on the objectives of judicial management. Hosted by Prof. Eduardo Oteiza, Prof. Li Hao (representing China), Prof. Hanki Sohn (representing Asia), Prof. Margaret Woo (representing North America), Prof. Remco van Rhee (representing Europe), and Prof. Antonio do Passo Cabral (representing Latin America) respectively presented their theoretical thinking of the relative practice of his/her country and the other countries in this continent. Each of the following four sessions focused respectively one topic as follows: case management mechanism, court structure, court's role in case management, and fact-finding and legal reasoning from perspective of judicial management. Each session has two general reporters, including one from China, and a discussant.

On the objectives of judicial management, Prof. Li Hao pointed out that the fundamental goal of case management is to improve the fairness and efficiency of the litigation system and improve the public's satisfaction with the government litigation system. Its direct goal is to improve the efficiency of handling cases on the premise that courts and judges handle cases independently in accordance with the law. Then he introduced two important systems in China's civil case management, namely, the trial time limit for courts and the proof time limit for the litigants. Prof. Hanki Sohn put forward his thoughts on the efficiency of judicial process and pointed out that the most useful work in case management is pre-trial preparation, which is also the development trend of many Asian countries at present. Prof. Margaret Woo briefly introduced the status and background of case management in the US, calling for more careful consideration of these questions: what is the purpose of civil litigation?Is it just to resolve individual disputes or is there some larger purpose? Is it merely to adjudicate private matters, or is it intended to serve the purpose of setting public norms? Is case management conducive to substantive justice? Is fairness likely to be sacrificed in the pursuit of efficiency? The answers to these questions will determine the approach to litigation management. Prof. van Rhee presented, the basic principles of civil litigation, established in the nineteenth century, said that litigation was to protect the rights of the individual but litigation focused only on private interests or the private interests of the most powerful, so this concept is slowly disappearing in Europe. He suggested safeguards to make effective use of scarce litigation resources and, comparing national legislation, pointed to Europe's tendency to settle disputes in an efficient, compound proportionality approach as a model. Prof. Cabral mainly discusses the case management system and possible new systems in the future from the perspective of Latin America, mainly focusing on the impact of litigation contract on case management and the reform of case allocation system.

On the topic of 'Case Management', Prof. Wang Fuhua pointed out that civil case management should stressed on cooperation between/among the litigants, their lawyers, and the judges, and that the application of new technologies such as the Internet provides an opportunity to reform trial pattern and help improve efficiency of case management. Prof. John Sorabji from the UK analyzed case management experiences and lessons in the common law and civil law countries, compared the case management system in different countries with detailed data and vivid stories, respectively discussed the purpose of case management and the way to realize, also shared the latest practice and development of several European countries.

On the session of 'Court Management', Prof. Fu Yulin from China introduced the internal structure of Chinese courts and the relationship between/among the tribunal of a specific case and the 'supervisors' or 'managers' as well as the relevant departments who are responsible for judicial management, especially the chief judges of the court and judicial committee. She mainly introduces the ongoing reforms of judicial mechanism in China and analyzes the background and prospect of the transition from judicial bureaucracy system to the so-called 'judicial responsibility system'. Prof. Emmanuel Jeuland from France, according to the data of America, Asia, Africa, and Europe, elucidated the court management mode that differs in the aspects of planning, budget, and management department. And he accordingly pointed out that the court's management over personnel is more suitable for the civil law countries, because this model can produce power concentration and increase effect of administration; while the aim of judicial management in common law countries is mainly to improve the judges' independence.

In the session on 'the Structure of Court System', Dr. Peter Chen from China (Hongkong) compared the prominent characteristics and differences of the court structure of mainland China and the district of Taiwan, Hong Kong, and Macao from perspective of the impacts of such factors as historical roots and affiliation of legal family, and he concluded that the premise of assessment over a specific jurisdiction's case management structure is that litigants often require the contents that are very similar to the civil justice system, including efficiency (avoid improper delay), reasonable cost-effective, suitable way for negotiation and settlement, fair share of cost of the lawsuit, proportionality of procedure, user friendly, and effective and easy enforcement system. Prof. Álvaro Pérez Ragone from Chile discusses the rules of efficiency and effectiveness, judicial independence, and the relatively procedural, cultural and structural arrangements in judicial system, based on more than a dozen national reports, he presented his comparative study and comments from various dimensions of horizontal and vertical management.

In the Session of 'Fact-Finding System', Prof. Zhang Baosheng from China stated that the purpose of court epistemology is to seek truth; logic is inductive reasoning and motive force is the interaction of prosecution, defense, and trial. He emphasized that fact-finding is an operation to discover minor premises of legal reasoning and the justification in fact-finding and legal reasoning. The proposed foreign speaker, Prof. Dmitry Maleshin from Russia, was absent from the conference for some reason and was replaced Prof. Alan Uzelac from Croatia as the main speaker, who made an in-depth theoretical extension on Chinese colleague's lecture. And Prof. Margaret Woo and Prof. van Rhee as co-discussants, brought the topic of fact-finding back to the framework of judicial management.

There's some explanation of the contents of this book, which partly differ from the conference. For the introductory session, Prof. Margaret Woo withdrew her report from this book because her report has been published in another collection published by the Springer. However, considering that her keynote speech has been repeatedly cited by other keynote speakers, keynote speakers, and commentators in this conference, to maintain the logical integrity between chapters. Here we specially provide the link of this article, Dr. Peter Chen' general report for the session 'court structure' has been published separately, so we invited Associate Prof. Chen Hangping of Tsinghua University Law School, who was the author of the report of Mainland China on this subject, to rewrite a report but focus on special courts and to leave the part of ordinary court structure to Prof. Fu Yulin's report on court management; and Prof. Fu Yulin revised her report substantially to conclude the amendment of the Court Organizing Law and the Judge's Law atfer the 2017 Conference. The report on fact-finding is quite different from the other parts of this book so it was recommended to publish separately. Considering all the above changes, in order to fully record such a valuable conference and commemorate each important participant, we have attached the agenda with the original emblem (devised by myself) into the book.

Five and a half years have passed since the conclusion of the Tianjin Conference, of which three years have been spent in the midst of the epidemic. Yet I still remember the twists of the conference preparation and the followed warm scene of the conference. As this book goes to print, I would like to extend my earnest thanks to all contributors. With the contact and push of Prof. Masashi Deguchi (Japan) who was the only IAPL presidium member from Asia, IAPL reached an agreement with

CCPLS that IAPL annual conference would be held in Beijing in June of 2017. I was appointed by the CCPLS to be the executive organizer of the conference to work under IAPL regulations and the related Chinese laws & policies. Since 2013, I started to work under the direction and guidance of IAPL's Chairman Prof. Loic Cadiet and CCPLS's President Prof. Zhang Weiping, which is the luckiest experience in my life, though I know it must be suffering time for Prof. Cadiet to read and reply 2000 emails from/to me during the four years. The unlucky experience we suffered was that we had to change the conference venue (changed from Beijing to Tianjin) and time (changed from May to November) due to some policy changes. The increased psychological pressure and workload can be imagined; actually, President Zhang Weiping undertook the pressure of funding and other pressures silently.

Thanks to our dear colleagues' complete understandings, confidence and supports from both IAPL and CCPLS, the China Law Society provided positive guidance and assistance in the international affairs especially for visa. Here I express special gratitude to Prof. Cadiet and Prof. Fernando Gascon (general secretary) from IAPL, and to Prof. Zhang Weiping and Prof. Li Hao (vice President) as well Ms. Qiang Meimei (secretary) from CCPLS. Tianjin University's timely help as the co-organizer made the conference possible and successful. Here I especially present my thanks to Prof. Sun Youhai, the dean of Law School, and the work team led by Ms. Lan Lan, Dr. Cao Yunji, Dr. Cao Jianjun, and the volunteer students. I appreciate all my colleagues and students of civil procedure field in Peking University Law School, especially to Associate Prof. Cao Zhixun, Dr. Li Man, Dr. Meng Xing, and Dr. Yu Zhaohui, who worked together with me all the time, and to Prof. Pan Jianfeng (the dean of Law School and vice president of CCPLS) and Associate Prof. Liu Zhewei, who back me up whenever and whatever I required for the conference. Moreover, my thanks shall give to Ms. Mao Ling who largely participated in the international communications, Dr. Bi Xiaoxiao and Dr. Lu Pei who partly participated in the material translations for the audience. None of the above participants was paid any cent of reward, though they must willingly bear the hardship and responsibility. My further gratitude shall leave to Mr. Min Weiguo, the Chairman of Desci Asset Management Group, who generously fund the rich gala dinner and acted as our assistant organizer for nothing. Finally, I would express my deep condolences to Prof. Cai Yanmin of Sun Yat-sen University who was always my cooperator in international communications and was one of the general reporters of this conference but left us during the preparatory period.

The editing process of the book is proved to be a hard work. It took us another four years to complete the English editing, proofreading, and revision by constantly communication with the authors and the professional translation companies who undertook the final language review and correction. Dr. Cao Zhixun, based on his fully responsible for the edition and translation of the conference reports, continued to act as the executive editor and undertook the main workload with his persistently excelsior input. During this process, our outstanding students, Mr. Wang Fengquan, Ms. Zhang Yang, and Ms. Li Yihui joined in the work of text proofreading, layout adjustment, reference style conversion of work; actually, King & Wood Mallesons also contributed to this book as a sponsor for that the professional proofreading fee was paid from the 'King & Wood - PKU salon' project fund. I would like to extend my sincere thanks to them and the contributors who are not listed in this book. Again, I express appreciation and respects to Prof. Zhang Weiping who should have been but rejected to be the co-editor of this book, though he was the general organizer of the whole project and specifically contributed much to selecting the theme of conference, topics, and reporters of each session which is the base of this book. I'm grateful to be a co-editor of Prof. Cadiet so that I could still work under his kind and honorable guidance.

Finally but importantly, I express my thanks to Prof. Margaret Woo and Dr. Peter Chan, the chief editors of 'The Contemporary Chinese Civil and Commercial Law Series' and by the Springer editors for approving the book and for their workload in organizing and participating in the professional review of this samples. The professional recognition and suggestions of the anonymous reviewers have encouraged us much more than expected. The editor Ms. Kowsalya Raghunathan for her assistance with great patience and kindness.

Let's expect of publishing and contributing a shining stone to the international communication and academic accumulation.

August 2023

Yulin Fu
Associate President of China Civil
Procedural Law Society
Beijing, China
fuyulin65@126.com

Contents

Judicial Management in Asia

Hanki Sohn

1 Prologue

Civil procedure is a national legal system administered by the state to resolve disputes between private individuals. The state does this by providing, within a limited budget, the physical and human resources to help resolve disputes.

Traditionally, the ideal implementation of the civil procedure centres around four key state objectives: impartiality, accuracy, promptness, and cost-effectiveness. However, the nature of the concepts of 'impartiality' and 'accuracy' are self-contradictory (antinomic) to the concepts of 'promptness' and 'cost-effectiveness;' therefore, it is very challenging to realise all four objectives equally. If the emphasis is placed on 'impartiality' and 'accuracy', the proceedings would take longer and result in higher litigation costs. On the contrary, if the emphasis is placed on 'promptness' and 'cost-effectiveness', this would hinder the fairness of the proceedings and, hence, affect the accuracy of the court judgment. However, all of the above-mentioned objectives should be taken seriously, and some countries have shown their intention to realise these objectives in their civil procedure codes.[1]

Looking back over history, it could be claimed that there has never been a single period in time when the parties to litigation were satisfied with the judgment of the court. It is worth noting that since the mid-twentieth century, most of the dissatisfaction with the civil procedure has been caused by the length of time acquired and the cost of litigation, the reasons for which are related to the exponential increase in the

[1] Article 1(1) of the Korea's Code of Civil Procedure stipulates that: 'A court shall endeavour to have the litigation procedures progress fairly, swiftly and economically,' while Article 2 of the Japan's Code of Civil Procedure stipulates that: 'Courts shall endeavour to ensure that civil suits are carried out fairly expeditiously, and parties shall conduct civil suits in good faith.'

H. Sohn (✉)
Law School, Yonsei University, Seoul, South Korea
e-mail: sonhk@yonsei.ac.kr

L. Cadiet and Y. Fu (eds.), *On Judicial Management from Comparative Perspective*, Contemporary Chinese Civil and Commercial Law,
https://doi.org/10.1007/978-981-19-8673-4_1

number of civil cases. To resolve the dissatisfaction regarding the delay and undue costs, states have spared no effort in reforming their case management systems.

However, for the ideal operation of the civil procedure system, it is not enough to improve the case management methods of the judge who hears the trial. The state should also consider the judicial system and court administration, alongside case management, to realise the ideal operation of the system.

If case management is crucial to the realisation of the concepts of promptness and cost-effectiveness, the improvement of the judicial system and court management are necessary elements for achieving impartiality and accuracy. In addition, the ideal operation of civil procedures is possible only through the efforts of the state(courts); the cooperation of the parties to the litigation is indispensable.

2 Case Management in Asia

The concept and method of case management in civil law jurisdictions that use the inquisitorial system are different from those in adversarial system. The role and function of a judge in civil law jurisdictions are different from those in the common law legal system. There is no such notion as 'sit-back passiveness' for trial judges. From the beginning of the lawsuit, the judge exercises full control over the litigation to address problems that occur during it. The judge's role and function in civil law jurisdictions is much more proactive than that in common law jurisdictions. The judge's power that allows him/her to control proceedings can be referred to as 'power of supervision' (*Prozessleitung des Richters*). Judges directly handle cases assigned to them using the power of supervision. The ambit of a judge's authority to conduct trials in many Asian countries can be categorised according to their purpose and objective: (1) supervision of the formalities of the proceeding[2]; (2) supervision of the procedure's legitimate(lawful) progression[3]; (3) supervision of the trial's rationality

[2] To secure the formalities (regarding external progress) of proceedings, a court has the authority to: (1) set and modify the trial dates; and (2) set, and prolong or shorten the time periods for some procedural activities. Also, under special circumstances, the court can discontinue and take over the procedure, or suspend the procedure entirely.

[3] To secure the legitimate (lawful) progression of the procedure, the court can: (1) evaluate whether the litigation requirements are being met; (2) the order to correct the written complaints; (3) transfer the case due to a breach (infraction) of jurisdiction; (4) evaluate the petition or written appeal, and (5) even dismiss the case.

and substantiality[4] (4) supervision of a concentrated(intensive) oral argument and speedy trial[5]; and (5) supervision of autonomous participation of the parties.[6]

One of the current issues of debate in Asian countries relates to the reinforcement of preparatory proceedings for the concentrated (intensive) trial.[7]

It is impossible to disregard the fact that cooperation between the judge and the parties is vital in a trial. Therefore, the courts need to exert the power of supervision in a respectful manner,[8] and should be careful not to abuse the parties' trust when exercising their authority in the preparatory proceedings.

3 The Preparatory Stage and Case Management

3.1 Preparatory Proceedings

Asian countries are striving to improve their preparatory procedures so that trials can be carried out promptly and cost-effectively. Notably, Japan is ahead of other countries in its current research and legislation, and possesses the most well-constructed system in the region.

Japan has various processes that form part of the preparatory stage, beyond the typical preparatory proceedings, namely: (1) the well-organised progress of court proceedings and a plan for trial[9]; (2) hearing the ancillary circumstances and process

---

4 To secure the rationality and substantiality of a trial, the court can: (1) restrict, separate and consolidate a procedure; and (2) ask parties for explanations or clarify the ambiguities on its own initiative.

5 To conduct concentrated (intensive) oral arguments and secure the speed of the trial, the court can carry out a preparatory proceeding beforehand and can dismiss the belatedly submitted materials for offence and defense. The court can establish a timetable for the presentation of specific arguments or evidence.

6 To encourage parties' autonomous participation in resolving the dispute, the judge provides recommendations for a reconciliation. If the case is deemed suitable or appropriate for mediation, it can be referred back for mediation (mediation can be initiated).

7 There are many pending issues that countries are constantly working on to improve their system, for example whether preparatory proceedings are necessary in all types of cases, how far the authority of the judge extends over the preparatory proceedings, and the sanctions to be imposed after the preparatory proceedings.

8 For example, the court might set a date for trial, but the date can be modified if both parties agree to it. In the situation of a case being transferred, the court shall respect the plaintiff's decision and transfer the case to another court as requested by the plaintiff. On some occasions, it is proper for a judge to set a time limit for the parties to submit their materials for offence and defense after consulting with both sides. Furthermore, Forcing the parties to reconcile or to command them to engage in mediation is beyond the judge's authority and should be refrained from.

9 Japanese legislation from 2003 requires court proceedings to be well-planned and well-organised. To achieve a proper and prompt trial, the court shall consult with both parties when formulating a plan for the trial if the case requires a number of complicated matters to be examined or if it has any other special circumstance. (Japan's Code of Civil Procedure, Article 147-3(1)). The

conference[10]; (3) preliminary oral arguments[11]; and (4) preparatory proceedings by means of documents.[12]

Korea revised its Code of Civil Procedure in 2002, adopting a new case management system that totally changed the framework of the trial system. This change was made following an empirical study showing that repeated trial dates in which the parties were unprepared and perfunctory were the main cause of unnecessary delays and undue costs of civil trials.

Under the new case management system, preparatory proceedings became almost a mandatory procedure[13] and the power of the presiding judge was substantially strengthened.[14] Exercising his/her strengthened power, the judge can grasp all relevant issues and evidence during this stage, and then only one trial date will be held thereafter, focusing on the interrogation of witnesses and both parties involved. Under this new model, the focus of civil litigation has switched from the trial to the preparatory proceedings. However, the Code of Civil Procedure was revised again in 2008 (Article 258-1), resulting in switching back to a trial-focused system, with the preparatory proceedings left to the judge's discretion.[15]

---

plan for trial must specify: (i) a time limit for arranging issues and evidence; (ii) a time limit for examining witnesses and the parties themselves; and (iii) a schedule of timing for concluding the oral argument and rendering a judgment. In addition, the plan for trial may specify a time limit for advancing allegations or evidence on a specific matter or on any other matters necessary for the well-organised progress of court proceedings.

[10] For formulating a plan for trial at the beginning of the procedure, a conference may be scheduled outside the date for the oral argument for both parties to attend, to confirm the list of referential items and consult on matters concerning the process of the trial (Japanese Rules of Civil Procedure, Article 95).

[11] The process of arranging issues and evidence during oral argument is called 'preliminary oral arguments' (Japan's Code of Civil Procedure, Article 164). During this process, the parties are able to determine the issues and evidence to be examined. As the preliminary oral argument is also part of the oral arguments, all documents presented during the preliminary oral argument are deemed to be litigation documents, and unlike in preparatory proceedings, restating them in the oral argument is not required.

[12] The court may refer a case to preparatory proceedings by means of documents, meaning proceedings for arranging issues and evidence through the submission of a brief, etc. without the appearance of the parties. This may be required when a party lives in a remote place, or when the court finds it appropriate for any other reasons (Japan's Code of Civil Procedure, Article 175).

[13] Under the 2002 'New Model,' preparatory proceedings are applied to all cases, regardless of whether it is a collegiate panel case or a single judge case, subject to a few exceptions where (1) a judgment is rendered without oral argument; (2) a court finds it unnecessary (simple cases); (3) a proceeding is conducted through services by public notice; or (4) the case involves a small claim.

[14] The presiding judge for the preparatory proceedings may, if he/she deems it necessary for the preparation for trial, render a ruling upon the motion of evidence, whether or not to adopt the evidence. Furthermore, the judge may also conduct an examination of evidence within the scope of the objectives of preparatory proceedings (Article 279(1)). However, the questioning of witnesses and parties should be conducted during oral trial, except in some specific situations (Article 281(4)).

[15] The main reason for this reversion is that the preparatory proceeding is not open to the public, though the outcome (win and lose between the parties) is actually decided in this proceeding. Many have criticised that this can violate the basic principle of civil procedure (principle of disclosure), and thus make the trials unreviewable.

3.2 *Use of Alternative Dispute Resolution (ADR) at the Preparatory Stage*

Many Asian countries use ADR at the preparatory stage as a form of case management and as a tool for fast and inexpensive resolution of cases.[16]

However, the courts should be very cautious when exercising their authority over preparatory proceedings which are not open to the public. Forcing the parties to reconcile or commanding them to resort to mediation is beyond the trial judge's discretion. However, the use of ADR generally contributes to a reduction in the backlog of cases and enables parties to resolve disputes in an amicable atmosphere. Therefore, the use of ADR should be encouraged.

4 Collection of Evidence and Case Management

In common law jurisdictions, where liberal discovery is practised, the main issue is how to control discovery, an important aspect of case management. The regulation of the scope, sequence, timing and methods of discovery through a discovery-planning conference (US FRCP Rule 26(f)) is a vital part of case management. In contrast, Asian countries that do not possess a discovery system have been traditionally criticised as being inconsiderate of plaintiffs who are the victims, for example in environment, medical malpractice and product liability cases. In such cases, the plaintiffs were often helpless as almost all the evidence was in the hands of the wrongdoer(s). Hence, in recent years, many Asian countries have tended to adopt the spirit of the discovery system by expanding the scope of the obligation to submit documents.[17]

Korea and Japan have, in principle, applied the obligation to submit almost all kinds of documents through recent amendment to their civil procedure laws.[18] Other than the expansion of the obligation to submit documents, Japan has also adopted

---

[16] In addition to Korea and Japan, many other Asian countries (Thailand, Indonesia, Malaysia, Cambodia, and Vietnam) use ADR before an oral trial.

[17] Nevertheless, in China, where the collection of some types of evidence is the responsibility of the court, much effort has been made to clearly specify the range of evidence that should be collected by the court.

[18] Both articles are similar (Korea's Code of Civil Procedure, Article 344-2 and Japan's Code of Civil Procedure, Article 220, no. 4). In the past, the obligation of submission was imposed on (1) documents cited by the parties in the lawsuit; (2) documents for which a party holds a right to ask the holder of the document to transfer or disclose; and (3) documents which have been prepared for the benefit of the applicant, or prepared in relation to a legal relationship between the applicant and the holder of document. Whereas general documents other than the aforementioned ones were not subject to the obligation of submission. But now, through the recent amendments, the obligation applies to almost all kinds of documents with only a few exceptions. But the scope of exceptions varies between Korea and Japan. For instance, in Korea, documents kept or held by a public official or ex-public official in connection with his/her duties are exempt from being submitted as a whole. In Japan, however, only documents concerning a secret relating to a public officer's duties, which is likely to harm the public interest or substantially hinder the performance of his/her public duties if

the interrogatory system from the United States' discovery system; Korea, however, did not adopt this.

According to Taiwan's Code of Civil Procedure, a party has the duty to produce the following documents: (1) documents cited by the parties in the lawsuit; (2) documents which the opposing party may require the delivery or inspection of pursuant to the applicable laws; (3) documents created in the interests of the party; (4) commercial accounting books; and (5) documents which are created regarding matters relating to the action.[19]

On the other hand, some Asian countries that have common law traits, use the discovery system in full or to a limited extent. The civil procedure law of Malaysia's Syariah Courts stipulates that the court may order any party to state, on oath orally or by affidavit, the document he/she has or has had in his/her possession or power relating to the matter in question, or to order any party to produce any document in his possession or power.[20]

5 Cooperation of the Parties and Case Management

It is impossible to resolve disputes promptly and cost-effectively through the judge's efforts alone: cooperation on the part of the parties and their litigation representatives is crucial too.[21] On top of the principle of good faith, all Asian countries have additional mechanisms to promote expeditious and cost-effective civil proceedings.

5.1 Change to the Principle Regarding the Submission of Litigation Materials

In the past, Asian countries generally adopted the principle of non-sequential submission regarding the submission of litigation materials (i.e. methods for offence or defense). Recently, however, many Asian countries have moved to the principle

---

submitted, will be exempted from the obligation of submission (Korea's Code of Civil Procedure, Article 344 and Japan's Code of Civil Procedure, Article 220).

19 Taiwan's Code of Civil Procedure, Article 344.

20 Malaysia's Syariah Court Civil Procedure (Federal Territories Act 1998), Article 85.

21 To emphasise the importance of this, an increasing number of Asian countries are proclaiming the principle of good faith in their laws. Korea adopted the principle of good faith in the 1990 amendment to its Code of Civil Procedure, Japan adopted the principle in a 1996 amendment, and China adopted in a 2012 amendment (Korea's Code of Civil Procedure, Article 1-2; Japan's Code of Civil Procedure, Article 2; China's Code of Civil Procedure, Article 13-1).

of timely submission.[22] To guarantee the timely submission of materials, the law generally gives the trial judge a right to dismiss the untimely produced litigation materials.[23] In many countries, the law also gives the trial judge the power to set a deadline for the party to submit his/her allegations or evidence. It is within the judge's discretion to decide whether or not to dismiss a belatedly submitted method for offense or defense. Even though this decision rests on the judge's wish to conduct a speedy trial, most judges are rather passive in exerting their authority in this matter.

5.2 Control of Dates and Time Limits

In Japan and Korea, default judgments will not be made even if one of the parties fails to appear on the trial date. In other words, both parties are deemed to be present at the trial, the argument is still carried out and judgment can still be made. In contrast to Japan and Korea, the civil procedural law of China recognises default judgments.[24]

In Asian countries, where neither party has appeared on the trial date, the action shall be deemed withdrawn and the proceedings can be closed, as long as certain conditions are met.[25]

Where a party does not keep to an invariable time limit, he/she loses the right to conduct the litigation. However, if a party was unable to meet the deadline due to a cause beyond their control, they may subsequently complement the originally intended procedural acts (for example, appeals to higher courts) within a certain period of time from the date on which such cause ceases to exist.

---

[22] Korea's Code of Civil Procedure, Article 149; Japan's Code of Civil Procedure, Article 157-1; Taiwan's Code of Civil Procedure, Article 196-2.

[23] To guarantee the timely submission of litigation materials, a proper enforcement mechanism is crucial. Where it is deemed that a party has delayed the conclusion of litigation by belatedly producing the means of offense (attack) and defense intentionally or by gross negligence, the court may dismiss the produced materials by its ruling, either *ex officio* or upon motion of the other party (Korea's Code of Civil Procedure, Article 149; Japan's Code of Civil Procedure, Article 157-1; Taiwan's Code of Civil Procedure, Article 196-2).

[24] If a plaintiff refuses to appear in court without justified reasons, the case may be deemed to have been withdrawn by him, and if the defendant files a counterclaim in the meantime, the court may make a judgment by default. If a defendant refuses to appear in court without justified reasons, the court may also make a default judgment (China's Code of Civil Procedure, Articles 143 and 144; Interpretation, Articles 234–241).

[25] In Japan, the action shall be deemed to have been withdrawn if neither party appears on the trial date and neither of them files a petition to reschedule the date within one month, or if neither party appears on the date on two consecutive occasions (Japan's Code of Civil Procedure, Article 263). In Korea, the lawsuit shall be deemed to have been withdrawn if neither party appears on the trial date on two occasions and neither of them files a request for a designation of another trial date within one month (Korea's Code of Civil Procedure, Article 268-2).

6 Court and Instance Management

Asian countries also have various specialised courts in addition to the common court. Specialised courts handle the same kinds of cases repeatedly and their procedures are thus standardised, which enables the courts to dispose of cases promptly and accurately. Thus, various specialised courts are theoretically desirable, although it is entirely dependent on the judicial resources a nation has available.

The three-tier system (three-instance system) prevails in Asia, with a few exceptions.[26] The most significant problem with this system relates to the appeals stages, especially the second appeal that is made directly to the Supreme Court. Some of the more common concerns include: is the second appeal a right or not?; what are the essential requirements for a second appeal?; and do second appeals cover fact-finding, or do they deal only with the legal aspects of the case? These issues are related to whether a second appeal to the Supreme Court is a fundamental right guaranteed by the constitution. Currently, however, the second appeal in Asia is restricted in various ways to alleviate the burden on the Supreme Court.

The development of modern IT technology is dramatically changing the landscape of the court process. In addition to the concept of the e-court, which uses IT technology for a trial, there are increasing numbers of so-called electronic lawsuits that start with e-filings and are handled electronically throughout the whole process, from trial to judgment. All of the Asian countries are taking a great interest in this.[27]

7 Different Rules for Different Types of Cases in Asia

It would not be an exaggeration to say that every civil case is different—whether in terms of number of parties/size, complexity, subject matter and the value in controversy; no two cases are identical. Such diversity raises the question—of whether it suffices to have only one set of rules and to allow the judge to tailor and manage individual cases according to the nature and type of the case, or whether different rules should be formulated for different types of cases. In this regard, the Asian countries are relatively active in making different rules for diverse types of cases.

---

[26] China and Vietnam use a two-tier system.

[27] In 2010, Korea promulgated the Act of Using Electronic Documents in Civil Litigation (abbreviated as the Act of Electronic Litigation), which allows e-filing. With this law, the era of e-filing started and the incidence of its use has sharply increased. According to 2015 statistics, the percentage of e-filing of patent-related suits reached 92.1, and 56.1% of ordinary civil cases were initiated with e-filing.

7.1 Summary Proceedings

To manage simple cases or small claims promptly and cost-effectively, Asian countries use summary proceedings, which are drastically simplified compared to ordinary civil proceedings. For example, in Japan, the Code of Civil Procedure sets out special provisions for trials conducted by the summary court.[28] Similar provisions can also be found in the civil procedure codes of China and Taiwan.[29]

Korea once had an Act on Handling Civil Cases using Summary Procedures, but the Act has since been abolished. However, trials for simple or small claims cases can be conducted through a single judge's subject-matter jurisdiction. These cases can therefore be handled promptly and cost-effectively compared to those cases being handled by a collegiate court. Cases that fall under the subject-matter jurisdiction of a single judge include (1) cases with value in dispute of under 200,000,000 won (approximately USD180,000); (2) claims concerning checks, bills and notes; (3) claims concerning loans brought by a financial institution as the plaintiff.[30]

7.2 Small Claims Procedure

Asian countries commonly use a simplified and speedy procedures to satisfy the rights of small claims creditors. Korea enacted the Trial of Small Claims Act in 1973 and since then has resolved cases via drastically simplified procedures. Likewise, Japan has special provisions on small claims in its Code of Civil Procedure,[31] while China has also created new rules on small claims under the chapter on summary proceedings in its Code of Civil Procedure.[32] The range of cases in which the small claims procedure apply is different in every country.[33]

Generally, in every country, small claims procedures are even simpler than summary proceedings. However, the appeal process varies between countries. For instance, Korea recognises only two reasons for a second appeal and is currently uses a two-tier system, while China does not permit appeals (using a single-tier system). In Japan, appeals are not allowed, but objections are.

---

[28] Japan's Code of Civil Procedure, Chapter 8, Articles 270–280.

[29] China's Code of Civil Procedure, Chapter 13, Articles 157–163; Taiwan's Code of Civil Procedure, Article 427–437(7).

[30] Korean Supreme Court Regulations on Subject-Matter Jurisdiction for Civil and Family Cases, Article 2.

[31] Japan's Code of Civil Procedure, Articles 368–381.

[32] China's Code of Civil Procedure, Article 162.

[33] In Korea, disputes of amounts under KRW 30,000,000 (approximately USD 28,000) are deemed to be small claims; small claims in Japan are those under JPY 600,000; and in Taiwan, those under NTD 100,000. As China is a huge country, the economic gap between regions is considered; small claims are those disputes of amount less than 30% of the annual average salary of employees of the relevant province, autonomous region, or municipality directly under the Central Government in the prior year.

7.3 *Procedures for Collective Dispute*

Collective disputes also arise frequently in Asian countries, and so all countries are well aware of the need to resolve collective disputes reasonably through litigation. Because the characteristics of collective disputes make it difficult to resolve them through the ordinary litigation procedures, countries have strived to formulate special procedures for collective disputes.

Korea, for example, has established the Securities-Related Class Action Act (2004) to resolve collective disputes concerning stock/securities,[34] as well as the Consumer Class Action Act (2007) and the Individual Information Related Class Action Act (2011) to protect the rights of consumers and to enhance the protection of personal information respectively.[35]

In Japan, in addition to the appointed-party system, the Special Provisions Concerning Large-Scale Suits, etc., have been adopted.[36] For its part, China has received attention from around the world for its recently adopted a public interest litigation system, in addition to the existing collective litigation system.[37]

8 Conclusion

It is true that recently, the main objective of case management has been to realise the ideology of speed and cost. The most inconvenient aspect of a civil lawsuit from the point of view of laypeople is that it is time-consuming and that litigations costs are high. Courts, for their part, are being put in a difficult position, facing a drastically increased number of cases. Undoubtedly, the need for case management has never been greater.

---

[34] The model of this class action is the United States' class action. However, strict supervision of the judge as a case manager applies. For example, the court may reject a representative party from acting in the litigation; the resignation of a representative party or a litigation representative is subject to the court's permission; and the representative party must also obtain the court's permission in circumstances where the representative party wishes to increase the number of litigation representatives. A court's permission is also necessary for the withdrawal of the lawsuit, settlement, waiver of claims, and withdrawal of appeals or waiver of rights to appeal (Korea's Securities-Related Class Action Act, Articles 22, 23, 26, 35, 38 etc.).

[35] Although the last two types of lawsuit are translated using the term 'class action,' they are not related to the class action concept in the Anglo-American legal system; however, they are based on the German *Verbandsklage*. Moreover, in the aforementioned securities-related collective dispute, compensation for damages is viewed as an element of subject matter. However, these two collective lawsuits can only be filed with the objective of prohibiting and suspending infringement; therefore, they differ from the securities-related collective dispute.

[36] Japan's Code of Civil Procedure, Articles 268–269(2).

[37] China's Code of Civil Procedure, Articles 53–55. Recently the standing committee of the national People's Congress decided to endow the people's prosecutor with the plaintiff's standing in public interest litigations(dated 27 June 2017).

However, the objectives of case management cannot be solely the expeditious and inexpensive resolution of cases. Therefore, judges as case managers should endeavour to manage their cases so as to secure actual justice for both plaintiff and defendant, and then render a judgment that corresponds to the substantive facts. Particularly in Asian countries, where the number of unrepresented litigants (litigants not represented by lawyers) is high, real equality between the parties should be guaranteed for substantively correct decisions. Therefore, it is necessary for the courts to properly exercise their power to request explanations to clarify the material aspects of the case and to ensure the streamlined flow of the proceedings.

Judges in civil law countries possess a fairly strong power of supervision. From the perspective of case management, the most useful tool for such judges is preparatory proceedings, and it is undeniable that preparatory proceedings are the focus of case management. The reinforcement of such proceedings is also a trend among most Asian countries. The following details should be taken into account in this regard.

First, not every case needs to undergo preparatory proceedings. Therefore, the judge assigned to the case should confirm the nature of the case promptly and meticulously, and decide whether the case requires preparatory proceedings or, in contrast, whether it should immediately go straight to trial.[38]

Second, we need to bear in mind the procedural characteristics of preparatory proceedings. Preparatory proceedings are not open to the public, which differentiate them from other supervisory tools. Hence, the problem of a judge wrongfully exercising his/her authority might occur during preparatory proceedings. In particular, the abuse of the judge's discretion is a serious matter. Moreover, we must not overlook the fact that the exercise of a judge's discretion during preparatory proceedings and the issue of whether the judge has exercised his authority properly are unreviewable.

Third, if the authority granted to the judge presiding over the preparatory proceedings is excessive, the handling of a case entirely relies on the judge's professional conscience, assiduousness and personal ability, which might then lead to distrust in the judicial system itself among laypeople. On the other hand, it is also a problem when judges do not exercise their power sufficiently strictly. In particular, the judge must lawfully impose sanctions on uncooperative parties who do not appear on the designated trial date, in order to prevent unnecessary delay and cost. This overly passive attitude of a judge must also be rejected. Lastly, if the preparatory proceedings end with simple preparations for the oral arguments, the function of it is too limited. Therefore, efforts to link the preparation process with ADR are essential, and the court should actively recommend settlement at the end of the preparatory proceedings and attempt mediation if necessary.

It is impossible to resolve all cases with one standard model of civil procedures. Using a one-size-fits-all approach will lead to applying a Cadillac procedure to a Chevy case, or its opposite, relying solely on the case-managing skill of the trial judge. Therefore, having different rules for different cases and regulating the judge's specific

[38] In relation to this, certain district courts in Korea have established and are running a division fully in charge of case management.

role and authority as a case manager are also effective for the ideal implementation of civil procedure.

It is necessary to improve the litigation system by incorporating highly advanced IT technology. The questions of whether electronic litigation can be entirely substituted for paper litigation or whether the complete digitalisation of litigation is desirable still leave room for further discussion. Nevertheless, the use of IT technology can certainly simplify and expedite proceedings and can reduce the courts' caseload.

Case Management and the Principle of Co-operation in Europe: A Modern Approach to Civil Litigation

C. H. Van Rhee

1 Introduction

The terminology 'Case Management' became fashionable in comparative legal studies in Europe as a result of the 1998 Woolf Reforms in England & Wales.[1] These reforms attracted a lot of attention in scholarly circles. It was noted that many of the Civil Law jurisdictions on the European Continent several or more decades earlier, and even the major European Common Law jurisdiction, were moving away from an idea that had dominated civil procedure in the non-Socialist states of Europe for a long period of time, this idea being that the parties are free to shape their civil lawsuits in the way they deem fit since civil litigation is (as a rule) about the protection of their private rights and duties over which they can freely dispose. The idea is forcefully expressed by a fundamental principle of civil procedure that was first formulated in the early nineteenth century by the Bavarian legal scholar Nikolaus Thaddäus von Gönner (1764–1827): the *Verhandlungsmaxime*, which can be translated freely in English as the adversarial principle.[2] The adversarial principle in its extreme form is harmful to justice since it only views the civil process from the perspective of the private interests of the parties (or, better, from the private interests of the most powerful party). This principle was in conformity with the role of the state in nineteenth century Europe, a state that only offered limited protection to its citizens, and then mostly to its propertied citizens. However, it contradicts the majority political view regarding the role of the state in present-day continental Europe, whereby the state is deemed to have an obligation to intervene actively when

[1] See Woolf (1995, 1996).

[2] Van Rhee (2018).

C. H. Van Rhee (✉)
Professor of European Legal History and Comparative Civil Procedure, Maastricht University, Maastricht, The Netherlands
e-mail: remco.vanrhee@maastrichtuniversity.nl

L. Cadiet and Y. Fu (eds.), *On Judicial Management from Comparative Perspective*, Contemporary Chinese Civil and Commercial Law,
https://doi.org/10.1007/978-981-19-8673-4_2

the interests of weaker groups in society are being jeopardised (i.e., the social welfare state).

In light of the above, it is surprising that the *Verhandlungsmaxime* remained a central principle in handbooks on civil procedure in Europe throughout the nineteenth and twentieth centuries. Most likely, this is due to the many exceptions to this principle that were admitted in Europe since its 'invention' by von Gönner, which made it, to a large extent, meaningless as an overarching principle of civil procedure. This also is demonstrated in many European jurisdictions where a new balance between adversarial and less adversarial elements in civil procedure has been sought since the end of the nineteenth century. This has resulted in a new principle of civil procedure, first formulated at the end of the twentieth century. The principle can best be described as the 'principle of co-operation', even though the very name 'co-operation principle' is only used in a few jurisdictions, notably in France (*principe de coopération*).[3] Although it is not seen in the 2005 Principles of Transnational Civil Procedure of the American Law Institute and UNIDROIT,[4] it seems that the principle is now also embraced in the 2021 Model European Rules of Civil Procedure of the European Law Institute and UNIDROIT[5]:

> Rule 2 (General) Parties, their lawyers, and the court[6] must co-operate to promote the fair, efficient and speedy resolution of the dispute.[7]
>
> Rule 6 (Role of the parties and their lawyers) Parties and their lawyers must co-operate with the court to promote a proportionate dispute resolution process.[8]

---

[3] Van Rhee (2017).

[4] See ALI/UNIDROIT (2005).

[5] See ELI/UNIDROIT (2021). Below, the Model Rules and the Commentary are cited. Quotation marks will not always be used when it is otherwise evident that reference is made to the Model Rules or the Commentary.

[6] The Model European Rules do not seem to make an express (only sometimes an implicit) distinction between 'court' and 'judge,' although such a distinction was suggested by one of the working groups preparing the Model Rules, i.e. the Working Group on Obligations of Parties, Lawyers and Judges ('Obligations Working Group' hereafter). In the Preamble of the draft of this working group, we read: 'It should be noted that rules referring to the court (as opposed to judges) include the powers and responsibilities of all existing court structures that ensure the good administration of justice in particular cases.'

[7] As regards the terminology 'fair,' 'efficient,' and 'speedy,' we find the following observations in the report of the Obligations Working Group (Rule 1, Comments): 'A precise definition of this terminology is hard to provide and may, in any event, even be dangerous. The terminology is flexible and should be interpreted in light of modern procedural standards. It should be read in the light of the procedural model that is envisaged by these rules. (1) 'Fair' includes the observance of modern procedural principles such as the duty of the parties to co-operate with each other and the court and the avoidance of manifestly ill-founded proceedings or the abuse of procedural rules for illegitimate purposes, (2) 'efficient' refers, amongst other things, to the use of resources in the least wasteful manner, (3) 'speedy' includes a time-frame which is reasonable given the nature, value and complexity of the case.'

[8] As regards the terminology 'proportionate,' we find the following observations in the report of the Obligations Working Group (Rule 1, Comments): "[P]roportionate' to a certain extent covers similar grounds as the terminology 'efficient' and 'speedy' taken together. 'Proportionate' is added

In the present contribution, the procedural model of the Model Rules will be discussed, especially where it concerns the effects of the principle of co-operation and case management (Sect. 3 below). First, some short remarks will be made on the historical context of the co-operation principle (Sect. 2 below).

2 A Procedural Model Based on the Principle of Co-operation

The starting point of a civil procedural model based on the co-operation principle is a political idea. It is the idea that civil procedure should be viewed from several perspectives: not only from the perspective of the litigants, but also from the perspective of society as a whole. This political idea is of course not new since it finds its roots in the writings of legal scholars such as the nineteenth century Austrian law professor Anton Menger (1841–1906) and the early twentieth century Austrian law reformer Franz Klein (1854–1926).[9] Admittedly, civil procedure aims at solutions for disputes on private rights and duties between private parties, but these solutions and the way they are reached may also influence other members of society. For example, the particular solution reached in a lawsuit generates case law that will influence the behaviour of third parties, whereas *the way* the solution is reached will also have consequences for third parties, e.g. where an inefficient use of court time in one particular case results in more limited means to decide disputes in other cases.

The various perspectives from which civil procedure can be viewed serves as a justification for a procedural model (1) that facilitates dispute resolution based on facts that come as near to the real facts in a dispute as possible, (2) that allows the court to take into consideration the correct legal rules, and (3) that contains guarantees for an effective and efficient use of the scarce resources available for litigation. Such a model cannot exist if the roles of the participants to a civil lawsuit (judges, parties, and their lawyers) are defined uniformly according to an overarching principle such as the adversarial principle. What is needed is a balanced approach to matters, defining the various roles of the actors in the various stages of litigation throughout the life of the civil lawsuit, and emphasising co-operation between these actors where it is necessary to achieve the three overarching goals just stated.

[to the original draft rule of the Obligations Working Group] in order to emphasise that different types of cases may require different use of resources and time.'

[9] Menger (1876), Klein (1891); Cf. Van Rhee (2005).

3 The Procedural Model of the Model European Rules[10]

The procedural model of the Model European Rules of Civil Procedure takes as its starting point that all participants in a civil lawsuit, i.e. the court, parties, and their lawyers, share the responsibility of putting an end to the dispute in a fair, efficient, and speedy manner.[11] The ELI/UNIDROIT working group entrusted with providing first drafts of the rules on the obligations of parties, lawyers, and judges ('Obligations Working Group' hereafter)[12] expressed this as follows:

> The rules [drafted by the Obligations Working Group] provide a modern approach to civil litigation in that they put the emphasis on loyal co-operation between the judge, the parties

[10] Below I will not discuss sanctions for the non-observance of the various obligations of parties and lawyers that are mentioned in the Model European Rules. It should, however, be noted that unlike the draft provided by the Obligations Working Group, the Model Rules do not regulate sanctions for *judges* in case they disregard their case management duties. Rules 11(3) and (4) drafted by the Working Group were not included in the Model European Rules. The former Rules read as follows: '11(3) A party may request that a competent authority transfer their proceedings to another judge where there is a failure on the part of a judge to carry out the general case management duty. 11(4) The parties may complain to relevant bodies for judicial conduct and discipline for investigation of alleged judicial failure to manage the case in an appropriate manner.' The Comments to these Rules read as follows: 'The third and fourth subsections deal with some of the consequences of a court's failure to carry out its case management duty effectively. This may occur, for instance, where the court has failed to issue any necessary case management order or if, due to its mismanagement of the case, the matter which is put before the court is not resolved within a reasonable time. Indeed, in line with the principle of loyal co-operation [the draft consistently refers to 'loyal co-operation' to better emphasise what behaviour is expected from the participants to a legal dispute], the party or the parties should openly discuss the management issues with the court and stimulate it to take action. Transfer of a case to another judge and, especially, complaints to competent disciplinary bodies, are appropriate only if a court's failure to adequately manage the proceedings is of a more serious nature. It should be noted that in some countries transferring cases may be difficult due to concepts of 'natural jurisdiction' and lack of competence by the court management to transfer cases (which, still, may be inevitable if the judge is unable to continue its work, e.g. due to sickness or other grounds).' The Working Group also stated (Rule 4, Comments): '… [S]anctions, if imposed on judges, do not affect their independence, since independence should be understood as independence in deciding the substance of the dispute between the parties and not as independence in managing the case procedurally.'

[11] ELI/UNIDROIT (2021, Rule 2). In draft Rule 2 of the Working Group it is stated that the lawyers must assist the parties to observe their procedural obligations. In the comments to this draft Rule we read: 'Assisting parties in the observance of their procedural obligations means, amongst other things, that lawyers should inform the parties of these procedural obligations as expressed in the Rules and of the consequences of non-compliance. Lawyers should not knowingly co-operate in any non-compliance with these obligations. If necessary, they should actively promote compliance by the parties. If a party persists in being non-compliant, this may ultimately mean that a lawyer has to terminate its relationship with that party.'

[12] This working group of the European law Institute and UNIDROIT was chaired by Professor Alan Uzelac and the author of the present contribution. Members of the Working Group were Emmanuel Jeuland (Paris), Bartosz Karolczyk (Warsaw), Walter Rechberger (Vienna), Elisabetta Silvestri (Pavia), John Sorabji (London) and Magne Strandberg (Bergen). The rules of the Obligations Working Group have served as a basis of part of the Model European Rules of Civil Procedure. They have been published with Oxford University Press (2021). It should be noted that not all suggestions of the Obligations Working Group have been adopted.

> and their lawyers. The rules are written from the perspective that judges, parties and their lawyers have a shared responsibility in putting an end to disputes in a fair, efficient, speedy and proportionate manner, either by way of settlement or by way of a court decision based on the true facts and right law. This means that the adversarial-inquisitorial divide is intentionally avoided. The underlying idea of the rules is that there is no mutually exclusive division of labour between the various participants in a civil lawsuit; there are only shared obligations. This means that apart from the parties, the court also has certain obligations regarding facts and evidence, whereas parties share the responsibility for the assessment of the pertinent legal issues with the judge. It is the duty of the lawyers to support the parties in the execution of their obligations. Lawyers' duties, however, go further than that as they also have to observe professional duties normally found in codes of conduct, to which the present rules refer where necessary.

In order to achieve this goal and to promote 'a proportionate dispute resolution process', the court, the parties, and their lawyers need to co-operate.[13] It is the court that must make sure that the dispute resolution process is indeed proportionate. To this end, it must not only consider 'the nature, importance and complexity' of the individual case at hand, but also its further caseload (other cases) to make sure that justice can be administered in all of these cases in a proper manner.[14] The latter is expressed as follows in Rule 5(2):

> In determining whether a process is proportionate the court must take account … of the need to give effect to its general management duty in all proceedings with due regard for the proper administration of justice.

The court should make sure that the least complex and costly methods are chosen to resolve disputes, if possible, outside the court by way of alternative dispute resolution.[15]

According to the Model European Rules, co-operation is already required before the case is brought to court, i.e. in the pre-commencement or pre-action stage.[16] In the Comments accompanying draft Rule 1 of the Obligations, it reads:

> Parties should observe their obligations not only during litigation but even before the case is brought to court (the pre-action stage) … In the pre-action stage the parties should co-operate in such a manner that the facts and the law underpinning their dispute are stated sufficiently, that available evidence is exchanged and that sufficient settlement attempts are undertaken before court action is initiated. Obviously, sanctions for non-observance of these obligations are not available in the pre-action stage, but they may be imposed when the case actually reaches the court (cf. the English pre-action protocols).

In the pre-action stage, the parties are required to co-operate with the aim of avoiding 'unnecessary disputes and costs, to facilitate the early consensual resolution of their dispute and, where such a resolution is not possible, the proportionate management of future proceedings …'[17] Co-operation in the pre-action stage may

---

[13] ELI/UNIDROIT (2021, Rules 2 and 6).

[14] ELI/UNIDROIT (2021, Rules 5).

[15] Cf. ELI/UNIDROIT (2021, Comments Rule 5).

[16] See Rule 22, Comments of the Obligations Working Group for a definition of the 'pre-action phase': '… the notion of 'pre-action phase' refers to the period after the dispute has arisen, but before the formal initiation of civil proceedings.'

[17] ELI/UNIDROIT (2021, Rule 51(1)).

imply that the parties make sure that their opponent is provided with 'concise details' of the claims and defences that may be brought if the case is taken to court, that disputed legal and factual issues are clarified and, if possible, narrowed, and that relevant evidence is identified.[18] In the pre-action stage parties may also discuss a timetable for the proceedings that may follow, make an estimate of the potential costs of litigation, and pay attention to prescription (statute of limitations), as well as jurisdiction, provisional measures, and 'any other procedural matter.'[19]

Attempting an amicable settlement is a central task for the parties and their lawyers.[20] Co-operation to resolve the dispute consensually is needed both in the pre-action stage, and when the case is brought before the court.[21] In order to make sure that the parties consider amicable settlement, their lawyers should inform them about consensual dispute resolution methods. The same lawyers should also provide assistance in selecting the most suitable method of consensual dispute resolution, and encourage its use where appropriate.[22] After the case has reached the court (therefore, after the pre-action stage), the court also has certain responsibilities with regards to the settlement. The Model Rules provide that 'the court must facilitate settlement at any stage of the proceedings' (in the Comments, it is stated that 'Early Neutral Evaluation' of the court may increase the possibilities of settlement)[23] and, just like the lawyers, inform the parties about the different types of settlement methods that may be used and suggest or recommend certain use of such methods. The court may also participate in settlement attempts, and assist the parties in reaching a consensual resolution and in drafting settlement agreements.[24] Assistance by lawyers and the court is important, since very often the parties themselves may not be aware of suitable methods of consensual dispute resolution and their benefits.

The above approach will most likely result in fewer cases reaching the state courts. And if cases are brought before these courts, it will mean that matters the parties can agree upon without the help of the court are not in dispute anymore. In other words, the dispute has been condensed: the court will consequently only have to deal with issues the parties have not been able to resolve in the pre-action stage.[25]

When in court, the parties and their lawyers should also display a co-operative attitude: they should 'contribute to the proper management of the proceedings.' This means that they must present their claims and defences, including facts and offers

---

[18] ELI/UNIDROIT (2021, Rule 51(2)).

[19] ELI/UNIDROIT (2021, Rule 51(3)). In the Rule, we read: '(c) consider issues of limitation'. A civil law audience may have preferred the terminology 'consider issues of prescription.'

[20] ELI/UNIDROIT (2021, Rule 3(a)).

[21] In the Preamble of the Obligations Working Group we read: 'The main rule is that parties must co-operate actively with each other in seeking to resolve their dispute consensually, both before and after proceedings have begun.'

[22] ELI/UNIDROIT (2021, Rule 9).

[23] See ELI/UNIDROIT (2021, Rule 10, Comment 1).

[24] ELI/UNIDROIT (2021, Rules 10 and 49(1)).

[25] ELI/UNIDROIT (2021, Rule 9(4)). The Obligations Working Group mentioned in its comments to its draft Rule 22: 'Where a settlement is not achieved, these steps may help in better management of the subsequent litigation proceedings.'

of evidence, and assist the court in the determination of the relevant facts and the applicable law 'as early and completely as possible and as appropriate to the careful conduct of litigation in order to secure procedural expedition.'[26] Different from the draft Rules of the Obligations Working Group, the Model Rules do not require that 'assertions of fact should take into consideration the opposing views [of the opponent party], if they were made known to the pleader.'[27] The Model Rules provide in Rule 53(6): 'The claimant *may* respond in a statement of claim to the defendant's defence as known from any exchange of arguments before commencement of proceedings' (emphasis supplied). Parties and their lawyers should furthermore abstain from procedural abuse and act in good faith.[28] In all stages of the proceedings, the court must monitor whether parties and their lawyers actually co-operate.[29]

Effective management of the case is the responsibility of the court,[30] albeit with the help of the parties.[31] It is specifically the task of the court to ensure that the

[26] ELI/UNIDROIT (2021, Rules 3, 47, 52ff and 87ff).

[27] Comments to draft Rule 12 of the Working Group. Draft Rule 12(1) reads: 'Parties are under a duty to identify the matter in dispute as early as possible, taking into consideration the views of the other party if these have become known to them.'

[28] ELI/UNIDROIT (2021, Rule 3).

[29] ELI/UNIDROIT (2021, Rules 4 and 48). See also ELI/UNIDROIT (2021, Rule 47, Comment 4): 'To ensure that parties fulfil their duty to co-operate properly, the court ought to monitor their conduct throughout the proceedings. It ought to require the parties to take such steps as it considers necessary to fulfil the obligation when it considers that such steps are necessary for the proper management of proceedings.' Cf. the Comments of the Obligations Working Group accompanying its draft Rule 3: 'Moreover, the court must monitor whether other participants in the lawsuit observe their obligations. Monitoring is a continual duty in so far as the court ought to ensure that procedural obligations are observed and that voluntary compliance with the professional obligations is secured throughout the entire course of the proceedings. Of course, continual monitoring does not imply that the court needs to check the progress of the case on a daily basis. It only means that throughout the proceedings the court should establish whether procedural timetables and procedural steps and actions, which were agreed or determined by the court, are being complied with, taking appropriate enforcement action if necessary. … In individual cases the court's duties have to be implemented by individual judges or panels of judges. This is an aspect of their judicial case management function. It is suggested that, in implementing this function, judges are monitored by the court: monitoring of adequate performance of this function does not touch upon the independence and impartiality of judges in decision-making. The courts themselves could be monitored by a Council for the Judiciary or a similar body that is independent of the Ministry of Justice.'

[30] ELI/UNIDROIT (2021, Rule 4).

[31] In the Preamble of the Obligations Working Group we read: 'Active management of proceedings under the court's direction also includes the duty to consult the parties and, wherever possible, secure their agreement on the form, content and timing of particular steps in the proceedings. The court's duty of active case management authorises judges to encourage the parties to identify the real issues in dispute, and to openly discuss with them the appropriate steps and methods for dealing with these issues. A case management conference is meant for consultations with the parties and their lawyers on such matters.' Part of the Comment to the Working Group's draft Rule 5 reads: 'As case management is an aspect of the court's *ex officio* or inherent powers, the parties' and their representatives' role is primarily a co-operative one. Parties may have a right to be heard before the court exercises its case management powers.' The draft Rules of the Obligations Working Group contain a Rule 10 entitled 'Co-operation in Issuing and Amending Case Management Orders.' Cf. ELI/UNIDROIT (2021, Rule 50(1) of the Model European Rules).

way the dispute is litigated is in conformity with what is at stake. This means that the court should make sure that the dispute resolution process is proportionate to 'the nature, importance and complexity of the particular case and of the need to give effect to its general management duty in all proceedings with due regard for the proper administration of justice.'[32] As stated above, the court should not only consider proportionality from the perspective of the individual case, but should also consider issues within the context of its wider workload. It should be noted here, that with a few exceptions, the Model European Rules do not provide procedural tracks for specific types of cases.[33] Such tracks are not necessary, since according to the Model Rules the judge and the parties can tailor the procedure to fit the individual needs of the case at hand.

A case management hearing (or case management conference) should be held as early as possible.[34] With regard to such hearings, the Obligations Working Group provided in its draft Rule 6: '… If requirements are met, the court must determine the claim on the merits at a case management conference[35] or immediately thereafter.'[36] In practice, this may mean that the case is decided on the merits at the first case management hearing scheduled. It seems that the possibility of such an early termination of the case may also be read into the Model Rules, where the drafters state in their Comments: 'In many cases proceedings may conclude with an early final judgment without there being any need for an elaborate concentrated final hearing.'[37]

Further case management hearings may be held if necessary, either with the parties attending in person, in writing, or by way of electronic means.[38] The structure of the proceedings as envisaged by the Model Rules is uncomplicated: there is a written pleading phase (meant for the submission of the statements of case), an interim phase which lasts until the closure of the proceedings, and a final phase for the final concentrated hearing and judgment.[39] Comment 3 accompanying Rule 61 states:

> The structure of the procedural model that underpins these Rules represents a clear rejection of discontinuous or of piecemeal proceedings, which involve a lengthy sequence of hearings, which result in unnecessary cost and delay. As a consequence, the fact that these Rules provide a discretion for the court to hold more than one case management hearing (see Rule 61(1)) should not be understood as an invitation to adopt a discontinuous, piecemeal approach to proceedings. The discretion to hold more than one case management hearing should only be exercised in appropriate circumstances, such as complex cases or where there has been an

32 ELI/UNIDROIT (2021, Rule 5).

33 ELI/UNIDROIT (2021, Rule 49, Comment 4).

34 ELI/UNIDROIT (2021, Rule 61).

35 The Obligations Working Group defined a case management conference as follows: 'A case management conference is the arena where the parties may exercise their right to be heard, in particular regarding matters relevant for the organization of the proceedings' (draft Rule 6, Comments).

36 In the Comment to this draft Rule, the Working Group states: 'If the case is sufficiently clear, the judge may determine the case on its merits at the case management conference.'

37 ELI/UNIDROIT (2021, Rule 61, Comment 1). Cf. ELI/UNIDROIT (2021, Rule 65).

38 ELI/UNIDROIT (2021, Rule 61).

39 ELI/UNIDROIT (2021, Rule 61, Comment 1).

unexpected change in the parties' original positions during the course of the proceedings. In such cases further case management hearings may be necessary to properly manage the proceedings.

Case management orders may be made on the court's own motion (usually upon consultation with the parties) or on application of a party. Case management orders can also be made immediately after the early case management hearing. If parties are not heard before the order is made, such parties may apply for reconsideration of the order or decision at a hearing or in writing. Normally, the court shall take the case management measures on which the parties agree. Varying or revoking a case management order may be done upon a party's motion, or even the court's own motion.[40]

The court's means of case-management include:

- giving the parties advice for the preparation of their case and make case management orders;
- scheduling case management conferences;
- determining the type and the form of the procedure;
- setting a timetable or procedural calendar with deadlines for procedural steps to be taken by parties and/or their lawyers;
- limiting the number and length of future submissions;
- determining the order in which issues should be tried and whether proceedings should be consolidated or separated;
- determining the separation of questions concerning jurisdiction, provisional measures, and statutes of limitation for early decision upon special hearings;
- considering necessary amendments regarding the parties' proper representation, the consequences of changes related to the parties to litigation, and the participation of third parties, intervenors, or other persons;
- considering amendments to the pleadings or offers of evidence in the light of the parties' contentions;
- requiring a party's appearance in person or requiring a party's representative, who should be fully informed of all matters relevant to the proceedings, to be present at a court hearing;
- addressing the availability, admissibility, form, disclosure, and exchange of evidence and, if adequate to the state of proceedings, (a) determine the admissibility of evidence, and/or (b) order the taking of evidence; or
- setting the timetable for a final hearing and the possible date by which the judgment will be given.[41]

Rule 11 provides that management by the court implies that the court must make sure that parties not only have a fair opportunity to present their case and evidence, but that they are also able to respond to the respective claims and defences and to any court orders or matters raised by the court.

---

40 ELI/UNIDROIT (2021, Rule 50). See also ELI/UNIDROIT (2021, Rule 61).

41 ELI/UNIDROIT (2021, Rules 49 and 61).

It is the task of the parties to put forward the relevant facts, but the court 'may invite the parties to clarify or supplement these facts.' Facts that have not been introduced by the parties can only be considered by the court if they are relevant and 'necessarily implied by matters of fact put forward by the parties or which are contained within the case file.' If such facts are considered, the parties should be given a reasonable opportunity to respond.[42]

Offering evidence of the relevant facts is the task of the parties. This means that the parties should, as a rule, offer evidence supporting the facts introduced by them. Where appropriate, 'parties and non-parties must contribute to disclosure and production of evidence', even if such evidence is advantageous for a party's opponent or for other parties (the rule *nemo contra se edere tenetur* is not part of the Model Rules).[43] The court may ask the parties to supplement their offers of evidence, and even suggest evidence. The court will order the taking of relevant evidence offered by a party whenever this is deemed necessary and appropriate, and by way of exception, courts may take evidence *ex officio*. The court may, amongst other things, decide about 'the sequence and timing of the production of evidence' in a case management order. The court may also determine the form in which evidence will be produced. It should afford the parties an opportunity to respond where it acts *ex officio*, and the parties must be given a fair opportunity and adequate time to respond to evidence that is presented.[44]

Appropriate case management measures for the disclosure of evidence and the taking of evidence before the final hearing are:

(a) the production and mutual exchange of documents;
(b) requests for written witness statements and their exchange;
(c) the appointment of a court expert and expert conferences between a court-appointed expert and experts appointed by the parties, or between court-appointed experts;
(d) requests for information from third parties, including public authorities; and
(e) personal inspection of evidence by the court.[45]

Although the rule 'ius curia novit' is observed, parties may present legal arguments supporting their claim or defence. The Obligations Working Group expressed this forcefully for parties represented by a lawyer. In the Preamble of the Working Group, one reads:

---

[42] ELI/UNIDROIT (2021, Rule 24). See also the Preamble of the Obligations Working Group: 'Apart from the parties, the court has certain responsibilities regarding facts …: the rules [of the Working Group] provide that the court may consider facts that appear in the case file even though they have not been used by the parties to build their argument, or may take evidence on its own motion if this is necessary for the proper adjudication of the case. This position follows the tradition, common to many European jurisdictions, of allowing the court discretion to actively intervene in factual … issues in order to eliminate injustice or an abuse of judicial proceedings. In the understanding of the drafters, these powers will be used only exceptionally. Thereafter, the court can only exceptionally request or permit additional facts … necessary to clarify the respective positions of the parties.'

[43] ELI/UNIDROIT (2021, Rule 25, Comment 5).

[44] ELI/UNIDROIT (2021, Rules 25 and 92).

[45] ELI/UNIDROIT (2021, Rule 62).

> The rules [of the Working Group] provide that both the court and the parties *should* contribute to the determination of the correct legal basis for decision-making. Parties *have an obligation* to present contentions of law, something which must be done in reasonable detail. The court may consider points of law on its own initiative if this is necessary for correct decision-making (emphasis supplied).

In its Comments to its draft Rule 17, the Working Group states:

> ... it is generally not sufficient to limit the parties' submissions merely to the bare presentation of facts on the expectation that the court will simply and passively identify the right legal provisions and apply them to the present case. Consequently, the old approach still influential in some jurisdictions, known under Latin saying *da mihi factum, dabo tibi ius*, is not supported in this Rule, at least when parties are represented by qualified lawyers. However, where parties are not represented by lawyers, the court is obliged to act in a more active manner and to assist the parties in identifying and clarifying their legal arguments.

Although the Model Rules differ from those of the Obligations Working Group in that they do not introduce a duty for the parties to supply legal argument,[46] it is hard to envisage a situation in which parties do not present such arguments, especially when represented by a lawyer. After all, the selection and introduction of relevant facts is not well possible without taking into consideration the legal arguments used in the case.

As soon as the court is satisfied that both parties have had a reasonable opportunity to present their case, it will close the proceedings after which, as a rule, no further submissions, arguments, or evidence are allowed.[47] The case is then ready for the final hearing.[48] This final hearing is a concentrated event, and takes place before the judge or judges who will give the final judgment. The taking of evidence is still allowed, albeit with some restrictions. The court determines the order in which issues shall be tried during the final hearing and is in charge of managing the proceedings. Parties must have an opportunity to submit their final conclusions including statements on the results of evidence-taking.[49]

4 Conclusion

The Model European Rules of Civil Procedure of the European Law Institute and UNIDROIT provide a modern approach to civil procedure which, according to its drafters, may be qualified as best practice. They take as their starting point the principle of co-operation and case management, and provide a procedural model that fits the leading political ideas in the European Union about the role of the state and its organs (such as the judiciary) tightly. This approach to litigation is far removed from

---

46 ELI/UNIDROIT (2021, Rule 26(1)): '...the parties *may* present legal arguments supporting their claim or defence' (emphasis supplied).

47 Cf. Rule 16(1) of the Obligations Working Group).

48 ELI/UNIDROIT (2021, Rule 63).

49 ELI/UNIDROIT (2021, Rule 64).

the liberal, laissez-faire approach to matters of the nineteenth century, and perfectly fits the 20th and 21st European models of the (liberal) social welfare state. The rules reflect the idea that the state is there to protect its citizens and that it should make sure that its services (here, the administration of justice through the state courts) are provided efficiently and proportionately. Within such a political context, it is to be expected that the Model Rules will flourish and be embraced by various EU institutions and Member States. Given the political differences in Europe, however, it may also be expected that the Model Rules will not be equally popular in all parts of Europe.

References

ALI/UNIDROIT (2005) Principles of transnational civil procedure. CUP, Cambridge

ELI/UNIDROIT (2021) ELI-UNIDROIT Model European rules of civil procedure. OUP, Oxford

Klein F (1891) Pro futuro: Betrachtungen über Probleme der Civilproceßreform in Österreich. Deuticke, Vienna

Menger A (1876) System des oesterreichischen Civilprocessrechts in rechtsvergleichender Darstellung. Hölder, Vienna

Van Rhee CH (2005) European traditions in civil procedure. Intersentia, Antwerp

Van Rhee CH (2017) Principe de coopération - co-operation principle. In: Jeuland E, Lalani S (eds) Lexicographical research in civil procedure. IRJS Editions, Paris, pp 207–214

Van Rhee CH (2018) Case management in Europe: a modern approach to civil litigation. Int J Proced Law 8(1):65–84

Woolf L (1995) Access to justice: interim report to the Lord Chancellor on the civil justice system in England and Wales. https://webarchive.nationalarchives.gov.uk/ukgwa/20060213222829/, http://www.dca.gov.uk/civil/interfr.htm. Accessed 1 Dec 2022

Woolf L (1996) Access to justice. Final report to the Lord Chancellor on the civil justice system in England and Wales. https://webarchive.nationalarchives.gov.uk/20060213223540/, http://www.dca.gov.uk/civil/final/contents.htm. Accessed 1 Dec 2022

New Trends and Perspectives on Case Management: Proposals on Procedural Agreements and Case Assignment Management

Antonio Cabral

1 Introduction

The yearning for a more adequate, speedy and effective judicial process has driven legal systems all around the world to rethink its rules and practices. Among the attempts of improval, case management consolidated itself in several jurisdictions as a tool to improve efficiency in civil procedure. And in many ways it has proven to be effective.

However, it is not simply a time for praise and rejoice of all the prior generations' efforts and achievements in the field of case management. We shall look back and give some thought on how this practice evolved. The aftermath could show us where things went wrong and what to correct.

My role, as introductory speaker, is to present what I understand to be the new trends in the field of case management. For this purpose, my aim is to lay out some classic assumptions that I believe to be the basis of the legal literature on the subject, and then identify possible blind spots and the possibilities for the development of case management activities over the coming years.

This introductory essay sets out to answer that question and proceeds as follows. Part I (infra Sects. 2–3) introduces and describes the traditional view of case management, sketching out its core elements: object, persons involved, goals and techniques applied as a management tool. Part I is thus primarily concerned with diagnosing the ways in case management has operated so far.

Part II (infra Sects. 4–7) poses, at a broad level, some of the procedural questions implicated by the new trends in case management. With examples in comparative perspective, this subpart critically examines and evaluates where the developing of the subject is heading, identifying scenarios useful to frame some of the problems and choices facing us today.

A. Cabral (✉)
Faculty of Law, Rio de Janeiro State University, Rio de Janeiro, Brazil
e-mail: antoniocabral@uerj.br

L. Cadiet and Y. Fu (eds.), *On Judicial Management from Comparative Perspective*, Contemporary Chinese Civil and Commercial Law,
https://doi.org/10.1007/978-981-19-8673-4_3

With this background in place, Part III (infra Sects. 8–9) outlines, as a mere preliminary suggestion, some proposals for improving case management in the following decades. My focus will be on: procedural agreements (negotiated procedure or procedure defined by contract), and case assignment management (relating the topic with both adjudication and court administration issues).

The paper then concludes by considering these further applications and potential objections to the proposed management tools.

2 What Is Case Management?

Case management constitutes the early and continuous control over a judicial process and its proceeding in terms of efficiency, in order to enhance speed and quality, as well as to ensure compliance. Case management depends on *planning*, and works by establishing objectives related to activities within the justice system that are suited to the attainment of these targets. These planned activities are to be performed in a resource-saving manner and accompanied by indicators that enable the control of the results. Constant monitoring in each step of the process is crucial to allow adjournments and adjustments.

3 Classic Assumptions of Case Management

I would like to briefly establish some of the assumptions of traditional legal writing—whether expressly stated or merely assumed—when describing case management.

3.1 Who Manages? Players Involved and Protagonism of State Bodies: Judicial *Case Management*

Subjectively, the study of the management task in a judicial proceeding frequently focuses on players from the judiciary. It is common to emphasise the jurisdictional role of the judge in a given case and the instruments at her disposal to make that procedure more efficient.

But it is also common to highlight the administrative side of those functions, either performed by the judge or by the judiciary, as an institution. Anyway, these management activities, although performed by judges, are described as an administrative role rather than jurisdictional. Case management, as we shall see, is a task that stays half way between adjudication and judiciary administration.[1]

[1] Jeuland (2017, pp. 7–8).

In one case or another, the *judge* is the *key management player*.[2] On the administrative side, while in some parts of the common law world, court administration has been delegated to professional managers, in the Roman-Germanic tradition (and that has always been the reality of Latin America as well), this task has been predominantly performed by judges with the assistance of the judiciary's personnel (civil servants or contractors), who are in practice responsible for these administrative functions.[3]

In recent years, seeking alternatives to the management of courts by judges, one can observe initiatives aiming to put other government bodies, such as those of the executive branch, in charge of case management. In the countries where this happens, there is a lot of controversy about whether the task of judicial case management, when not performed by judges, could lead to a violation of the separation of powers, allowing forms of constraint, pressure or external influence to be imposed on judicial decisions.[4]

On the other hand, regarding the procedural management powers within the jurisdictional sphere (adjudication), it was in common law legal systems that, in order to exercise those objectives of efficiency, judges were granted powers to define the manner in which procedural legal acts are to be performed with more flexibility, adapting them to the circumstances of the case at hand.[5] The widespread belief was that, in order to achieve greater efficiency, case management had to be implemented by an extensive control of litigation—and its formalities—exercised by the managing judge (the so-called 'court control of litigation').[6] It is deemed that, if a judge is to

---

[2] Many authors still depict the judge as a passive umpire or a detached decisionmaker, but the increasing discretion related to case management powers show that the judge becomes more and more another 'strategic player in the litigation game,' as Bone highlights: Bone (2007, pp. 1996–1997).

[3] Jeuland (2017, pp. 17ff), Röhl (1998, pp. 242ff).

[4] Ferejohn (1999, pp. 353–384).

[5] Mainly in the USA, but also in England since the reforms resulting from the Woolf Report. See Flood et al. (2007, p. 143). The full content of Woolf's final report can be seen in: http://webarchive.nationalarchives.gov.uk/+/http://www.dca.gov.uk/civil/final/contents.htm. Judicial powers are exemplified in Part 3 of the Civil Procedure Rules. In legal literature, Clarke (2009, pp. 33–49). In the United States of America, there was no provision in statutory law, but the constant concerns of legal scholars and of the Judiciary with economic aspects led to a progressive acceptance of judges' procedural management powers, always with regard to greater efficiency of the results. See Resnik (1982, pp. 374 ff, 419–431), Marcus (2008, pp. 2274–2275). In Brazil, Gajardoni (2008a, b, pp. 162ff), Ono (2016, p. 3).

[6] According to Van Rhee, '(1) The specific nature of the case should determine to a large extent the rules, directions and orders that govern the proceedings; (2) The rules, directions and orders of proceedings should to a large extent be determined by the judges, parties and attorneys involved in the case and not by detailed legal provisions; (3) The court should have the necessary procedural discretionary powers to manage the case; (4) The court's direction should be discretion in the weak sense, that is to say, the court should use its powers for a specific goal, i.e., to achieve the disposition of the dispute fairly, efficiently, and with reasonable speed.' Van Rhee (2008a, b, pp. 3–4). About the subject, Andrews (2003, p. 333), Sorabji (2017, pp. 1ff), Resnik (1986, pp. 524, 534–535 (with strong criticism)), Dodge (2014, p. 333), Almeida (2011, p. 289), Barbosa Moreira (2001, pp. 185–186), Amendoeira (2006, p. 55), Cabral (2010a, b, pp. 150–153).

exercise her jurisdictional powers aiming at efficiency, she must be assured prerogatives that allow her to conduct and adapt the manner in which procedural acts are performed in order to attain optimal results.

One speaks of *judicial* case management, the management power a judge has to waive formalities, change deadlines, interfere in the order of the production of evidence, etc.[7] In some jurisdictions, case management powers of judges involve court rulemaking,[8] with judges' discretion to define procedure rules,[9] and extends to the appointment of litigation committees, sequencing of issues, setting a timetable for pretrial discovery, summary judgment, etc.[10]

In the wake of these trends of the common law legal systems, the Brazilian Code of Civil Procedure (CPC) incorporated judicial case management in Art. 139, VI, allowing the judge more flexibility in the rendering of deadlines and the taking of evidence; and also, in articles 69 and 55 § 3, enables joinder of claims on efficiency grounds.[11] In some proceedings, the judge can choose on efficiency grounds to stay or to process satellite litigation together with the original case (Art. 685, sole paragraph).

The new statute established in Art. 357 a 'procedural phase' for the organisation of the procedure, especially pretrial activity, in which the judge: defines the issues of fact that the parties will need to prove; decides what kind of evidence will be admissible; determines the burden of proof, which can be distributed dynamically on a case-by-case basis (Art. 373 §1°); and establishes the legal issues relevant to the

[7] Jeuland (2011, p. 98), Papier (2001, p. 1093), Gajardoni (2008a, b, pp. 119ff), Shetreet (1989, pp. 295, 299, 303–304), Silva (2010, pp. 137ff), Carvalho (2015, pp. 273ff), Didier (2016, pp. 118ff), Cahali (2013, pp. 44, 203ff).

[8] In the USA, professional court administration began soon in the first half of the twentieth century, enabled by the broad normative power of the judiciary to regulate its own activities, even in many aspects of its budget. Congress holds a sort of 'veto power' by producing statutes that revoke provisions of the courts. An interesting approach of the US system in a civil law perspective can be found in Röhl (1998, pp. 243–244).

[9] Bone (1999, p. 917). About the different systems regarding discretionary case management powers of the judge, see Sorabji (2017, pp. 38ff).

[10] Bone (2007, p. 1968).

[11] If no other evidence is needed, the Code of Civil Procedure grants the judge the power to decide the case on the merits (whether totally or partially) by summary judgments, i.e., without a trial hearing or taking of testimonial or expert evidence (Arts. 354 and 356). In Brazilian legal literature, see Marinoni et al. (2015a, b, p. 47), Gajardoni et al. (2015, p. 72). Didier (2001). Didier Jr. speaks of a 'jurisdictional adaptation of the procedure.' Didier (2016, p. 119), giving other examples of normative provisions that reinforce the normative basis of this adaptability. In the same sense, Bedaque (2006, pp. 63ff, 109–112), Oliveira (2013), Cabral (2010a, b, p. 63). This principle of adaptability is provided for in the Portuguese Civil Procedure Law for quite some time, allowing the judge a more flexible management of procedural formalities. This flexibility exists in Portugal since the previous Code of Civil Procedure (Art. 265.°-A (princípio da adequação formal): 'Quando a tramitação processual prevista na lei não se adequar às especificidades da causa, deve o juiz oficiosamente, ouvidas as partes, determinar a prática dos actos que melhor se ajustem ao fim do processo, bem como as necessárias adaptações'), and the new Code of Civil Procedure from 2013 introduced an intense duty of judicial case management for the judge (Art. 6). In the Portuguese legal literature, Geraldes (2012, p. 93). In France and Norway one can note this progressive quest for flexibility in the last decades. See Cornu (1998, pp. 391–393), Valguarnera (2008, pp. 888, 891, 893–894).

judgment on merits. In complex cases, the Code of Civil Procedure provides that the court should set a date for a hearing to allow the parties to discuss the organisational issues with the judge (Art. 357 §3º).

The overall intention is to grant the judge powers to manage the proceedings, assuring greater adaptability and flexibility of the formalities, which can result in a more suitable and efficient judicial process, in step with the calls for an effective access to justice.[12]

While many legal scholars are favourable to the management attitude of judges,[13] this emphasis on judicial case management has attracted a lot of criticism.[14] Especially in countries where the posture of the judge is more restricted and passive, one takes into consideration the risk of a magistrate, when taking on an intense management task, transmuting her activity, transforming from judge to manager until she becomes more of an interested player, perhaps the most important stakeholder, and certainly the most powerful.[15] The risk of compromising impartiality would be, from this perspective, immense.

In my view, such risks can be mitigated nowadays, because the management functions can be exercised beyond the debate between self-restraint and judicial activism. Within the paradigm of the principle of cooperation, one can overcome the dichotomy between activism and 'guarantism', or between the prevalence of public or private interests (publicism vs. private ordering), with the practical advantage of all the players (partial, impartial, interested or not regarding substantive law) being brought together by the common goal of having the proceedings conducted in a correct, efficient and just manner.[16]

From this point of view, the management of proceedings by the judges would not represent a risk to their impartiality or independence, but rather a natural and necessary activity for the administration of justice in the contemporary world,[17] aiming to afford greater efficiency and effectiveness to the results of the procedure.[18]

As can be easily seen, whether in adjudication or performing judiciary administration, in either case there is a widespread view that the management task is predominantly a *state* activity. Whether conducted by the executive branch or by the judiciary itself, the parties to court proceedings are *beneficiaries*, but not active players in the case management activity.

---

[12] Oliveira and Mitidiero (2012, pp. 74ff), Medina (2015, p. 115).

[13] Peckham (1981, pp. 770–773).

[14] Molot (2003, pp. 29ff).

[15] McGovern (1997, p. 1869).

[16] It's important to remember that, even in the common law tradition, where a greater passivity of the judge could be seen in the past, the behavior and the role of the judge have been modified more recently in light of the cooperation principle.

[17] Machado Alves (2016, pp. 73, 76).

[18] Fix-Fierro (2003).

3.2 *Object of Case Management: What to Manage?* **One-Case** *Management and* **Conflict** *Management.* **Court** *Management: Administration of Court Structures and Bodies*

With regard to the object of case management, there are two focal points of study and practices around the world.

On one hand, in the judicial sphere, there is a concern for the *existing* court proceedings, devising techniques to handle them judicially or extrajudicially. This practice could be described as *one-case management* or *conflict management.* One seeks to resolve a dispute *already brought before* the courts for them to decide; and, more and more, one wishes to provide a *suitable* solution, acknowledging the importance of arbitration for certain disputes, and having the humility to perceive that the best way of resolving a conflict may not necessarily be the judicial alternative, but also instruments of amicable resolution, promoting mechanisms such as mediation,[19] conciliation (within or outside the courts), collaborative law,[20] etc.[21]

On the other hand, there are increasing studies on the management of judicial structures, which has been termed *court management.* Court management is understood as the administration of staff (human resources, recruitment of civil servants, disciplinary proceedings) and budget of the court, infrastructure (real estate, construction, maintenance and security of the court buildings), and management of IT equipment and technology.[22]

The expression 'court management' has been entrenched in practice[23] because, in recent years, this aspect of the management activity has focused on the possibility of the courts expanding their structure, sectors and benches, promoting the qualification and training of judges, clerks and other court officials.

Court management, thus, relates to shaping management practices and improving court organisation. The legal duties that a judge carries out in a democratic state ruled by law depend on minimal structures to exercise her competences. Therefore, the legal system must concern itself with assuring *suitable organisational conditions*. Thus,

---

19 Cabral (2017b, pp. 342–359).

20 Cabral and Cunha (2016, pp. 471ff).

21 This trend has been highlighted in several of the reports written for this IAPL conference. See Sorabji (2017, pp. 39ff), Chan (2017, pp. 16ff), Perez-Ragone (2017, pp. 18ff).

22 Jeuland (2017, p. 1).

23 'Court management' may be an inaccurate term because this variant seeks to innovate not only within the judiciary itself, but also in institutions that are connected to the justice system, such as lawyers' associations, public defenders' services, the public prosecutor's office, mediation and conciliation centres etc. Some scholars reported some misunderstanding over the expression. Jeuland (2017, pp. 10ff). See also Perez-Ragone (2017, pp. 16–17). The term brings some confusion in a comparative analysis of the Chinese speaking countries, which have different traditions (some influenced by civil law jurisdictions such as Portugal and Germany, some with English background). See Chan (2017, pp. 9ff), Wang (2017, p. 1).

procedural efficiency becomes a goal to be sought also in the definition, planning, structuring and development of court management and organisation.

3.3 *When to Manage? Pre-trial and Post-trial Case Management*

With regard to the stages of proceedings, the case management task encompasses both the initial stages (the filing of the suit and the presentation of the defence by the parties), and the fact-finding phase for the gathering of evidence. This is known as *pre-trial case management*. However, there is also case management activities at the execution or enforcement phases, known as *post-trial case management*.[24]

3.4 *Goals of Case Management. Efficiency and Speed. Caseflow Management*

In a goal-oriented perspective, the legal literature that broaches case management states that the concerns with case and court management take into account the desired objectives of this activity.

One speaks mainly of efficiency, the calculation of cost–benefit (economy) and the aim of processing cases within a reasonable timeframe. The need to manage the large number of pending cases is also mentioned, which, in many countries, renders the workings of the judiciary almost impracticable. This is referred to as *caseflow management*.

The emphasis on each of these goals depends on the object and on the moment when the management activity is implemented. For example, pre-trial case management is concerned with cost and time reduction; whereas post-trial case management is predominantly concerned with effectiveness and efficiency.[25]

---

[24] Resnik (1982, pp. 391, 413–414). The differences are not only in terms of purposes; according to Resnik, they are observed also in respect to initiative and effects: 'In both, judges Interact informally with the litigating parties and receive information that would be considered inadmissible in traditional courtroom proceedings. Management at both ends of the lawsuit takes time and increases judges' responsibilities. Nevertheless, the two management stages are dissimilar in many respects. Predecision management is initiated usually by the judge; postdecision supervision begins more often at a litigant's request. Pretrial management occurs much more frequently, but posttrial intervention tends to be more far reaching in its effects. Unlike pretrial management, post-trial activity occurs within a framework of appellate oversight, public visibility, and institutional constraints that inhibits overreaching.'

[25] Resnik (1982, pp. 391, 413–414).

3.5 Methods and Techniques. Adaptable Formalities, Cost Management, Time Management

In order to achieve these objectives, the legal system would have to adopt *atypical techniques*,[26] and various methods to implement case management have been theorised and tested in practice.

On one hand, in order to guarantee efficiency, it would be necessary to afford the procedure greater adaptability to the specificities of each dispute. Ordinary proceedings, often long, slow and burdensome, could no longer satisfy the peculiarities of each conflict, which, in the last few decades of the twentieth century, led to the proliferation of special proceedings, that is blocks of legislated rules that the parties could opt for (instead of the ordinary proceeding), and that would provide more *substance-specific*—and, therefore, more suitable—procedural handling to areas in which substantive law did not fit the generalised format of the ordinary proceeding.

Besides the various and diversified proceedings, depending on the substantive law litigated in each case, many legal systems, especially in the civil law tradition, experienced the establishment in statutory law of several types of summary and fast-track proceedings, among which the small claims model was widely disseminated.[27]

On the other hand, to reduce costs, the management activity is commonly associated with the *formal loosening* of procedures. Reducing formalism and attributing some margin of flexibility to the proceeding would enable the prevention of nullities of procedural legal acts, making it feasible for judicial procedure to better serve the interests of an effective dispute resolution, solving the litigated substantive legal issues, instead of getting lost, as an end in itself, in comings and goings, procedural setbacks, and judgments to dismiss on purely formal grounds. A more flexible procedure would contribute to adaptability and would be more suitable to provide effective relief.

To guarantee an adequate caseflow management and the court control of time and speed of proceedings, case management powers of the judge allows her to set a calendar,[28] sometimes in a consensual manner with the parties in a pre-trial preliminary or preparatory hearing.[29] In Brazil, the new Code of Civil Procedure provides for the possibility of the judge and the parties to agree upon a timetable for the performance of procedural legal acts (Art. 191), including the taking of forensic evidence (Art. 357 §8°).

As regards the reduction of costs, a lot of studies have been undertaken on *cost management*, the management of procedural costs.[30] This management is now operated by procedural cost allocation orders and decisions to distribute and invert

---

26 Didier (2008, p. 41).

27 Sorabji (2017, pp. 45ff), Chan (2017, pp. 13ff), Wang (2017, pp. 23ff).

28 Resnik (1986, p. 523).

29 Uzelac (2008, pp. 87–88).

30 Davis and Garrett (2014, pp. 483, 488–489), Wang (2017, pp. 22–23).

cost burdens among parties and third-parties.[31] In the past decades, cost allocation has been strongly influenced also by litigation agreements such as legal expenses insurance and third-party funding.

4 Different Object: *Multiple-Cases M*anagement

Traditionally, the problem of the excessive number of cases pending before the courts, from the perspective of court management, was mainly dealt with by establishing court practices for the whole tribunal: the management of civil servants, structure, budget, etc.

However, in the judicial sphere, management was dealt with from the perspective of each law suit. The systemic benefit of increasing efficiency of various proceedings was in reality the *effect* of the management of individual actions rather than an autonomous goal of the management activity. If judges could implement a suitable pace for each action, conducting the proceedings to their conclusion within a reasonable timeframe, without unnecessary costs and with the fulfilment of all the fundamental guarantees of the parties, the optimal resolution of each case would have a large-scale impact assuring that many other law suits would also be conducted accordingly. Therefore, the repercussion of case management on court management was not the goal of the case management activity, as the latter was envisaged on a case-by-case basis.

In recent times, adjudication mechanisms of jurisdictional nature (applicable by a judge within judicial proceedings) are beginning to flourish and develop also to enable the *management of many procedures at once.* An example are the standard-solution procedures, proceedings for the resolution *en bloc* of multiple claims on the same issue of fact or law, such as test claims, model proceedings, pilot-judgements and the like.[32]

Through the use of these techniques, case management is targeted from a macro-procedural view, in what could be called *multiple-cases management*. The biggest difference is that these techniques promote large-scale solutions, albeit as a function of adjudication, that is *jurisdictional* and not administrative activities (like court management), with all the differences of principles and guarantees between these two spheres.

---

[31] Hurst (2009, pp. 171–181), Machado Alves (2016, p. 194).

[32] Cabral (2016c, pp. 263–281).

5 Evolution of the Purposes of Case Management. Efficiency and Fundamental Guarantees of the Parties. The Balance Between Legality and the Reduction of Formalism

With regard to the goals of the management activity, some lines of thought can be developed.

An initial reference is that applying efficiency to adjudication does not mean abandoning the fundamental guarantees of procedural law. The balance between efficiency and guarantees follows the precept that procedural law is aimed at the protection of legal rights, and must indeed provide it in an effective and efficient manner, but always respecting the constitutional rights of all stakeholders.[33]

That is why the quest for efficiency cannot stem from a purely quantitative concept, focused only upon swiftness and cost reduction in order to satisfy government priorities. The savings logic has limits, and concern over efficiency and the outcome of judicial processes cannot allow the fundamental guarantees of the due process of law to be breached or overlooked.[34]

Furthermore, efficiency is *instrumental*, and for that reason is related to the objectives one hopes to achieve through adjudication.[35] These aims involve both public interests and the interests of the parties, all of which must be considered and weighed.[36] One must then reject the utilitarianism that considers only the collective good and disregards the individual,[37] and seek to reconcile efficiency and guarantees in both perspectives.[38]

Therefore, case management could never forego the fundamental guarantees of procedural law. Efficiency must be viewed as an adjustment in the allocation of resources in order to maximise the exercise of these fundamental guarantees. To this effect, efficiency itself takes on the dimension of a guarantee, provided it is understood to be a way of optimising substantive rights. Efficiency is a fundamental principle

---

[33] This is the tone of the procedural system proposed by Marinoni et al. (2015a, b, pp. 39ff). See also Sodan (2005, p. 766), De Cristofaro (2010, pp. 282–305). In a perspective that I consider outdated, Thomas Roth sees a contradiction between procedural effectiveness and the principle of the lawful judge, giving priority to fixed statutory rules of competence, understanding that the legislator decided that they were 'more effective' for certain sort of cases. Roth (2000, pp. 95–100).

[34] Pflughaupt (2011, p. 28). Marcus says: 'one may resist the siren song of efficiency.' Marcus (2008, p. 2255).

[35] Carvalho (2015, pp. 273ff), Barber (2013, p. 567).

[36] It is interesting to observe how judges' independence is frequently invoked more as an individual right of the magistrate than from a systemic perspective of its relevance for the functioning of the judiciary. We must see the aspects of the lawful judge not only from a unique prism, but considering all the aspects in which the principle of the lawful judge actually protects individuals (control of arbitrariness, security, equality, impartiality, previsibility, coherence, efficiency). In this sense, Röhl (1998, pp. 245–246, 249).

[37] Eidenmüller (1995, pp. 320–321).

[38] Greco (2012, p. 24).

and also a *limit* for the formal loosening of procedural techniques for managing purposes.[39]

Against the background of these assumptions, it appears that the classic principle of legality, based on legislative (statutory) rules established prior to the case, is unable to meet the human necessities of our times, demanding efficient, dynamic and adaptable procedural instruments. The application of procedural rules nowadays depends on variable case-specific elements that cannot be entirely foreseen by statutory law.[40] Hence the need for procedural techniques to aim for a paradigm that goes beyond strict legality and encompass some level of discretionary judgements.[41] However, it should be emphasised that efficiency does not act against legality: this opposition is illusory. On the contrary, efficiency aims to establish a *finalistic legality*, that promotes the practical results the legal system wants to achieve, but always within the framework of lawfulness.[42] So efficiency is not synonymous with subjectivism, arbitrariness, absence of control.[43]

6 New Players Involved in Case Management. The Parties as Key Players: Litigation Agreements and No-Case Management

The changes in the goals, in the techniques and the methods have also modified the role of the players in charge of case management.

This shift is natural within the framework of the principle of cooperation in contemporary civil procedure, that constraint all actors (judges and parties). In fact, if all the stakeholders are called to share responsibility for the management of the proceedings, judicial case management does not exhaust the topic because the parties should also be key players in this task.[44]

In this perspective, I would like to talk about one topic which has been increasingly studied and expands as a great global trend: litigation agreements (also called contract procedure or negotiated procedure), possibly the most evident proof that procedural management has often a *leading role of the parties*. Through the negotiation of the proceedings rules, parties seek to outline a format of proceeding that suits their interests, adapting the judicial process in order to render it more efficient. That is, something similar to arbitration but in the realm of judiciary processes.

---

39 Cunha (2014, p. 79).

40 Pflughaupt (2011, p. 313).

41 Bettermann (1959, pp. 558ff), Marx (1969, p. 73). About the subject, Storme and Hess (2003).

42 Câmara (2013, pp. 42–43).

43 Diez-Picazo Gimenez (1991, p. 116).

44 Tatiana Alves remembers that a case management approach exclusively focused on the judge's activity does not exhaust the subject. Machado Alves (2016, p. 84).

One of the advantages of this technique is to afford greater predictability to proceedings. The legal rules of the, as yet, potential judicial procedure are anticipated at the moment of signing a contract. At this point, the dispute may not even exist, and may never actually come about in practice. However, the parties provide from the outset the proceeding that will govern the dispute arising from the contract, should that dispute reach the point of being filed in court. The judicial process begins, so to speak, long before the proceedings in court.

The Brazilian new Code of Civil Procedure is possibly the most important legislation about this subject. Article 190 states as follows:

> Art. 190. When the action deals with rights that permit the resolution of the dispute by the parties themselves, the parties can stipulate changes in the procedure to adapt it to the specific requirements of the case and can agree upon their burden, powers, procedural legal rights and obligations, before or during the proceedings.
>
> Sole paragraph. Whether upon request or on its own motion, the judge shall control the validity of the agreements set forth in this article, denying their application only in the case of nullity or abusive inclusion of such terms in adhesion contracts or in cases where any of the parties is in a manifest position of weakness.

And article 200 states:

> Art. 200. The legal acts of the parties consisting of unilateral or bilateral declarations of will shall immediately produce the constitution, modification or extinction of procedural legal rights.

Articles 190 and 200 pose *general clauses* for procedural agreements, which enable the parties to agree upon the procedure (and their legal situations) without being limited to specific provisions.[45]

Procedural agreements are a very powerful management tool, although it has not been yet thoroughly approached in the studies about case management.[46] The Brazilian Code of Civil Procedure shows how agreements can serve as a case management instrument in litigation. For example, in the organisational phase, in which the parties and the judge come together to manage pretrial activity, article 357 §2 provides that the parties can agree on the issues of fact that will be debated, or submit to the court a choice of law agreement, which is binding to the judge.

But there are other features of litigation agreements worth highlighting because they introduce a major paradigm change to the activity of procedural management.

On one hand, case management always reflected a concern with the management of cases that have already been filed. With litigation agreements, provided that contracts can be signed prior to the occurrence of the dispute, case management begins to deal with cases that have not yet reached the courts. Instead of managing pending disputes, one intends often to *avoid* litigation. Preventing, rather than curing, is something that could be seen as *no-case management*.

---

[45] Cabral (2016a, 2016b).

[46] For example, among all general reporters, only Sorabji mentioned the subject. Sorabji (2017, pp. 62–63). In China, Wang reports that there is little space for the parties to convene on proceedings, for the judges tend to play a leading role in the definition of procedural rules. Wang (2017, pp. 20ff).

On the other hand, litigation agreements also change the logic of the adaptation through special proceedings. If formerly, adaptation of judicial proceedings was a legislative task, with the creation of statutory special proceedings that would better fit the peculiarities of substantive law, nowadays, these special proceedings become increasingly unnecessary, as the formal loosening and adaptability of procedure begin to move towards the ordinary proceeding. In other words, if the creation of statutory special proceeding rules was once based on the inflexibility of the ordinary proceeding, now that the ordinary proceeding becomes more flexible and adaptable, we are closer to seeing the death of special proceedings.[47]

7 New Structures

7.1 Court Management and Allocation Efficiency: A Global Trend of a New Public Judiciary Management. Justice Outsourcing and Privatization

The quest for more efficiency of the judiciary has been strongly noted in today's world. The traditional approach, limited to strict legality, does not meet the demands of modern society. The need of 'new judicial public policies' has been exhorted for quite some time.[48] In Europe, there is currently a strong tendency for the application of *new public management* also to court management.[49]

---

[47] Another aspect of the topic which has been little explored concerns the fact that these procedural agreements represent a rearrangement of the relationship between substantive law and procedural law. Litigation agreements can, indirectly, increase or reduce the costs of the implementation of rights, by rendering their enforcement more or less difficult; and they can establish a new evidentiary logic (burden of proof, evaluation of evidence, etc.), causing an impact on substantive law because they change the prognosis of spontaneous compliance with the rules. In the normal exchanges of any contract, an improvement in the procedural legal position of one party could represent an advantage gained by the opposing party in another point of the negotiations, e.g., in aspects of substantive law, such as a price reduction. A consumer could negotiate a lower price by agreeing to clauses that allow greater 'seizability' of her assets or easier attachment in execution proceedings. Therefore, it may not deal merely with the choice of more efficient procedures: the parties frequently agree on procedure against a backdrop of the expectation of the impact of those provisions on substantive law. And, mainly in contracts signed prior to the emergence of the dispute, contractually designing the future in-court proceedings may generate incentives for individual behaviour. By undertaking obligations and regulating procedure, the parties are indirectly delineating incentives that favour compliance with their legal obligations. This aspect of litigation agreements has been little studied (a fortunate exception is the interesting analysis carried out by Dodge (2011, pp. 727, 731–732, 739), but indicates that litigation agreements is not only a form of conventional case management, but also a means of reshaping or remodelling the interactions between procedure and substantive law.).

[48] The movement has started in the early 1980s. See Santos (1985, p. 125).

[49] Hoffmann-Riem (1997, pp. 4ff), Scott and Sturm (2006, p. 566).

This new public management movement requires efficiency parameters for state performance, which involve not only the effectiveness of management, but also transparency (openness, dialogue, communication) and accountability.[50] The manager must work with diagnoses of the problems and the establishment of plans and targets, seeking to achieve standards of quality defined on the basis of developed indicators.[51] The motivational leadership of teams of officials and advisors is encouraged.[52] In addition, there must be strict control of results in order to review the judicial policies previously adopted.[53] And all this would be applicable to the judiciary.

The calling for a new public judiciary management was observed in Australia, New Zealand and England,[54] and spread throughout several European countries such as the Netherlands, Belgium, England, France and Germany.[55] In the majority of the countries that implemented the guidelines of the new public judiciary management, there have been reports of positive experiences with this type of court administration, and the fear that there could be some type of undue interference in judicial activity or judges' independence has proven to be purely speculative.[56]

The new public judiciary management encompasses, in the field of procedural instruments, a quest for greater flexibility and adaptability, but the movement wishes to implement increased qualification of the staff responsible for the court administration. In recent times, whether by hiring professional administrators, economists, accountants, etc., transferring functions to private persons (*justice outsourcing*)[57] or by instituting bodies outside the judiciary for the administrative and budgetary management (such as *management committees* or *councils*, sometimes independent of the of the court itself[58]; or *court managers*, with more or less autonomy in relation

---

[50] Hess (2006, pp. 143ff), Hoffmann-Riem (1997, p. 5), Eifert (1997, pp. 75ff), Contini and Carnevali (2010, pp. 1–2, 6, 12).

[51] Contini (2010, pp. 111ff), Fabri et al. (2005), Ng et al. (2008, pp. 58–64), Porcelli (2009), Sodan (2005, pp. 766–767), Pauliat (2008, p. 108), Röhl (1998, p. 241), Loth and De Werd (2003, pp. 318–319).

[52] Costa (2016, p. 317).

[53] Langbroek (2007, pp. 112–113), Contini and Carnevali (2010, pp. 7–8).

[54] In Germany, Röhl (1998).

[55] Loth and De Werd (2003, pp. 318ff), Hoffmann-Riem (1997, pp. 5–6), Langbroek and Fabri (2007, p. 16).

[56] Loth and De Werd (2003, p. 319).

[57] A growing practice in the field of execution proceedings. See Uzelac (2010, pp. 86–87), Yarkov and Abolonin (2010, p. 225), reporting on several countries where that happens: Estonia, Latvia, Lithuania, Slovakia, Hungary, Czech Republic, Macedonia and Slovenia among others.

[58] Mäurer (2000, p. 68), Langbroek (2007, pp. 112–113). It is important to highlight that court management does not need to be carried out necessarily by the judiciary itself (*judge-only*). We could imagine commissions or committees formed by members of both the judiciary and parliament. In the traditional debate, judicial independence and judges' accountability are values considered to be clashing values. Trying to tackle this issue, Contini and Mohr (2007, pp. 28, 39ff). About the relationship between judiciary budget and judges independence, Douglas and Hartley (2003, pp. 441–453), Baar (1999, pp. 399–351), Wheeler (1979, pp. 134–149).

to the decision-making bodies of the court[59]), or even by the enhanced qualification of the judges themselves for this administrative task.[60]

The transferring of management activities to a technical body of professional administrators and accountants tends to increase efficiency, as judges do not normally have expertise for these tasks and their proper training demands costs and time. On the other hand, adjustments in policies are more likely to be made when the manager and their teams can be changed if the planned outcomes are not achieved. This would be much more difficult when judges are those responsible for court management because they cannot be removed for a lack of managerial results.

In Latin America, however, this has been hardly ever seen: in most courts, judges or judiciary civil servants remain as those responsible for court administration. There is a strong lobby and even resistance from the corporation's side, especially judge's associations, against any kind of justice outsourcing or privatization.

7.2 *Specialisation of Courts*

Especially with regard to the *court management* aspect, i.e. focused on the *court structures*, many legal systems around the world are betting on the establishment of *specialised* units.

Specialisation is a professional practice based on the quest for knowledge and techniques to the extent that they can be exercised on a relatively high level when compared with other decision-making centres.[61] Thus, specialisation should not be confused with qualification or training.[62]

The most common form of specialisation has been that of attributing exclusive subject-matter jurisdiction to certain courts.[63] This specialisation sometimes redounds to independent branches of the judiciary (e.g. Administrative jurisdiction or Labour and Military Courts),[64] but is much more frequent when implemented in

[59] Karpen (1999, pp. 993ff), Papier (2002, pp. 2587–2590), Pauliat (2008, pp. 96, 99, 101, 108), ContinI and Carnevali (2010, pp. 7–9), Jeuland (2017, pp. 21ff).

[60] Kramer (2001, p. 3449), Loth and De Werd (2003, p. 318).

[61] In similar sense, Uzelac (2014, p. 148).

[62] See different acceptances for the term specialisation in Baum (2009, pp. 1671–1675).

[63] Uzelac (2014, p. 148), Mak (2008, p. 2).

[64] In some countries, as in Germany, there are lots of specialised courts. There is, in federal level, a common justice (civil and criminal) and other branches of administrative justice, a general (or residual) branch, the *Verwaltungsgerichtsbarkeit,* with subspecialisation in social security, tax and financial and labor. Lately, a court specialised in trademarks and patents was created (*Bundespatentgericht*). In France, there is specialisation based on concentration, with exclusivity, of commercial causes (*tribunaux de commerce*), and labor causes (*conseils des prud'hommes*). Foignet (1932, pp. 11–13), Perrot (2006, pp. 3–11, 123ff), Vincent and Guinchard (2003, pp. 330ff), Solus and Perro (1991, pp. 435ff), Couchez (2008, pp. 34ff), Héron and Le Bars (2006, pp. 499ff, 757–758). In Brazil, it's common to question the maintenance of certain judiciary branches which are too expensive and maybe could be fused to other courts. The best example, without any doubt, is the Military Justice, which number of processes absolutely does not justify its existence.

some subdivisions of trial (first instance) and appellate courts, such as a chamber or panel that is specialised by subject matter.[65]

7.2.1 Benefits of Specialisation Derived by the Parties and by the System

The specialisation of courts brings many benefits. On one hand, it enables the attainment of greater speed and efficiency not only by assigning more complex cases to judges experienced on that topic, but also because the repeated analysis of similar issues may encourage judges to develop routines, to establish performance models and extend their knowledge on the same issues.[66]

There is therefore a gain in *every single procedure* as decisions tend to be rendered faster and with greater technical quality. But the effect *on the system* is also positive. When filing a lawsuit before a generalist judge, the parties tend to enormously broaden their arguments, and are often inclined to bring experts to explain the topic, not only to 'instruct' the judge on the matter, but also to pave the way for an appeal against a potentially unfavourable decision. Contrarily, when the dispute is brought before a specialised judge, lawyers trust her ability to understand the dispute and tend to reduce their activities, for example decreasing the length of their pleadings, which saves costs and time.[67]

Thus, by offering the parties specialised structures, allowing them to file complex and specific claims before these trial and appellate courts, proceedings flow more naturally and without mishaps. From a different perspective, specialisation removes the obstacles that these very lawsuits constantly produce in a court of full and generalist competence, reducing, in these and other courts, the processing time of all the other procedures.[68] The gains for the judiciary (as a whole) are evident.

Another advantage of specialisation is that it gives rise to a greater *uniformity* of decisions, which favours *integrity* and *consistency* of the legal system (as advocated by the precedent model of the brazilian CPC, Articles 926 and 927).[69]

7.2.2 Disadvantages of Specialisation

One cannot deny that specialisation also has its disadvantageous effects on the framework of court management and the division of competences among judges.

---

[65] In Brazil, within State jurisdiction, the division of competences between the Tax, Civil, Family, and Commercial Courts is well known. Within the Federal jurisdiction, in the various circuits, there are specific courts for social security, environmental, agrarian, tax and tax foreclosure, intellectual property and trademark, home loan system matters, or matters regarding the Hague Convention on the Civil Aspects of International Child Abduction, among others.

[66] Rottman (2000, p. 23), Zimmer (2009, p. 2), Mac, Kerošius et al. (2014, pp. 209ff).

[67] Zimmer (2009, pp. 1–2).

[68] Fabri and Langbroek (2007, p. 312), Zimmer (2009, p. 1).

[69] Baum (2009, pp. 1675–1676), Gramckow and Walsh (2013, p. 6), Zimmer (2009, p. 2).

One of the dangers of excessive specialisation is the distortion of concentrating all the expertise on a specific matter in the hands of a single judge. This is what happened in Brazil in criminal proceedings with courts specialised in money laundering and financial crimes, which normally have jurisdiction over a whole Judicial District (which can encompass an entire State of the Federation). In these courts, what one notes is that the judge becomes the personification of justice.

Another negative side of specialisation with an excessive concentration of competences is that it generates an absolute isolation of judges,[70] who become so specialised that, due to 'tunnel vision'[71] or to cognitive and interpretation biases, tend to loose versatility and reduce their capacity to reach suitable decisions in a more general scenario, or fail to consider other arguments and variables in an interdisciplinary or systematic perspective, aspects that could be equally relevant for the solution of the case.[72] Furthermore, this isolation hampers 'dialogue' between the courts, which can prevent or delay the evolution of law.[73]

There are other deleterious effects of specialisation, constantly pointed out in legal literature: the risk of loss of independence or impartiality by the 'capture' of specialist judges by lawyers or companies who are repeat players in that field[74]; loss of self-awareness of the judiciary as a 'single body of judges;' elitist feelings or personal discouragement, in the sense that certain types of specialisation can make judges feel more or less prestigious than others[75]; career problems for an ultra-specialised judge to continue in the appellate courts, when promoted, if the same specialisation does not exist in the higher instances; excessive cost of the specialisation[76]; difficulty in terms of geographic accessibility to the specialised courts for the parties, which would speak out against this concentration due to the heavy burden of requiring that they travel to large urban centres,[77] among other negative aspects.[78]

---

[70] Baum (2009, pp. 1677ff).

[71] The term is used in economic law to refer to superspecialised organs' characteristic of not tackling problems from a larger perspective.

[72] This is the discussion found in Oldfather (2012, pp. 848, 858ff, 871ff).

[73] Mak (2008, p. 6). Posner remembers that specialisation restricts a cross-exchange of ideas between courts. Posner (1983, p. 787).

[74] Komesar (1994, pp. 145–146), Zimmer (2009, pp. 3–5). About lobby groups and the external influence that could produce this capture, Baum (2009, p. 1679), Posner (1983, pp. 783–784). Speaking not about capture, but actually of corruption, Gramckow and Walsh (2013, p. 8).

[75] Uzelac (2014, p. 154). One should notice that some authors question whether specialisation makes the judge more prestigious. In their opinion, broader competences mean more power, and prestige. Oldfather (2012, pp. 860–861).

[76] Damle (2005, p. 1275).

[77] That is a problem that can become alarming in a continental-size country as Brazil, as already observed in Russia: Terekhova (2014, pp. 178–179).

[78] For example, it is said that decisions from specialised judges tend to be more complex and not so understandable to the general public. Kerošius et al. (2014, p. 220), Silvestri (2014, pp. 166ff). See critics to specialisation in Rottman (2000, pp. 22–27).

Despite this criticism, the overall balance has been of general agreement that, if well conducted, specialisation brings more benefits than harm to judicial organisation.[79]

8 Case Assignment Management. Functionality and Management of the Rules Governing the Allocation of Competences

One of the topics that I can envisage as a proposal for further development is *case assignment management*, that is, developing forms of distributing cases among judges and courts to achieve an optimal result, not only in terms of quantity but also in terms of quality (competence/jurisdiction rules management).

Upon analysis of many systems from a comparative perspective, one can note that efficiency in the allocation of competences is greatly neglected in many of them, reduced almost to dividing equally the dockets among judges of equal subject-matter jurisdiction, a purely quantitative approach. This paradigm must be broken in favour of more functionality and flexibility.

Functionality is an intrinsic characteristic not only of case management[80] but also of the most fundamental objectives of the system of competences, which is structured and based on the attainment of a suitable division of tasks among the various decision-making centers.[81]

A more functional and flexible system enables the performance of *case assignment management*, distributing or attributing it according to efficiency parameters for an optimal organisation and distribution of work.[82]

The functionality that I propose must be obtained with the *coordination* of competences aimed at *both the internal purposes of a case,* as well as a combination of competences from a macro perspective, for the *management of several cases.*

The experience in some legal systems shows such a change of paradigm. More and more courts around the globe think on different ways of designing judicial structures and allocating resources to them in order to enhance management results through a better case assignment.[83]

The idea is, on one hand, to focus on the main competences and distribute or delegate the related functions or those that are not core tasks of a typical judicial

---

79 Carpi (2014, pp. 73ff), Santos (1985, pp. 129–130). A critical view that deserves reference is that of Uzelac (2014, pp. 155, 160), asserting that there is no evidence that specialisation actually leads to more quality and efficiency.

80 McGovern (1986, pp. 440ff).

81 Sabatini (1961, p. 953), Mitidiero (2013, p. 13).

82 That is Elaine Mak's definition (Mak 2008, p. 2), along with Hol and Loth (2004, pp. 67–89).

83 Scott and Sturm (2006, p. 566). Describing this court management process in USA, Finland, Holland, Singapore and later in the European Union, Albers (2009, pp. 58ff), Langbroek and Fabri (2007, p. 16).

role.[84] Furthermore, new rules, principles and judicial practices have proved that it is possible to reconcile, within the framework of the lawful judge, guarantees and efficiency, applying a more flexible system of competences (with adaptability and techniques of decentralisation and coordination),[85] but nevertheless rational and suited to contemporary challenges.[86]

8.1 Redefining the Principle of the Lawful Judge

Case assignment management raises questions on its compatibility with the principle of the lawful judge, which is traditionally based on some widespread assumptions, ideas upon which its lawfulness rests:

(a) the rules of jurisdiction must be provided for *in a norm* (whether written statutes or precedents) and could not be determined by judicial decisions on a case-by-case basis;
(b) that norm must be *previous* to the case at hand, excluding *post factum* case assignment;
(c) the norms of competence must be clear and establish predictable powers to the judges, excluding the exercise of judicial discretion in case assignment;
(d) the rules of competence ought to be *inflexible* to the greater extent possible; therefore, once the claim has been brought before the judiciary, the competence of the court stablelizes itself and could not be altered (*perpetuatio iurisdictionis*).

This format seems to be outdated. In many judicial systems, in common law and civil law jurisdictions, one can see several procedural mechanisms that authorize case assignment to be determined by judicial decisions or litigation agreements, allowing discretionary allocation of cases among judges on efficiency grounds, and permitting changes and transfer of jurisdiction even after the case has started before a certain court.

In France, for example, to achieve a more efficient court management, *ex post facto* changes of jurisdiction are permitted.[87] In Holland, since the implementation of intense legislative and structural reforms, the judiciary was reshaped with changes in the manner of appointing judges and in court management (both in terms of organisational, and financial or budgetary aspects).[88] The touchstone has been the quest for a higher level of expertise of the judges and greater flexibility in their

[84] About this issue, Karpen (1999, pp. 989–990), Eifert (1997, p. 81).

[85] Kramer (2001, p. 3449).

[86] Harmonizing efficiency and fundamental guarantees of the parties is also a concern of Mak (2008, p. 4).

[87] Renoux (1993, p. 169).

[88] Loth and De Werd (2003, p. 318), Contini and Mohr (2007, p. 35), Langbroek (2007, p. 105). The described indicators and statistics show that this was a fruitful experience. Van Dijk (2014, pp. 10–12, 15). Information in English about the Dutch legal system in https://www.rechtspraak.nl/English. Accessed 1 Dec 2020.

performance.[89] In the system of competences, there is provision for the possibility of a cooperative exchange among judges of various courts, who can be moved from one court to another.[90]

To the same effect, the Belgian judiciary underwent a major reform in 2014, which focused on a better case and court management, quality and efficiency of procedures and services.[91] As regards the system of competences (jurisdiction rules), the *mobility* of judges is now in effect. This mobility can be *internal,* within a district, as judges are appointed not only primarily to fill the vacancies of one court, but also the vacancies of all others. They can, therefore, be called upon to act in any court of that district if the president of the higher court so determines. But there is also the possibility of *external* mobility, i.e. outside the territorial boundaries of the district (horizontal) and even to higher appeal instances (vertical) when the judge is transferred to other districts or to courts of appeal. In the cases of external mobility, as there is no ordinary appointment of the judge in that district (neither primary, nor secondary), the appointed judge must agree to the assignment.[92]

In England, the attribution of competences is based on the pursuit of maximum efficiency.[93] And the logic of the distribution of work among judges is that of the ad hoc assignment of cases,[94] which makes the system very dynamic and flexible.

Of course, the legal culture in those places is not equal to every other legal system, and maybe in these wealthy and developed countries the system often works because one does not feel the need to establish mechanisms to ban the manipulation of competences.[95] But the logic underlying all these initiatives is based on the ideology of affording greater deference to the initiatives of the courts, in the name of efficiency, and to look for new techniques for the adaptation of court structures and case allocation, seeking alternatives to the traditional forms of case assignment.

Well, if based on the traditional format of the principle of the lawful judge, a quick look at some of these legal systems would lead the observer to conclude that many of them might violate recurrently the principle. And one could say that the principle does not protect the individuals anymore, since case assignment, transfer and changes of competence are made after the case has been brought before an initial court (*ex post facto*), by means of judicial decisions (not only legislative norms) and sometimes with discretionary standards.

So we ought to ask ourselves whether all these instruments are to be considered unconstitutional or against international treaties; or if we should reassess and redefine

89 Van Dijk (2014, p. 6).

90 Fabri and Langbroek (2007, p. 296), Mak (2008, p. 3). This mobility is a characteristic of Dutch judicial organization. Langbroek (2007, p. 108).

91 Voet (2014, p. 137).

92 Voet (2014, p. 140).

93 Section 14 of the *Crown Court Manual,* p. 2, available in https://www.judiciary.gov.uk/wp-content/uploads/JCO/Documents/Protocols/listing_crown_court_manual_050705.pdf. Accessed 1 Dec 2020.

94 Müssig (2009, pp. 377–379).

95 Eser (1995, pp. 263–264).

the principle of the lawful judge, for it to actually protect people that seek adjudication as a means of conflict resolution.

I think that in contemporary civil procedure, efficiency in case assignment is compatible with the principle of the lawful judge, but only if the principle is redefined in its scope and content.

I propose that the principle of the lawful judge is to be interpreted as the prohibition of unpredictable case assignment and manipulation of competence rules. The principle nowadays demands that jurisdiction rules must be: (1) *objective* and *impersonal*, excluding case assignment depending on the person involved; (2) *non variable* or *unchanging*, meaning that they must apply to similar cases and circumstances.

The principle of the lawful judge should not prohibit allocation of cases or transfer and changes in competence of pending cases for efficiency purposes, but as long as it guarantees (3) *predictability* and *participation* of the parties in the determination of jurisdiction. Taking part and being able to influence decisions about case assignment (contradictory principle and the right to a fair hearing) would reduce objections of insecurity and unpredictability.

8.2 Between Microjustice and Macrojustice: Efficiency and the Redefined Principle of the Lawful Judge

Departing from the structure that I proposed for the principle of the lawful judge, it is possible to reconcile efficiency and fundamental guarantees in court management and case assignment management.

Efficiency in case management brings together a micro-procedural perspective (geared towards the optimal resolution of each case) and systemic considerations.[96] If the efficiency of judicial relief leads to the rationalisation of material and human resources[97]—because its application was optimised—, the efficient management of each case contributes, in scale, towards the increased effectiveness of the workings of the judiciary as a whole.[98] Therefore, there is an 'internal saving' that reflects on the efficiency of the entire system.[99]

In this scenario, by using the parameters of allocation efficiency, a jurist can take into account the internal and external variables of the case. This combination is absolutely indispensable to the justice system in the contemporary world for two reasons. Firstly, because it authorises the judge to undertake judgments of efficiency

---

96 Didier (2008, p. 41).

97 Greco (1999, p. 62).

98 Pflughaupt (2011, p. 23).

99 Mettenheim (1970, pp. 15–17). About the subject, Schumann (1973, p. 277). In page 279–280, he says: 'Die Prozessökonomie ist (...) miβverstanden, wenn sie vom je einzelnen Prozeβ her begriffen wird. Prozeβökonomisch ist nur die Gestaltung, die sich mit den institutionellen Zielen des Prozesses verträgt. Manch Prozedieren mag im Einzelfall sehr 'ökonomisch' sein, bringt aber insgesamt nur Nachteile oder sogar den Prozeβ als Institution in Gefahr.'

regarding competence beyond the purely binary view of (competent/not competent), a gradual principle-related perspective (cooperative and coordinative in the multi-institutional sense)[100] that involves a comparative and inter-procedural analysis of competences.

On the other hand, this intersection between the case and the system in considerations of efficiency allows the judge to make use of arguments that are not strictly jurisdictional (being able to draw on those related to court management) in order to decide on the rules for case assignment.[101] Hence, on the relationship between efficiency and competences, it should be noted that efficiency in civil procedure imposes that we consider not only jurisdictional aspects[102] but also those of court organisation and administrative management.[103]

8.3 *Flexibility and Adaptability: Balance Between Efficiency and Guarantees. Can It Be Achieved by the Proposed New Approach of the Principle of the Lawful Judge?*

We have seen that procedural efficiency imposes a *performance guideline* in terms of adopting *atypical techniques* in order to provide the judicial process with an optimal

---

[100] This point has already been noted by scholars of the so called 'structural litigation,' in procedures in which the judiciary, in order to provide appropriate relief, must engage in cooperative activities in partnership with many social and State players. About the subject, in Brazil, Arenhart (2015b, pp. 211ff), Ferraro (2015, pp. 56–61).

[101] Pflughaupt (2011, pp. 282, 291–294).

[102] Didier (2008, pp. 36–37), Ávila (2005, pp. 19–24).

[103] Theodoro (2011, p. 33). Some authors consider jurisdiction a 'public service.' In this sense, Redenti and Vellani (2000, pp. 138–139). This vision is usually followed by more prominent considerations about procedural efficiency. Remo Caponi affirms: '(…) Essa mudança de perspectiva – a *Justiça* de função estatal a *serviço público* – faz com que o sistema político seja chamado hoje, mais urgentemente do que no passado, a responder às *expectativas de eficiência provenientes dos usuários do serviço judiciário* e, portanto, a medir e a incentivar a sua qualidade, a sua produtividade etc. Essa perspectiva reage ainda com a própria elaboração e conformação dos princípios jurídicos do processo que tendem, hoje mais do que no passado, a extrair de seu bojo a visão de uma *gestão eficiente*, em que pese a escassez de recursos dedicados à Justiça. Um exemplo sobressai nesse campo: a inclusão na Itália da duração razoável do processo entre as garantias constitucionais (Art. 111, § 2.°, da Constituição) pode e deve representar de forma direta a *constitucionalização* do *princípio da eficiência*. (…).' (Caponi 2011, pp. 400–401). This perspective is very frequent in French legal literature. Bandrac (2003, pp. 1096–1097). Cadiet and Jeuland say: 'À côté des principes d'organisation, l'ordonnancement judiciaire comporte des principes de fonctionnement qui sont essentiellement fondés sur la notion de *service public*. Fonction étatique, la justice est, naturellement, un service public; elle l'est souvent dans les deux sens du terme, organique (l'institution) et matériel (l'activité) lorsque la fonction de juger est exercée par une juridiction étatique (…). Mais parce qu'elle est un service public, la justice doit fonctionner conformément aux principes communs à tous les services publics: la continuité et l'égalité.' Cadiet and Jeuland (2013, p. 40). We do not think this idea to be essential to defend that the judge, while exercising his jurisdictional powers, should be guided by efficiency criteria.

solution. These techniques operate in accordance with various legal doctrines, but have the common goal of providing more flexibility and adaptability.[104]

The requirements of greater flexibility and adaptability also of jurisdiction rules (competences) reflect a new trend[105] which has been apparent for a fairly long time and has become increasingly necessary due to the complexity of contemporary society and to the high-level specialisation of the judiciary.

Flexibility of the system of competences means mitigating formal rigour, optimising the procedural legal acts performed by the court lacking jurisdiction and preserving their effects, to the greatest extent possible, in the competent court (*translatio iudicii*).

On the other side, adaptability entails the possibility of changing or transferring jurisdiction during the proceedings, flexibility in the appointment of judges and composition of benches and panels, and waiver of statutory rights in favour of models of proceedings carved by the parties through litigation agreements.

In sum, it is a matter of case assignment and determining jurisdiction on the basis of criteria of efficiency,[106] which were not found in the primitive concept of the lawful judge,[107] but which can nowadays be compatible with that principle.[108]

In fact, this new scope of protection of the principle of the lawful judge allows the reconciliation of guarantee and efficiency, and it is therefore possible to argue that flexibility and adaptability are characteristics of case assignment in today's procedural law.

Indeed, it is possible for the new trends of the competence system to function within this flexible and adaptable framework without relinquishing the necessary protection of the essential core of the principle of the lawful judge. For instance, allowing discretion in case assignment does not mean absence of control; fostering the activity of itinerant judges specialised in complex cases does not waive the establishment of objective criteria for the selection of those judges and the assignment of cases to them; the requirement that the competences should be provided for in a general and previous rule does not imply the impossibility of modifying jurisdiction once the procedure has begun, provided this alteration is predictable and unchanging, equally applicable to any other future case where similar circumstances are observed.[109]

---

[104] Jacobs (2011, p. 899).

[105] Van Rhee (2008a, b, pp. 58–59), Leisner (1995, p. 287), Bohn (2011, p. 16): 'Gegen den 'Perfektionismus' des gesetzlichen Richters werden Argumente wie die Praktikabilität und Zweckmäβigkeit einer flexibleren Fallzuteilung bemüht. Ziel ist es, das bestehende Spannungsverhältnis zwischen formalisierter Fallzuteilung und effizienter, ermessensgebundener Fallzuteilung zu erörtern und kritisch zu würdigen.'

[106] Bruns (1964, p. 1887).

[107] Arndt (1959, p. 171).

[108] See the critical view of Jeuland (2011, p. 88). With some concessions to flexibility.

[109] Schulze-Fielitz (2008, p. 660).

8.4 Delegation and Coordination of Competences

8.4.1 Definition and Admissibility

Jurisdiction delegation is the declaration by which a judge attributes another state body or person the power to perform legal acts that would correspond to the exercise of her own competences.[110] By means of jurisdiction delegation the delegator judge transfers voluntarily the *exercise* of the competence,[111] not the competence itself,[112] in order to coordinate with the delegatee for a more suitable adjudication.

Jurisdiction delegation is usually based on efficiency grounds, when the court considers that the transfer *in totum* or *ad actum* of competences to another institution or person could produce a more efficient result.

Jurisdiction delegation is more common than one would assume. It is first of all, a very old practice. It could be observed in Roman Law in several of its phases,[113] and was frequent in Europe during many centuries.[114] In Canonic Law, competence delegation was admissible and could be implemented through the *comissio* even to organs non regularly invested of jurisdictional powers. It was the opposite of the *remissio*, which represented the delegation of functions to stable and permanent organs, and therefore called 'ordinary' judicial bodies.[115]

Of course all these examples were based on the understanding of adjudication as equivalent to the sovereign power of the monarch or feudal lord, an attribute of his property that could be transferred and transmitted to others.[116]

After the consolidation of the rule of law in contemporary legal systems, the notion of adjudication as a public function—exercised to protect not only private but also

---

[110] Gelsi Bidart (1958, p. 256).

[111] Gelsi Bidart (1958, p. 257). In public law, see the opinion of Jellinek (1969, pp. 41ff).

[112] The delegator judge does not loose jurisdiction. That is why one should reject Heinrich Triepel's thesis that delegation would always be *translative*, and would lead to the loss of competence, through its exercise by the delegatee *in her own name*. Triepel (1942, pp. 23–24, 36–38, 41–42, 51). Supporting Obermayer (1956, p. 625). Against Triepel (1997, pp. 498–499).

[113] Triepel (1942, pp. 10–13), Heinz (1997, pp. 496–497), Chiovenda (1993, p. 79), Pérez López (2011, pp. 134ff). Some passages of Roman sources point to the same conclusion. Digest (book I, 21, 'De officio eius, cui mandata est iurisdictio,' or 'The office to whom jurisdiction is delegated'), divided state powers that would be transmissible from those that could not; and admitted jurisdiction delegation 'Quaecumque specialiter lege vel senatus consulto vel constitutione principum tribuuntur, mandata iurisdictione non transferuntur: quae vero iure magistratus competunt, mandari possunt.'

[114] The *iudex pedaneus*, to whom the practice of some procedural legal acts was delegated, could be pointed out as a similar type of delegation. See Tucci and Azevedo (2001, p. 140). The commentators and glossators used to draw a distinction between the delegation of competence for all cases (*ad universitatem causarum*) and the delegation restricted to one case (*ad unam causam*). Picardi (1985, pp. 766–767).

[115] Picardi (1985, pp. 775–777), Triepel (1942, pp. 17–19). In Canonic Law, the Pope had the adjudication power and he could delegate (and order a transfer back) every case submitted to ecclesiastical courts. Tucci and Azevedo (2001, pp. 99–100).

[116] Van Bynkershoek (1737).

public interests—began to make adjudication to be seen as a legal duty of judges,[117] what led to the conclusion that adjudication was impossible to decline (the prohibition of a *non liquet* judgment).[118] Because of that, jurisdiction provisions would have to be indelegable,[119] and the competent judge could not transfer her sentencing powers to another decision-making center.[120]

Nevertheless, in many legal systems one can see really frequently the delegation of procedural legal acts and sometimes a wide delegation of most (if not all) jurisdictional powers to other judges and private persons,[121] such as notaries.[122]

In Brazil, competences delegation begins at the Constitution, which authorizes delegation of jurisdictional legal acts to other staff members of the Judiciary (with the exception of final judgments). The Constitution also allows the Supreme Court to delegate competences regarding the enforcement of its own decisions and sentences. But there are several other examples of delegation of pre-trial gathering of evidence by means of rogatory letter or letter of request. The Code of Civil Procedure provides for other cases of delegation regarding the rescissory action (Art. 972).[123] These have been identified as a true type of delegation.[124]

In many countries, in enforcement proceedings there is a widespread tendency of jurisdiction delegation. Sometimes, legal systems attribute functions to private persons[125]; some other times, the creditor herself acts as a director or manager of the execution,[126] with powers to subdelegate.[127] Many European legal systems permit attachment issues to be conducted and decided by the *huissier de justice*,[128] the *Rechtspfleger* and *Gerichtsvollzieher*,[129] or enforcement agents (in Portugal, the *agente de execução*) among other similars. The most important example is perhaps the Swedish National Enforcement Agency, in charge of execution proceedings for the enforcement of court judgments, arbitral awards, administrative decisions and other

---

117 Schönke (1951, p. 145), Gelsi Bidart (1958, p. 242).

118 Carneiro (1980, p. 13), Didier (2016, pp. 179–180).

119 Chiovenda (1993, p. 79), Kern (2017, p. 117), Greco (2015, pp. 114–115), Cunha (2013, pp. 28–29), Didier (2016, pp. 177ff).

120 Marinoni et al. (2015a, b, p. 148).

121 Some authors have studied the possibility of judical competences being transferred by outsourcing and other types of partnerships. Cf. Hoffman-Riem (2001, pp. 36–46), Gilles (2000, pp. 1388, 1418).

122 Yarkov and Abolonin (2010, p. 228).

123 See Barioni (2016, pp. 2266ff), Cramer (2016, pp. 1431–1432).

124 Marques (1974, p. 75), Greco (2015, pp. 82, 115).

125 See Perez-Ragone (2014, pp. 648–649).

126 Jellinek (1892, p. 238).

127 Subdelegation is a subsequent transfer of competences from the delegatee to the subdelegatee. Cf. Obermayer (1956, p. 625), Triepel (1942, pp. 121ff), Rasch (1957, p. 338).

128 Donnier and Donnier (2003, pp. 38, 58–60, 169–174), Hippeli (2013, pp. 182–186), Couchez (2003, p. 60).

129 Jellinek (1892, pp. 234, 238).

titres.[130] In common law jurisdictions, execution powers are delegated to masters, bailiffs, sheriffs, enforcement officers[131] and the like.[132]

Jurisdiction delegation in execution proceedings can improve efficiency not only because of some specific functions requiring expertise the judge not often possess, but also because the delegatees usually are not bound by the borders of the court district and can perform their activities in many courts and different places.[133]

In Brazil, the new Code of Civil Procedure enables the transfer of powers to a court administrator or a judicial depositary with managing authority over attached or seized assets (Arts. 159–161).[134] Art. 861 §3° provides for an administrator (or trustee) for the selling of company shares; and Art. 862 permits the nomination of a manager in case the establishment or the whole business (the activity included) is attached.[135] In execution proceedings, the auction can be conducted by a private broker or accredited auctioneer appointed by the court (Art. 879, I e 880). In all these cases delegation of powers to someone that has to report back to the delegator judge abound.

But also in collective and class actions, especially in the so-called structural litigation (when it comes to correct or change public policy and reform administrative bodies and structures), judges tend to create adjudicatory facilities to whom some jurisdictional powers are transferred, and also delegate functions to agencies or masters.[136]

These examples could be easily described as jurisdiction delegation, which proves that there is nothing strange about delegation of judge's powers. Of course, we cannot forget that legal systems sometimes restrict the object of the delegation, preventing judges to delegate the power to decide the conflict, that is, to sentence the case on the merits. In some jurisdictions, the possibility to delegate jurisdictional powers depends on the delegatee or on the type of the legal act to be performed: some admit only simple functions to be delegated and only to court officials, clerks, trainees, civil servants and judiciary's staff in general[137]; if they were to be delegated to another judge, fewer objections arise; if the delegatee is a private person or entity, or even an administrative state body, some legal systems forbid the transfer of adjudicational

[130] Hess (2010, p. 44).

[131] In England and Wales, the experience with the High Court Enforcement Officers has been reported as an enormous success. See Turner (2010, pp. 137ff).

[132] Brazil (1986, pp. 394ff).

[133] That is what happens with the Dutch court bailiffs. See Jongbloed (2010, p. 181).

[134] Arenhart (2015a, p. 362).

[135] Arenhart (2015b, pp. 224–229).

[136] Brazil (1986, p. 394ff), Resnik (1991, p. 63).

[137] Perez-Ragone (2017, p. 29), Jeuland (2017, p. 20).

prerogatives.[138] Anyway, these restrictions, where applicable, do not exclude the possibility of jurisdiction delegation.[139]

Indeed, if we propose a system of competences more adaptable, functional and with combinatory and convergent powers (based on coordination and not exclusivity), the managing of competence rules or case assignment management should encompass jurisdiction delegation techniques.

8.4.2 Objections Against Jurisdiction Delegation

Although a common and ancient practice, jurisdiction delegation faces vehement utterances of rejection. Especially in civil law jurisdictions, objections to the delegation of competences are frequently raised by legal scholars.[140]

Some authors reject the possibility because it would change the lawful judge, violating parties procedural rights to see the case be conducted by that court previously and abstractly determined in a statute.[141] Jurisdiction delegation would mean the 'commission' of a sentence to an ad hoc state body or person, determined on a case-by-case basis.[142] That would represent an 'extraordinary tribunal', created *ex novo* or with its competences enlarged to decide specific cases that did not fall into its original jurisdiction. This would also violate the principle of the lawful judge because the delegatee organ would not be a 'permanent' and regular court.

The argument is based, as one can easily see, in an old conception about the principle of the lawful judge, developed to avoid manipulation of competences in authoritarian states. Nowadays, as we have seen, the preoccupations of proceduralists all over the globe tend to lead to another perspective, focused on efficiency, which is also compatible with the principle of the lawful judge.[143] Jurisdiction delegation should be admissible if it respects the contemporary scope of the principle (to protect objectivity, impersonality and invariance, as well as predictability and participation over case assignment).

---

[138] In Brazil, for instance, there is an express constitutional restriction: all jurisdictional legal acts but can be delegated to clerks or civil servants of the judiciary except decisions and sentences. See Art. 93, XIV of the Brazilian Constitution.

[139] Of course there would be cases in which no delegation could be implemented, especially if the competence would interfere with subject matters that can only be decided by judges ('reserva de jurisdição,' *Richtervorbehalt*). That varies a lot from country to country, but are usually linked to arrest, emprisonment, coercitive measures, etc. Cabral (2017c).

[140] Triepel (1942, p. 95), Sabatini (1961, p. 956), Gimeno Sendra (1988, p. 56), Schenke (1977, p. 121). In common law countries, jurisdiction delegation is much more frequent. See Chayes (1976, pp. 1300–1301).

[141] Marinoni et al. (2015a, b, p. 148), Didier (2016, p. 177).

[142] Gelsi Bidart (1958, pp. 261–262).

[143] Pinho (2000, p. 13).

Other critics say that jurisdiction delegation would harm the separation of powers.[144] The activity of pronouncing what the Law is should be exclusive of judiciary bodies, and it would be impossible to delegate it even to administrative entities with some decisional powers (like agencies).[145] There would be, in this perspective, a normative command imposing a 'functional division' that would prohibit any organisational mixture between courts and other institutions, whether persons or state bodies.[146] Only the Constitution would be able to attribute jurisdiction to other entities,[147] especially non-judicial ones, and jurisdiction delegation could never be granted by a judicial decision in a specific case.[148]

The argument is not convincing because it would only impede delegation to non-judicial organs, but not delegations within the judiciary (e.g. among judges). And even regarding delegation to non-judicial institutions, the objection does not consider the contemporary notion of separation of powers, understood not in an organic sense, but rather in a functional way of attributing basic models of activities to rationalize state organisation.[149] This scenario leaves some room to accommodate and reallocate tasks to organs that would not correspond to those, in that fundamental distribution of the Constitution, to whom those functions would be most commonly trusted.[150] Separation of powers in today's legal systems should be based in this functional approach, focusing on coordination and complementariness.[151]

To argue against jurisdiction delegation, some legal scholars also stress that once the State has prohibited individuals (with rare exceptions) to self-defend by force their legal rights, it would have a legal duty to provide adequate and effective relief whenever solicited by the interested parties, and therefore adjudication would be non declinable (impossible for the judge to render a *non liquet* judgment), and for the same reason the judges' competences would not be delegable to other state bodies or private entities or persons because it would mean a *denial of justice.*

I do not agree. It seems to me that the argument confuses adjudication with jurisdiction (or in civil law terms, confuses jurisdiction with competences). What

---

144 Santos (2007, p. 72).

145 Jacobs (2011, p. 890), Henkel (1968, p. 13).

146 Jauernig and Hess (2011, p. 41), Wilke (2007, p. 639).

147 Canotilho (2002, pp. 651ff), Dinamarco (2016, pp. 545, 552).

148 Gajardoni et al. (2015, p. 168).

149 Guinchard (2003, p. 1104), Wilke (2007, p. 637), Cabral (2014, pp. 562ff), Küster (1949, pp. 402ff).

150 Hesse (1995, p. 211): 'Den damit gegebenen verschiedenartigen Erfordernissen der Aufgabenbewältigung entsprechend unterscheidet die Verfassung die drei Grundfunktionen der Gesetzgebung, der Vollziehung und der Rechtsprechung. Diese Unterscheidung hat keinen Ausschließlichkeitscharakter. Sie bezeichnet bestimmte Grundtypen der Art der Aufgabenerfüllung. Sie enthält keine abschließende Umschreibung der verfassungsmäßigen Funktionen, sondern läßt Raum für weitere wie etwa die der Kontrolle, der Mitwirkung der politischen Parteien bei der politischen Willensbildung oder der Bildung und des Wirkens der öffentlichen Meinung. Sie darf auch im Blick auf die einzelnen Funktionen nur in einem typisierenden Sinne verstanden warden, weil die sachgemäße Erfüllung der Aufgaben starre Grenzziehungen nicht zuläßt.'

151 Cabral (2014, p. 564).

cannot be subject to delegation is adjudication power, not competences. And one must remember that jurisdiction delegation transfers only the *exercise* of competences, not the competence itself. The judge retains adjudication over the case; hence, the judge retains even jurisdiction (competence) over the case, provided that she can revoke the delegation and perform the delegated legal act herself. So jurisdiction delegation does not mean a denial of justice because it does not represent a permanent transmission of adjudicational powers, but only an episodic cession of the exercise of one or more of its competences.[152]

8.4.3 Oversight as a New Function Performed by the Judge: Supervision as a Jurisdictional Activity

Another objection to jurisdiction delegation is that it would somehow harm judicial independence.[153] Judges would no longer be independent if their functions were to be performed by exogenous institutions.

However, we have seen that the judge does not delegate adjudication, only the exercise of her competence. Nevertheless, this argument raises another interesting debate. If the delegator judge does not lose her adjudicational powers, and not even jurisdiction itself, which kind of functions are left to exercise?

I think jurisdiction delegation promotes an organisational change of judicial activities regarding the case: before delegation, it would be up to the delegator judge a *primary analysis* of the subject-matter; after delegation, she performs an *oversight*[154] activity, also described as monitoring or supervision.[155]

Judicial oversight of the delegatee is the form of adjudicational functions that the delegator judge performs after jurisdiction delegation.[156] Her analysis of the subject matter will no longer be primary anymore, but only *secondary*.[157]

Judicial oversight of the exercise of the delegated competence preserves the separation of powers (for it maintains the judiciary as the final decision-maker), but allows the first inputs to be brought before the delegatee (an institution or entity more suitable to perform that competence with efficiency[158]); the delegated activity will only be controlled by the judge after a former debate had already taken place.

---

[152] Pinho (2000, pp. 11–13).

[153] Perez-Ragone (2017, p. 29).

[154] Mbazira (2009, pp. 222–223), Roach and Budlender (2005, pp. 325ff), Resnik (1982, pp. 391, 394), Mcgovern (2005, pp. 1387–1388), Cole (2000, p. 1217) (despite defending an administrative nature of the supervision task); Gilles (2000, p. 1434).

[155] Verbic (2013, pp. 275ff). The judicial supervision can be corrective of the activity of the delegatee. In Sweden, for example, the National Enforcement Agency is monitored by the judiciary. See Hess (2010, p. 53).

[156] Roach and Budlender (2005, p. 335). One can envisage supervision performed by other branches. In some countries, there are executive agencies in charge of this monitoring functions. See Jongbloed (2010, pp. 194–196).

[157] In similar sense Rodotà (1985, p. 184).

[158] Brazil (1986, pp. 411, 417ff).

Well, jurisdiction delegation is a very complex topic, and we will not be able to approach all aspects. I shall return to the subject in detail in other specific texts. Here I would like to highlight the possibility of using jurisdiction delegation as a technique of case assignment management.

8.5 *Managing Mass Litigation*

One of the new trends in case assignment management is the search for new tools to administrate mass litigation. Some advocate that the best solution is to focus on class arbitration as a model: the managing solution for mass litigation would be to take proceedings out of the judiciary.[159] There is no need to remember the problems that the costs of those arbitration proceedings represent, which shows this might not be a viable alternative for poor and developing countries.

8.5.1 Consolidation and Centralisation of Similar or Repetitive Claims

Another group of techniques that has been conceived to manage the court system refers to the loosening of the rules governing jurisdiction to aggregate cases in which discussed the same issues of law or fact.[160]

We can see the rise of mechanisms for the consolidation and centralisation of individual proceedings, even after the definition of the jurisdiction of each one of them, that is, regardless of the *perpetuatio iurisdictionis*.

Examples of these are the multidistrict litigation orders in the USA, the centralisation of multiple actions in Brazil (via assignment or transfer to another court), or the consolidation in Portugal, under which several actions pending before different trial and appellate courts are joined for fact-finding and taking of evidence, or for a joint trial.[161]

These are all types of aggregation of claims[162] with the aim of managing a number of cases on similar subject matters to assure uniformity of the final result, and to reduce costs and time to reach a final solution.[163] And they refer to case assignment management because of the possibility of discretionary judicial decisions, on a case-by-case basis, transferring jurisdiction from one court to another.

---

159 Strong (2013), Roque (2014).

160 The idea is to foster relief for a larger number of people at once. Mcgovern (1983, pp. 5–9).

161 Cabral (2017a).

162 Aggregation in a broad sense occurs in any case in which more than one person or entity is a plaintiff or a defendant. Resnik (1991, p. 23). On the other hand, Yeazell (1989, p. 44), rejects such a wide approach because it would mask 'an important distinction between voluntary joinder and involuntary participation,' which brings questions regarding 'free riders' and 'kidnapped' participants.

163 Resnik (1991, p. 37).

But these tools are different from the class or collective actions model. In fact, during the twentieth century, the emergence of class actions and similar types of collective redress was seen as an empowerment mechanism of associations and institutions to seek judicial protection for collective rights. However, the more recent forms of aggregation of claims are clearly seen as a management instrument and often have the sole goal of expediting pending procedures.[164]

8.5.2 New Role of the Judge. Lawyers Networks and Committees. Claims Resolution Facilities

I tried to demonstrate before that litigation agreements have proven that the changes in goals and tools of case management caused impact on the players involved in this management activity.

Furthermore, if management is to be shared with the parties, one can recognize legal duties (not only legal powers) to the judge.[165] This gives rise to the issue of judges' accountability, something that goes beyond the reasoning of judicial decisions, and which involves dialogue, openness to the participation of society, transparency[166] and responsiveness.[167]

For example, court administration cannot be imposed top-down, it must instead be in contact with the legal community and the local population, not only for the purposes of participative budget management, but every time court management decisions can impact on access to justice (e.g. decisions regarding the specialisation of courts).[168]

The new methods and techniques that have emerged to improve case management have also required a reformulation of the forms of subjective interaction between all stakeholders who participate in judicial proceedings, calling for a new theory on the relationships between the parties and third parties.[169]

Networks and committees of lawyers are often seen in procedures for the resolution of repetitive claims, consolidation and centralisation of cases.[170]

---

164 And more and more, class actions, that in their origin, were seen as an empowerment, are starting to be looked at as a management tool as well. See Resnik (1991, pp. 47–48).

165 Machado Alves (2016, p. 193).

166 Voermans (2007, pp. 148–159).

167 Contini (2007, p. 27), Corder (2001, p. 202ff). In another text, Contini and Mohr try to differentiate judges' accountability. See Contini and Mohr (2008, pp. 61, 86).

168 An important example on this subject is the Swedish legal system. See Hagsgård (2014, pp. 993–1014). In a more general perspective, see Contini (2010, pp. 111ff).

169 The topic is too broad to be dealt with here. In fact, there are new and diverse roles that can take part in a procedure, such as that of the *amicus curiae*, a non-interested third-party. Social participation in public hearings starts to come up more often, and the possibility of switching roles (in which the same player changes roles in the same claim, sometimes supporting the interests of the plaintiff, sometimes supporting the interests of the defendant). Cabral (2009, pp. 7ff).

170 Some plaintiffs and defendants have already an aggregative form before they enter litigation. That is the case for corporations, voluntary associations and governamental units and bodies. See

Other interesting managing tool is to craft innovative structures to facilitate the resolution of complex claims before the courts. In the U.S., one can observe the so called *claim resolution facilities*, agencies or entities created and structured to process claims related to a specific case, some of which have a potential funding source.[171] By means of these mechanisms, litigants pool resources and coordinate their activities and somehow simulate the position of a repeat-player.

This had also impact on the functions that are to be performed by the judge. In mechanisms such as consolidation and centralisation of procedures, the role of the managerial judge is to act as a facilitator, cooperating with all stakeholders, some of which might have expertise e specific talents for the new challenges that jurisdiction faces in the contemporary world.[172]

In structural litigation, especially in execution or enforcement phases, it is pretty usual that the judge establishes a dialogue with other players in order to adapt her own decisions and to obtain full but realistic compliance to it.[173] One should avoid, in these kinds of procedures, the so called 'one-shot remedies.'[174]

In complex litigation, the judge must also develop tools and make the proper infrastructure available for the communication among parties and between them and the court, including the use of technology to enhance case management (e.g., computer systems and softwares for filing motions electronically, sending text messages, which are particularly important for parties that reside in other places other than the transferee court).[175] The judge can also create a regional or national database for relevant documents of the case, with a user-friendly format, that allows storage and access to all evidence already gathered and that would be common to all parties (for example, video of the recorded testimonies and depositions).[176] I could envisage also the producing of websites of the case,[177] with information in simple and accessible language about the conflict and as to how should the individual be entitled to a similar right.[178]

Resnik (1991, p. 23). Here I would like to emphasise the eventual gathering and the formation of structures just for the purposes of litigation.

[171] McGovern (2005, p. 1316), Resnik (1991, p. 38), Hensler (1990, p. 175), Peterson (1990, p. 113).

[172] Dodge (2014, p. 368).

[173] McGovern (1986, pp. 440ff).

[174] Tushnet (2008, pp. 36–42), Roach and Budlender (2005, p. 325), Chayes (1976, p. 1292).

[175] Technology in case management has been reported in many countries. See Wang (2017, pp. 31ff).

[176] This was already implemented in the U.S. multidistrict litigation. See Mcgovern (1997, p. 1864). On cooperation and facilitative judging, Dodge (2014, pp. 342–344).

[177] Rothstein and Borden (2011, p. 8).

[178] In Brazil there were a few cases in which informative hotsites e websites were created on line, but this initiative is very recent. In criminal matters, see the Operation Car Wash ('Operação Lava a Jato,' the biggest corruption case in the world) website (http://lavajato.mpf.mp.br); in the field of class actions, a good example is the collective action of coal mines ('Ação civil pública do carvão') (https://www.jfsc.jus.br/acpdocarvao/index.php).

9 Court Management

9.1 *Specialisation and Case Assignment: The Lawful Judge as the Judge with Expertise on the Subject Matter*

In the traditional literature of procedural law, the technical capability or expertise of a judge have never been considered within the scope of the principle of the lawful judge. The parties would not be entitled to a specialist judge who is familiar with the subject matter of the litigation.[179] However, if efficiency is compatible with the principle of the lawful judge, one must ask in what terms and to what limits the legal system aims to find a more qualified judge with specific knowledge to decide the case. On the basis of efficiency, one of the ways to implement this, in many cases, is to attribute competence to *specialised* courts.[180]

Indeed, an increasing qualification of judges has been noted as a characteristic of contemporary judicature.[181] As an outcome of this qualification, judges are selected and trained bearing in mind the performance of functions that the adjudicative activity will require from them in their daily working life.[182] Even so, they deal with general knowledge, and in practice they are faced with other challenges that cannot be included in theoretical studies. Furthermore, legal systems can change over time, and, for this reason, practical training and theoretical refresher courses are a constant and unquestionable need.[183]

Nevertheless, regarding specialisation, more than training and qualification, I want to highlight the importance of the specific nature of the subject of this training, so that the judge may become a true specialist on some topics.

[179] The traditional opinion is expressed by Thiedemann (2003, p. 233).

[180] Gramckow and Walsh (2013, pp. 1ff).

[181] Guiliani (1988, pp. 603–604, note 15). Some say it resulted from the historical evolution of the principle of the lawful judge (the process that led to 'permanent' courts becoming 'established' or 'natural' or 'ordinary' courts gave rise to a 'career' of the judge). Picardi (1985, p. 781). There is a concern of the magistracy with seeing this 'profissionalisation' as a 'functional improvement,' not as a loss of power, a bureaucratization of the judges that would bring them next to the other public servants, what could reduce their function in the frame of State's institutional arrangements, sterilising the judiciary in a political sense. About this subject, Giuliani and Picardi (1987, pp. 272, 283).

[182] In Brazil, professional career judges are selected by means of public civil service exams, which already focus the assessment of candidates on the content deemed useful for the performance of their judicial functions.

[183] Nunes and Bahia suggest training of judges should precede statutory reforms. Nunes and Bahia (2009, pp. 121–122).

In effect, the increasing need for specialisation occurs not only because no country can indefinitely increase the number of judges[184] due to budgetary constraints,[185] but also due to the complexity and variety of contemporary problems, that produce a large number of intricate topics with which judges are faced and for which specific training would be both time-consuming and costly if it were offered indiscriminately to all judges.[186]

Specialisation on these complex topics becomes a requirement for efficiency in the contemporary world. The lawful judge, from the perspective of an optimal allocation of resources and procedural techniques, must, in many cases, be the judge with the necessary expertise to provide suitable judicial relief.[187]

9.2 Variants of Specialisation. Need for Emphasis on the Specialisation of Judges, Rather than of Courts

As already seen, the focus of specialisation activity, within the sphere of court management, has been on the specialisation of courts (court bodies, chambers, benches) or entire trial or appellate courts.

Another aspect that needs to be further studied and practised, as it can also contribute towards an efficient case assignment management, is *specialisation with emphasis on the judge*.[188]

In many countries, it is common for certain subject matters to be assigned to lay judges or justices of the peace. France and Belgium have them for labour and

---

[184] Studies on the impact of the number of employees and productivity of judicial staff on the overall court performance are inconclusive. See Mitsopoulos and Pelagidis (2007, pp. 219–244), Rosales-López (2008, pp. 231–251), Gomes et al. (2016, p. 13).

[185] In some countries like The Netherlands, efficiency turned to be an objective due to budgetary constraints. Van der Grinten (2012, pp. 279, 285ff).

[186] Oldfather (2012, pp. 854ff). Specialisation is a very difficult subject, and it may vary according to the comprehension that one has of the principle of the lawful judge, which varies in comparative law depending on the characteristics of each judicary system. In some countries for example, there is no court specialisation: all judges are generalists and are part of the same judicial body, being capable of adjudicating in various branches. It is not surprising that, in those systems, the notion of a lawful judge is totally different from that existent in Brazil. Fabri and Langbroek (2007, pp. 300–301).

[187] Of course that, although specialisation is an important element to provide functionality and efficiency to the system, specialisation itself is not enough to reach a correct decision and an efficient result. Technical knowledge is not the only relevant predicate to the task of judging: abilities such as analysing information, evaluating evidence, inquiring witnesses, conducting hearings, writing understandable decisions, these are all important features as well. In this sense, Posner (1983, p. 778).

[188] Uzelac (2014, p. 149). Commenting the South African experience, Van Loggerenberg says that we must not only think of the variety of services (in the *multidoor* or *multiaccess* logic), but also of the variety of tasks attributed to judges and the variety of their capabilities and expertises (*multitasked* and *multi-skilled*). Van Loggerenberg (2014, pp. 187–188).

commercial matters,[189] Denmark and Sweden for labour claims,[190] and Holland for lease issues.[191]

Brazil has also had justice of the peace since the Imperial Constitution of 1824. Nowadays, its competence is defined in Art. 98, II of the Constitution, as is limited to the performance of marriages and conciliation activities of a non-judicial nature.[192]

Besides justices of the peace, one must remember the lay judges, also provided for in the Brazilian Constitution within the scope of the small claims courts (Art. 98, I of the Constitution). Despite the provision for an elective 4-year mandate for justices of the peace, which would assure them a certain job security, lay judges do not have the same assurances as professional judges (like stability or lifetime tenure), and for that reason I have doubts as to whether assigning them more functions would be a good alternative as a guideline for specialisation in civil procedure, at least from a Latin American perspective.

Besides lay judges and judges of the peace, comparative analysis provides other good practices in the field of the specialisation of professional judges.[193]

The French, English and Dutch procedural systems implemented forms of *specialisation of judges* (not only of the courts).[194] Judges that are specialised in one topic can be assigned to work not only in the trial or appellate court to which they are regularly designated, but also in others.[195] In this manner, the specialised jurisdiction (competence) is detached from a specific court or bench.

In England and Whales, the distribution of competences, besides being case-specific and discretionary, takes into consideration the personal knowledge of each judge, her experience and technical abilities.[196] It was there that the so-called *ticketing system* was developed,[197] enabling judges to try cases where there is a greater need for specialisation if they prove to have the expertise or if they had specific training on the matter. By means of qualification courses, judges obtain a *ticket* or *certificate* to be assigned to cases in which that specific subject matter is litigated.[198]

---

[189] Vincent and Guinchard (2003, pp. 330ff). In Belgium, this competence is even larger, involving disputes about neighborhood rights, alimony, rights and duties of spouses, consumer relationships etc. About the subject, Voet (2014, pp. 131, 134).

[190] Gramckow and Walsh (2013, p. 4).

[191] Mak (2008, p. 6).

[192] This makes room for state law, at the initiative of the State Courts of Appeals, to regulate other functions for the justice of the peace, but the majority of States of the Federation have not, to date, drafted rules about the justice of the peace.

[193] Reporting some good experiences from the German Federal Constitutional Court, which the author understands that could also be applied to the United States federal courts, Damle (2005, pp. 1291ff). See also Gramckow and Walsh (2013, pp. 10, 21ff).

[194] Fabri and Langbroek (2007).

[195] In most legal systems from the countries we had the opportunity to study, this possibility is not usually admitted. Expressly bringing the subject to the debate, Kerošius et al. (2014, p. 212).

[196] Bohn (2011, pp. 136–137).

[197] Langbroek and Fabri (2007, p. 21).

[198] Fabri and Langbroek (2007, pp. 301, 312).

I believe that some of these specialisation practices focused on judges can be adopted in many countries with a good prognosis of success. And that would be a way to enhance case assignment management.

And there would be no violation of the separation of powers or of the independence of the judiciary. Specialisation, when defined by the courts themselves by their self-organisation powers, does not raise questions about external interference on the distribution of competences.[199] On the other hand, if the assignment of specialised judges complies with parameters that preserve the principle of the lawful judge, there is no problem with regard to the independence and impartiality of those judges.[200]

Finally, it should be remembered that this aspect of specialisation aimed at judges, and not at the courts, may provide an organisational alternative for certain matters which, due to their complexity and specificity, deserve a specialised analysis but perhaps do not occur in sufficiently significant quantity to justify the specialisation of a court or a whole tribunal just for that topic. This is what occurs, in many places, with class actions.[201]

I would like to suggest some alternatives to develop the topic, as follows.

9.3 Lists of Specialisations of Judges: Efficiency due to Expertise and Objectivity by Random Distribution

One proposal that can be easily implemented in many legal systems is to *list specialised judges by subject matter* (those topics whose technical complexity requires specific training) and to whom cases could be assigned regardless of the court to which the judges would ordinarily be nominated to.

The first step would be to *select the judges* who would integrate specialisation lists. And, from among the judges found on the list, case assignment would be a *random* distribution by the drawing of lots or by other criteria, provided these parameters

[199] Barber (2013, pp. 567–568): 'Identifying democracy and competency as two of the necessary, though not sufficient ingredients for a successful state gives us just enough to begin to explain the classic demands of the separation of powers. It explains why we need different types of institutions, wielding different types of power, staffed by people with different talents and qualities. (…) There is a good explanation, grounded in the point of the state, as to why the state needs an array of institutional forms, why these institutions should exercise the powers they possess, and why different types of qualification should be required of the officers who act in those bodies. The usual demands of the separation of powers can be couched in terms of *suitability.* Institutions and powers should be created that are *suitable* to the achievement of the state's characteristic purpose. Powers should be allocated to those institutions that are most *suitable* for their exercise. The type of person chosen to act in these institutions should be *suitable* for the type of power the institution exercises.'

[200] This is the conclusion in some other countries. Kerošius et al. (2014, p. 211).

[201] Therefore, one cannot agree with Mendes (2006, pp. 276–277), that suggests only specialisation of courts.

are *objective, impersonal* and *unchanging*.[202] Thus, the idea is to guarantee objectivity and impersonality of case assignment among the judges on the list, with the concomitant increment of the decision-making expertise in complex cases involving the areas of law in which very specific knowledge is necessary.

The assignment on the list could occur at the request of the plaintiff or by litigation agreements signed by both parties. Faced with an agreement between the parties (which, in this case, must be prior to the filing of the lawsuit), there would be no offence to the principle of the lawful judge because there was consent and predictability.

When case assignment on the list is made at a request of the plaintiff, if the defendant objects to this form of assignment, the judicial body responsible for deciding the conflict of jurisdiction can control whether the case is complex and the subject matter specific enough to justify prioritising efficiency; if it reaches the conclusion that there are no grounds for attributing competence on the list, the case shall be assigned freely, off the list, by regular rules for the allocation of workload among judges.

Some criteria may also be suggested for drawing up the lists and for the assignment of judges. I would like to propose six parameters, without claiming that they are exhaustive.

(a) *qualification certificate*—one must develop the means to assess whether a certain judge actually has the relevant knowledge for that type of specific litigation,[203] a procedure to certify the expertise of the judge on the subject matter of the dispute, which can be done by means of proof of a master's or LL.M. degree, a doctorate, or participation in specific courses.

(b) *refresher courses for judges and periodic updating of lists*—it is important that the specialisation of judges be renewed, with frequent refresher training. For this purpose, one can consider the renewal of the selection every two or three years, requiring new certification in order to make up the list. The expertise of the judge must be tested through methods of continuous reassessment and improvement, especially as the complexity of the law in the contemporary world means that case law may change, legal scholars produce more legal writings and legislation itself can vary, both on a national and international level, leading to an undeniable need for continuous training. The lists must, therefore, be drawn up periodically, with new certification at the end of the period.

(c) *broad access of judges to the make-up of the list*—it is vital that there be no manipulation of the composition of the lists through nepotism or personal preferences. In order to follow a logic of impersonality, the candidacy of judges to be included on the list must be accessible by all. If there is a large number of judges interested in participating, one could consider the possibility of a mandate or rotation on the lists.[204]

---

[202] An automated electronic case assignment does not consider judges' technical specialisation, as observed by Romboli (1993, pp. 68–69). About false assumptions regarding specialisation, Oldfather (2012, pp. 851ff).

[203] Baum (2009, p. 1676).

[204] This measure is suggested to avoid ultra-specialisation and a sort of 'saturation' of the magistrate's expertise due to an overspecificity of the subject-matter. Some authors criticise long-term stability of specialised judges, what happens in every system where judges are entitled to lifetime

(d) *objective criteria for the selection of specialist judges*—the criteria used to gauge expertise must be, as far as possible, objective, impersonal and unchanging, reducing subjectivism in the choice of judges who will participate on the list. The selection must also be formally justified.
(e) *disclosure and transparency*—the lists and the reasoning for the selection must be widely disclosed, published not only in the official press but also in the courts' electronic websites on the internet.
(f) *objective and impersonal criteria for the assignment of cases to judges on the list*—it is further necessary, once the list has been drawn up, that objective and impersonal criteria also be determined for the assignment of cases to the judges on the list. These criteria can be the random electronic assignment or others, but shall always comply with the parameters of objectivity, impersonality and invariance.[205]

When a case is assigned to a judge by virtue of the listed specialisation, there shall be numeric compensation, by which another case assigned to that judge shall be reassigned (this 'compensation' can be easily implemented through electronic computer software).[206]

Through the numeric compensation of cases assigned according to the list, there would be no management problem as this manner of assignment would not inflate the number of cases accumulated by one or few courts, 'punishing' the good judges who sought training and 'rewarding' the judge who did not apply to be included on the list (whether because she does not wish to be assigned complex cases, or simply because she did not seek training on specific subject matters).

9.4 *Specialised Itinerant Judges to Act in a Sporadic and Case-Specific Manner*

Another possibility for the adaptation of judicial structures that we believe to be compatible with the lawful judge and procedural efficiency is the use of groups of itinerant judges, who are to be appointed not only to cover the annual leave and other

---

tenure and can only be removed or appointed elsewhere if they ask or agree to it. Zimmer (2009, pp. 5–6).

[205] Regarding litigation agreements, I should envisage the possibility of parties agreeing not only the assignment among the judges of the specialised list, but also agreeing to assign a specific magistrate from the list. Parties would define not only the organ (such as in forum selection clauses), but the person of the judge herself. Would that be possible? I am inclined to answer the question affirmatively. In this case, the conventional norm would derogate the need of objective and impersonal criteria to case assignment to one of the judges among those on the list (letter 'f' in the text). The only downside of this choice would be a possible practice of *judge shopping*. However, in the countries with more flexibility when it comes to case assignment, this problem has not been observed, although the theoretical issue deserves close attention. See Langbroek and Fabri (2007, p. 16, 307).

[206] Other authors suggest compensations and awards to be offered to judges whose productivity is based on specialisation, perhaps giving them some days off or cash bonuses. Mäurer (2000, p. 69), Weth (1997, pp. 971ff).

absences as substitutes, but also to meet additional staffing needs due to an excessive workload (such as in hearings and sentencing campaigns).

The idea here is to assure *functional mobility* with greater flexibility in the management of court structures, allowing judges to move from court to court to analyse very specialised cases or assist overburdened courts, acting jointly with the judge presiding over these cases.[207] In this way, without excluding the judge to whom the case was originally assigned, a more efficient performance is enabled in terms of quality.

To the effect argued here for the establishment of groups of specialised itinerant judges, there are some good practices in comparative law that can serve as a reference. In Holland, for example, there is a successful experience with mechanisms of this nature, with the possibility of transferring judges from one court to another if the management committees of both appellate courts consent.[208] There is also provision for 'traveling judges' to try certain types of actions in various locations, being able to carry out a joint settlement of claims involving multiple actions on the same issue of law or fact.[209]

In Lithuania, there has also been reported the possibility of reallocating judges and transferring competences to other courts on the grounds of efficiency, when it is proved that the case will be settled faster and more economically in the transferee court, especially if that is the location where most of the evidence to be gathered can be found.[210]

9.5 Specialisation Without Isolation or Concentration of Competences

At this point, I wish to suggest some factors that seem important to guide the judicial organisation as regards specialisation.

Firstly, one must avoid precisely the means most commonly used in many countries to specialise courts, which is the *concentration* of competences, imposing the idea of attributing *exclusive jurisdiction* to some court over one subject-matter.

The logic of the concentration of competence in a single court is that of *exclusivity*. But that is not the only way to proceed towards specialisation.[211]

The concentration of competence by specialisation does not conform to the most contemporary trends in procedural law as regards jurisdiction which is moving

---

[207] This characteristic has been seen as fundamental to assure efficiency in court management. Langbroek and Fabri (2007, p. 17).

[208] Fabri and Langbroek (2007, p. 296). In France, legislation has historically provided some rules like those. See Foignet (1932, pp. 37–38).

[209] Mak (2008, p. 3).

[210] Art. 34, paragraph 2°, (1), Lithuanian CPC. About the subject, Kerošius et al. (2014, p. 212, note 13 and p. 213 note 15, highlighting), however, that competence transfers are exceptional in practice.

[211] Damle (2005, p. 1271).

towards less exclusivity and greater flexibility, functionality and coordination. There is urgent need to think of ways of allocating competences based on the *combination* of judicial prerogatives. For all the above reasons, the technique of concentration of competences by specialisation does not appear to be the most advisable.

Furthermore, an intense concentration of competences could isolate the judge, creating a sentiment of 'castes' or 'elitism', or even foster the image of a 'vigilante.' It is also important for specialisation not to 'isolate' the jurisdiction, taking away from the judge the examination of more general issues. As we have seen, this can capture the expert judge through the jargon and the influences of the specialised environment,[212] with the additional risk of the specialist judge losing sight of the more general legal disputes, whose arguments can be of great value to the adjudication under her jurisdiction.

For this reason, it is suggested that the specialised court receives and analyses related issues and proceedings (satellite jurisdiction due to joinder, counterclaims etc.), or that the court should take on specialisation over more than one subject matter.[213]

On the other hand, the concentration of competences at a single location renders access to justice more difficult, forcing many litigants to travel to the venue of the specialised court. Therefore, I would propose the creation of one specialised court per subject matter in various judicial districts or subsections. But that depends, of course, of budget constraints and economic possibilities.

9.6 *To Specialise, Not to Specialise, How to Specialise? Complexity, Quantity and Frequency as Relevant Factors*

The global move towards specialisation has generated a concealed notion that specialisation is unavoidable, and that the debate should limit itself to identifying to what degree and in what subjects this specialisation should take place. However, the cost of specialisation, the number of cases, the risk of making access to justice more difficult and all the disadvantages previously described can point to the contrary. Although some measure of specialisation may be efficient, it is possible that, in some cases and for certain subject matters, the best court management decision is *not to specialise* court structures at all.[214]

As to the criteria used by the courts to decide whether or not to specialise, one must initially analyse the *complexity* of the cases. Simple cases can probably be well

[212] By the risk of capture, some authors defend that the solution for some issues should be in charge of a generalist judiciary, not of specialised regulatory agencies. About the discussion, see Eskridge (2013, pp. 428ff).

[213] Defending specialisation formats that do not withdraw judge's general vision, Zimmer (2009, p. 5), Mak (2008, p. 7).

[214] Or adopting alternatives, such as itinerant judges. Against the euphoria over specialisation, see Uzelac (2014, pp. 156–157).

dealt with by generalist courts, preferably scattered throughout the country (with trial courts and benches in various locations in order not to infringe the rights of the parties and not to obstruct their access to justice and the right to a fair hearing).

Besides the complexity of the litigation, one must also verify the *quantity* (the number of cases by subject matter) and the *frequency* with which the claims are filed, as the number of proceedings and the consistency with which they turn up before the courts for trial are circumstances that must be taken into account for specialisation purposes.

Combining these factors, one can reasonably conclude that: (1) *complex and recurring* cases will be better decided by specialised courts (more scattered throughout the country, without exclusivity or concentration); (2) *complex and sporadic* cases will be better decided by a small number of fixed specialised courts (concentration) or by specialised itinerant judges (coordination).[215]

If there is a large quantity and frequency of claims filed, but without complexity, perhaps one should not specialise, with the problem of quantity being tackled with other managing mechanisms (such as test claims, model proceedings and other forms of standard-solution procedures).

10 Concluding Remarks

Since its development, case management has been dealt with enormous enthusiasm and fascination. Its widespread application and approval as a tool for enhancing efficiency should lead, however, to caution and warning against hasty solutions that might cause more harm to fundamental guarantees than benefits in terms of effective results.

In this essay, I tried to outline the main features of case management, as seen in legal literature, but also new trends that can be observed worldwide. In the end, I proposed some developments in the field of case assignment management, court management and litigation agreements (contractually-designed proceedings).

But I have depicted a story with a wide brush, and I do not intend it to lead to ubiquitous and universal conclusions. Moreover, an amalgam of less tangible institutional factors, contrary trends and specificities of every legal system may show that the world is far more complex than this tiny picture suggests and presents.

Rethinking case management is not just a question of making sense of what is the 'state or the art' in legal theory and judicial practices. Although it is important to know what has been already done, it is also relevant to supply some sort of framework for evaluating the path that took as this far and to point out to which way we should proceed in the crossroads of the years to come.

Some of the possible new tools of managing conflicts and procedures highlighted here are not immune to objections and often raise a lot of questions about their limits and possibilities. However, the tensions canvassed above are at least a starting

[215] Mak reaches a partially similar conclusion: Mak (2008, p. 5).

point to the development of these topics, and I hope, also for our discussion in this conference.

References

Albers P (2009) Quality assessment of courts and the judiciary: from judicial quality to court excellence. In: Uzelac A, Van Rhee CH (eds) Access to justice and the judiciary: towards new European standards of affordability, quality and efficiency of civil adjudication. Intersentia, Antwerp

Almeida D (2011) O case management inglês: Um sistema maduro? Revista Eletrônica de Direito Processual 7:283–335

Amendoeira Jr S (2006) Poderes do juiz e tutela jurisdicional: A utilização racional dos poderes do juiz como forma de obtenção da tutela jurisdicional efetiva, justa e tempestive. Atlas, São Paulo

Andrews N (2003) English civil procedure: fundamentals of the new civil justice system. OUP, Oxford

Arenhart SC (2015a) A tutela coletiva de interesses individuais: Para além da proteção dos direitos individuais homogêneos, 2nd edn. Revista dos Tribunais, São Paulo

Arenhart SC (2015b) Processos estruturais no direito brasileiro: Reflexões a partir do caso da ACP do carvão. Revista de Processo Comparado 2:211–229

Arndt A (1959) Die Gesetzlichkeit des Richters. Deutsche Richterzeitung, 171ff

Ávila H (2005) Moralidade, razoabilidade e eficiência na atividade administrativa. Revista Eletrônica de Direito do Estado 4:1–25

Baar C (1999) The development and reform of court organization and administration. Public Admin Dev 19(4):351–399

Bandrac M (2003) In: Guinchard S et al Droit processuel: Droit commun et droit compare du procès, 2nd edn. Dalloz, Paris

Barber NW (2013) Self-defence for institutions. Camb L J 72(3):558–577

Barbosa Moreira JC (2001) Uma novidade: O Código de Processo Civil inglês. In: Temas de direito processual: Sétima série. Saraiva, São Paulo, pp 179–189

Barioni R (2016) Da açao rescisória. In: Wambier T, Didier F, Talamini E, Dantas B (eds) Breves comentários ao Código de Processo Civil, 2nd edn. Revista dos Tribunais, São Paulo

Baum L (2009) Probing the effects of judicial specialisation. Duke Law J 58(7):1671–1675

Bedaque JRdS (2006) Efetividade do processo e técnica processual. Malheiros, São Paulo

Bettermann KA (1959) Die Unabhängigkeit der Gerichte und der gesetzliche Richter. In: Bettermann KA et al (eds) Die Grundrechte: Handbuch der Theorie und Praxis der Grundrechte, vol 3. Duncker & Humblot, Berlin, pp 558ff

Bohn K (2011) Der gesetzliche Richter als rechtsstaatstragendes Prinzip in europäischen Staaten: Eine Untersuchung der Fallzuteilung unter besonderer Berücksichtigung Englands. Peter Lang, Frankfurt am Main

Bone RG (1999) The process of making process: court rulemaking, democratic legitimacy, and the procedural efficacy. Georget Law J 87(4):887–955

Bone RG (2007) Who decides? A critical look at procedural discretion. Cardozo L Rev 28(5):1961–2024

Brazil WD (1986) Special masters in complex cases: extending the judiciary or reshaping adjudication. Univ Chic Law Rev 53:394–423

Bruns R (1964) Zur Auslegung des Art. 101 Abs. 1 Satz 2 Grundgesetz: Das Recht auf den gesetzlichen Richter. NJW 1884

Cabral A (2009) Despolarização do processo e zonas de interesse: Sobre a migração entre polos da demanda. Revista Forense 404:7ff

Cabral A (2010a) Nulidades no processo moderno: contraditório, proteção da confiança e validade prima facie dos atos processuais, 2nd edn. Forense, Rio de Janeiro

Cabral A (2014) Coisa julgada e preclusões dinâmicas: Entre continuidade, mudança e transição de posições processuais estáveis, 2nd edn. Juspodivm, Salvador

Cabral A (2016a) Convenções processuais. Juspodivm, Salvador

Cabral A (2016b) Les conventions sur la procédure en droit processuel brésilien. Revue internationale de droit compare 68(3):629–648

Cabral A (2016c) Standard-solution procedures and mass litigation. Int J Proced Law 6(2):263–281

Cabral A (2017a) Juiz natural e flexibilização de competência: flexibilização, delegação e coordenação de competências no processo civil. Thesis (Rio de Janeiro), Universidade do Estado do Rio de Janeiro

Cabral A (2017b) Mediation und Schlichtung nach brasilianischem Recht. Zeitschrift für Vergleichende Rechtswissenschaft 116(3):342–359

Cabral A (2017c) Per un nuovo concetto di giurisdizione. In: Briguglio A et al (eds) Studi in onore di Nicola Picardi, vol 1. Pacini Giuridica, Pisa

Cabral A, Cunha L (2016) Negociação direta ou resolução colaborativa de disputas: "Mediação sem mediador." Revista de Processo 259:471–489

Cabral TNX (2010b) Flexibilização procedimental. Revista Eletrônica de Direito Processual 6:150–153

Cadiet L, Jeuland E (2013) Droit judiciaire privé, 8th edn. Lexis Nexis, Paris

Cahali CES (2013) O gerenciamento de processos judiciais: Em busca da efetividade da prestação jurisdictional. Coleção Andrea Proto Pisani, vol 10. Gazeta Jurídica, Brasília

Câmara AF (2013) O direito à duração razoável do processo: Entre eficiência e garantias. Revista de Processo 223:42–43

Canotilho JJG (2002) Direito constitucional e teoria da constituição, 5th edn. Almedina, Coimbra

Caponi R (2011) O princípio da proporcionalidade na justiça civil: Primeiras notas sistemáticas. Revista de Processo 192:397–415

Carneiro AG (1980) Jurisdição: Noções fundamentais. Revista de Processo 19:9–22

Carpi F (2014) Specialisation of judges as an efficiency factor in civil justice. In: Adolphsen J, Goebel J, Haas U, Hess B, Kolmann S, Würdinger M (eds) Festschrift für Peter Gottwald zum 70. Geburtstag. C.H. Beck, München

Carvalho F (2015) O princípio da eficiência no processo coletivo: Constituição, microssistema do processo coletivo e o novo Código de Processo Civil. In: Milaré É (ed) Ação civil pública após 30 anos. Revista dos Tribunais, São Paulo

Chan PCH (2017) Framing the structure of the court system in the perspective of case management. In: IAPL Conference 2017 (unpublished)

Chayes A (1976) The role of the judge in public law litigation. Harv Law Rev 89(7):1281–1316

Chiovenda G (1993) L'idea romana nel processo civile moderno. In: Saggi di Diritto Processuale Civile: 1894–1937, vol 3. Giuffrè, Milano

Clarke A (2009) The Woolf reforms: a singular event or an ongoing process? In: Dwyer D (ed) The civil procedure rules ten years on. OUP, Oxford

Cole SR (2000) Managerial litigants? The overlooked problem of party autonomy in dispute resolution. Hastings L J 51(6):1199–1263

Contini F (2010) The reflective court: dialogue as key for 'quality work' in the Swedish judiciary. In: Langbroek P (ed) Quality management in courts and in the judicial organisations in 8 council of Europe member states: a qualitative inventory to hypothesise factors for success or failure. CEPEJ, Strasbourg

Contini F, Carnevali D (2010) The quality of justice in Europe: conflicts, dialogue and politics. Italian National Research Council: Research Institute on Judicial Systems

Contini F, Mohr R (2007) Reconciling independence and accountability in judicial systems. Utrecht L Rev 3(2):26–43

Contini F, Mohr R (2008) Judicial evaluation: traditions, innovations and proposals for measuring the quality of court performance. VDM, Saarbrücken

Corder H (2001) Seeking social justice? Judicial independence and responsiveness in a changing South Africa. In: Russell PH, O'brien D (eds) Judicial independence in the age of democracy: critical perspectives from around the world. University of Virginia Press, Charlottesville
Cornu G (1998) La codification de la procédure civile en France. In: L´art du droit en quête de sagesse. PUF, Paris
Costa EJdF (2016) Comentário ao art. 191. In: Câmara HM (ed) Código de Processo Civil Comentado. Almedina, São Paulo
Couchez G (2003) Voies d'exécution, 7th edn. Armand Colin, Paris
Couchez G (2008) Procédure civile, 15th edn. Sirey, Paris
Cramer R (2016) Comentário ao art. 972. In: Cabral AdP, Cramer R (eds) Comentários ao novo Código de Processo Civil, 2nd edn. Forense, Rio de Janeiro
Cunha LCd (2013) Jurisdição e competência, 2nd edn. Thomson Reuters Revista dos Tribunais, São Paulo
Cunha LCd (2014) A previsão do princípio da eficiência no projeto de novo Código de Processo Civil Brasileiro. Revista De Processo 233:65–84
Damle SV (2005) Specialize the judge, not the court: a lesson from the German constitutional court. Va L Rev 91(5):1267–1311
Davis LA, Garrett PA (2014) Case time and cost management for plaintiffs in multidistrict litigation. La L Rev 74(2):483–505
De Cristofaro M (2010) Case management e riforma del processo civile, tra effettività della giurisdizione e diritto costituzionale al giusto processo. Rivista di Diritto Processuale 65(2):282–305
Didier F Jr (2001) Sobre dois importantes, e esquecidos, princípios do processo: Adequação e adaptabilidade do procedimento. Revista dos Mestrandos em Direito da UFBA 224–238
Didier F Jr (2008) Apontamentos para a concretização do princípio da eficiência do processo. Revista Magister de Direito Civil e Processual Civil 52:41
Didier Jr F (2016) Curso de Direito Processual Civil, vol 1, 18th edn. Jus Podivm, Salvador
Diez-Picazo Gimenez I (1991) El derecho fundamental al juez predeterminado por la ley. Revista Española de Derecho Constitucional 31:116
Dinamarco CR (2016) Instituições de Direito Processual Civil, vol 1, 8th edn. Malheiros, São Paulo
Dodge J (2014) Facilitative judging: organizational design in mass-multidistrict litigation. Emory L J 64:329–382
Dodge JL (2011) The limits of procedural private ordering. Va Law Rev 97:722–799
Donnier M, Donnier JB (2003) Voies d'exécution et procédures de distribution, 7th edn. Lexis Nexis, Paris
Douglas J, Hartley R (2003) The politics of court budgeting in the States: is judicial independence threatened by the budgetary process? Public Admin Rev 63:441–453
Eidenmüller H (1995) Effizienz als Rechtsprinzip: Möglichkeiten und Grenzen der ökonomischen Analyse des Rechts. Mohr Siebeck, Tübingen
Eifert M (1997) Das neue Steuerungsmodell – Modell für die Modernisierung der Gerichtsverwaltung? Die Verwaltung 30:75
Eser A (1995) Der 'gesetzliche Richter' und seine Bestimmung für den Einzelfall: Rechtsvergleichende Beobachtungen und rechtspolitische Überlegungen zur spruchkörperinternen Geschäftsverteilung. In: Eser A, Kullmann HJ, Meyer-Grossner L, Odersky W, Voss R (eds) Straf- und Strafverfahrensrecht, Recht und Verkehr, Recht und Medizin: Festschrift für Hannskarl Salger. C. Heymanns, Köln
Eskridge WN Jr (2013) Expanding Chevron's domain: a comparative institutional analysis of the relative competence of courts and agencies to interpret statutes. Wis Law Rev 2013(2):411–454
Fabri M, Jean J-P, Langbroek P, Pauliat H (eds) (2005) L'administration de la justice en Europe et l'évaluation de sa qualité. Monchtrestien, Paris
Fabri M, Langbroek PM (2007) Is there a right judge for each case? A comparative study of case assignment in six European countries. Eur J Legal Stud 1(2):292–315
Ferejohn J (1999) Independent judges, dependent Judiciary: Explaining judicial independence. South Calif Law Rev 72:353–384

Ferraro MP (2015) Do processo bipolar a um processo coletivo-estrutural. Master thesis, Universidade Federal do Paraná

Fix-Fierro H (2003) Courts, justice and efficiency: a socio-legal study of economic rationality in adjudication. Hart, Oregon

Flood J, Whyte A, Banakar R, Webb J (2007) Case assignment in English courts. In: Langbroek PM, Fabri M (eds) The right judge for each case: a study of case assignment and impartiality in six European judiciaries. Intersentia, Antwerp

Foignet R (1932) Manuel élémentaire de Procédure Civile, 11th edn. Rousseau, Paris

Gajardoni FdF (2008a) A flexibilização do procedimento processual no âmbito da common law. Revista de Processo 163:161–178

Gajardoni FdF (2008b) Flexibilização procedimental: Um novo enfoque para o estudo do procedimento em matéria processual, de acordo com as recentes reformas do CPC. Atlas, São Paulo

Gajardoni FdF, Dellore L, Roque AV, Oliveira JR ZDd (2015) Comentários ao CPC de 2015: Parte geral. Metodo, São Paulo

Gelsi Bidart A (1958) Competencia y delegación. In: Scritti giuridici in memoria di Calamandrei, vol 2. CEDAM, Padova

Geraldes ASA (2012) Temas da reforma do processo civil. In: Julgar Nº 16 (Jan-Abr 2012). Coimbra, Lisboa, pp 47–97

Gilles ME (2000) Reinventing structural reform litigation: deputizing private citizens in the enforcement of civil rights. Colum L Rev 100(6):1384–1453

Gimeno Sendra V (1988) El derecho constitucional al juez legal. In: Constitución y proceso. Tecnos, Madrid

Giuliani A, Picardi N (1987) Professionalità e responsabilità del giudice. Rivista di Diritto Processuale 42(2):249–299

Gomes AO, Guimarães TA, Akutsu L (2016) The relationship between judicial staff and court performance: evidence from Brazilian State Courts. Int J Court Adm 8(1):12–19

Gramckow H, Walsh B (2013) Developing specialized court services: international experiences and lessons learned. Justice and Development Working Paper 81946

Greco L (1999) A execução e a efetividade do processo. Revista de Processo 94:34–66

Greco L (2012) Novas perspectivas da efetividade e do garantismo processual. In: Souza MCXd et al (eds) O novo Código de Processo Civil: O projeto do CPC e o desafio das garantias fundamentais. Elsevier, Rio de Janeiro

Greco L (2015) Instituições de Processo Civil, vol 1, 5th edn. Forense, Rio de Janeiro

Guiliani A (1988) L'ordo judiciarius medioevale (Riflessioni su un modello puro di ordine isonomico). Rivista di Diritto Processuale 43:598–614

Hagsgård MB (2014) Internal and external dialogue: a method for quality court management. Oñati Socio-legal Series 4(5):993–1014

Heinz KE (1997) Delegation und Mandat: Eine rechts- und verfassungstheoretische Untersuchung. Der Staat 36(1):495–520

Henkel J (1968) Der gesetzliche Richter. University of Göttingen, Thesis

Hensler DR (1990) Assessing claims resolution facilities: what we need to know. Law Contemp Probl 53(4):175–188

Héron J, Le Bars T (2006) Droit judiciaire privé, 3rd edn. Montchrestien, Paris

Hess B (2006) Effektiver Rechtsschutz vor staatlichen Gerichten aus deutscher und vergleichender Sicht. In: Gottwald P (ed) Effektivität des Rechtsschutzes vor staatlichen und privaten Gerichten. Gieseking, Bielefeld

Hess B (2010) Different enforcement structures. In: Van Rhee CH, Uzelac A (eds) Enforcement and enforceability: tradition and reform. Intersentia, Antwerp

Hesse K (1995) Grundzüge des Verfassungsrechts der Bundesrepublik Deutschland, 20th edn. Heidelberg

Hippeli M (2013) Privatisierung des Gerichtsvollzieherwesens. C.F. Müller, Hamburg

Hoffmann-Riem W (1997) Wahrheit, Gerechtigkeit, Unabhängigkeit und Effizienz – das Magische Viereck der Dritten Gewalt? JZ 52(1):1–8
Hoffman-Riem W (2001) Modernisierung von recht und justiz: Eine herausforderung des gewährleistungsstaates. Suhrkamp, Frankfurt am Main
Hol A, Loth M (2004) Reshaping justice: judicial reform and adjudication in the Netherlands. Shaker Publishing B.V., Maastricht
Hurst P (2009) Costs orders as a case management tool. In: Dwyer D (ed) The civil procedure rules ten years on. Oxford University Press, Oxford, New York, pp 171–181
Jacobs M (2011) In: Stein F, Jonas M (eds) Kommentar zur Zivilprozessordnung, 22nd edn. Mohr Siebeck, Tübingen
Jauernig O, Hess B (2011) Zivilprozessrecht, 30th edn. C.H. Beck, München
Jellinek G (1892) System der subjektiven öffentlichen Rechte. J.C.B. Mohr, Freiburg im Breisgau
Jellinek G (1969) Die Lehre von den Staatenverbindungen. Scientia, Aalen
Jeuland E (2011) Le renouveau du principe du juge naturel et l'industrialisation de la justice. In: Frydman B, Jeuland E. Le nouveau management de la justice et l'indépendence des juges. Dalloz, Paris
Jeuland E (2017) Toward a new court management and the rise of the court manager—general report. In: IAPL Conference 2017 (unpublished)
Jongbloed AW (2010) The Dutch Court Bailiffs Act eight years after its introduction. In: Van Rhee CH, Uzelac A (ed) Enforcement and enforceability: tradition and reform. Intersentia, Antwerp
Karpen U (1999) Brauchen wir einen Gerichtsmanager? In: Isensee J, Lecheler H (eds) Freiheit und Eigentum: Festschrift für Walter Leisner zum 70. Geburtstag. Duncker & Humblot, Berlin
Kern CA (2017) Der gesetzliche Richter – Verfassungsprinzip oder Ermessensfrage? Zeitschrift für Zivilprozeβ 130(1):91–120
Kerošius V, Simaitis R, Vėbraitė V (2014) Specialisation of judges and the lenght of proceedings: Lithuanian approach. Zeitschrift für Zivilprozeβ International 19:209–227
Komesar NK (1994) Imperfect alternatives: choosing institutions in law, economics and public policy. University of Chicago Press, Chicago
Kramer B (2001) Modernisierung der Justiz: Das Neue Steuerungsmodell. NJW 54:3449–3453
Küster O (1949) Das Gewaltenproblem im modernen Staat. Archiv des öffentlichen Rechts 75(4):397–413
Langbroek P (2007) Case assignment in Dutch courts. In: Langbroek PM, Fabri M (eds) The right judge for each case: a study of case assignment and impartiality in six European judiciaries. Intersentia, Antwerp
Langbroek P, Fabri M (2007) Internal case assignment and judicial impartiality: Comparative analysis. In: Langbroek P, Fabri M (eds) The right judge for each case: a study of case assignment and impartiality in six European judiciaries. Intersentia, Antwerp
Leisner W (1995) 'Gesetzlicher Richter' – vom Vorsitzenden bestimmt? Problematisches Richterrecht aus den Vereinigten Großen BGH-Senate. NJW 48:285–289
Loth MA, De Werd MFJM (2003) Teilaspekte der Gerichtsorganisation in den Niederlanden im Überblick. Deutsche Richterzeitung 81(9):315–321
Machado Alves T (2016) O gerenciamento processual no Código de Processo Civil de 2015: mecanismos para a gestão cooperativa da instrução probatória e integração da atuação dos sujeitos processuais. PhD thesis, Universidade do Estado do Rio de Janeiro
Mak E (2008) Balancing territoriality and functionality; specialisation as a tool for reforming jurisdiction in the Netherlands, France and Germany. Int J Court Adm 1(2):1–8
Marcus RL (2008) Cure-all for an era of dispersed litigation? Toward a maximalist use of the Multidistrict Litigation Panel's transfer power. Tul L Rev 82:2245–2296
Marinoni LG, Arenhart S, Mitidiero D (2015a) Novo Código de Processo Civil comentado. Revista dos Tribunais, São Paulo
Marinoni LG, Arenhart S, Mitidiero D (2015b) Novo curso de processo civil, vol 2. Revista dos Tribunais, São Paulo
Marques JF (1974) Manual de Direito Processual Civil, vol 1, 2nd ed. Saraiva, São Paulo

Marx E (1969) Der gesetzliche Richter im Sinne von Art. 101 Abs.1 Satz 2 Grundgesetz. De Gruyter, Berlin
Mäurer U (2000) Justiz – Aufbruch oder Abbruch? Ressourceneinsatz und Arbeitsleistung der Justiz. Deutsche Richterzeitung 65ff
Mbazira C (2009) Litigating socio-economic rights in South Africa: a choice between corrective and distributive justice. Pretoria University Law Press, Pretoria
Mcgovern F (1986) Toward a functional approach for managing complex litigation. Univ Chic L Rev 53(2):440–493
McGovern FE (1983) Management of multiparty toxic tort litigation: case law and trends affecting case management. The Forum 19:1–23
McGovern FE (1997) Rethinking cooperation among judges in mass tort litigation. UCLA Law Rev 44:1851–1870
McGovern FE (2005) The what and why of claims resolution facilities. Stanf Law Rev 57(5):1361–1389
Medina JMG (2015) Direito processual civil moderno. Revista dos Tribunais, São Paulo
Mendes A (2006) O juiz competente e a especialização judicial no Código-Modelo de Processos Coletivos. Revista de Processo 133:267–277
Mettenheim C (1970) Der Grundsatz der Prozeβökonomie im Zivilprozeβ. Duncker & Humblot, Berlin
Mitidiero D (2013) Cortes superiores e cortes supremas: do controle à interpretação, da jurisprudência ao precedente. Revista dos Tribunais, São Paulo
Mitsopoulos M, Pelagidis T (2007) Does staffing affect the time to dispose cases in Greek courts? Int Rev Law Econ 27(2):219–244
Molot JT (2003) An old judicial role for a new litigation era. Yale L J 113(1):27–118
Müssig U (2009) Recht und Justizhoheit, 2nd edn. Taschenbuch, Berlin
Ng GY, Velicogna M, Dallara C (2008) Monitoring and evaluation of courts activities and performance. Int J Court Adm 1(1):58–64
Nunes DJC, Bahia AGMF (2009) Eficiência processual: algumas questões. Revista de Processo 169(34):116–139
Obermayer K (1956) Zur Übertragung von Hoheitsbefugnissen im Bereich des Verwaltungsbehörden. Juristen Zeitung 11(20):625–630
Oldfather CM (2012) Judging, expertise and the rule of law. Wash Univ L Rev 89(4):847–900
Oliveira CAA, Mitidiero D (2012) Curso de processo civil, 2nd edn. Atlas, São Paulo
Oliveira GP (2013) Adaptabilidade judicial: A modificação do procedimento pelo juiz no processo civil. Saraiva, São Paulo
Ono T (2016) A flexibilização procedimental: uma comparação entre os sistemas jurídicos brasileiro, inglês e português. Revista de Processo 254:407–427
Papier HJ (2001) Die richterliche Unabhängigkeit und ihre Schranken. NJW 54(15):1089–1094
Papier HJ (2002) Zur Selbsverwaltung Der Dritten Gewalt. NJW 55(36):2585–2593
Pauliat H (2008) Le modèle français d'administration de la justice: distinctions et convergences entre justice judiciaire et justice administrative. Revue française d'administration publique 125(1):108
Peckham RF (1981) The federal judge as a case manager: the new role in guiding a case from filing to disposition. Calif L Rev 69(3):770–773
Pérez López X (2011) La delegación de jurisdicción en el derecho romano. Edisofer, Madrid
Perez-Ragone Á (2014) The conflicts between the fundamental rights of the creditor and the debtor. In: IAPL Seoul Conference 2014
Perez-Ragone Á (2017) An approach and general overview to framing the structure of the court system and case management—general report. In: IAPL Tianjin Conference 2017 (unpublished)
Perrot R (2006) Institutions judiciaires, 12th edn. Montchrestien, Paris
Peterson MA (1990) Giving away money: comparative comments on claims resolution facilities. Law Contemp Probl 53(4):113–136
Pflughaupt M (2011) Prozessökonomie: Verfassungsrechtliche Anatomie und Belastbarkeit eines gern bemühten Arguments. Mohr Siebeck, Tübingen

Picardi N (1985) Il giudice ordinario (le variabili nella tradizione del diritto comune europeo). Rivista di Diritto Processuale 8(9):802–809

Pinho JC (2000) Breve ensaio sobre a competência hierárquica. Coimbra, Almedina

Porcelli F (2009) Measurement of technical efficiency: a brief survey no parametric and non-parametric techniques. Paper, University of Warwick. http://citeseerx.ist.psu.edu/viewdoc/download?doi=10.1.1.232.4843&rep=rep1&type=pdf. Accessed 1 Dec 2020

Posner R (1983) Will the federal courts of appeals survive until 1984? An essay on delegation and specialisation of the judicial function. South Calif L Rev 56:761–791

Rasch E (1957) Festlegung und Veränderung staatlicher Zuständigkeiten. Die Öffentliche Verwaltung (12):337ff

Redenti E, Vellani M (2000) Diritto processuale civile, vol 1. A. Giuffrè, Milano

Renoux TS (1993) Il principio del giudice naturale nel diritto costituzionale francese. In: Il principio di precostituzione del giudice. Quaderni del Consiglio Superiore della Magistratura, vol 66

Resnik J (1982) Managerial judges. Harv L Rev 96(2):374–448

Resnik J (1986) Failing faith: adjudicatory procedure in decline. U Chicago L Rev 53(2):494–560

Resnik J (1991) From cases to litigation. Law Contemp Probl 54(5):5–68

Roach K, Budlender G (2005) Mandatory relief and supervisory jurisdiction: when is it appropriate, just and equitable? S Afr L J 122(2):325–351

Rodotà S (1985) Attuali asimmetrie del sistema istituzionale e legittimazione del potere giudiziario. In: Poteri e giurisdizione: Atti del sesto congresso nazionale. Jovene, Napoli

Röhl KF (1998) Vom Gerichtsmanagement zur Selbstverwaltung der Justiz. Deutsche Richterzeitung 241–250

Romboli R (1993) Teoria e prassi del principio di precostituzione del giudice. In: Il principio di precostituzione del giudice. Quaderni del Consiglio Superiore della Magistratura, vol 66

Roque A (2014) Arbitragem de direitos coletivos no Brasil: Admissibilidade, finalidade e estrutura. PhD thesis, Universidade do Estado do Rio de Janeiro

Rosales-López V (2008) Economics of court performance: an empirical analysis. Eur J L Econ 25:231–251

Roth T (2000) Das Grundrecht auf den gesetzlichen Richter. Duncker & Humblot, Berlin

Rothstein BJ, Borden CR (2011) Managing multidistrict litigation in products liability cases: a pocket guide for transferee judges. Federal Judicial Center, Judicial Panel on Multidistrict Litigation

Rottman DB (2000) Does effective therapeutic jurisprudence require specialized courts (and do specialized courts imply specialist judges)? Court Rev 37(1):22–27

Sabatini G (1961) La competenza surrogatoria ed il principio del giudice naturale nel processo penale. Rivista italiana di diritto e procedura penale 4:946

Santos BS (1985) Introdução à sociologia da administração da justiça. Revista de Processo 37(21):11–44

Santos MA (2007) Primeiras linhas de direito processual civil, vol 1. Saraiva, São Paulo

Schenke WR (1977) Delegation und Mandat im Öffentlichen Recht. Verwaltungs Archiv 68:118–168

Schönke A (1951) Lehrbuch des Zivilprozessrechts, 7th edn. C.F. Müller, Karlsruhe

Schulze-Fielitz H (2008) In: Dreier H (ed) Grundgesetz-Kommentar, vol 3, 2nd edn. Mohr Siebeck, Tübingen

Schumann E (1973) Die Prozeβökonomie als rechtsethisches Prinzip. In: Paulus G et al (eds) Festschrift für Karl Larenz zum 70. Geburtstag. C.H. Beck, München

Scott J, Sturm SP (2006) Courts as catalysts: rethinking the judicial role in new governance. Columbia J Eur L 13:565–594

Shetreet S (1989) Adjudication: challenges of the present and blueprints for the future. In: Lindacher WF et al (eds) Festschrift für Walther J. Habscheid zum 65. Geburtstag. Gieseking, Bielefeld

Silva PE (2010) Gerenciamento dos processos judiciais. Saraiva, São Paulo

Silvestri E (2014) Judicial specialization: in search for 'the right judge for each case?' Russ L J 2(4):165–175

Sodan H (2005) Das Spannungsverhältnis von Qualität und Quantität in der Justiz. Die Öffentliche Verwaltung 18:764–771

Solus H, Perrot R (1991) Droit judiciaire privé, vol 3. Sirey, Paris

Sorabji J (2017) Managing claims—general report. In: IAPL Tianjin Conference 2017 (unpublished)

Storme M, Hess B (eds) (2003) Discretionary power of the judge: limits and control. Kluwer, Mechelen

Strong SI (2013) Class, mass and collective arbitration in national and international law. OUP, Oxford

Terekhova L (2014) Grounds for the specialisation of courts and judges in Russia. Russ L J 2(4):176–186

Theodoro H Jr (2011) Curso de direito processual civil, vol 1, 46th edn. Podivm, Rio de Janeiro

Thiedemann H (2003) The 'lawful judge': a comparative survey on the allocation of cases to judges in South Africa and Germany. Verfassung und Recht in Übersee 36(2):228–260

Triepel H (1942) Delegation und Mandat im öffentlichen Recht. W. Kohlhammer, Stuttgart

Tucci JR, Azevedo LC (2001) Lições de processo civil canônico (história e direito vigente). Revista dos Tribunais, São Paulo

Turner R (2010) A model for an enforcement regime: the high court enforcement officers of the supreme court of England and Wales. In: Van Rhee CH, Uzelac A (eds) Enforcement and enforceability: tradition and reform. Intersentia, Antwerp

Tushnet M (2008) Weak courts, strong rights: judicial review and social welfare rights in comparative constitutional law. Princeton University Press, Princeton

Uzelac A (2008) Reforming mediterranean civil procedure: is there a need for shock therapy? In: Van Rhee CH, Uzelac A (eds) Civil Justice between efficiency and quality: from ius commune to the CEPEJ. Intersentia, Antwerp

Uzelac A (2010) Privatization of enforcement services: a step forward for countries in transition? In: Van Rhee CH, Uzelac A (eds) Enforcement and enforceability: tradition and reform. Intersentia, Antwerp

Uzelac A (2014) Mixed blessing of judicial specialisation: the devil is in the detail. Russ L J 2(4):146–164

Valguarnera F (2008) Le riforme del processo civile in Norvegia: Qualque riflessione comparativa. Riv Trimest Dirit Proced Civ 62(3):885–912

Van Bynkershoek C (1737) Questions of public law (trans: Tenney Frank), book 2, chapter 12. http://lonang.com/library/reference/bynkershoek-questions-public-law/bynk-212/. Accessed 1 Dec 2020

Van der Grinten P (2012) A Dutch perspective on civil litigation and its harmonisation. In: Kramer XE, Van Rhee CH (eds) Civil litigation in a globalising world. Springer, Hague

Van Dijk F (2014) Improved performance of the Netherlands judiciary: assessment of the gains for society. Int J Court Adm 6(1):83–99

Van Loggerenberg D (2014) Specialization of South African judges and courts: multi-skilled, multitasked, multiaccess? Russ L J 2(4):187–203

Van Rhee CH (2008a) Dutch civil procedure: reform and efficiency. In: Van Rhee CH, Uzelac A (eds) Civil justice between efficiency and quality: from ius commune to the CEPEJ. Intersentia, Antwerp

Van Rhee CH (2008b) Introduction. In: Van Rhee CH (ed) Judicial case management and efficiency in civil litigation. Intersentia, Antwerp

Verbic F (2013) El remedio estructural de la causa 'Mendoza:' Antecedentes, principales características y algunas cuestiones planteadas durante los primeros tres años de su implementación. Revista Anales De La Facultad De Ciencias Jurídicas y Sociales De La UNLP 43:267–286

Vincent J, Guinchard S (2003) Procédure civile, 27th edn. Dalloz, Paris

Voermans W (2007) Judicial transparency furthering public accountability for new judiciaries. Utrecht L Rev 3(1):148–159

Voet S (2014) Belgium's new specialized judiciary. Russ L J 2(4):128–145

Wang F (2017) The history and future of civil judicial management in China. In: IAPL Tianjin Conference 2017 (unpublished)
Weth S (1997) Prämien für gute Richter. In: Prütting H, Rüssmann H (eds) Verfahrensrecht am Ausgang des 20. Jahrhunderts: Festschrift für Gerhard Lüke zum 70. Geburtstag. C.H. Beck, München
Wheeler R (1979) Judicial reform: basic issues and references. Policy Stud J 8(1):134–149
Wilke D (2007) Die Rechtsprechende Gewalt. In: Isensee J, Kirchhof P (eds) Handbuch des Staatsrechts der Bundesrepublik Deutschland, vol 5, 3rd edn. C.F. Müller, Heidelberg
Yarkov V, Abolonin V (2010) Enforcement in Russia: a short outline. In: Van Rhee CH, Uzelac A (eds) Enforcement and enforceability: tradition and reform. Intersentia, Antwerp
Yeazell S (1989) Collective litigation as collective action. U Ill L Rev 41(1):43–68
Zimmer MB (2009) Overview of specialized courts. Int J Court Adm 2(1):46–60

Towards a New Court Management?

Emmanuel Jeuland

1 Introduction

Management in the sense of controlling and directing a team to reach an objective has existed since time immemorial. The art of management may be traced in many civilizations and in many cultures since the times of the monumental construction of the pyramids in Egypt.

Court management may be defined as the administration inside the court and outside the case. We will see, though, that the concept is not completely settled in the countries studied. It is inside the courts, so court management does not concern the general administration of justice (which is within the purview of the Ministry of Justice, judicial councils, etc.). It is outside the cases, so court management does not deal with the administration of cases, the so-called case management. Yet, these three fields belong to the same category of judicial management or judicial administration, and there is some overlapping and even confusion especially between national judicial management, court management and case management (in Chile and in India, for example, case management seems to be understood as largely encompassing part of court management[1]; court administration is often seen in academic papers as synonymous with judicial administration).

In a descriptive approach, it can be said that court management deals with leadership inside a court, the relationship between the judges and court staff, the allocation of cases, the evaluation of judges and court staff, the court budget, the real estate, the maintenance and security of the building, the new technology, human resources and judicial communication. Court management deals with the different councils and assemblies of the court as well as with specific planning. A distinction between the

[1] See Chilean Report.

E. Jeuland (✉)
Sorbonne Law School, Université Paris 1 Panthéon-Sorbonne, Paris, France
e-mail: emmanueljeuland@wanadoo.fr

L. Cadiet and Y. Fu (eds.), *On Judicial Management from Comparative Perspective*, Contemporary Chinese Civil and Commercial Law,
https://doi.org/10.1007/978-981-19-8673-4_4

inside perspective and the outside perspective may be drawn, but this does seem to me very clear. For example, the relationship the court has with the media and other stakeholders belongs to the outside perspective; but what about the court budget if the court is not autonomous and depends on the ministry for funding? Another way to define court management would be to take a negative approach and say that a function that is not a true judicial function (to adjudicate a case) belongs to court management.[2] Still, sometimes the dividing line between court management and procedural rules is not clearly drawn.[3]

This General Report is based on fifteen national reports (outside China) and different specific information, papers and books about other interesting nations (more to be said of them shortly). There are two Asian countries, one large and one small (India and Singapore). There is a national report from a country that belongs to both Asia and Europe (Russia). There are two reports from Africa (Algeria and Benin) and three reports from the Americas (Argentina, Chile and the United States). Lastly, there are seven national reports from European countries which are Member States of the European Union, three from the north-west (the Netherlands, Germany, England and Wales), one from the central south-west (France), one from the south-west (Spain), and two from the central east (Hungary and Poland). There are four national reports from common law countries (England and Wales, India—even though in India there is some hesitation to characterize the entire judicial system as belonging to the common law tradition, since there is a written constitution, codes and many specialized courts which are quite independent of the supreme court—Singapore and the United States). It is important to stress these differences because the approach to court management may vary according to the organization, the tradition and the location of the country studied.[4] For example, the role and the regime of the public prosecutor vary according to whether a country belongs to the civil law family or the common law family. Even some expressions are difficult to translate, for example 'judicial public service' is not used very much outside of France (in France, the judiciary has been a judicial public

[2] See Chilean Report.

[3] See Chilean Report.

[4] Here is a list, with titles and email addresses, of the national reporters. German Report: Professor Christoph Kern, University of Heidelberg, christoph.kern@ipr.uni-heidelberg.de; Spanish Report: Dr Marco de Benito, marco.debenito@ie.edu, Professor of Law, IE University, Madrid; Indian Report: Professor Yashomati Gosh, National Law School University in Bangalore, yashomati@nls.ac.in; Chilean Report: Pablo Bravo-Hurtado, Maastricht University, the Netherlands, pablo.bravohurtado@maastrichtuniversity.nl and Ramón García Odgers, Catholic University of Concepción, Chile (this national reporter would like to attend the conference in November); Benin Report: Joseph Akuesson, Doctor, University Paris 1 and University of Abomey Calavi (Benin), akuessont@yahoo.fr; Algerian Report: Mostapha Maouene, Professor at the University Djilali Liabès - Sidi bel abbès, maouene_mostefa@yahoo.fr; United States Report: Etienne Nedellec (after a research project carried out in the United States), PhD Student at the University of Paris 1, etiennenedellec@gmail.com; Dutch Report: Chantal Mahe, Lecturer, University of Amsterdam, c.b.p.mahe@vu.nl; Argentinian Report: Leandro Gianini, Professor, University La Plata Buenos Aeres, lgiannini@gmail.com; England and Wales Report: Gar Yein Ng, Doctor, University of Utrecht (expert in English law), G.Ng@law.uu.nl; Singapore Report: Yap Cai Ping (Ms), Assistant Director, Legal Policy Division, Ministry of Justice, YAP_Cai_Ping@Mlaw.gov.sg; Russian Report: Professor Svetlana K. Zagaynova, Ural State Law University, usla.mediator@gmail.com;

service just since the statute of 18 November 2016, previously it was only a judicial service). Another important source of difference is whether a country has a federal structure or not. When the structure is federal or based on regions, the approach to court management may vary according to the different regions or states (United States, Argentina, Spain, Germany, etc.).

The information, papers and books also drawn upon for this General Report are about Australia, Belgium, Brazil,[5] Norway[6] and Switzerland. Australia is one of the most advanced countries whose approach to court management is closely similar to the US model. Belgium's approach is in between that of France and the Netherlands, and it is trying to find is own way.[7]

The national reports comprise the responses to a questionnaire of eleven questions which were constructed objectively and neutral in tone, and not orientating towards new public management or old-school administration of the courts.[8]

French Report: Emmanuel Jeuland; Polish Report: Bartosz Karolczyk, Lawyer, Warsaw, bkarolczyk@law.gwu.edu and Kinga Flaga-Gieruszyńska, kingaflaga@gmail.com, dr hab. Kinga Flaga-Gieruszynska, prof. US, Head of the Chamber of Civil Procedure, Faculty of Law and Administration, University of Szczecin, Poland.

[5] I would like to thank Antonio Cabral for his very interesting insights on the Brazilian system.

[6] I would like to thank Magnus Stranberg for his very interesting insights on the Norwegian system. The organization of the tribunal is very flexible and may vary; in case of backlogs, temporary judges may be hired (which raises the question of potential conflicts of interest, since these judges, hired for 6 or 12 months, may have worked for private companies and could return to private companies afterwards). The assistants of judges (usually after University) may adjudicate a case, even a criminal case, on their own.

[7] I would like to thank Florian Roger for the information he provided on the Belgian system.

[8] 1.What is the conception of court management in your country? Is there a difference between court management and administration of the tribunal?

2. What are the roles of the court staff (judges, prosecutors, assistants, clerks, judicial officers, mediators, etc.) as far as management of the court is concerned?

3. What are the relationships among them (judges, prosecutors, assistants, clerks, judicial officers, mediators, etc.) as far as management of the court (competition of power, diarchy between judges and public prosecutors, between court managers and the head of the judges)?

4. What are the interactions on a day-to-day basis between court staff as far as management is concerned? Are there frequent meetings, for example?

5. Staff Management and Judicial Independence: Who manages: the head of the judges of the jurisdiction, the head of the court clerks, the public attorney? Who manages what: real estate of the tribunal building, maintenance of the building, new technology, security of the building, human resources, communications? Does the organization allow the judge to remain independent (e.g. workload objectives, indicators)?

6. Allocation of the cases and Appointment of the Judges (professional judges, lay judges, etc.). Is it a unilateral allocation of the cases made by the head of the tribunal or is there a commission, which allocates the cases to the judges and divisions of the tribunal? Are there objective criteria to allocate cases (name of parties, number of the case, subject matter, etc.)?

7. Evaluation, Accountability and Responsibility of judges and courts: What is the impact of bonuses, assessments, statistics, disciplinary sanctions in case of failure to meet the objectives?

8. Economic Budget of the Courts and the Justice System: What is the national budget of the justice system? What is the budget of a small, medium and large court? The different parts of the budget: for the jails, the courts, the national school, etc.?

The primary observation of this General Report is that court management is becoming a common concern everywhere in the world as part of the efforts to avoid backlogs, unreasonable duration of proceedings and costly litigation. It seems that the tasks of management are more and more given to a specialized clerk (the director of clerks) while the role of leadership remains in the hands of the head of the court. The management we are considering is a new management based on indicators, objectives and evaluations coming from the new public management, itself coming from the private business approach (in the United States, Japan, Belgium) or the planned economy approach similar to that of the communist approach to management (Russia, Benin to a certain extent). The relationship between new court management and the independence of judges is not an explicit concern in every country. Nevertheless, it seems that there may be a conflict between the two. The question I would ask is: Can the courts manage in the same way as a business does? If so, then the judge and the staff could refer all their activities to certain business cases and measure precisely the cost of each case. The parties would be clients and the court would be client-oriented. For some reason, it seems that it is more natural in English to say that the parties are 'clients' than in other languages. But the real question is: Is there a risk in this for the rule of law and the principle of due process?

The answer is that court management has to be specific to the court, or else the new public management has to be adapted. So, court management is not the new management implemented as usual in other organizations. The peculiarity of justice has an impact on the type of management. The national reports confirm that the court belongs to a very specific kind of organization, one which involves three publics: citizen, judge and staff. The university and the hospital belong to this category as well, with student, scholar and department, and patient, doctor and administration. It is said of this kind of organization that it has a loosely coupled organizational structure with certain specificity: the high intellectual level of the agents, an unclear chain of command, the need for discussion and negotiation, grey zones of hierarchy between staff and judges, unpredictable alliances and changes in public expectations. It is management in a state of uncertainty. One of the drawbacks of this kind of organization is that in the event of difficulty it reacts by closing in on itself, becoming a bunker, a citadel to protect itself from political power or media scrutiny.

This organization also varies, depending, for example, on whether the public prosecutor has a role to play in court management or is considered an outside professional. What is specific to justice is that the 'product' involves the independence and more than that the autonomy of judges. The scholar does not have to be impartial and independent of power in the same way as the judge has to be. But the scholar may have the freedom of speech that the judge does not have in a particular case for

9. Is there a concern about the emotions of the court staff (threats, security, etc.)? If so, how is this issue tackled? (Is there a special group composed of doctors, psychologists and other people, or a commission on hygiene and security?)

10. Is there a general assembly, a governing council (composed of staff and stakeholders, such as a bar representative, a media representative, a city hall representative in the court)?

11. Is there compulsory or voluntary planning for several years in the courts? If yes, who is responsible for initiating and carrying out the plan?

confidentiality reasons. A doctor has independence and responsibility when making a medical decision, but the doctor does not have to be independent of power. Moreover, justice involves a certain procedure by which to get a judgment, which implies respect for fundamental principles such as a fair trial, the cooperation principle and the right to be heard.

Court management has to take into account all of this specificity. As a result, it seems that the court is rarely totally autonomous. There are, for example, central bodies that intervene in court management, such as the executive power, which may interfere especially through the Ministry of Justice and at times the Ministry of the Economy. Then there is the question of the role of Information Technology in court management, where managerial decisions in the field of IT may have an impact on case management.

Taken all together, I would suggest that there is no clear-cut agreement about the meaning of court management and the choice of words to describe it in the same way in different countries.

The administration of justice is rooted in history. In the West, it may have been taken very seriously in canonical justice, since there was a real concern to administer the Church as a body, and so too the abbeys. This organization has been seen as the origin of the industrial and disciplinary organization, in particular by Foucault and Musso. There is an anomaly in the common law since the word 'court' used to 'reflect the close connection between the judiciary and the monarchy', given that the same word was used when speaking of 'the court of justice' as when speaking of 'the royal court.' Court administration especially in the English colonies (Canada, Australia, Singapore and India) was carried out by the executive power.[9] One can speak of the executive model. An important shift seems to have occurred, from this executive model to a management model, in order to gain more independence. Scientific management was invented by Frederick Taylor and at the same time by a French mining engineer named Henri Fayol at the end of the 19th and the beginning of the twentieth century. An important debate in the United States during the 1930s led to the creation of an independent branch of power with the establishment of the administrative office, which was to deal with the administration of the federal courts, leaving the independence and management of state courts to each state. This shift towards the management model was triggered not only by any concerns for independence of the courts, but also by an aggregation of political interests in the United States called progressivism which appeared in all spheres of society against the rise of big business and labour unions.[10] Even quality control management later formulated by the American guru of the modern corporation Peter Drucker aimed at fostering the independence of business from state power.

Court administration in civil law countries seems to have quite a different history. New management tools are used mainly by the state power. Philipp Langbroek, a Dutch specialist in court administration, considers that the judge in civil law countries

---

[9] Martin (2014, p. 5). In France, the equivalent word *cour* is still used for the court of appeal and the Court of Cassation.

[10] Graham (1993, pp. 3–25).

is a civil servant as a consequence of the Napoleonic legacy.[11] It seems to me that the position of the civil law judge as a civil servant goes farther back in time to the Roman-canonical tribunals. In these courts the judge was a priest as were the parties much of the time. These judges were part of the Catholic Church's hierarchy. It may well be that the French influence at the time of Napoleon secularized this organization, but it did not create it. As a matter of fact, the judge in civil law countries is still part of a sort of hierarchy. As a result, the courts are not autonomous. The budget may be more or less decided at the central level. The rules of management are fixed by the central body as well. In this situation, the pressure for higher productivity may impede the judge from having enough space for review of case law and seminars or to give sufficient time to a difficult case. The executive model is still present, but it takes the form of the management model through the new public management. The management model is not a way for the judiciary to be more independent, but a way for the central body to get more power over the court. As a result, there is a temptation to give more power to court managers without the control of the judge. This trend can be seen in Spain, Chile and the Netherlands. This distinction between the common law approach and the civil law approach can be seen according to the famous distinction made by Damaška between hierarchical and coordinate justice.[12] Court administration will be different in a hierarchical, usually centralized system from that in a coordinate, usually more decentralized and flexible system.[13] However, the Damaškian distinction is not totally helpful since for the topic of court management it may be misleading. It seems that the system is vertical in civil law countries and horizontal in common law countries. In civil law countries, there is not a true hierarchy between judges, since they are all independent. Nevertheless, the court of appeal is a superior court which adjudicates a second time in fact and law. Conversely, in common law countries, the coordination involves a superiority of the judge upon the parties and the staff—like a god[14]; whereas the civil law judge is a civil servant not essentially superior to the parties and the staff. Moreover, the system of justice is not necessarily decentralized in common law countries.[15] At least what can be said is that there is a centrifugal force in civil law countries and a centripetal force in common law countries. The former tends to hierarchy and unity and to be top down, the latter tends to decentralization and autonomy and to be bottom up (especially in the United States).

So, the question may well be: Are we going towards a new court management and therefore towards the management model? The answer is not obvious, since the problem is not the same in civil law countries and common law countries. I would

[11] Langbroek (2017).

[12] Damaška (1986).

[13] Damaška also divided systems between those which implement public policy and those which are dispute-solving. I am not sure that this distinction may be used on the topic of court administration.

[14] Jacob (2014).

[15] The system of justice is not decentralized in England and Wales. In the United States, there are differences depending on the state between a centralized or decentralized system, with sometimes after unification a period of decentralization even at the federal level: see Gazell (1993, pp. 79–97).

try to demonstrate that there is a subdivision to draw between the civil law court management model and the common law court management model. The influence of the common law court management model on the civil law court management model may lead to tensions in court. Then there are also many countries in between civil law countries and common law countries. For example, in Norway there is a civil law system, but the tradition is closer to the common law. The organization of the court is flexible and may vary. The courts are quite independent with a court administration central body which is not located in Oslo but in Trondheim. The chief judge may hire deputy judges, and even judges, although formally that is a decision taken by the Minister of Justice. It has to be said that in Norway one becomes a judge in his/her late thirties, quite similar to what occurs in common law countries.

In any event, the encounter between court management and procedural law is not an easy one. One hypothesis would be to say that management interferes with law and procedure. For example, the allocation of cases among sections may be essential for the result of one case. One section of the court may favour a conservative solution while another is more progressive. A totally different hypothesis would be to say that management and procedure are complementary. In a way, court management is part of procedural law and so the allocation of cases could be challenged by a remedy. Court management would be a kind of internal law to the court, but a kind of law nonetheless. An Australian judge, Wayne Martin, has demonstrated that almost all aspects of court administration could have a procedural effect: allocation of cases, IT, the architecture of the building, data collection and statistics, security. As a matter of fact, it is impossible to draw a clear-cut line between judicial activity and court administration.[16] In Martin's view, all that should be considered purely administrative is the buying of office furniture and such office supplies as pens and file folders. I came across an example in France where the file folder had a procedural significance. At the Paris Court of Appeal, the judges liked transparent folders, because it was easy to read the name of the case at the top and to clearly see the different parts of the file. In fact, in English they are precisely called clear view folders. However, the budget was so low that it was not possible to continue to buy that kind of file folder. The transparent folders disappeared, replaced by cheaper opaque folders, and the judges complained, but to no avail. The procedural effect is that it is more difficult to find a case in a pile since you have to open all the folders.

Another small example comes from Norway, where a chief judge wanted to impose the requirement that the hearings in his court should start at 9 o'clock in the morning and no longer at 9:30 so that more cases could be handled each day. One judge complained that this would be an infringement of his constitutional right to deal with his cases the way he wanted to. I think that there is no administrative decision in a court without potential impact on judicial activities. For this reason, the leader of the court has to be the judge even though there is a court manager. At the same time, a party should have recourse against an administrative decision any time the decision directly affects the interests of the party. The Canadian Supreme Court has decided that only the functions directly related to the adjudicative process such as

[16] Martin (2014, p. 17).

the assignment of judges, the scheduling of trials and the allocation of courtrooms should be under the control of the judiciary.[17] I would prefer a more abstract criterion based on the impact of the administrative decision on the interests of the parties. In France, recourse can be brought in front of the Court of Cassation against a judicial administrative act (*acte d'administration judiciaire*) on the basis of abuse of power. The Council of State considers that it has no jurisdiction since there is a principle of separation between the civil and criminal courts and the administrative courts. Nevertheless, the administrative court could have jurisdiction over a purely administrative decision of the court. For example, a judges union brought an action before the Council of State when judges' bonuses were created by a governmental decree.

Then there are different styles of management. The new management based on objective indicators and assessments does not have the same relation with law as the old-fashioned administration of law. So maybe the administration of law did not interfere with procedural law whereas the new public management may endanger procedure. For example, if a judge has to reach a certain number of judgments, he or she is under pressure and may judge more quickly and with less attentiveness to each case. More strikingly, the judge may try to set aside or dismiss some cases for procedural reasons in order to have a better score. It seems that some judges in Australia, France and Poland are sometimes tempted to refuse to join more than one case at the same time for statistical reasons. We could call this trend the managerialization of justice.

Nonetheless, the majority of the national reports stress the point that court management does not impede respect for procedural principles. It should even foster higher quality and more reasonable time in respect of them. The dangers of managerialization seem to be felt in France, Germany and even the Netherlands, but not in the United States or Australia. Could it be possible that the common law is more at ease with new management than the civil law? Since the judge is appointed at a certain mature age, usually forty-five or older in common law countries, and sometimes with the legitimacy of election, there is no risk of competition between court leadership and court management, and so between court management and procedural law. Conversely, in civil law countries judges are chosen at a much younger age, around twenty-three, and without electoral legitimacy. As a result, there is a risk of competition between law clerks and judges. In France, for example, as in Spain or Chile, the importance of the director of the court clerk's office is increasing as he/she gets management powers. The director may have the same academic degree as the judge and sometimes has taken but failed to pass the national examination for judges.[18]

Maybe the old-fashioned court administration was in line with secret written procedure. In a way (allow me to be provocative), the civil law judge is already a kind of administrator. Thus, there is difficulty in making a good connection between the clerk's office and judges. There may be tension. Procedure is becoming more and

[17] Valente v the Queen, [1985] 2 SCR 673.

[18] In France, there may be directors of law clerk's offices who prefer management to adjudication of cases, but it is a new trend.

more managerial with case management, and the director of the court clerk's office is becoming a manager. It seems that there is a risk of conflict between them in some sort of diarchy. It would be easy to say that management is about organization and that administration is about the institution in a very strong, symbolic sense.

It should be mentioned that there also exist critical management studies. Assessments, statistics and indicators are discussed by scholars specialized in management. There may be opposition between new management and procedure since new management may sometimes be criticized, because some elements of new management are not applicable to procedure. For example, is it reasonable to limit the number of judges in a court for budgetary reasons while at the same time the judicial branch of government is obliged to adjudicate cases in a reasonable time? The answer is that it depends on the conception one has of procedure. If one favours managerial principles such as efficiency, rapidity, even quality, then one may be in favour of new public management based on objective indicators, benchmarking and the like. I observe that in every national report there is a concern for the traditional principles of procedure such as independence, impartiality and the natural judge. New public management is favoured by liberal economists who base their analysis on the rational agent even though now it is said that the economic agent is not always rational. It seems to me that a third model of court administration is possible. After the executive model and the management model, I would propose, based on the national reports, a relational model. This relational model of management goes with a relational approach to procedure.

It is possible to have a relational approach to procedure in a very broad sense, meaning that the procedure, in itself, creates a legal bond, the procedural bond, between the parties under the aegis of the judge. This bond is made to transform a legal relationship existing on the merits and which is litigious. In order to achieve this goal an effective fair trial is necessary; each party has to be heard a sufficient amount of time. Court management, which complies with this relational approach to procedure, is a relational management, which does not mean a genial and delicate management. It means that staff and judges have to cooperate at the level of the court. The principle of cooperation goes beyond case management. This relational management does not rest on a purely rational agent who has to be in competition with another to be efficient, but on a rational and emotional agent, who interacts with the other. Taking into account the emotions of the staff and judges in participating in the adjudication of a case has gained growing interest in North America for about the last fifteen years.[19] One result of this has been the formation of court committees and the holding of regular meetings (By the way, one of the problems here, which

[19] Through the movement Law and Emotion, on the growing importance of the topic of emotion in law, see Grossi (2015, pp. 55–60); see as well concerning the emotions of court staff as a terra nova Maroney (2012, pp. 481–488): 'If we were to look at the legal decision-makers whose emotions really matter most, and most frequently, I think we would be looking at judges, clerks, prosecutors, defense attorneys, civil litigators, mediators, police officers, probation officers, court room deputies, expert witnesses, legislators and so on.'

was not addressed in the questionnaire, is the salary of the staff[20]). Many things still need to be studied. At the end of the day, I think that court management is the way to deal with legal relations in the courts with citizens, legal professionals, the staff and other judges. It is a non-litigious task having a strong influence on procedure and requires competences, which are not all legal.

It seems that the same thinking is leading to a new court management in many countries, but that the goals are not always the same, and a divide may exist between civil law countries and common law countries (Sect. 1). There is not necessarily one type of new court management, but perhaps several types. The concept is differently understood, in a certain way, according to the country studied. I could even say that there are some misunderstandings especially when the word management is used outside the common law realm (Sect. 2). Then, the level of the countries studied in terms of management tools varies considerably from the most advanced, if I take the word advanced in a truly neutral way in accordance with the management model, to the not advanced at all. The understanding of what court management is may vary a great deal, and once again a line may be drawn between common law and civil law countries (Sect. 3). The professional in charge of court management is not always the same, and more and more there is a court manager even though the head of the court remains almost everywhere the judge (an example is the Netherlands, discussed in Sect. 4). The role of the council and the assembly as far as court management is concerned may vary enormously (Sect. 5). The day-to-day relationships between staff and judges may be informal or formal (Sect. 6). The concerns are not exactly the same in each studied country. We will see that there are different styles and difficulties, and I will stress the potential conflict between independence and new court management. We will see whether there are conflicts between traditional tools such as court administration, procedural law and judicial organization (Sect. 7). The allocation of the cases and the appointment of the judges (professional judges, lay judges, etc.) may comply with the principle of the natural judge, but may also try to take into account the necessary specialization of judges (Sect. 8). The evaluation, accountability and responsibility of both judges and courts are growing (Sect. 9). It is quite difficult to determine the budget of courts in comparison to the justice system and it seems that courts are rarely autonomous in this domain (Sect. 10). The psychosocial risks and security issues are more or less taken into account (Sect. 11). Moreover, court planning is not present everywhere (Sect. 12). In conclusion, it will be possible to state that there is not a new public management everywhere and on every issue, that the conception of court management may vary, but generally speaking in many countries there is rising interest in a managerial approach to court with a new character: the court manager and perhaps the fall of the traditional clerks dedicated to the authentication of the judgment. It is not obvious that the management model is going to be applied in every jurisdiction. Certain countries seem to be hesitant. I suggest that eventually the relational model will fit the needs of the courts better than the management model.

[20] The gap in salary between judges and staff is very important. This gap may result in tension between the two.

2 General Interest in a New Court Management

All the national reports show that there is general interest in a new court management because of the failure of the current judicial system. I will take several examples where the trend is striking.

In Western countries such as England and Wales, the Netherlands, the United States, Australia, Canada, Norway and Switzerland, the management model has been the answer to the backlog of cases and judicial costs. At the same time, it seems that in the common law countries the management model is seen as the way to get beyond the executive model.[21]

It is interesting to then turn to non-Western countries, where one sees that it is essentially a matter of backlogs.

In Algeria, a long process led from a new constitution in 1996 to a judicial reform that transformed the judiciary into a real power, whereas formerly it was only a function of one sovereign power. This process, according to the Algerian reporter, is in line with the concern to deal with the backlog of cases in a qualitative way that respects the fundamental principles of procedure and the equity between the users of the public service. The tools used to reach these objectives are based on the jurisdiction of the court and judges, specialization of judges and the management of the court using new technology and human resources.

In Chile, the topic of management has become an important part of discussion and reform because of the congestion in the courts. Judicial management, as special subject matter in Chilean procedural law, was born in 2000 with the reform of criminal procedure, which introduced a completely new system. This reform created a new prosecutorial agency (*Ministerio Público*) with investigative and prosecutorial functions, and a new public defence system. In addition, legislative changes modified the entire structure of the lower criminal courts and incorporated professional administrators, separating the judges from the management of these organizations. Budgetary issues also had an impact on the creation of a new model. For those reasons, the new criminal court organization gives the entire management of the procedures to a professional in the management field once the cases get to the court. A court manager (*administrador*) is in charge of court administration, and the judge's time, to schedule cases. Furthermore, this manager is the chief of the administrative staff. All the staff and the manager himself/herself come from the professions in the management and administration fields. This administrative structure, in the charge of the court administrator, relates to the judges through the Presiding Judge and the Committee of Judges. In that context, the reform not only separated the jurisdictional task from the managerial task, but also took away from the judges the control over their working time. Parties' lawyers, who previously dominated the progress of litigation, lost influence too. The separation between judicial and managerial functions was justified based on a cultural shift, in which courts should abandon their old autarchic and formalistic practices. After discussion and with the passage of time, the system received good evaluations and the best practices were replicated in the

[21] Martin (2014, p. 5).

reforms to other courts, such as those that handle family (in 2004) and labour (in 2009) disputes. The Supreme Court enacted several rules called Performance Acts (*Actas de Gestión*), destined to standardize the best practices regarding scheduling of hearings by separating and categorizing the different cases that enter the system. The scarce empirical evidence available shows that the use of these techniques or case management tools has achieved a positive effect by diminishing the congestion in the courthouses and reducing the time frame of cases.

In India, the Constitution, through its preamble, guarantees to citizens *Justice*—economic, political and social. But even after sixty-five years of independence substantive justice has not been achieved for the vast majority of Indian citizens. In the specific area of the justice delivery system the courts are faced with the problem of large backlogs and pendency of cases. At present, there are more than 22 million cases pending in various courts across the country. On average, the length of time for a case from the date of filing to the final disposal bridges the lifespan of an individual. Often it is said that litigation in India is handed down from one generation to the next as part of inheritance. Under the separation of powers doctrine, the judiciary is an integral part of the Indian state and adjudication of disputes is part of the core functions of the State. Independence, fairness and competence of the judiciary are the cornerstones of the Indian legal system. But the large number of pending cases has crippled the working of the judiciary and has had an adverse impact on the timely delivery of justice. The right to a speedy trial is an integral part of the fair trial; it is also fundamental to international human rights doctrine. The backlog of cases has resulted in the dilution of the right to access timely justice and is an erosion of the rule of law values, all of which has adversely affected the common people's faith in the justice delivery system.

If we examine the problem of pendency of cases, we find that there are many causes for the delay in disposing of cases. These causes include the shortage of judges, human resources and adequate facilities, the need for modernization of equipment, the litigation explosion, increases in legislative activity, the accumulation of first appeals, delays in filling vacancies in the High Courts, inadequate infrastructure, the failure to provide adequate forms of appeal against quasi-judicial orders, the lack of priority for disposal of old cases, the failure to utilize the grouping of cases and those covered by rulings, the granting of unnecessary adjournments, the plurality of appeals and hearings by division benches, as well as the increase in population.[22] That is the reason why at the moment there is an increasing interest in court management in India. At present, various efforts are being made to bring about reforms in the justice delivery system. The fundamental points of reform are based on achieving the three-fold goals of (a) making the judicial system 'five plus free' (i.e. free of cases more than five years old) by addressing the 26% of cases that are older than five years; (b) shortening the average life cycle of all cases; and (c) substantially upgrading court management systems. The Vision Statement prepared by the Department of Justice focuses on two major judicial reforms—increasing access by reducing delays and arrears (the backlog of cases) in the system, and enhancing accountability through

[22] Arrears Committee 1990.

structural changes and setting performance standards and capacities. The Action Plan provided under the Vision Statement identifies the following as the major areas of reforms: creation of a National Arrears Grid; focus on selection, training and performance assessment of judicial personnel and court management executives; efficient utilization of the judicial system and existing infrastructure through effective manning, planning and timely management by increasing the use of technology and management methods, procedural changes, management and administration. But the solution is mainly a matter of case management and therefore of scheduling; it is not court management in the strict sense.

The example of Benin is interesting as well because it shows the priorities in developing countries. The average case duration is two to three years at first instance, two years in appeal, two years at the Supreme Court (in Porto Novo). There were about 7 million inhabitants in the African nation in 2002; there are 11 million today. There is not a direct and expressed will to unclog the courts. But this goal is in mind in the willingness to reform the judicial map. Before 2002, Benin had eight first instance tribunals and one court of appeal. Following the new statute on judicial organization of 2002, there are now twenty-eight first instance tribunals and three courts of appeal (but only 18 of the 28 tribunals are settled). Additionally, since 2016 there is an administrative section in the tribunals and the courts of appeal. More and more judges are being recruited (80 this year). The procedure of divorce cannot exceed six months; in summary proceedings, the decision should be taken within one month even though the average duration of summary judgments is one year. Furthermore, there is a project underway to create commercial courts. As a whole, the solutions to the problems are not based on court management but on the creation of new courts.

In Brazil, for around ten years judges and court staff have been willing to undergo training in management in order to properly run the courts. In some courts, though, there are still managers who are civil servants; the judge who is the head of the court is still the chief of the administration of the court and of the director of the court clerk's office.

The management model seems to be gaining influence, but has not developed everywhere to reach the same goals. Despite this general interest in court management, there is still a misunderstanding in the vocabulary.

3 Misunderstanding in the Vocabulary

The concept of management itself comes from Western culture and language. Today, it is used worldwide in business companies, and more and more in public administration. The word seems to be quite straightforward, and so 'court management' seems to be a clear concept used even in non-English-speaking countries (such as Belgium); however, it is not a clear-cut concept.

Different countries may have a different understanding of the concept. There is the problem of the words themselves. Management is an English word of Latin,

Italian and French origin. It is now used in French, Spanish and in languages all over the world with the English spelling (sometimes, as in France, with a more or less proper British accent when spoken), but not always exactly with the English meaning. One of the reasons for this is that there is not exactly the same set of words under consideration in the different Indo-European languages from which it is derived.

In English, the two main words to be considered are administration and management. The former is used for a higher purpose than the latter; it is determinative of what the executive in performing the latter can and cannot do, and its scale is the long-term. In French, Italian and Spanish there are three words to be considered: administration, management and *gestion*. One of the founders of modern management, Henri Fayol, who I mentioned earlier, authored a book titled *Administration industrielle et générale*. Interestingly enough, his book has been translated twice into English, in 1930 as *Industrial and General Administration* and then again in 1949 as *General and Industrial Management*. Management tends to replace administration in French when it comes to the five functions described by Fayol: planning, organizing, staffing, controlling and directing. It tends to replace the word *gestion* as well, which is a specific Italic word meaning 'being in charge.' It is close to 'running a business' in English. So, now in France management means at the same time leading, administering and managing in the day-to-day sense or 'executing' in the English sense. Today, the management pronounced in French with an English accent appears to be more modern. It seems to me that this problem of language is very important when it comes to the comparison of different countries, since we are not talking about exactly the same thing even though we believe we are discussing the same matter when we use the same word 'management.'

What is at stake is important, because there is a general trend, as we are going to see, in the development of court management all over the world. But are we talking about the leadership in a court or the day-to-day running of a court and not about the judicial activity of a court?

The word management is English, but it comes from the French word *ménage* or *manège*. There is an ambiguity in the word in and of itself. Its etymology is debated. *Ménage* means housekeeping and used to mean dealing with the economic situation of a family (a *ménage* is still a couple in French). However, the *Oxford English Dictionary* considers that the origin of management is the French *manège* coming from the Italian *maneggiare*, which derives from the Latin *manus* (the hand), which is a horse riding arena sometimes called 'manege' in English or a carousel for children. Yet again, the same dictionary considers that the French *ménasgement* influenced the English word management in the seventeenth and eighteenth centuries. Well, the first meaning signals that the court will be considered a family or a company; it is mainly an economic matter to be handled. The second meaning signals the idea of leadership in the word management, and even dressage or training, since in a *manège* horses are trained in a particular regimented manner.[23] One thing that is beyond debate, though, is that the word 'man' does not enter into the etymology of management so that it would thus clearly be a matter of human resources.

[23] On this different etymology see Hoad (1996, p. 279).

The word administration comes from the Latin *administrare* and *ministare* (the one who serves) which meant 'give a hand' to the religious. Administration of justice was used in the fifteenth century in France. It was used as well and is still used in French to say 'take the evidence.' The modern sense of public administration comes from the French Revolution.

In Italian, the word *gestione* is used as well, but it is not equivalent to management. Management understood as directing is one aspect of *gestione*, and administration is limited to dealing with information to build the memory of the organization. Information is the input for the managerial decision.[24]

In Spanish, there are several words, *dirección*, *gestión*, *administración* and *gerencia* which may translate management. Behind each word there is a different agent: the director directs, and the administrator has a higher rank than the director in a firm.

In German, *die Verwaltung* is the running of an estate or other asset. *Betriebswirt* is the management of a business, *Betriebswirtschaft* is the science of management, while quality management becomes *qualität* Management in German. There are as well *die Leitung* and *die Fürhung*. So again, there is a set of words (and the relationships between these words are not exactly the same in every language). This is an original situation. The word *Verwaltung* is important in German and it means at the same time management and administration; it is a unique word for 'management and administration.' *Verwalten* translates at one and the same time: administration, management, governance and the running of.[25]

Moreover, the culture of management is not the same everywhere. In Germany, management is not a separate science of engineering. The German management style is still based on consensus, collegiality, quality-oriented, committed to long-term prospects and loyalty to the company. It is results-oriented as in the United States, more aggressive and quick to change.

In Brazil, the expression 'case management' is often encountered, but the Portuguese gestão do procedimento (running of the procedure) is used as well for judicial measures. The word administração is used to characterize an administrative decision (administração judiciária).[26]

But even in the United States the meaning of court management is not so obvious and the conception may vary.[27] Court management is sometimes synonymous with court administration (as in the National Center for State Courts' Institute for Court Management) or refers to the day-to-day running of a court as compared to the general policy of court administration. This issue of terminology is important, for in France, Italy and Spain management is considered something having to do with

---

24 See Argentinian Report.

25 See German Report.

26 In Norwegian, the word management is not used in courts; *ledelse*, close to leadership, or *styring*, close to steering, are used along with *admistrasjon*, in a practical sense the day-to-day running of the court.

27 Interview at the National Center for State Courts (NCSC).

leadership and governance of the court, whereas in the United States management is limited to the day-to-day running of the court even though there is some ambiguity even there.

4 The Conceptions of Court Management

The conception of court management is not clear everywhere, even where it is used (it is not used in Benin and Algeria, nor in Singapore). It is often confused with the administration of justice as a whole at the national level (Argentina, Russia) or regional level (Argentina again, and Germany) and/or with case management (Chile, Norway[28]). The concept does not seem to be totally settled[29] (England and Wales, Germany, France, India). Even the word court in the expression 'court management' may be debated. For example, in Spain there is a common office for a number of tribunals in charge of managing a case (without judges) before the case is allocated to a judge in a court.

4.1 Conceptions of Court Management in Common Law Systems

In the United States, the preferred expression is the administration of justice and the word management is used for the day-to-day activity carried out by the court manager, who is not the head of the court.

In England and Wales, the conception of court management is an evolving one. There is currently a reform programme underway (since 2015). It has three goals: 'delivering more efficiency and high performing court administration, meeting the needs of the public as well as providing significant benefits to the taxpayer and the legal profession.'[30] Interestingly enough, in this official phrase there is no difference between court management and administration of the court.

In Singapore, the Constitution establishes the legislative, executive and judicial branches of government. The judiciary consists of the Family Justice Courts, the State Courts and the Supreme Court. The management of the courts is the responsibility of the Chief Justice, who performs this function independent from the other branches of government. While the Ministry of Law works closely with the courts when considering law reform proposals, the Ministry does not influence the management of the courts.

---

[28] For example, the chief judge can take back a case from a judge who is not sufficiently diligent: Is this action part of the case management or the court management?

[29] See German, Chilean and Argentinian Reports.

[30] Handcock (2014).

Court administration is preferred to court management in the United States. At the federal level the main body is the Administrative Office of U.S. Courts, again the word administration is favoured. Nevertheless, the National Center for State Courts has a Management Institute for State Courts. The word management deals more with day-to-day organization, and the word administration is the general word. Thus, there is not really the idea of leadership in the word management. Usually there are court managers whose duties include dealing with the human and material resources of the court. They are not judges and they are not the leader of the court (often they work in the court under a contract, which can be terminated if necessary).

Court administration has developed along so many different paths in so many different settings that it is not possible to identify one ideal model. It is, however, possible to identify the various elements in a court administrative system: a court of last resort that makes administrative policy for the judicial branch, often reflecting this policy in court rules, directives or orders; a chief justice who generally serves as an executive overseer to ensure that court policy is implemented; a state court administrator whose office provides administrative support to the chief justice and the courts in implementing policy and in serving various other administrative or legal functions; chief judges of trial courts and intermediate appellate courts who administer the operations of their respective courts in conformity with the policy set by the supreme court and by the court they serve; trial court administrators and trial court administrative offices that provide the principal, but not the sole, assistance to the chief judges in implementing their administrative responsibilities. In federal courts:

> Day-to-day responsibility for judicial administration rests with each individual court. By statute and administrative practice, each court appoints support staff, supervises spending and manages court records. The chief judge of each court oversees day-to-day court administration, while important policy decisions are made by the judges of a court working together. The clerk of [the] court is the executive hired by the judges of the court to carry out the court's administrative functions. The clerk manages the court's non-judicial functions according to policies set by the court and reports directly to the court through the chief judge. Among a clerk's many functions are: maintaining court records and dockets, managing court information technology systems, paying all fees, fines, costs, and other monies collected into the U.S. Treasury, administering the court's jury system, providing interpreters and court reporters, providing courtroom support services, sending official court notices and summonses. [This last function is interesting since it seems that it is a procedural function and not an administrative task.][31]

The difference between administration and management of the court does not count very much is these examples where court management does not refer to something totally new.

---

[31] NCSC, Judicial administration, individual courts.

4.2 Conceptions of Court Management in Civil Law Systems

In Algeria, the expression court management is not used, but *gestion administrative judiciaire* is, which means judicial administrative management (in the strict sense of day-to-day activity).

In Argentina, the concept of court management may be confused with the concept of administration of justice. The concept of court management, as normally used in Argentina, includes diverse situations that can be divided into two groups of concern.[32] The first one is related to the strategic planning of the judicial system, the application of general resources and services needed to its actual functioning, and the design and administration of the budget of the judiciary. The second one is related to the management of each judicial organ. This second expression deals with multiple aspects of each court's running, organization and division of labour. It does not refer to the administration of the judicial system as a whole, but to problems such as the definition of the roles that will occupy each of the staff members of a first instance court, a court of appeal or a supreme court. This second group of concerns could be referred to as 'court management stricto sensu.' In general, this mission is developed by the judge of each court of first instance or, in some cases, by the president of a tribunal with plural composition (for example, the president of a court of appeal).

In Benin, the courts have an autonomous budget integrated into the budget of the Ministry of Justice. The administrative and financial management is assigned to the head of the tribunal. It is not a new court management, but the old court management. Having visited a court of appeal in Benin, I would say that justice is still largely based on oral debate.

In Chile, judicial performance and court management have not been the object of major studies by Chilean legal scholars.[33] A symptom of this is that, in Chilean legal language, there is no shared terminology or uniform concept to point at these aspects of the courts' functioning. A prominent exception among this scarcity of literature is Vargas, for whom court management comprises all the aspects of the courts' functioning, which are necessary to the efficient and effective delivery of judgments. These aspects include the structure of the courts, workflow, division of labour, distribution of tasks and competences, among others. The goal is to configure these management aspects to increase quality and speediness, taking advantage of the available resources of the court.[34] Vargas's concept is broad and points at all the aspects that are necessary to produce a jurisdictional response to the dispute before the court.

Overall, Chilean scholarship has not developed clear conceptual differences between case management and court management. Instead, any topic associated with court performance is labelled as 'administration' issues. Here we will distinguish between *court* management and *case* management. *Court* management points at the general managerial aspects which apply to all courts as a whole, such as the

[32] See Argentinian Report.

[33] See Chilean Report.

[34] Vargas (2006, p. 79).

rules on the appointment of judges, their training and promotion, the availability of human and material resources, performance measurements, among others. *Case* management, instead, points to the tools that judges have to manage the dispute at hand. Currently in Chile, however, this distinction is not frequently made. Quite the contrary, every aspect which does not strictly relate to dictating a judgment tends to be confused with general court management or court administration. In other words, particular case management issues blur within the broader notion of court management.

In France, there is an interesting shift in the choice of words. During the nineteenth century and until quite recently (before 2000), the general expression was judicial administration. It applied mainly to the administration of justice led by the Ministry of Justice. It encompassed the administration of each court (in fact the clerks were a private body until 1960, the court building belonged to the town organization, so the head of the court had nothing to administer except the allocation of cases). The management of the case existed but was considered part of the judicial and procedural power of the judge to prepare the case file (*mise en état*, to be judged of the case). In 2001, a tax statute imposed objectives on the judiciary (in terms of duration and quality). From then on the new public management applied to the judiciary and the expression judicial management tended to replace judicial administration. There is a clear distinction from case management, which is older and has a different name (*mise en état*), but not with the national judicial management. The word management is understood in a broad sense as the leadership of the court and as the administration of the court. However, it appears more and more that the director of the court clerk's office has management powers as well. So the question was addressed as to potential conflict between the director of the court clerk's office and the head of the tribunal. But this is mainly a matter of vocabulary, since in French the word 'management' has a very broad meaning which encompasses leadership. Sometimes the expression 'intermediary management' is used to describe the head of a section or services. Court management is used, but not totally distinguished from judicial management as a whole. In Quebec, the word management is not considered French and not recommended by the Quebec office of the French language (especially as a synonym of 'cadre', manager).

In Germany, court management understood as the administration of staff (human resources, e.g. recruitment of staff, supervision, disciplinary proceedings), infrastructure (e.g. construction and maintenance of court buildings; also the acquisition of material such as furniture, stationery and IT equipment) and budget planning is among the secondary duties of judges, and apart from jurisprudence. However, there is no clear distinction between such internal tasks and the broader term *Justizverwaltung*, which encompasses a federal state's justice ministry's competences over the courts. These uniquely include the authority to issue directives, thereby making certain elements of *Gerichtsverwaltung* a means of external management.[35] A committee of judges conducts the administration of the tribunal, understood as the

[35] Wittrek (2006, pp. 16–18).

development of a distribution plan. Thus, administration of the tribunal is a competence reserved exclusively for certain judges. Hence, there is no comprehensive concept of court management in Germany.

In Russia, in a purely hierarchical approach to justice, court management is understood as the implementation of a system of measures of an organizational, personnel, financial, logistical or other nature with the aim of creating conditions for the complete and independent administration of justice. The principle of independence of the court system grounds the conception of court management in Russia. This means that only the community of judges should govern all bodies responsible for the community. The judicial branch is supposed to be autonomous as much as possible. The basic provisions of self-government are the following: according to the 2002 Federal Law on Organs of the Judicial Community, the All-Russian Congress of Judges is the supreme body of the judiciary. The Judicial Department at the Supreme Court of the Russian Federation is a body of the federal judiciary which provides support for courts and other bodies of the judiciary. It also coordinates financing of the justices of the peace. The Judicial Department of the Supreme Court of Russia is responsible for the administration of the courts, such as the selection and training of judicial candidates, working with law institutes, and the qualifications of judges and other court officers. It is expected to enhance the independence of the judicial branch. It also supports the Council of Judges and the Supreme Qualifying Collegium. The Court Department at the Russian Federation Supreme Court carries out its activities directly or through regional divisions, which are located in every region of Russia. Each federal court includes a judicial office, which should be established by the court's chairperson with the consent of the Court Department at the Supreme Court. There is no administration of the tribunal as a special purpose court. Therefore, there is no difference between court management and administration of the tribunal.

In Spain, strictly speaking, there is no notion of court management. It goes without saying that courts exercise their jurisdictional authority (*potestad jurisdiccional*) based on the principle of independence. Having said that, a number of practical issues, such as the assignment of human and material resources, the location of the courts, the organization of the work, etc., do require some 'administrative' activity, sometimes referred to generally as the 'administration of the administration of justice' (*administración de la administración de justicia*). The traditional first instance court model was unipersonal: a judge led and presided over the court's office (*Juzgado*) and worked with the assistance of the relevant staff: a court secretary (*Secretario Judicial*, broadly equivalent to the French *greffier*) and other assistant officials. These courts were specialized according to their jurisdictional order (civil, criminal, administrative, labour) and sub-specialized as required (insolvency, family, etc.), as decided by one of those courts acting as the provincial coordinating authority (*Juez Decano* or *Decanato*). The different courts of appeal (up to the Supreme Court and the Constitutional Court) were the only truly 'collective' entities.

Organic reforms dated 2003, 2009 and 2015 have profoundly altered this model and designed an entirely new organization, still in the process of being implemented. The new model distinguishes three types of activity: (a) 'procedural' activity: the handling of lawsuits in everything except judgments and other important decisions; (b) 'jurisdictional' activity: the power to make judgments and other important decisions; and (c) 'administrative' activity: the management of human resources, computer media and other material means.

The centre of gravity of the new model is the so-called 'procedural' activity. A provincially centralized office (*Servicio Común Procesal*) now handles the lawsuits. This new office does not include judges. In fact, it is physically separate from the old courts, where the judges remain. The *Servicio Común* is staffed with a new state corps of civil servants that has replaced the old state corps of court secretaries, the *Letrados de la Administración de Justicia.* With the only exception of hearings and major decisions, the *Servicio Común* handles the entire procedure directly with the parties' attorneys in an autonomous manner, without judicial supervision (apart from the possible appeal of the *Letrados*' decisions). The structure of the new corps is strongly hierarchical and based on the discretional appointment of all members holding directive responsibilities. The *Letrados* are assisted by inferior categories of civil servants.

Once 'processed', the file is sent to the judge, who will hold the hearing or make the decision, assisted by a smaller group of civil servants (*Unidad Procesal de Apoyo Directo*). This strictly speaking decision-making power constitutes the new narrow meaning of 'jurisdictional' activity.

Besides these two basic units, a third one (*Unidad Administrativa*) manages human resources, computer media and material means; in a word, this unit carries out 'administrative' activity.

The idea of 'court' has therefore been dramatically altered over the last fifteen years. The complete disappearance of the old unipersonal courts is only a matter of time, as the new model continues to be implemented at different speeds depending on the region.

The Spanish example is fascinating, since it shows how a hierarchical system may lead in terms of separation between different professions. The ambiguity of the expression 'court management' and the difference in understanding are going to have consequences on the person in charge of court management.

5 The Professionals in Charge of Court Management

Everywhere, the leader is the judge, the head of the court. As far as court management is concerned, the role of the public prosecutor may vary. Everywhere, there is a director of the staff playing more and more the role of court manager. However, the chief judge in the common law system may have more autonomy and power than his/her counterpart in civil law countries.

5.1 Leadership by the Head of the Court or by a Committee?

Everywhere, the leader is the judge (France, Germany, Norway, the United States, etc.). It may well be that the situation is more clear-cut in common law countries. In Singapore, the Chief Justice heads the judiciary. The State Courts and Family Justice Courts are each led by their Presiding Judge. The Chief Executive of the Office of the Chief Justice oversees the efficient running of court operations and the provision of effective services to court users. There is a diarchy in certain civil law countries, and the importance of an executive board is growing (Belgium, the Netherlands). In Germany, the president of the court, his staff (assigned to the executive power) and the committee (*Präsidium*) composed of judges (assigned to the judicial power) as well as presidential and judicial councils perform the main tasks of court management.[36] The president of the court has the most important position in court management. He/She has supervisory powers over judicial and non-judicial staff and carries out all general business of court management. There is no legal regulation; moreover, the amount of particular competences such as the nomination of lay judges, authorization of secondary employment, etc., determines the president's power in court management. The committee is mainly responsible for the allocation of cases and the appointment of the judges' disciplinary tribunal.

In the Netherlands, since 2002, all the courts except the Supreme Court have at their head a central body: *Raad voor de rechtspraak* (RvdR). Two judges and one non-judge compose the court council for a term of six years (and then three years more). They are appointed by royal decree upon the proposal of the Ministry of Justice. Membership on the council may be revoked by a royal decree, which Bovend'Eert considers to be an infringement of the separation of powers. This council is competent for the budget and the running of the building (security). They have to take into account the exception of the independence of the judges (*onafhankelijkheidsexceptie*) and not interfere in litigation. The council oversees the quality of justice and the uniform implementation of the law. Several courts (Groningen and Rotterdam) put in place pilot programmes such as family judge or family mediation to improve the quality of justice. The council is responsible for the structure of the court (sections and the composition of them). Its decisions may be registered in the court rules of procedure[37] and the working order. This council is the hierarchical authority of the court.

Following the Dutch model, in Belgium each court has an executive committee composed of the head of the court, the director of the court clerk's office and the head of each division of the court (another committee is composed of members from the public prosecutor's office).

[36] See German Report.

[37] Beware, it is a false friend, since there are no civil procedural rules in this text.

5.2 *The Role of the Public Prosecutor*

In terms of the hierarchy and organization of the courts, one of the key points is whether the public prosecutor is considered part of the court. This issue is not linked with the distinction between common law countries and civil law countries. Rather, it has to be said that the public prosecutor has a role to play in court management only in civil law countries. In this situation, the public prosecutor body is highly hierarchical.

In many countries such as England and Wales, Brazil, Singapore and Norway, prosecutors are not members of staff, nor are they part of the judiciary. In England and Wales, prosecutors are barristers who are 'officers of the court' and are expected to comport themselves appropriately. Prosecutors, as part of the criminal justice system, would fall under the Better Case Management system and would be subject to such procedures and management system under that policy. In Singapore, the public prosecutor is not a member of the court staff. Nonetheless, the public prosecutor assists the court in the administration of justice by gathering the necessary information and presenting the prosecution's case to the court for its consideration in the course of criminal proceedings.

In the Polish legal system, prosecutors, judicial officers (bailiffs) and mediators are located outside the structures of the courts. In Germany, the prosecutors are subordinated to the Ministry of Justice. On the one hand, they are subject to instructions from the Minister; on the other hand, their status approaches that of a judge. However, the prosecutor in his/her special position has no function concerning the main areas of court management.

In Algeria, Belgium, Benin and France the public prosecutor brings the criminal actions on behalf of the society. In France, there is a so-called diarchy specially to decide the hearing agenda. Also in France, the conception of court management is hierarchical with a diarchy, almost a 'triarchy.' The head of the public prosecutors participates in the preparation of the hearings: date, hours, number of cases, etc., and supervises the other public prosecutors. There may be tension between the head of the court and the head of the public prosecutors since usually the latter wants to have many more cases than the former. The director of the court clerk's office (the one who manages human resources, building safety and maintenance, etc.) helps the chief judge. In large tribunals, the head of the tribunal may have a general secretary, usually a judge, to help with managing the tribunal. In Benin, the head of the court has to consult and inform the public prosecutor in order to maintain a cordial atmosphere.

5.3 *The Role of the Staff*

Another key point to explain the differences is the role and nature of the staff. It is not totally clear, but there seems to be a very real hierarchy in civil law countries between the judges and the staff, and a certain specialization of function in common law countries.

In Argentina, the organization of the court is generally based on a vertical structure. Almost exclusively, the judge, who has the ability to assign different tasks that must be performed, determines the roles in the judicial office. According to the common tradition in court organization, the judge assigns tasks by taking into account the hierarchy of law officials and other employees that work in the office. The number of them, in first instance courts, ranges from 10 to 15 on average, which includes 3 or 4 lawyers. The more complex tasks are assigned to law officials and employees of a higher position: the Chief Officer (*Jefe de Despacho*), a Senior Officer (*Oficial Mayor*) and a First Officer (*Oficial Primero*). The other tasks are assigned by the judge to the rest of the employees. In principle, the clerk and/or the 'auxiliary lawyer' control due compliance with such tasks, and frequently they delegate certain supervisory tasks to the chief officer or the senior officer.

In Hungary, the presidents of general courts, courts of appeal and the *Kúria* (Curia) are the employers of the judges and law enforcement employees of that given court. Judges and law enforcement employees are subordinated to the court executives, who can apply disciplinary and other sanctions (e.g. withdraw work-from-home and other benefits, request reports on activities and official documentary evidence in writing to verify that he/she is not subject to any disqualifying factors, order professional and disciplinary examinations) against the judges and law enforcement employees. Only judges can be court executives (presidents of the courts).

In France, the judge may have assistants to help in legal research. Their position title is 'assistant of justice.' Recruited for two years (the contract may be renewed twice), they work part-time and earn between €450 and €500 a month (usually they are university students in their fourth or fifth year of study, or doctorate candidates). They have no management powers. Then there are the clerks and civil servants. The head of the court has management powers over the staff, but a judge is not clearly the superior of a clerk. They are distinct professions. Thus, tension may exist between clerks and judges.

In England and Wales, the clerk is responsible for assisting the judge and managing the courtroom, ensuring it runs smoothly and that everyone is in the right place at the right time. The clerk implements any updates and informs the judge, and prepares all the case papers for the judge to make sure they are fully prepared for court. The ushers are often the first point of contact and are responsible for preparing the courtroom, checking that witnesses, defendants and lawyers are present, calling defendants and witnesses into court and administering oaths. 'Sworn ushers' are also responsible for escorting the jury to and from the courtroom, being on duty outside the jury room and handling messages between the jury and the judge. The Court Enforcement Officers[38] are responsible for enforcing Magistrates Court orders, which may require them to seize and sell the offender's goods to recover outstanding debts.

[38] Different arrangements at different levels, e.g. sheriffs, but outsourced.

The Security Officers are responsible for the control of access doors and gates to ensure that only authorized persons and vehicles are permitted access to court, conducting entry searches of all persons entering court buildings via public entrances, and preventing and dealing with security incidents.

In Germany, the role of judicial officers (*Rechtspfleger*) is assigned by federal law (*Rechtspflegergesetz*) and has a wide range of different tasks, performing executive management, among them.

In Singapore, the court staff are also members of various committees and carry out various projects together to further the objectives of facilitating access to justice and the efficient administration of cases. For example, the various State Court Committees meet regularly to plan and carry out their respective projects: Corporate Social Responsibility Committee; Divisional Planning Units and Divisional Knowledge Management, Library and Training; Eco Committee; Staff Benefits Committee; Staff Welfare Committee; and Workplace Safety and Health Committee.

In Singapore, the Infrastructure and Court Services Directorate strategizes the use of resources and services that best support the hearing process. It includes the Digital Transcription Services Section, Interpreters Section and the Office Management section. This directorate oversees the maintenance of the building. The Corporate Services Directorate oversees human resources, the administration section, security section, procurement section and the library. The Office of Public Affairs oversees the planning and execution of public engagement and communication efforts so as to position the Supreme Court as a forward-thinking and outward-looking organization with effective public service delivery. The Finance Directorate promotes proper stewardship of the Supreme Court's resources. The Strategic and Planning Policy Directorate sets long-term and sustainable goals, and conducts research to identify emerging trends regionally and internationally. The Internal Audit Directorate promotes a culture of risk awareness and ensures the adequacy of internal controls and compliance. The Computer and Information Services Directorate aims to be at the forefront of new IT trends and developments, as well as to anticipate and render IT solutions for the organization. The Legal Directorate reports to the Registrar of the Supreme Court, and it oversees the processing and maintenance of all court documents and records, and makes these available to court users. It also provides administrative support to the Registrar to ensure the efficient and expeditious disposition of all cases.

In the Netherlands, each court has an administrative department competent in support functions and administrative matters. This department is not led by a judge but by another kind of civil servant. For example, the Amsterdam tribunal has a department for support functions, which comprises ten administrative offices. Some national councils offer support functions as well.[39]

---

[39] See Dutch Report.

5.4 Court Managers or Not?

In Australia, England and Wales, and the United States, court managers are responsible for managing the day-to-day operation of the court, for example ensuring excellent customer service and the efficient running of court administration. They are also responsible for building and maintaining partnerships with the judiciary and external agencies, and promoting engagement with the local community.

In the United States, the state courts have a head of the court, who supervises, and a director of the court. A chief judge generally serves as an executive overseer to observe whether policies are implemented. We can also find state court administrators. Their office provides administrative support to the chief judge by implementing policy. Most states, through statute or constitutional provision, designate the chief justice of the court of last resort as the chief executive officer of the court system. Some chief justices involve the full court in most administrative decisions; other chief justices make many unilateral decisions, keeping the full court informed and occasionally asking for support on controversial issues. The power and authority of chief justices vary according to the method by which they are selected, their tenure and the degree of unification within the court system. Perhaps the most important factor in the power of a chief justice is the degree of court unification. Strong vertical lines of authority running from the supreme court down through the trial court system buttressed by control over the trial court budget can greatly enhance the authority of the chief justice and the supreme court. The chief justice does not have time to get involved in the day-to-day administration of the court system and operates through the administrative office of the courts and various committees. The principal managerial deputy of the chief justice is the state court administrator. Ideally, the chief justice and the state court administrator operate as an executive team. In actual practice, some state court administrators are not delegated much authority. Procedural rules of the courts have serious administrative and financial implications, but they do not deal specifically with administrative matters that transcend the processing of individual cases. Courts, therefore, promulgate administrative rules, such as a set of rules to govern court personnel management or standards for disposing of cases within specified time periods.

Some states, to enhance the authority and prestige of the office of state court administrator, give the position to a judge. Generally, however, a person other than a judge is selected. At first, courts tended to choose lawyer-administrators from the legal culture with which judges were familiar. Over time, courts have been more willing to choose professional managers as administrators.

All court administrators are to some degree involved in planning, organizing work to achieve objectives, staffing the administrative office, and directing and supervising persons who are on the staff. However, the actual functions of an administrative office vary, particularly in regard to trial court activities. In a system with a unitary budget and vertical administration, the administrative office of courts may provide many services to trial courts; in other states, administrative office contact with trial courts is quite limited. Moreover, some state court administrative offices deliberately remain small, leaving many aspects of court administration at the local level. Among the typical functions of court administrative offices are personnel management, financial management and budgeting, case-flow management throughout the system, automation of office management, jury management, public education, information management and dissemination, records management, research and advisory services, inter-governmental relations and secretarial services to judicial committees. In the federal system, the Director of the Administrative Office, who is appointed by the Chief Justice of the U.S. Supreme Court in consultation with the Judicial Conference, serves as the chief administrative officer. Congress vested many of the judiciary's administrative responsibilities in the Director. Recognizing, however, that the courts can make better business decisions based on local needs, the Director delegates the responsibility for many administrative matters to the individual courts. This concept, known as 'decentralization', allows each court to operate with considerable autonomy in accordance with policies and guidelines set at the regional and national levels.

In civil law countries, the head of the court has a double function. In Germany, the court president, as the court manager in the proper sense, is the head of judges at the same time. He/She has a hybrid status concerning the management of the court. The judges perform their court management functions assigned by federal and state law through the committee and the Council of Judges. In the Netherlands, the head of the court is not really a judge during his/her mandate. Actually he/she has a double function, both judicial and administrative. In Russia, heads of court are responsible for organizing court management. In this case, they have to combine the functions of two positions: court manager and judge.

In France, the director of the court clerk's office manages the court on a day-to-day basis. The director has no traditional clerk functions (authentication of judgments, writing the record of the hearings). Although before he/she was a court clerk, the director has now become the manager of the court. He/She deals with human resources (relating to law clerks and civil servants, not judges and the public prosecutor). There is not really a diarchy, but more or less a hierarchy between the head of the court and the director of the court clerk's office (the change of name to director is very recent).

There is a diarchy in Poland: the management of the courts is basically divided between two persons, i.e. the president of the court and the director of the court, who handles matters that are not the responsibility of the president. The specific rules regarding appointment of the president differ depending on the court, but generally the president is appointed by the Minister of Justice from among all the judges of the court, and with the approval of the general assembly of judges from that court. The director is appointed and dismissed by the Minister of Justice (thus, this is a political appointment; this is a very recent change in the law). The president generally handles all matters pertaining to the leadership of a court, in particular all matters pertaining to adjudication (administration of justice). The director generally takes care of all financial, fiscal and property matters of the court, so administration in the strict sense. Thus, if the president wants money, he/she needs to go to the director. In the Polish legal system, judges who perform administrative functions (president, vice president, department chair, etc.) influence the management of the court. At present, the tasks of the president of the court include, among other things court management and representation of the court outside the court (except for matters falling within the competence of the court director), in particular: to direct the administrative activities of the court in the scope specified in regulations; to determine the needs of the court necessary to ensure the proper functioning and efficient performance of the court's duties; to entrust judges, court assessors and court auditors with their duties and to release them from the duties; to analyse the judicial decisions of the court in the level of its uniformity and inform the judges and assessors about the results of this analysis, and in case of finding significant discrepancies in judicial decisions, to inform the First President of the Supreme Court about them. In turn, the tasks of the court's director include: to direct the administrative activities of the court within the scope specified in regulations; to perform tasks assigned, on the basis of separate regulations, to the head of the unit in the field of finance, economy, financial control, management of state treasury property and internal audit in these areas; to determine, in consultation with the president of the court, the location and number of posts in the court departments in which court employees are employed—judges, court assessors, court auditors, professional curators, assistant judges. The president of the court is in charge of all the judges in a court, and in practice can make a judge's life better or worse. In particular, the president appoints judges to the position of chief judge of a particular division. It is commonly said that all judges who hold these positions generally adjudicate far less that a general (line) judge, but make better money. Therefore, there is certain resentment towards chief judges. The relationship between the president of the court and the director of the court is not clearly defined and depends on the practice developed in the particular court. However, the director of the court is significantly independent of the president of the court, since the supervisor of the director of the court is the Minister of Justice. Not all district courts, which are the lowest level of the judiciary, have a court director appointed.

In England and Wales, the key relationships are between court managers and the lead judge of the court (court managers are usually assigned several courts to manage in a region). As highlighted in a CEPEJ study 'Quality Management in courts and in the judicial organisations in 8 Council of Europe member States', in the England and Wales Report, well-run courts had good interactions between the court managers and lead judges.

The court manager deals with all the administrative matters. In Spain, under the new model, the administration is entrusted to the *Unidades Administrativas*. These units are presided over by the new *Letrados* (old court secretaries) and do not include judges. These units are designed, created and organized by either the Regional Secretaries of Justice, in the regions with competences over the administration of justice, or the Ministry of Justice, in the regions without competences over the administration of justice. Collective courts, such as all courts of appeal, including the Provincial Courts of Appeal, the Regional High Courts and the Supreme Court, retain their previous administrative autonomy.

In Russia, judges do nothing but administer justice by resolving cases. Therefore, they do not participate in court management. Clerks and judge assistants only fulfil subsidiary functions while administering justice. All judicial officers in a particular court, who are subordinate to the chairperson, are responsible for all organizational and logistical issues that occur. As a consequence, there is no competition over power or a diarchy between judges and other members of the court staff. Judges are separated from having to solve court management problems.

In Chile, a distinction has to be made between the management of the *reformed courts*, and the *non-reformed courts*. The Supreme Court—through a special management office, named *Corporación Administrativa del Poder Judicial* (CAPJ)—manages the human, financial, technological and material resources of the Chilean court system as a whole. In the reformed courts, four different organs handle management: the Committee of Judges (*Comité de Jueces*), the Presiding Judge of the Court (*Juez Presidente*), the Court Manager (*Administrador de Tribunal*) and the Heads of Departments (*Jefes de las Unidades*). These organs should coordinate their management functions based on the rules laid down by the legislature, the Supreme Court's practice directions (*autoacordados*) and the guidelines dictated by the same management organs, which can be found in the Annual Plan or in particular resolutions. For example, each court manager (*Aministrador del Tribunal*) at a local level should follow the general policies dictated by the Supreme Court's CAPJ. These general policies regulate issues such as staff appointment, evaluation and management of human and material resources, and elaboration of performance statistics, among others. The *non-reformed courts* have a staff comprised of, at least, one court manager, one head of department and administrative personnel, in the reformed areas. In the civil courts, non-reformed yet, there is no clear division between jurisdictional and managerial functions. The court staff is not specialized in different departments. The organization is pyramidal, in which the judge at the top supervises the overall functioning of the court staff.

5.5 *Court Managers at the Regional Level*

Between the sphere of judicial administration and the sphere of court administration, there is room for judicial management at the regional level. On this matter, the situation of Spain is interesting. The regions that have assumed judicial competences provided by statute have notably increased their powers in the new model, as they are responsible for the design, creation and organization of both the centralized procedural offices (*Servicios Comunes Procesales*) and the administrative units (*Unidades Administrativas*), as well as the working hours, organization, management, inspection and management of personnel serving these units. The reforms have notably increased the presence of the executive branch—both central and regional—in the judiciary. Even though some authors have expressed doubts about the very constitutionality of the new model, the process continues to be implemented with the consensus of all the most relevant political parties at both the state and the regional levels. Historically, in the old unipersonal courts, the relationship between the judge and the court secretary was generally harmonious. One of them (the judge) held undisputed authority, whereas the other (the court secretary) was subordinated, but retained functional autonomy to authenticate or certify the files and, most importantly, manage the budget of the court through the predetermined tariffs earned from the parties. The judge's fixed state salary was normally inferior to the court secretary's variable income from court tariffs. This balance was undermined in the historical process that made the court secretaries dependant on a fixed state salary, and eventually was destroyed when, in 1985, court tariffs were abolished. Court secretaries, who were used to earning more than judges, suddenly earned less. And their natural subordination remained. They fell into a deep identity crisis. Comparative grievances became the norm. Soon they started to demand a certain equal participation in authority with judges, as well as emancipation from judicial supervision. Resolving this tension has been one of the driving forces behind the new model of administration of justice. In the new model, there is no possible diarchy or competition over power between judges and court managers, as court management has been altogether removed from the sphere of influence of judges and placed under the authority of the central and regional executive powers through the transformation of the old corps of court secretaries into the new hierarchical, discretionally appointed state corps of *Letrados de la Administración de Justicia.*

In France, there is a regional administrative office (SAR) which deals with human resources, real estate and advises the courts.

In the United States, the state courts of last resort decide the policy the lower courts will follow. The chief justice with the help of the state court administrator will implement those policies. But, even if the highest court normally makes the administrative policy for a state court system, it rarely allots much time for consideration of administrative issues (because the highest court is primarily concerned with the adjudication of cases). The role of the highest court is then to approve or disapprove the policy recommendations that are presented by the lower courts, often at the request of the highest court itself.

6 The Role of the Council and Assembly as Far as Court Management Is Concerned

There is a great variety among countries as far as the council and assembly is concerned. It seems that their role is growing in the management model especially to take into account stakeholders.

In some countries, there is no general court assembly (Russia, Chile). Sometimes there is a court council where the court staff and stakeholders are present (England and Wales, France, the Netherlands). There may also be a committee composed only of judges (Germany, Poland). There is often a national committee of judges with management powers (Belgium, the Netherlands) or an independent agency (Norway, Sweden, Ireland).

It seems that in the traditional approach of civil law countries there is seldom an assembly, and if it does exist, it is mainly composed of judges. Court administration is connected to the Ministry of Justice. Quite recently, independent agencies have been created in certain countries to improve court management and the independence of the judiciary (Sweden, Norway) following the US model.

6.1 No Assembly

In Russia, there is no general assembly or a governing council. The judges are responsible only to the Russian Federation authority. Other authorities' representatives are not supposed to interfere in the administration of justice or court management. Chairpersons may conduct meetings, briefings or press conferences with other representatives in case of need. All meetings are held only for the reasons of exchanging or giving information and they are organized by judicial officers.

In Chile, there is no equivalent to the Spanish, Italian or French Council of the Judicature, in which the different stakeholders of the judicial system can have representation. The, so to speak, 'internal government' of the Chilean judicature is in charge of the Supreme Court through its special management office. The Supreme Court appoints the members of this office. Therefore, other stakeholders—e.g. prosecutors, lower court judges, the government or the legislature—have no right to a voice nor to vote in this internal government of the judiciary. Certainly, this lack of representation of the other stakeholders creates political tension in Chile, particularly between lower court and higher court judges.

In Singapore, there is no general assembly. Nevertheless, there is a strong working relationship between the judiciary, the bar (as represented by the Law Society of Singapore) and the Attorney-General's Chambers.

6.2 Council of the Court Staff and Stakeholders

To take into account stakeholders is something that belongs to the new management model. Nevertheless, in many countries 'stakeholders' are not represented at all in the administration of justice (Spain, Benin, Germany, etc.). I do not see a divide between civil law countries and common law countries on this matter. In England and Wales, there is Her Majesty's Courts and Tribunals Service Board, which is composed of executive members, non-executive members, judicial members and a Ministry of Justice representative member. There are no media representatives or city hall representatives in court. However, past research shows that there have been some innovations to connect to the public through the use of 'service level agreements', which take into account specific performance review by lawyers, police, and prosecutors.' In 2016, there were also initiatives taken on outreach and communication with the wider society, a judicial communications office with an annual press conference, publication of judgments (though not all), TV broadcasting and the creation of a judicial website and intranet.[40]

In France, there is a general assembly of judges, which has a power of recommendation only. The general assembly encompasses the general assembly of the judges, the general assembly of the public prosecutors, the general assembly of clerks and the general assembly of civil servants (civil servants have no judicial competence). There is a permanent committee board composed of representatives of the general assemblies. Recently (Art. R212-64 COJ, Decree 26 April 2016), the court council was created to open the door to the stakeholders (the bar, towns, associations, representatives of the penitentiary administration, etc.). Benin also has a general assembly, which is composed of judges and clerks and which takes certain decisions.

In the Netherlands, there are three assemblies: the court assembly with consultative power (composed of the judges of the court), a court committee representing all of the staff (*Ondermingsraad*, since 2002) and a committee composed of stakeholders from outside the court, for example, the Gueldre court has a committee (*De Raad van Advies*) made up of a law professor of Leiden University, a consultant in product innovation, a doctor and a management professor from Amsterdam.

6.3 Committee Composed of Judges

In Germany, the courts have no governing council composed of non-judicial stakeholders. The judge's council has a say in such matters as preventive health management, the duration of convalescent leave, vacation schedules and various 'soft' management concerns. Committees composed of both judges and staff are typically formed for such informal tasks as organizing internal holiday celebrations or similar events.

In the Polish legal system, common courts are organizationally separated, so in their structures there are no representatives from other professional corporations, public administration, etc. The judges form a judicial self-government, whose bodies are: the general assembly of judges of appeal, the general assembly of regional judges and the gathering of the judges of the particular court. In addition, court boards are formed inside court structures. The boards include only the judges of the particular court (five in the court of appeal, eight in the regional court, four of which are district court judges operating in the area of the relevant district court). The tasks of colleges (both courts of appeal and regional courts) include in particular: expressing opinions on candidates for the position of the head of training and the position of spokesperson for the courts, and expressing opinions on the dismissal of persons

[40] Judiciary of England and Wales (2016, pp. 30–31).

from those positions; and also expressing opinions on the professional behaviour of judges and commenting on cases of judges violating ethical standards.

6.4 A National Committee of Judges

This matter belongs more to judicial management than to court management. Nevertheless, it is important in order to understand the style of the court management. Traditionally in civil law countries, the Ministry of Justice is in charge of judicial management (France, Germany), which may raise an issue of independence. Strangely enough, England and Wales have only recently created a Ministry of Justice (2005). There are more and more independent national bodies to deal with judicial management (Ireland, Norway, Sweden, the United States Hungary, etc.). In certain countries, judicial management is performed by the council of judges (the Netherlands) or by the supreme court (Chile, the Council of State in France for administrative justice).

In Hungary, the National Committee of Justice (OBT) functions as the supervisory body for the central administration of the courts. In addition to its supervisory tasks, the OBT also takes part in the management of the courts. OBT meetings convene monthly. It has its own budget. Every judge may attend its public meetings, but the judicial staff (court clerks, court secretaries, court officials, manual labourers) are not represented, and they may not be present even as an audience.

In the United States, in regard to the state courts, the Conference of Chief Justices (CCJ) was founded in 1949 to provide an opportunity for the highest judicial officers of the states to meet and discuss matters of importance in improving the administration of justice, rules and methods of procedure, as well as the organization and operation of state courts and judicial systems, and to make recommendations and bring about improvements on such matters. Membership in the Conference consists of the highest judicial officer of each of the fifty states, the District of Columbia, the Commonwealth of Puerto Rico, the Commonwealth of the Northern Mariana Islands, and the territories of American Samoa, Guam and the Virgin Islands. The Conference is governed by a board of directors and has several standing, temporary and special committees to assist the Conference in meeting its objectives. In 1983, the board of directors voted to adopt a non-profit corporate form of organization. We can also find the Conference of State Courts Administrators (COSCA), established in 1955 and dedicated to the improvement of the state court systems. Its membership consists of the state court administrator or equivalent official in each of the fifty states.

The Judicial Conference of the United States is the national policy-making body for the federal courts. The statute establishing the Judicial Conference states that it will: comprehensively survey business conditions in the courts of the United States; plan assignments of judges to or from courts of appeals or district courts, where necessary; submit suggestions to the various courts that promote uniform management procedures and the expeditious conduct of court business; and continuously study the operation and effect of the general rules of practice and procedure in the federal courts. The Conference also supervises the Director of the Administrative Office of the U.S. Courts in his/her role as the administrative officer of the courts of the United States. In addition, certain statutes authorize the Conference to act in a variety of specific areas dealing with the administration of the courts. There is also the Circuit Judicial Council at the regional level. It oversees the administration of courts located in that circuit. The chief circuit judge serves as chair, while an equal number of other circuit and district judges comprise the judicial council. Each judicial council appoints a circuit executive who works closely with the chief circuit judge to coordinate a wide range of administrative matters in the circuit. This detail shows that the goal is more to coordinate than to dominate as in the civil law system.

7 The Interactions on a Day-to-Day Basis Between Court Staff

In certain countries, meetings are not legally compulsory or organized in advance. In all the countries casual and informal meetings are possible and very useful. It is difficult to say whether meetings are more organized or favoured in common law countries than in civil law countries as a matter of fact. However, meetings fit better in the coordinate system, and there have traditionally been very few meetings between judge and staff in civil law countries. The management model based on quantitative indicators and assessments does not necessarily call for meetings, whereas the relational or cooperative model assumes meetings.

7.1 Informal Interactions

In many countries, interactions are usually casual and informal. In Argentina, on a daily basis, communication between court employees and officials with respect to office management is merely casual or promoted by an external requirement. In general, there is no mid- or long-term internal planning in need of constant monitoring. Work meetings around this subject are not common, since a culture of management is still in the initial stage. Therefore, internal communication channels are not highly developed. As a result, evaluation, correction and several aspects of court office management generally are undertaken unsystematically, which often leads to contradictions or perplexity at different levels. In Argentina, there are no fixed or rigorous patterns regarding functional relationships between court staff. They depend on the managerial criteria adopted by each judge. In some cases, the judge assumes a strong management profile and receives daily reports from the clerk, law assistants or other employees of the court. In other cases, the judge isolates himself/herself from office management issues, so the clerk or the law assistant receives the periodical reports. Depending on the degree of delegation, this kind of information is channelled to the chief officer or senior officer of the court.

In Hungary, the President of the National Court Office supervises the courts' activities and exercises the employer's rights in respect of the presidents (except the President of the Curia). Judges tend to keep their distance from their presidents. Only the president's personality and collegial behaviour can remedy this situation: if the president does not take the initiative to establish a close relationship with the employees, he/she functions clearly only as a real inspection body, and because their careers depend on it, judges keep their distance for good reason. Court executives do not interfere with the professional work of the judges; they only have control over the quantitative and efficiency parts of their work. Law enforcement employees who are not judges are in almost total existential dependence on the presidents of the courts. Professional executives (the head of a college, the president of a chamber) are court executives as well who direct, help and supervise the professional work. Judges are essentially on the same level and have a collegial and proper relationship with their executives.

In Poland, at the national level there are no standards developed in this area, but in individual courts it is a matter of procedure developed by successive court presidents and court directors who work together at the intersection of their competences.

In Russia, judicial officers, according to the chairperson's orders, fulfil the day-to-day interactions relating to court management matters. Chairpersons, with the consent of the Court Department at the Russian Federation Supreme Court, also assign duties to the judicial officers. The officers are in charge of various aspects of court management according to their specialization. Chairpersons organize meetings with judicial officers if needed. Each chairperson decides for himself/herself how often these meetings should take place. In case of a small problem (e.g. lack of paper, problems with the computer) experienced by a judge, he/she is allowed to apply directly to the officer responsible.

In United States state courts, most courts periodically set aside a few hours for administrative issues. They also propose various policies that will be submitted to the highest court for approval.

7.2 *Formal Interactions*

In England and Wales frequent meetings are highly likely. The better run courts have positive and constructive interactions.

In France, the number of meetings between court staff depends on the head of the tribunal. Some of them like to have a meeting once a week with the clerks, directors and the public prosecutor although not necessarily all together. Some of them do not organize many meetings, maybe one per month. There are no strict rules on this matter. However, there is a dialogue between management of the courts of appeal and the Ministry of Justice to prepare the budget. There are also meetings between the heads of the first-level courts and the head of the court of appeal to prepare for the dialogue by management with the Ministry. This system is highly hierarchical.

In Spain, in the new model the role of the Ministry of Justice and the Regional Secretaries of Justice in the administration of justice has been strongly reinforced. The decisions regarding human, electronic and material resources are now essentially made on a political level. The decisions are taken by consensus between *both* the Ministry of Justice *and* the Regional Secretaries of Justice on the most important matters. These decisions will then be implemented by the hierarchical, discretionally appointed *Letrados* or by the administrative units (*Unidades Administrativas*) themselves, concerning day-to-day management, these units being created by either the Ministry of Justice or the Regional Secretaries of Justice in their respective territorial areas of influence, and presided over by a *Letrado*.

In Germany, in smaller courts, informal interaction between court staff and judges/public prosecutors typically occurs during coffee breaks. Another form of communication encountered is weekly meetings (*jours fixes*) of the president, vice president, head of management, head of legal training and other office holders.

In Hungary, there are two forms of interactions: formal interactions (professional conferences, sessions), including the professional session of the heads of colleges (compulsory, four times a year), the plenary session of judges (annually), sessions of heads of groups (generally once a week/once in a fortnight); and informal interactions (open door), including heads of groups—presidents of chambers—deputy heads of colleges, which are open to addressing any problems (professional or personal) on a daily basis, and they can report to the court executives. This is the preferred form of interaction to handle problems on a confidential basis, which helps to avoid writing problems down immediately (expiration of time limits, professional problems, personnel conflicts, technical difficulties, e.g.). Judges prefer this method because since it is more confidential, it is more effective, and faster. It is less unpleasant and it has a preventive aspect.

In the Netherlands, as required by the rules of procedure, the court council has to have at least twelve meetings a year according to a scheme proposed by the head of the court. There are ad hoc meetings as well.

8 Staff Management and Judicial Independence

Some countries hold the view that management and independence may overlap, so they protect the judges (Hungary). Other countries think there is no risk at all of interference between court management and the independence of the judiciary (Germany). In certain situations, there are conflicts between the council in charge of judicial management and the Ministry of Justice (Argentina, the Magistrate's Council).

8.1 No Threat to Independence

In Benin, the tribunal handles operating expenditures. The Ministry of Justice handles investment expenditures. This distinction does not impede independence, which must attach to the chief judge and to the head of the court, taking into account the good administration of justice.

In Germany, concerning the federal courts, the ministries with the Minister of Justice represent the head of court management. Subordinate to the ministry is the president of the court, who is the head of the staff. Material concerns and requirements such as the maintenance of buildings, furniture, technical equipment, stationery and literature are in part subject to *Gerichtsverwaltung*. These tasks are generally not perceived as posing a threat to judicial independence. Needless to say, the tasks of the judges in this respect are purely organizational; the executive (*Ministerialverwaltung*) allocates the budgets to the courts. The court president exercises the *Hausrecht* (a somewhat idiosyncratic term meaning the right of the householder to determine who shall be allowed or denied access). This right also includes all sorts of security measures varying in intensity, the admissibility of which is unilaterally agreed upon. Judicial independence is granted only concerning jurisprudence in its narrow sense. Administration and management of the court as an executive task are not encompassed. Notably, public prosecutors do *not* have a stake in these areas of *Gerichtsverwaltung*.

In Russia, chairpersons carry out staff management. It is not considered interference into judicial independence.

Building maintenance (construction, repair), facilities, provision of equipment, vehicles, computer software and information support are carried out by the Court Department at the Russian Federation Supreme Court through its regional divisions.

The Federal Bailiff Service, a federal body of the executive power, provides security of court buildings and trial order in courtrooms. Generally, bailiffs are not subordinate to judges, and judges do not govern the Service. However, during the trial, the judge, being the main governor of the proceedings, may well give obligatory orders to the bailiff on the discipline of the participants.

Generally, judges are appointed to their positions by the President of the Russian Federation. Justices of the peace and judges of regional constitutional courts and charter courts may be either appointed or elected (it depends on the regional legislation). Judicial officers are appointed to and removed from their positions on the chairperson's orders. They are considered to be employees. The judicial officers under the supervision of chairpersons carry out the interior (within the court system) and exterior (with the mass media) communications. These rules are believed to keep judges independent from any interference. Moreover, there are some restrictions on judges' communications for the purpose of ensuring their independence.

In Singapore, the Chief Justice, the Judges of Appeal and the Judges of the High Court are appointed by the President on the advice of the Prime Minister. The Constitution of Singapore provides that judges have security of tenure. The law determines their remuneration and other terms of office (including any pension or gratuity) will not be altered to their disadvantage after their appointment. Judicial Commissioners of the Supreme Court may be appointed for a specified period and may exercise the powers and perform the functions of a Judge of the High Court. They are independent and impartial, and uphold the rule of law.

8.2 *Some Threat to Independence*

In Argentina, the Magistrate's Council was created through the 1994 Constitutional Reform. It is one of the main expressions of the 'Euro-influenced' 1994 amendments to the 'American style', original Constitution of 1853. The Magistrate's Council, among other powers, manages the resources of the judiciary and executes the budget that the law assigns to the administration of justice. The Supreme Court has repeatedly put limits around the Council's attributions, creating in some cases a public conflict between the two organs. In multiple administrative resolutions (*acordadas*), the Supreme Court has stated that although the 1994 amendments assigned the Magistrate's Council the task of general administration and budget execution, it did not modify the role of the Supreme Court as 'head of the judiciary', responsible for its 'governance.' According to this self-defined understanding of the Supreme Court, that responsibility includes, for example, the exclusive attribution to issue final decisions in the field of functional reorganizations and remuneration of judges, judicial staff and employees of the judiciary. This means that the Supreme Court remains chiefly responsible in the field of the human resources of the judiciary. For that reason, it is fair to say that the management of the judiciary at the federal level in Argentina has two main referents: the Magistrate's Council (in charge of a sort of general administration) and the Supreme Court (head of the judiciary and chief of its governance). This tension has led to some conflicts between them, in which the Supreme Court has had, almost every time, the last word, suspending or nullifying in some cases administrative decisions of the Council.

In Spain, since it is the Spanish government that determines the regions' budgets each year after negotiations based on political, not clear-cut parameters, all political players normally seek to maintain a certain level of consensus. The new organization has reinforced the roles of both the central and the regional executive powers, and the newly reorganized court secretaries (*Letrados de la Administración de Justicia*). Correlatively, the system has objectively narrowed the judges' scope of authority, as they are now excluded from both the day-to-day procedural handling of cases and most administrative decisions. By losing authority in those realms, the judges' independence has also been indirectly affected.

In England and Wales, a member of staff of Her Majesty's Courts and Tribunals Service (HMCTS) will manage estates, maintenance, new technology (which will be a centralized issue and mainly outsourced to the private sector), security, human resources and communications. The judiciary remains independent within the organization. The Lord Chancellor and the Lord Chief Justice as well as the Senior President of Tribunals do not intervene (whether directly or indirectly) in the day-to-day operations of HMCTS and have placed the responsibility for overseeing the leadership and direction of it in the hands of its board. The Chief Executive is responsible for the day-to-day operations and administration of the agency.

Furthermore, the Framework Agreement between the independent judiciary and HMCTS sets down that the protection of judicial independence is paramount in any activities of HMCTS and the Ministry of Justice.

In Hungary, the professional direction of the judiciary is fundamentally different from the administrative conduct of duties. There is no overlap between them, which protects judicial independence. Judges (and even the court executives as well, who adjudicated before their posting and will adjudicate after it) strongly require and protect this system, which is considered evident.

In Poland, the organization is problematic. The administrative tasks of the courts are: to ensure the proper technical, organizational and property conditions for the functioning of the court and the performance of the court's tasks; to ensure the proper conduct of the internal administration of the court, directly related to the performance of the duties of the court. Those are the responsibilities of the court's director and subordinate clerks. In turn, the administrative supervision over the activities of the courts can be divided into external supervision, administered by the Minister of Justice through the supervisory service, which is composed of judges delegated to the Ministry of Justice, and internal supervision performed by the president of the court. Nowadays, the powers of the Minister as an executive body are predominant also because most of the administrative functions in the common courts have been entrusted to the presidents of the courts, that is, to the bodies appointed and subordinate to the Minister of Justice. At the same time, the influence of the president of the court on the finances of the court was limited by the introduction of the director or financial manager of the court, who directly submits to the Minister when it comes to the tasks and powers of disposing of the budget of the courts. However, certain administrative functions were left in the hands of collegial bodies, selected in whole (general assembly) or in part (board) by the judges themselves. It must be borne in mind that administrative supervision activities cannot enter the area where the judges and the assessors are independent.

8.3 Accountability of Judges

Bonuses are granted to judges in certain countries—France, Spain and Poland for example. They depend on controls in place in respect of the performance of judges. Management controls exist in certain countries (France, the Netherlands and Argentina). It more often involves the hierarchy in civil law countries. In Argentina, there are jurisdictions in which the concrete experience in management 'control' comes from the top and concentrates on supervision aimed at avoiding judicial delay. In other cases, judicial management offices have more comprehensive missions (for example modernization of procedures and justice services) or are complemented by planning departments.[41]

In Hungary, statistical data relating to judges are available to the general public. The amount of work they perform is available too. For measuring and evaluating the quality of the judicial work beyond the statistics, there is a detailed and legally regulated inspection of judges. Its set of predetermined criteria have been renewed, unified and objectified in recent years (they include court session visits and monitoring of files, legal examination of fifty random cases, inspection of statistical data relating to individual judges). Inspections are conducted in a transparent manner at the local level by fellow judges. Some inspectors have a light touch, others go by the book, and the standards are not always equal; nevertheless, inspection outcomes determine the career advancement of the judge. This results in increased conformity by judges with the professional standpoint taken by second instance inspectors and motivates the interest of the judges in maintaining a good relationship with them.

Accountability for the maintenance of the buildings falls to the presidents of the general courts (twenty county-regional courts), the presidents of the courts of appeal (there are five) and the president of the *Kúria* (one). High-budget projects (restorations, the purchase of new buildings) proceed with the approval of the President of the National Court Office so that it can be incorporated into the budget of the judiciary. This is a completely centralized system. Building management is overseen at the national level. Any meaningful local development or modernization can only be achieved with the approval of the National Court Office (otherwise there are no funds available).

In Spain, judges retain ample autonomy as regards workload objectives. In 2003, a law was passed which regulated the remuneration regime of judges. That same year, the General Council of the Judiciary drafted a law which would regulate the measurement of the productivity of judges. However, it was annulled by the Supreme Court in 2006 and has not yet been replaced. The measurement system that is currently used—a provisional arrangement accepted by associations of judges and the General Council—is based solely on the number of decisions issued by each judge. In any event, the bonus or a variable part of the judges' salary that mirrors this measurement system is extremely limited (not more than 2% of their total salary).

In France, the organization allows the judge to remain independent up to a certain point. There are indicators and workload defined for each judge by the head of the tribunal (under the pressure of the objective of a certain number of cases each year). It has no immediate impact on the independence of the judges. Nevertheless, under the quantitative pressure, judges may work more quickly than they would like and may leave for their successors the complicated cases at the bottom of the pile (interviews). There is an individual assessment of each judge every two years which determines the future of their careers. Bonuses which exist have been seen as a threat to the independence of the judges, since a judge depends on the head of the court for a part of his salary. A case against bonuses was brought to the Council of State, which

[41] See Argentinian Report.

decided that the bonus was acceptable. As a result, all judges receive almost the same amount of bonus.

In Brazil, the courts and the National Judiciary Council establish 'metas', objectives, which may vary: they may deal with economy of office paper usage or electric energy, sometimes they deal with certain types of actions related to, for example, corruption or the environment (this programme was launched in 2012 and evaluated in 2015). The New Civil Procedure Code addresses the principle of efficiency (Art. 8); Article 69 allows the joining of cases for efficiency reasons.

9 Assignment of Judges (Professional Judges, Lay Judges, etc.) and Allocation of Cases

There are two kinds of countries as far as assignment of judges and allocation of cases is concerned. There are countries where the principle of the natural judge applies and others where it does not apply. At first, the principle was used by the courts of appeal (called 'Parlements' then) to impede the king from interfering in a case. The first set of countries look to the potential complexity of cases and the second set looks to some objective criteria even though not compulsory according to the constitution. The tendency is to render the system more objective and at the same time to take into account the complexity of cases. Traditionally, the principle of the natural (or lawful) judge does not exist in common law countries (or in certain countries somewhat close in legal perspective, such as Norway and France). The issue of allocation of cases involves distinguishing the assignment of judges from the allocation of cases in itself. It is an irony of history, according to one Italian scholar, that the principle seems to have originated in France during the *Ancien Régime* but does not exist in France anymore.[42]

9.1 Assignment of Judges

The appointment of judges is a question pertaining to judicial management. The assignment of judges in a court is certainly a matter pertaining to court management. The assignment may be decided by the head of the court (France), the general assembly (Benin) or the committee (Germany) depending on which body has the power to decide (see Sect. 4). The divide between common law and civil law does not have an impact on this matter.

In Benin, the general assembly decides the position of judges in the court. In France, each year the head of the tribunal decides on the assignment of judges to the different divisions on the advice of the general assembly. In a similar way, in England and Wales the Presiding Judges are responsible for the overall assignment

---

[42] Alavazi del Frate (1999).

of the judiciary and the allocation of cases on their circuit. The protocol setting out the Responsibilities of Resident Judges and Designated Civil and Family Judges makes clear that the Resident Judge has the general responsibility, subject to the guidance of the Presiding Judges, within his/her court centre for the allocation of criminal judicial work, to ensure the just and efficient despatch of the business of the court or group of courts. This includes the overseeing of the assignment of judges to the court or group, including the distribution of work among all the judges assigned to that court.[43] In Poland, the assignment of judges to the departments and the scope of their duties fall within the competence of the president of the court (of appeal in courts of appeal, and in the regional and district courts, the president of the regional court), who determines, among other things, the assignment of judges, court assessors and court auditors. The president of the court does so, taking into account the specialization of the judges (as well as that of court assessors and court auditors) in the recognition of different types of cases, the need to ensure the proper placement of judges, court assessors and court auditors in court departments, and even the distribution of their duties and the need to ensure effective court proceedings.

In Germany, both professional judges and lay judges, as far as provided by federal law, are assigned to their respective chambers in the distribution-of-business plan made by the committee. In this regard, no difference is made between professional and lay judges. One exception to the self-given distribution-of-business plan practice concerns the Federal Constitutional Court.

In the federal system of the United States, each federal judge is commissioned to a specific court. Judges have no authority to hear cases in other courts unless they are formally designated to do so. Because of heavy caseloads in certain districts, judges from other courts are often asked to hear cases in these districts.

9.2 Allocation of Cases Among Tribunals

In the United States federal and state courts, case allocation is based on the respective division: the Civil Justice Division receives civil cases, the Criminal Justice Division receives criminal cases, a Community Justice and Tribunals Division may handle community justice issues such as those relating to the community, harassment and small claims, and additionally there are state court centers for dispute resolution.

Sometimes the allocation of cases seems to be almost a jurisdictional rule. In Argentina, the general rule on allocation of cases is to draw from among the tribunals that may be competent over the case. That mechanism is considered useful to prevent arbitrary appointment of a judge that could lead to a violation of the right to a 'natural judge.' Normally, each jurisdiction has an office that carries out an automatic drawing process to determine the tribunal in which the case will be heard (General File Reception offices).

[43] See England and Wales Report.

To prevent 'forum shopping', the system determines the draw and sends the case to that same tribunal. If, for example, this judge considers that the new case has no connection with the previous case, he/she has to send the case file back to be redrawn.

The system serves two main purposes. The first one, as anticipated, is to strengthen the right to a natural judge (Art. 18, National Constitution of the Argentine Republic), preventing arbitrary assignment and forum shopping. The second one is to rationalize the workload. The latter is achieved by instructing the system to send an equal number of cases to the different tribunals that may have jurisdiction over the case.

9.3 *Allocation of Cases Inside the Court*

Common law countries do not know the principle of the natural judge as the main civil law countries apply the principle. Countries in between (e.g. Norway) do not have this principle in their tradition, which can lead to domestic controversy. The concept of natural justice which exists in the common law is close to the fair trial and impartiality principles but is not precisely the right to have a judge assigned objectively. This principle requires that the court be constituted prior to the beginning of the trial. In Germany, it is the principle of lawfulness which dates back to the nineteenth century.[44]

9.3.1 Countries with the Natural Judge Principle

In Argentina, when the body is divided into chambers or panels, as it happens, for example, in the courts of appeal, the same court that selects the chamber that will hear the case draws the case. There are also mechanisms of allocation of appellate courts by 'shifts', which means that each case will be delivered to the chamber that is 'on shift' when it arrives. Supreme courts have different mechanisms of case allocation, depending on their structure and organization. There are some provinces in which the supreme court is divided into chambers based on specialization, so the allocation will depend on the matter involved in each case. Other supreme courts are organized in unified bodies with no chambers or panels, such as the Federal Supreme Court or the Supreme Court of Buenos Aires Province. In this hypothesis, allocation by random draw, as a general rule, serves the purpose of defining the order in which to study the case and deliver each written vote.

In Germany, the committee (*Präsidium*) of each court basically conducts the allocation of cases. The composition of those committees as well as the appointment of their members and the method of decision-making is regulated under federal law. As a central function of this committee, federal law also governs the allocation of cases in the form of a distribution-of-business plan. The committee has to define the allocation of the chambers and the criteria for distribution of business among them.

---

[44] Shetreet and Forsyth (2011, pp. 496–497).

This plan has to ensure that each case is allocated by objective criteria in advance so that any manipulation is precluded. Possible criteria for the distribution of business and allocation of cases are: time of arrival, subject area, initial letter of the name of a party, in sequence, etc.

In Chile, the reformed courts allocate cases to each courtroom according to general guidelines, approved every year by the Committee of Judges based on the proposal of the Presiding Judge. Specifically, the court manager implements case allocation based on these general guidelines. In these courts a master calendar system operates, not a single calendar. In other words, there is no single judge who takes care of the entire case, from the filing to the disposition. Instead, different judges may intervene in different parts of the proceedings depending on their specialization. In that sense, the reformed courts do not have a proper allocation of 'cases' to particular judges, but the allocation of 'tasks' among them. Furthermore, the Case Management Department (*Unidad de Administración de Causas*) is in charge of the remaining tasks of scheduling of hearings and deadlines for each case. The efficiency of this allocation system depends on grouping cases that have common elements, such as the same parties, similar legal matters or complexity level. Accordingly, a 'typology' of cases is used by court managers to guide the allocation of cases and to estimate the duration of hearings, among other procedural decisions.

In the Netherlands, since the reform of 2013 the inner organization of courts is no longer organized by statute. The courts benefit from a large amount of autonomy. The key words of the reform are concentration and differentiation of the offer of justice. Each unit of the court has several categories of cases. The executive board establishes the criteria upon which to allocate cases; the chief of a unit may adapt the criteria to the local situation. The general objective is to allow the courts to answer to the demands of citizens in terms of cases and volume. The allocation order indicates for each kind of case the location of the hearings, the section in charge and the planning. Usually there are a civil law department, a criminal department and an administrative department. The assignment order is published. The executive board may derogate from the orders in the event of issues relating to the availability of judges or if a specialization is needed. A case or a kind of case may be allocated to another section on a temporary basis. The head of the department may opt for another allocation of a case on account of the complexity of the case or if a special expertise is needed. It is a mixed solution, which is interesting: the principle of the natural judge may have exceptions, in particular for specific expertise in the management model.

In Spain, as regards 'jurisdictional' activity, the allocation of cases (*reparto*) is made by predetermined rules among the several courts having subject matter, territorial and functional jurisdiction. The *Sala de Gobierno* section of the relevant Regional High Court approves and publishes the allocation rules previously proposed by the Meeting of Judges. This section can suggest the modification of the rules when deemed appropriate. The main criteria are (a) the subject matter, as some courts are specialized; and (b) the identification number, i.e. the number given to the file upon the first 'procedural' activity. The actual allocation is carried out under the supervision of the dean judge (*Juez Decano*), who in turn is assisted by the court secretary appointed for that purpose. As regards the 'procedural' activity—i.e. the activity within the *Servicio Común*, the centralized provincial procedural bureaucracy that handles all cases—the allocation rules are far from clear. It seems that the *Letrado Director*—a discretionally appointed civil servant—will be, to a large extent, free to choose the team of *Letrados* and other minor civil servants who will handle each case, having regard for their personal skills and competences. It may be interesting to point out that the shift to the management model seems to go against the principle of the natural judge.

9.3.2 Countries Without a Strict Natural Judge Principle

In France, each year the head of the tribunal decides on the assignment of judges to the different sections. Then the cases are allocated to the competent section. If there are two sections having the same competence (in large courts), the rule to dispatch the case is objective (usually one new case out of two for one section and the other case for the other section). The principle of the natural judge (or lawful judge) does not really exist in France, at least not in the Constitution. The head of the tribunal is allowed to assign the judges and allocate the cases as he/she wishes. It is rare for a matter to rise for discussion. The advantage of this system is that the head of the court may allocate a very complex case to a much-experienced judge or specialized judge. The annual distribution-of-business plan made by the head of the court is not a judgment or an administrative document, so there is no recourse against it (except a never used recourse for abuse of power). This document is sent to the general assembly to get its recommendation, but the head of the court has the last word.

In Hungary, every court must establish rules on case allocation and make them accessible to the public. The automatic nature of signalization is expected; however, nowhere is it guaranteed. The system can be manipulated and it will not be traceable afterwards. This has a positive side, notably the specification. The executive who allocates the cases knows the strong and weak sides of each judge (for example, the presence of the press, resilience under heavy workload, knowledge about a specific type of case, personal difficulties such as illness or family matters); but there is a negative side to this which is the unequal distribution of hard and easy cases, the deliberate helping or obstructing of someone. The system can be manipulated such that a certain case may be allocated to a specific judge or a certain individual concerned with a case may be allocated the case, and thereby control the 'luck of the draw' element.

In England and Wales, the allocation of cases is subject to procedural law in both civil and criminal procedure, and is a judicial function. In civil law, they are allocated to specific tracks, and in criminal law to particular courts depending on the seriousness of the crime.

In Poland, the allocation is unilateral and generally unregulated. There is an ongoing discussion about changing this procedure. There are no objective criteria.

According to the changes planned in the Polish judiciary, the allocation of cases will take place on the basis of the rules specified in the regulations of the functioning of the common courts assigned by the Minister of Justice after consultations with the National Council of the Judiciary. The regulations define, among other things, detailed rules for the allocation of cases, including: how to draw a case, how to divide a case into categories in which a random allocation occurs, how to reduce the assignment of tasks on the basis of functions and justified absences as well as the grounds for temporary suspension of the allocation of cases. From a technical point of view, this process will be supported by a special electronic system (according to its creators—modelled on Germany), which is supposed to properly 'weigh' particular issues and theoretically lead to a situation in which none of the judges will be overly burdened in relation to other judges of the same department. The effectiveness of this solution is unknown, because it has not yet been implemented (statutory changes are in the publishing stage). It is also intended to strengthen the principle of constancy of the composition of the adjudicating panel, except for special fortuitous events, such as the chronic illness of a judge.

In Russia, the rules of case allocations between judges depend on the court type. In commercial courts, there has been a computer allocation system in operation since 2005. The courts of general jurisdiction have a different tradition. The chairpersons or heads of the colleges (there are basically three colleges—civil, administrative, criminal) allocate cases to the judges under their supervision. There are several criteria of allocation: for example, the territory which a particular judge is responsible for and subject matter. Lay judges (jurors) are chosen from the electoral register.

In Singapore, to more effectively manage the caseload, the Supreme Court has implemented a modified docket system. This affords the judges a degree of specialization and enhances the court's ability to cope with the ever-increasing complexity of the law, especially in specialist and technically difficult areas, such as intellectual property, construction, and banking and finance. It also ensures that issues can be anticipated early on in the life cycle of a case and actual hearings can then be more focused on the substantive issues.

In United States state courts, judge assignment methods vary, but all courts use some type of random case allocation procedure and manage caseloads so that each judge in a court receives roughly an equal caseload.

10 Evaluation, Accountability and Responsibility of Judges and Courts

A distinction may be drawn between the responsibility for management tasks and the question of assessments and bonuses of judges.

10.1 Responsibility for Management Tasks

The expression 'responsibility for management tasks' may be understood as a description relating to the person in charge of management tasks, and as the disciplinary sanction of judges and staff in case of management mistakes. The judge has a general responsibility which is not limited to management tasks and is usually protected by the constitution.

10.1.1 General Responsibility of Judges

In Algeria, judges are evaluated and may be sanctioned if they commit a fault. In a criminal matter, alternative ways to deal with cases have been put in place. The quality of judgments seems to have increased and the motivation of judges is better than in the past. Information technology has been introduced (videoconference, digitalization of files, a web platform for each court since 2015). As a result, the work methods have been streamlined.

In Argentina, in order to reinforce judicial independence, there is a constitutional principle of stability of tenure, by which judges hold their offices during good behaviour. When magistrates breach that standard of conduct (committing crimes or failing to perform their duties) they can be subjected to different forms of impeachment or disciplinary mechanisms, depending on each jurisdiction.[45]

In France, when a judge commits a serious error a disciplinary procedure is possible in front of the judicial council (there are several findings of fault each year, but the sanctions are rarely severe, the worst may be to be deleted from the rolls of the magistrates body or forced into early retirement). A citizen who proves to have suffered harm because of an error made by a judge may bring an action for liability against the French State (there are several cases a year, especially when the duration of the trial was not reasonable).

10.1.2 Specific Responsibility for Management Tasks

In the event a court does not meet objectives, the ramifications may vary: cuts in the allocation of resources for the court (England and Wales), an increase in the allocation of resources (France, if it is justified), education of the chief judge (Russia), positive incentives only for the court that meets the objectives (the Netherlands, Belgium ongoing discussions), disciplinary measures against judges or staff (Argentina, Poland). It is difficult to draw a line between civil law countries and common law countries on this matter. It may well be that common law countries rely on case management more than on court management. The careers of judges are especially at stake in the 'hierarchical' system of the civil law. In comparison, there is much less sanctioning of judges in the common law system.

---

[45] See Argentinian Report.

Specific Responsibility for Management Tasks in Civil Law Countries

Since judges are civil servants in civil law countries, the consequences of bad court management seem to fall mainly on the careers of judges (Germany, France). There is a general tension between (and debate over) the natural judge principle and workload calculations (France, Poland, Switzerland, Germany).[46] In a hierarchical system, sanctions on a judge may be disciplinary. Sometimes the judge may be obliged to take an education course (Russia).

In Germany, the comparison of the number of cases processed is a key factor in the evaluation of judges. As such, it is a viable method by which to prepare staff reports. Due to the different degree of the legal complexity of a given case, however, such a quantitative comparison requires comparability of the cases decided. It appears questionable whether these ideal requirements can really be met; even if they are, there remains a considerable amount of subjectivity. Notwithstanding these hindrances to a level playing field, there is little doubt in academic discussion that there must be at least one type of objective variable for the evaluation process of judges and that these methods do not impose a threat to judicial independence if carefully and correctly applied. Overwhelmingly, a judge's industriousness is only of importance for promotional decisions, as these are made on the basis of staff reports. Thus, with the exception of the entering phase, evaluation bears only indirect consequences.[47]

In France, each year the tax bill imposes new objectives on the judiciary in terms of duration and quality. There are six indicators (number of new cases, number of cases treated, duration by case, caseload, rate of admission at the judicial register of crime, rate of second appeal). The Minister checks the realization of objectives given each year according to these indicators in management dialogue with courts of appeal. Each court of appeal has an informal management dialogue with each tribunal (civil high court, small claims court, labour court, commercial court) in its jurisdiction. In each court, the president tells each judge the number of cases he/she has to write each year. This depends on the subject matter, the types of cases, etc. A working group was set up to fix a method to calculate the weight to be given to cases. This working group composed mainly of judges failed to provide a solution because of disagreement among its members. The consequences for the judges have affect, mainly, on their career advancement.

If a court does not reach the objectives, the dialogue with the court of appeal may lead to an increase in the allocation of resources. A head of a court explained that one year he preferred not to reveal the good results of his court so as not to risk having his resources cut. In France, as in Argentina or Italy, an attempt at mediation before bringing a case to the court is compulsory. The sanction is the non-admissibility of the case, which is rather serious. Again, it could be a matter of court policy to decide whether or not the sanction has to be strictly applied. Sometimes a detail may lighten a question: in many jurisdictions in France external mediators were located outside

[46] On the debate between the natural judge versus workload calculus see in Switzerland, Lienhard and Kettinger (2016, pp. 62–79).

[47] See German Report.

the court until the heads of the courts realized that it would work better within the symbolic atmosphere of the court.

There may be consequences for the court itself in terms of budget, but this can lead to a paradoxical situation (France, Belgium). The mediation policy may be a matter of court management.

In Argentina, each judge is responsible for the office management of the court that he/she runs. In collegial structures (for example courts of appeal), the president mainly exercises this responsibility. Some administrative managerial duties of the judge over 'his/her' court structure are considerable, but the supervision of efficiency goals is, as a matter of fact, very limited. Those objectives are generally limited to checking compliance with time limits provided for the different types of decisions, according to deadlines established in the procedural codes. Argentina has an expanded model of pre-judicial mandatory mediation in force, with some differences, in almost every jurisdiction. This model imposes on the plaintiff, prior to the filing of a suit, the requirement to go through a mediation process before a private or public mediator who, in most of the jurisdictions, is not part of the judicial staff. For the rest of the judicial officials and employees there are different disciplinary regimes for analysing their misconduct. At the federal level, the Supreme Court, the courts of appeal and the first instance judges have a general disciplinary power over officials and employees. For that purpose, there are special offices to conduct investigations, sometimes within the Magistrate's Council.[48]

In Norway, the judge can refer a case to a mediator, but, except in one specific court, he/she usually prefers to mediate himself/herself. It could be said that the general policy of a court with regard to mediation is that it is a matter of court management, especially since mediation could alleviate the number of cases, and so have a positive impact on the court budget.

In Belgium, there is on-going reflection over the sanction to be given to a court that does not reach the objectives. To cut into the allocation of resources could be counterproductive. An alternative idea would be to give incentives to the courts that meet the objectives, such as an additional allocation.

In Chile, each year the Presiding Judge of the Supreme Court gives a public speech in which he/she reports on the functioning of the court system during the previous period, both the jurisdictional and management aspects. Another mechanism of control is the personal inspections (*visitas*) conducted by higher court judges on the premises of the lower courts. Finally, judges and court staff can be held liable as a result of infringement of their legal duties, which implies disciplinary sanctions.

In the Netherlands, each year the executive board meets once or twice to assess the functioning of the court. The national body in charge of supervising the courts stands in a position of authority in relation to the executive board. One scholar considers that this control infringes the constitutional principle of separation of powers.[49]

In Poland, the judge holds disciplinary responsibility. Official offences may also be delinquent actions or omissions related to the excessive length of proceedings

48 See Argentinian Report.

49 See Dutch Report.

conducted by the judge, improper performance of administrative functions and breach of the financial management of the court. In addition, the directors of the courts and other clerks are responsible for their own actions. The main instruments for verifying the implementation of administrative tasks are periodic qualification assessments, which also assess the effectiveness and usefulness of the employee in achieving the objectives related to the management of the courts. A negative result of the assessment may result in the consequences provided in the provisions of the labour law, including loss of employment.

In Russia, there is no evaluation, accountability and responsibility for courts. Only the federal authority decides whether a court should exist or not. All courts are financed and equally provided with all necessary resources according to the court's hierarchy. Statistics reports are important but do not have a significant role in respect of responsibility. A judge's personal responsibility and accountability may lead to various disciplinary sanctions up to his/her removal. In case of bad records or failure to meet objectives, the judge may be obliged to take an education course aimed at correcting these faults. There is mainly a moral aspect as to the impact of bonuses, assessments and statistics for judges.

Specific Responsibility for Management Tasks in Common Law Countries

It is not clear whether the consequences of bad management are totally different in common law countries. There may be cuts in the budget as well (England and Wales), but no sanctions on the judges themselves, taking into account the authority of judges in the common law system (England and Wales, USA). Certain common law countries stress the importance of case management more than court management (India). When the judge is elected, a record of bad management may be a campaign argument (USA).

In England and Wales, the impact appears to be on the allocation of resources to the courts. There is no disciplinary sanction against judges for failure to meet objectives. The system is undergoing fundamental structural reform at the moment due to severe budget cuts—moving to an IT-based model with less access to traditional court hearings.

In India, pendency and arrears (backlogs) of cases are serious problems for the Indian judicial system. According to the recent estimates of the National Judicial Data Grid, a total of 24,247,103 cases are pending before various courts in India of which 7,815,594 cases are civil in nature and 16,431,509 are criminal cases. It has been estimated that more than 16% of the cases are pending beyond the time frame of five years, of which almost 10% have a pendency period exceeding ten years. In recent years the government has made serious efforts to reduce pendency in the courts. A Vision Statement was adopted in 2009 by the central government setting out the government's focus on two major judicial reforms—increasing access by reducing delay and arrears in the court system, and enhancing accountability through structural changes and setting performance standards and capacities. An Action Plan provided under the Vision Statement identified the following areas as the major areas of reforms: creation of a National Arrears Grid/identification of arrears; identification of bottlenecks in crisis areas; tackling the bottleneck areas; adoption of innovative measures for expeditious case disposal; focussing on the selection, training and performance assessment of judicial personnel and court management executives; effective planning and timely management by increasing the use of technology and modern management methods; procedural changes; management and administration. It was recommended that civil cases be divided into three or four tracks along the suggested guidelines. Additional recommendations included the appointment of a judge for the purpose of monitoring the entire process, from the allocation of cases to the different tracks, to the taking of appropriate decisions, in order to ensure that the cases are disposed of within the period fixed for each track. The draft rules also granted flexibility to the judges to determine the time frame of individual cases based on the complexity of the case. Almost twenty-one state judiciaries adopted the concept of Case Flow Management and framed their own rules for ensuring timely justice. It seems that case flow management pertains more to case management than to court management.[50]

In Singapore, the Supreme Court sets targets for waiting periods in various court processes as part of its commitment to provide quality public service. These targets are reviewed annually to ensure that they are realistic and aligned with international benchmarks. The Supreme Court endeavours to achieve at least 90% compliance with all targets set. For the past few years, the set targets have all been consistently met.

In the United States federal circuit, federal judicial oversight mechanisms deter and prevent fraud, waste and abuse, and address mistakes should they occur. Oversight mechanisms also promote compliance with ethical, statutory and regulatory standards. By statute, responsibility for administering the third branch of government rests with the Judicial Conference of the United States, regional circuit judicial councils; the individual courts themselves and, in specified areas, the Director of the Administrative Office of the U.S. Courts. Internal safeguards exist at the local, regional and national levels to deter waste and wrongdoing, and enable detailed performance assessments. In state courts, where many judges are elected officials, the sanction for bad management could be not being re-elected. It seems that one of the defects of the American system is that the election of judges is becoming more and more based on the political party to which the judge is attached. As for the court manager, he/she is generally recruited by the chief judge on a contractual basis, so that the court manager may be easily fired in case of bad management performance.

10.2 Judges—Assessments and Bonuses

The assessment of judges leads to bonuses in a limited number of countries (France, Benin, Chile, Hungary, Poland and Spain), mainly civil law countries where judges are perceived as civil servants.

[50] See Indian Report.

Bonuses do not appear to be present in Germany. Swiss scholars do not touch upon bonuses. In Benin, judges claim frequently to get a bonus. There, judges' salaries have doubled in ten years.

In Chile, since 1998 all court personnel have been under a legal scheme of economic incentives known as 'performance bonuses' (*bonos de gestión*), which are awarded based on institutional efficiency and collective goals (*Metas de Eficiencia Institucional* and *Metas de Desempeño Colectivo*). The criteria to award these bonuses include, for example, the reduction of delays in proceedings and waiting times in public attention services, and training, among others. Both judges and court staff propose these goals on an annual basis. A special committee (*Comision Resolutiva Institucional*) comprised of members of the judiciary and the Ministry of Public Finance (*Ministerio de Hacienda*) approves their proposals. There are several ways to check the accomplishment of these performance goals. If a court does not accomplish the goals, however, the judges and court staff will not suffer any proper sanction other than the loss of the annual bonus.

In France, there is an evaluation of the judge every two years. The bonus for each judge should depend on the court assessment. As a matter of fact, the amount of the bonus is about 10% of the salary of each judge (heads of court do not like to use this tool as a means to attain the objectives) and does not change (although it is less than 10% for the youngest judges and more for the judge in charge of a particular big case). The evaluation will be used when considering whether or not to promote the judge. Among the criteria to evaluate a judge there is managerial competence (especially for intermediary management). Sometimes the head of a court asks a judge to give him/her two judgments so that the president can assess their quality. One judges union brought an action in front of the Council of State against the very idea of the bonus, claiming that it was contrary to the principle of independence. The Council of State considered that the bonus was acceptable since it did not concern the judicial work of the judge.

In Hungary, there is minimal economic incentive and only then in broader programmes, for example in the programme for serviceable court systems, which means that judges get a predetermined bonus for an above-average closing of old cases. Advancement in their judicial career is accompanied by greater bonuses: appointment as a president of chamber increases the salary by 25–35–45% on each level, for life, which is very significant; on each level there is a 20% increase in income; appointment as head of a group/head of a college means an increase in salary by 20–40%, but for only six years.

In Spain, the legal framework for the remuneration of judges is still in the making. Currently, the bonus for over-performing judges is extremely limited, while in practice no sanctions are imposed on underperforming judges other than the missed opportunity of receiving a bonus.

In Poland, the effectiveness of the work and the professional competence of the judge in the methodology of work and the culture of the office, as well as the specialization in the identification of particular types of cases and the fulfilment of particular functions, are subject to assessment (assessment of the judge's work). The judge's work is assessed taking into consideration: the efficiency and effectiveness of the activites undertaken and the organization of work in case recognition or other tasks or functions; culture of the office, including the personnel culture and work organization culture, and respect for the rights of the parties or participants in the proceedings during the recognition of cases or performing other tasks or functions; how the statements are formulated when issuing and justifying judgments; and the process of professional development. When assessing the work of the judge, the type and complexity of the assignments or tasks entrusted to him/her, the workload and the conditions of work throughout the period covered by the assessment are taken into account. It is extremely important that the scope of assessing the judge's work cannot enter into the field in which the judge is independent. This means that when it comes to the judge's decisions only the statistics relating to whether they were upheld or overturned by the superior courts are analysed. The president of the court furnishes the judge with the assessment of his/her work, including, in particular, performance evaluation and summary, drawing up an individual professional development plan for the judge, which covers a period of not less than four years. The clerks and other court employees and prosecutors are subject to periodic qualification assessments as well. Assessments are made by the director of the court or the prosecutor, taking into account the opinion of the immediate superior and the qualification commission appointed by the director of the court, or the prosecutor.

11 Economic Budget of the Courts and the Justice System

As far as the budget is concerned, it is quite easy to get information on the national budget of the judiciary, but it is much more difficult to obtain a true idea of the budget of one specific court. A comparison between the systems is, consequently, not easy to make, and there are sometimes anomalies. In the future, there should be a specific general research undertaken on the budgets of the judiciary. The framework of this General Report is already too broad to go into great detail about this particular subject. According to the European Commission for the Efficiency of Justice (2016 CEPEJ Report with 2014 statistics), justice costs €64 per inhabitant. What counts in the CEPEJ Report is not the amount but the autonomy of the courts as far as the budget is concerned. It seems that in the civil law system heads of the court do not have a great influence on the court budget and have no margin of manoeuvre to spend this budget. In common law countries, a court often has high fees as one source of revenue.

11.1 Budget Autonomy in Civil Law Countries

The reform of the judiciary in Algeria has led to a constant increase in the budget allocation since 2014. There are more and more beneficiaries of legal aid and the free assistance of lawyers and other legal professionals. The criminal reform of 2015 created alternative measures which reinforce access to justice through pre-court action consultation. Judicial mediation is used more often since it is now more clearly understood. Aid for the victims of terrorist attacks is provided through a national fund. Multi-year planning for reform of the justice system increases the budget so as to provide sums to improve the material and human resources of the judiciary. There are national schools to educate judges and staff at the initial stage of their careers and during their careers. Agreements have been concluded with European countries, especially France, to get experience in the transformation of the judiciary, in particular in the field of the administration of justice.[51]

In Belgium, the College of the Courts discusses the budget with the Ministry of Justice. The budget is €675 million a year. The College distributes the funds to the courts and the tribunals (49 entities) according to the management project plan (the average by entity is €13 million). There are three management contracts (with the Court of Cassation, with the public prosecutors, and with the courts and tribunals). Overall, it is a process of empowerment (autonomization) of the 49 entities, and it is a model of business management in the context of a civil law country. In France, the heads of court were promised that they would be autonomous in managing their budgets. Now, however, the funds allocated are dedicated to such and such expenses. (As a result, there are stories in France of heads of court who could not have a corridor painted (Poitiers), repairs made to restrooms (in a suburb of Paris) or buy a deep fryer for a court in the north of France, near Belgium, where fries are the basic food: to resolve these issues, it is said that a ministerial decision was needed.)

In Benin, the budget is very low (around 1% of the national budget, which for 2017 is CFA2,010 billion, or €3.06 billion; thus 1% of €3.06 billion is around €30 million. But normally the national budget has been around CFA1,500 billion, or €2. 29 billion and so about €22 million).

In Chile, the general budget of the judicial branch for 2017 is about US$800 million. The budget of the judges' training school (*Academia Judicial*) is about US$5.3 million. The jails—either publicly administered or private concessions—have a budget of US$770 million. Unfortunately, the statute on the budget of the judiciary does not break down the numbers for each type of particular court.

In France, the budget of the judiciary ranks 37th out of 48 listed by the Council of Europe. There are approximately €3 billion for civil and criminal justice (the budget for administrative justice depends directly on the Ministry of the Economy; a recent study shows that a civil case costs €600 less than an administrative case). All in all, there are about €1 billion for civil justice. There are ten Operational Budget of Programmes (BOP) in the metropole regions, but the size varies a lot and the number of courts differs. In Lyon, for example, there are several courts of appeal and many civil high courts at the first instance. This budget does not cover the salary of the staff and judges, nor the real estate of the tribunals. Thus, the budget for the operation of regional courts is about €150 million (logistics, maintenance, new technology, travelling expenses of judges and staff).

---

[51] See details in the Argentinian Report.

There are 41 BOP, but only 10 large ones covering France (about 10 BOP deal with French territory outside the metropole; one BOP for the Court of Cassation has a budget of about €50 million), so each large BOP has a budget of approximately €10 million. Efforts are being made to save money (stamps, for example, are no longer used, which is forecasted to save more than €2 million in 2017). In interviews, several directors of clerks said that it is difficult to find funding for something necessary or new (example: a wall which needs to be repainted). So as a whole, it is difficult to determine the budget of each tribunal, because its budget is part of a more general budget at the level of a BOP. There is a budget of €400 million for investment (e.g. a new building). In the BOP Centre East (in 2012) there appeared 4 courts of appeal (Lyon, Grenoble, Chambéry, Riom), 21 civil high courts, 33 small claims courts, 27 labour courts, 770 judges (localization 2012), 2,182 clerks and civil servants (localization 2012), a €190,000,000 payroll, €46,000,000 justice-related expenses, and €27,300,000 for current operations.

The budget for each tribunal is allocated according to the number of full time personnel.

There is as well a regional administrative service, which for each court of appeal coordinates human resources, training of the staff, software of accountancy (Chorus) and computer equipment. The civil justice budget increased by 20% between 2007 and 2015 (activity increased 3.2%); at the same time, the budget of administrative courts increased 42% (activity increased 8%). Generally, it could be said that the heads of court have very little autonomy in terms of the budget.

In Germany, the budget for the Federal Justice System (including the five highest courts as well as the Federal Constitutional Court, the Justice Ministry and the Federal Prosecutor's Office) in 2016 was €745,492,000. As a consequence of the federal system in Germany, each federal state has its own economic budget. In the state of Baden-Wuerttemberg, for example, the budget for the justice system in 2016 was €1,651,161,900. From this total amount €791,408,200 were spent on courts and public prosecutors. Baden-Wuerttemberg counts 21 public prosecutor offices and approximately 153 courts, including local, district and higher regional courts as well as various sorts of specialized courts (labour, finance, administration, social/welfare). Some of these have 'outposts' inside the buildings of other courts in other cities, while the prosecutors' offices are usually integrated into a court, and some local courts share buildings with district courts. However, the buildings themselves are the property of the State, and the state-level finance ministry provides for the purchase and major renovations of the court buildings in its budget. The budget of a single court depends heavily on the number of employees. Given that the size of a local court (Amtsgericht) can range from family-size staff to hundreds of employees in big cities (Hamburg, for example), the numbers vary accordingly. There is, however, a fair amount of anecdotal evidence stemming particularly from judges that there is an urgent need for more judicial posts. In general, the autonomy of regions seems to be greater in Germany than the autonomy of the courts themselves as far as the budget is concerned.

In Hungary, the basis of any court's internal budget is that it is approximately 90% personnel costs. There is a predetermined number for employees based on the number of cases a court handles. Maintenance costs (cost of overhead, mandatory insurance fees, etc.) and the funds for small-scale information systems development are almost always around 8–9% of the budget. This means that only 1–2% of the budget is available for any local development, event, representation or economic incentive programme. In practice, there is no room for individual planning, the support of the National Court Office is needed for every project (such as conferences, a sporting day, acquisition of new servers or installation of air conditioners). This is also true for technical and other types of equipment. Thus, on the local level the room for spending is tight, while on the national level the budget of the National Court Office shows just the reverse, 10% personnel costs and 90% for investments. Again, the financial autonomy of the courts is limited.

In the Netherlands, in 2016 there were 1.6 million new cases. The budget was about €1 billion and the number of employees was 9,622 of which 2,360 were judges, or 14 judges for every 100,000 inhabitants (there were about 7 judges for every 100,000 inhabitants in France). The executive board of the court draws a provisional budget which has to be approved by a national body (RvdR). The courts may gain financial autonomy if they surpass their objectives. Also, they can keep a cash reserve. What was seen as a good idea before the financial crisis of 2008 now appears less interesting since there is no evidence that the reserves of the courts are sufficient.

In Poland, in 2017 the state budget relating to the common courts includes 11 courts of appeal, 45 regional courts and 319 district courts. The budget of the Ministry of Justice is €543 million.[52] In Warsaw, the expenditures of the courts are about €196 million (there are €83 million of revenue).

In Russia, all federal courts are financed from the federal budget. The subject courts (justices of the peace, regional constitutional courts and charter courts) are financed from the subject budget according to their location. All judges have the same status and, therefore, are paid from the federal budget. The exact sums of money are not known. There are some criteria in respect of the budgets of the courts: location of the court, the court's level in the court hierarchy, how many judges work there, the number of cases the court hears annually, etc. The budget items for jails, the courts and national schools are different and independent from each other.

In Spain, it is worth bearing in mind that the complex organization of Spanish justice hinders the accounting of expenditures. The public justice budget in Spain is made up of the sum of the budgets of the central administration (including the Ministry of Justice and the General Council of the Judiciary) and the regions with competences in regard to justice. However, there is no single, consolidated national budget covering all administration of justice. A body coordinating budget information regarding justice is missing. There are not even uniform criteria to determine what expenses should be accounted to justice. Regional justice budgets often appear combined with non-justice items. As a consequence of this, it is difficult to know the public expenditure actually incurred in justice matters throughout Spain and, consequently, to compare them with those offered by other countries. The justice budget in Spain ranged from €2,200 million in 2004 to €3,800 million in 2010. Likewise, the

---

[52] See Polish Report.

percentage representing the total justice budget with overall state and regional expenditures ranged from 0.67% in 2004 to 0.79% in 2010. And as a percentage of GDP per inhabitant, the budget in respect of justice per inhabitant represented 0.26% in 2004 and 0.34% in 2013. Both figures show important increases. The detailed budget by court is more difficult to obtain. There is no directly available information in this regard which should consolidate the many different items of expenditures—judicial salaries, salaries of personnel from different administrations, valuations of real estate in ownership, leases, material means, etc.—that come together in a given court.

11.2 Budget Autonomy in Common Law Countries

In England and Wales, the Ministry of Justice in general will receive £6.9 billion for the current budget year, but this should be reduced down to £6 billion by 2020. The funds are split between the criminal justice system (including prisons, youth justice, prosecution services, etc.) and Her Majesty's Courts and Tribunals Service, among other services. Budgets for the courts, at this time, are being invested in real estate and technology. However, the courts generate an income through court fees based on 'full cost recovery; that is the use of fee income to recover the full cost of the court system minus the cost of fee remissions (waivers). Fee remissions ensure access to justice for those that cannot afford a fee.'[53]

In Singapore, in 2017 the proposed budget allocated to the judiciary, comprising the Supreme Court, State Courts and Family Justice Courts, is $376,743,700 (about €227 million). The Singapore Prisons Service is under the purview of the Ministry of Home Affairs, which has a proposed 2017 budget allocation of $547,262,300.

In United States state courts, in almost two-thirds of the states, the judiciary presents its budget request directly to the legislature. In almost three-quarters of the states, the judiciary has the discretion to manage and administer appropriated funds without restrictions of detailed budget line items. The state general fund is the primary source of court funding in approximately two-thirds of the states. In these states, the level of funding for the trial courts is determined by the state legislatures: the state funds trial court judges, judicial support staff, clerical staff, technology and operating expenses. In some of these states, the probation department is included in the judiciary's budget. Counties usually provide the courthouses, along with their maintenance.

In the other states, a mix of state and local funding supports the trial courts. In all but a few states, the state funds the salaries of the trial court judges. In most states, the state funds the cost of developing and enhancing technology. The state funds trial court clerk staff and judicial support staff in three-fourths of the states. The counties or municipalities fund the cost of providing and maintaining the courthouses in two-thirds of the states.

[53] See England and Wales Report.

In the federal system, Congress has given the judiciary the authority to prepare and execute its own budget. The Administrative Office, in consultation with the courts and with various Judicial Conference committees, prepares a proposed budget for the judiciary each fiscal year. The proposal is reviewed and approved by the Judicial Conference with an accompanying set of detailed justifications. By law, the President must include the judiciary's proposed budget as a part of the unified federal budget submitted to Congress each year. The President may comment on the judiciary's budget request, but the proposal must be transmitted to Congress without change. The congressional appropriations committees conduct hearings at which judges and the Director of the Administrative Office frequently present and justify the judiciary's projected expenditures. After Congress enacts a budget for the judiciary, the Judicial Conference approves a plan to spend the money and the Administrative Office distributes funds directly to each court, operating unit and programme in the judiciary. Individual courts have considerable authority and flexibility to conduct their work, establish budget priorities, make sound business decisions, hire staff and make purchases, consistent with Judicial Conference policies. The budget for Fiscal Year 2016: on 18 December 2015, the President signed into law the Consolidated Appropriations Act of 2016 (Public Law 114-113). The Act provided the Judiciary with $6.78 billion in discretionary appropriations, a 1.2% increase over the previous fiscal year.

12 Psychosocial and Security Risks

Generally speaking, psychosocial risks are not expressly taken into account but are part of the human resources functions. Security is another concern. I have evidence that there are more psychosocial risks for judges and staff in civil law countries than in common law countries. Nevertheless, in this field the impression is more important than the scientific facts.

12.1 Psychosocial Risks

In Chile, among the training programmes for court staff, certain courses are devoted to stress management and the emotional aspects involved in teamwork, public attention services and the resolution of labour disputes. However, the courts do not have a special team of medics or psychologists to handle emotional problems of the court staff. As regards threats and security, the courts for which this matter is a particular concern usually have metal detectors and judicial police (Gendarmes) guarding the entrances, and they provide security and order in the courtrooms.

In France, a young judge at the national school of the judiciary learns that he/she ('she' in more than 60% of the cases) must keep his/her emotions under control. Recently, judges have received a 'green telephone number' which they can call to reach a psychologist in case of need. There are no statistics on the psychosocial risks although the staff (but not the judges or the prosecutors) do receive support from a committee on hygiene and security in dealing with them. The theme of the judge and the emotions is now somewhat in fashion in France since *Justice Poetic*, a book by Martha Nussbaum, was translated into French. The author says that the better training for a judge is to read novels so that she/he is more able to learn the complexity of emotions. The emotions must not be kept at bay, but used reasonably in the appreciation of the facts. It is said sometimes that the judge must manage her/his emotions, but it is not clear whether the emotions are a matter of management for the leaders of the court. There would be a risk for the independence of judges.

In Argentina, aspects related to the physical, mental and emotional health of court staff are analysed by a special health department that reports to the General Administration of the judiciary or the Supreme Court itself, as it happens, for example, at the federal level or in Buenos Aires Province. This department promotes routine controls and makes suggestions on health care issues. It also has an important role in medical, illness or accident leave matters. Additionally, it offers lectures and courses relating to healthcare at work and campaigns against smoking and a sedentary lifestyle, for example.

In Benin, there are no medical staff available in court, but there is a 'social' agent assigned to deal with personnel issues.

In England and Wales, this is not information that is easily obtained from the documents. England and Wales have stringent rules of public health and safety, and these are incorporated into all organizations. Security at courts includes metal detectors and screening of hand-carried items; however, these measures are not in place at the Supreme Court. What is of concern in the documentation available is that of staff development in terms of training and promotion.

In Hungary, there is no one whose task is to monitor the psychological and emotional condition of the employees of the court. On the other hand, there is an occupational doctor who can make referrals to a specialist. There are also local initiatives for recreation, examples of which include: the opportunity to play table tennis, recreation rooms, an occupational physician, the opportunity to get a special discount card for sports equipment shops, and sports days (both national and local).

In Russia, there are a number of legal propositions about security guarantees for judges. In the event a judge is threatened or having other problems in respect of his/her security, the police are called upon to intervene. There is no special staff (psychologists, psychiatrists or other doctors) in courts. If someone experiences emotional problems, the person is expected to solve the problem privately.

In Singapore, court staffs are valued, and there are various staff events throughout the year to give the staff opportunities to get to know their colleagues better. The Staff Welfare Committee and Staff Benefits Committee also oversee the well-being of the court staff. The Singapore Judicial College also runs various training programmes to develop the skills and knowledge of the court staff.

In Spain, in 2015 a plan on risk prevention in the workplace for those engaged in a judicial career was approved. This plan seeks to identify the particular characteristics of judicial activity—the lack of an office timetable, the unlimited number of cases allocated to each judge, the stress caused by potential aggression and harassment, etc.— along with general risks associated with office work and the use of computer equipment. Currently, a new plan is being negotiated. In 2016, a protocol was also issued against discrimination, sexual harassment and in fact all forms of harassment and violence in the judicial career sector. In the implementation guide, the appointment of persons called to exercise the position of 'confidential advisers' is recommended and actions are foreseen to advise and support those who have suffered the aforementioned behaviours.

12.2 Security Risks

In Germany, security guards as well as actual police power can be found in many courts. Yet, there are rather big differences between states. In North Rhine-Westphalia, for instance, court entrances are heavily secured. Other states such as Baden-Wuerttemberg still take a rather lax stance. There are, however, units of specially trained police personnel that can be ordered to any court as a preventive measure. It is also on a case-by-case basis that security measures are individually adapted. In many places, judges have been equipped with security buttons on the underside of their desks.

In Poland, there are no organizational structures that deal with issues of emotions, sense of security, etc., of the judges and other court employees. The safety of judges and the courts is subject to judicial police duties, in particular the protection of public safety and order in courts and prosecutors' offices, and the protection of the life and health of judges, prosecutors and other persons who perform their duties resulting from the implementation of the tasks of the judicature. Within the scope of their tasks, the judicial police cooperate with, among others, court employees, prosecutors and the Prison Service.

13 Court Planning

Although national plans abound (Hungary, Singapore), court planning is not found everywhere (Germany); but it does seem to be increasing and can be compulsory (England, Russia, the Netherlands), or not (France, USA). It could be said that the plan is compulsory in hierarchical systems, but the divide between common law countries and civil law countries is not clear on this matter. The example of France is interesting to this extent: there is compulsory planning for the administrative courts but only voluntary planning for the civil and criminal courts (*projet de juridiction* since 2016). Now, the administrative system is much more hierarchical than the civil and criminal systems. The initiative is taken by the head of the court in concert with all judges and staff, it is submitted to the advice of the general assembly and it fixes objectives for several years to improve the service given to the citizen, taking into account the independence of the judges. In the United States, court planning depends on the committees and the tasks they are assigned, whether in the state court system or the federal system. There is usually a non-compulsory business plan covering a three-year period. At first, the American practice was a strategic plan of twenty years; now it is usually three or four years with a specific objective (a new building, acquisition of IT, communications and so on).

However, in England and Wales there is compulsory planning: Her Majesty's Courts and Tribunals Service. They have to produce a business plan once a year. With bi-annual budgets set by the Chancellor of the Exchequer (finance department), the courts need to produce a plan, and several reports are generated by the court system in general. This example shows that the English system is quite hierarchical.

In Belgium, the College of the Courts distributes the amount of the budget to the courts and the tribunals according to the management project (of three years' duration). The contract is concluded with objectives especially in terms of arrears. The management project is compulsory and pertains to the new management model as it is applied in civil law countries.

In Chile, well-defined planning began in 2009 with the new scheme of jurisdictional and administrative roles, together with a more intensive use (and understanding) of management tools. The most important experiences are two. The first is the Five-Year Plan (2011–2015) in which the Supreme Court defined long-term planning for the entire court system. The document of that Plan defined the mission, vision and values of the court system in a participative manner. The Plan required that each court define the concrete objectives, goals and indicators for each single year period. Still, the strategies for the mid- and long-term are yet incipient, with rather limited monitoring and control. The President Judge—based on the proposal of the court manager—approves an Annual Working Plan (*Plan Anual de Trabajo*) (the second experience) which defines a standardized system of workflow. The goal of this Plan is to increase the number of hearings through a distribution of workload that takes advantage of the particular skills of the court staff. The Plan is approved by the Committee of Judges. The management organs are in charge of monitoring the implementation of the Plans within each court, and these organs can be held responsible for achieving the performance goals. Furthermore, a 'visiting' judge from the local court of appeal may inspect the performance of the lower courts according to these Plans too.

National planning is found in many countries (Benin, Hungary). In Benin, there is a national scheme prepared by the Directorate of Planning at the Ministry of Justice.

In Hungary, the justice system has an obligation with regard to annual monetary planning which is regulated by law. This includes the non-financial titles (education, conferences, professional training abroad, language courses, missions, acquisition of books, magazine subscriptions, etc.). The President of the National Court Office prepares the plan and the Parliament, upon the proposal of the Minister of Finance, votes whether to accept it. The Minister of Finance is not obligated to propose the plan.[54]

---

[54] See Hungarian Report.

In the Netherlands, the executive board establishes an annual plan and a multi-year plan of activity with a provisional budget.

In Russia, there is compulsory planning for the upcoming year for each court separately. However, the planning for several years is voluntary. Chairpersons carry out both types of planning. They appoint people responsible for carrying out the planning: the heads of collegial courts, senior clerks and judicial officers. In the event that objectives are not met, they answer to the chairperson.

In Singapore, the State Courts' Strategic Planning and Technology Division works with the Divisional Planning Units to formulate long-term plans and improve court processes, procedures and services for court users. Scenario planning exercises are also carried out to identify and prepare for possible situations which might arise in the future. The exercises enable gaps in the existing strategies to be identified and improved.

In Germany, on the level of individual lower courts, there is no such planning. Budget plans are usually devised for two-year periods. If anything, long-term planning occurs on the level of appellate courts and in the justice ministries.

In Spain, the administration of justice is currently focused on implementing two profound, systemic reforms: (a) transitioning from the old, unipersonal court model to the new model based on provincially centralized, case-handling bureaucracies; and (b) transitioning from the paper-based litigation to electronic, paperless litigation. This can be seen on the website of the Ministry of Justice. These systemic reforms are led and implemented by a diversity of territorial and corporate powers. Some regions have competences over the 'administration of the administration of justice' and some do not; likewise, the Ministry and the General Council of the Judiciary sometimes have overlapping functions. Each of these entities generates a number of annual, triannual, quinquennial general plans as well as numerous implementation plans, status reports, sectorial plans and plans to reform specific aspects of the system.[55]

14 Conclusion

There is an increasing interest in court management. More and more there is specialized staff in court management. It seems to be needed in order to diminish the backlog of cases and also the duration of cases in many countries. The content of court management (human resources, IT, real estate, communication, objectives and indicators) is universal, but sometimes court management is understood as encompassing the leadership of the court or case management. It does not mean that the courts are autonomous, at least in civil law countries. It is usually difficult to know their specific budgets. Courts are subordinate to superior bodies and more and more

[55] See Spanish Report.

under a national independent body specialized in the administration of justice. Nevertheless, there are great differences between countries. Some countries are not developing the new public management in court involving objectives, indicators, assessments, bonuses and budget (Benin, Germany, Russia and India). Other countries are quite advanced in this field (the Netherlands, Belgium, Chile, France, England and Wales, Singapore, Spain, the USA). Lastly a group of countries is developing tools of court management, but may be at an early stage (Algeria, Argentina, Brazil and Poland). There are some concerns in different countries about the tension between court management and the independence of judges, but it cannot be said that there are major problems. It seems that in common law countries judges are independent and have authority, whereas in civil law countries judges are civil servants. The paradox is that in common law countries the management model has been built by the judiciary to get more independence from the executive power; whereas in civil law countries the management model could increase the executive and centralized power and threaten the independence of the judges as civil servants. Therefore, there are two kinds of management model: a civil law management model and a common law management model. However, this distinction does not apply very well to the German system where the management model is not influenced by Anglo-American business management. It does not apply, either, to the English system which is in fact centralized and quite hierarchical. I could be provocative and say that the Dutch system is becoming more common law-like, whereas the English system is becoming more civil law-like. There are so many cross influences that it is difficult to draw the line.

At the end of the day what remains is a conviction. I believe that autonomy is an important value in support of the independence of the judge. The management model does not seem to foster much autonomy except in its intentions (in France, Belgium or the Netherlands). It seems that the management model is favoured by the executive power more than by judges. Autonomy of judges and the court does not mean that the judges should work alone. We need to improve the relationship between judges and the staff and stakeholders in many countries. I would be in favour of a relational model of management fostering the autonomy of judges and staff.

I will conclude with two specific examples. In Chile, the professionalization of the administration of the courts was a central objective in the implementation of different reform processes. In that context, the practical needs associated with oral proceedings—such as scheduling hearings, the uninterrupted presence of the judge, the use of courtrooms, the registry systems and the personnel operating them, plus the parties, lawyers, witnesses and experts that should attend the oral hearings—generated the necessity (and opportunity) to use management tools. In this way, the concept and operation of court management were received in the system through the reforms to criminal procedure. Professional court administrators have been key to the judicial reforms and instrumental in better case processing and court administration. From now on, court management is in the charge of professional managers, who develop interesting innovations and understanding about case flow management as the essential business of the courts. However, these reforms and the radical separation between jurisdictional and managerial functions discourse, justifying the removal of the old culture of the judges, have created the idea that management is something related only to general court management. In this way, judges do not have an important role due to their lack of managerial training. This idea can now be a problem if the justice system tries to advance to a more sophisticated case management, where the judge must be involved in the progress of the case.

The complexity and deep implications of the implementation of the new court management system and case management in any judicial system seem to lead judicial reforms to recognize it institutionally, and also define and articulate the different spaces that should be regulated by 'legal rules' and those that should be regulated by the judicial system on its own. This is a subject that uncovers crucial questions of policy, principle and theory largely left unaddressed and unanswered, especially in those areas where competing principles, rights, interests or values need to be prioritized or traded off. Likewise, that management system must allow balancing the accuracy of the judicial decisions against the length and the costs, including the workload of the system.

There is no perspective for a specific sort of litigation such as complex litigation. A management system with this feature seems particularly justified in the area of complex litigation for the forthcoming civil procedural reform in Chile where this kind of problem is more frequent than in family or labour matters.

Indeed, it is possible to observe problems regarding the lack of comprehension and experience in using this tool, which tied to a formalistic application of managerial acts facilitates decisions that are not adequate for the particular needs of the cases, which ultimately impacts the quality of the measures and the procedural rights of the parties. In addition, the rules of these acts have been applied as though they were legal rules and not as general criteria of performance. The incentive regime in the lower courts, which depends rather on the quantitative term of the cases, has contributed to this situation. Finally, the organizational criteria are not always known, and in some cases are dissimilar within the same courts.

This development has raised criticism and resistance. An important number of judges, especially lower court judges, have criticized the way these managerial acts have been set down. As mentioned before, the acts set down by the Supreme Court are mandatory for the judges even when those acts are not a law, and for that reason they think that it goes against judicial independence. The lawyers also manifest objections regarding the restrictions that this system imposes over the discretion they have in the litigation of their own cases. Finally, a portion of the community of legal scholars has criticized this from the approach of due process and judicial independence.

A recent law in Chile on electronic proceedings, in practice from last December in the civil courts, also shows this trend to increase judicial control over the pace of litigation with the introduction of principles such as efficiency, multi-functionality of the judicial employees, speediness and opportunity in procedures and judgments.

However, the civil procedure reform is facing important challenges. On the one hand, the culture and practice of the legal actors remain anchored in the mind-set of the written, de-concentrated procedure in which the judge remains passive and delegates to the court staff. On the other hand, the Bill Project does not make a clear divide between jurisdictional and managerial tasks.

In India, the importance of Case Flow Management Rules has been a part of academic discussion for a significant amount of time. It has been more than a decade since the first Case Flow Management Rules were drafted and announced by the High Court of Himachal Pradesh, and since then followed by many others. But there has been a failure in the effective implementation of the case management practices in ensuring timely disposal of cases. The high rate of judicial pendency and arrears clearly raises crucial questions regarding the applicability and adequacy of the case flow management rules in ensuring timely disposal of cases. In this context, it is important to emphasize the need for commitment on the part of the different stakeholders in the justice delivery system to ensure that the cases are handled in a time-bound manner from the stage of filing to final disposal. The state governments and the High Courts need to work in a harmonious manner to ensure that adequate resources are made available for building the necessary court infrastructure and appointment of qualified managerial staff that will assist the judges in monitoring the progress of the cases and review the process of timing. The existing case flow management does not create any special mechanism monitoring system apart from creating a tracking system and time period for tracking cases. All responsibility of monitoring and reviewing has been left to the existing court administration system and places additional burdens on the already over-burdened judges. At present, the responsibility for court administration, which includes data collection and management, lies with the judge, who may not be equipped to perform this task. In the absence of appointment of specific and specialized 'court managers', the proper implementation of the case flow rules will be illusory.[56]

Eventually, the real issue seems to be the impact of the new public management and IT on the motivation of judges and court staff. There are psychosocial risks and sometimes a risk that the efficiency of justice leads to inhuman justice. Court management should not be purely technical and quantitative. But the qualitative approach is not always easy to carry out. Which indicators are the most useful (rate of appeal, rate of second appeal)? In certain countries, the backlog involves a quantitative approach to diminish the arrears and duration (India, maybe Italy). Case management may be more urgent than court management. In the most advanced countries, in terms of new public management, the qualitative approach is needed (the Netherlands, France, the USA, Belgium) but difficult to master (in the USA sixty indicators of quality had been proposed, but only a handful of indicators are used, and those with great caution).

I would personally call for a relational approach to court management.[57] This means that what counts is to improve the network of relationships between judges and staff, judges and citizens, judges and lawyers, etc. Rather than a quantitative approach, interviews with stakeholders may help to assess the quality of relationships inside a court. Efficiency is not a goal in itself and could even be dangerous if it was only a matter of economy. The solution would be to avoid justice as much as possible

[56] See Indian Report.

[57] See in the Bibliography the relational approach of organization and law.

through mediation. However, litigation is not an illness, it is a crisis which can be useful for society and the law, in particular to improve the law. Unilateral power using IT (email, tele-work, open data, etc.) exercised by the head of the court or quite often by a national body specialized in court administration may put at risk the cordial atmosphere in the court. Even security concerns may lead to inhuman situations; for example, in a new court building in Germany the necessity to have one entrance for the victim, one for the public, one for the judge, one for the perpetrator led the architect to design a courtroom without natural light, which is so important to the creation of a cordial atmosphere.

Relational power (Robert Meste) takes into account the fact that the relationship affects the person who exercises a power as much as the person who receives an order. It is more complicated. It implies time to allow discussion, but at the end of the day it may be more efficient than unilateral power if the quality of justice is higher.

References

Alavazi del Frate P (1999) Il giudice naturale. Prassi e dottrina in Francia dall'ancien regime alla Restaurazione. Viella, Roma

Damaška MR (1986) The faces of justice and state authority: a comparative approach to the legal process. Yale University Press, New Haven

Gazell JA (1993) A current status of state reform: a national perspective. In: Hays SW, Graham CB (eds) Handbook of court administration and management. Marcel Dekker, New York, pp 79–97

Graham CB (1993) Reshaping the courts: traditions, management theories and political realities. In: Hays SW, Graham CB (eds) Handbook of court administration and management. Marcel Dekker, New York, pp 3–25

Grossi R (2015) Understanding law and emotion. Emot Rev 7:55–60

Handcock P (2014) HM courts & tribunals service business plan. https://www.gov.uk/government/uploads/system/uploads/attachment_data/file/386415/hmcts-business-plan-2014-15.pdf. Accessed 14 Mar 2017

Hoad TF (ed) (1996) Concise dictionary of English etymology. Oxford University Press, Oxford

Jacob R (2014) La grace des juges: L'institution judiciaire et le sacré en Occident. Presses universitaires de France, Paris

Judiciary of England and Wales (2016) Lord chief justice's report. https://www.judiciary.gov.uk/wp-content/uploads/2016/11/lcj-report-2016-final-web.pdf. Accessed 14 Mar 2017

Langbroek P (2017) Court administration in Europe—management in a different context. Int J Court Adm 8(3):1

Lienhard A, Kettinger D (2016) La justice entre le management et l'Etat de droit: Résultats du projet de recherche 'Fondements d'un bon management de la justice en Suisse.' Stämpfli/Nomos/Verlag Österreich, Bern-Baden-Baden-Wien

Maroney T (2012) Law, emotion, and terra nova: Neal Feigenson as both radical and reformer. Quinnipiac L Rev 30:481–488

Martin W (2014) Court administrators and the judiciary—partners in the delivery of justice. Int J Court Adm 6(2):3–18

NCSC, Judicial administration, individual courts. http://www.uscourts.gov/about-federal-courts/judicial-administration. Accessed 1 Dec 2020

Shetreet S, Forsyth C (2011) The culture of judicial independence: conceptual foundations and practical challenges. Martinus Nijhoff Publishers, Leiden-Boston
Vargas JE (2006) La reforma a la justicia civil desde la perspectiva de las políticas públicas. Revista Sistemas Judiciales 11:73–92
Wittrek F (2006) Die Verwaltung der Dritten Gewalt. Mohr Siebeck, Tübingen

An Approach and General Overview to Framing the Structure of the Court System and Case Management

Álvaro Pérez Ragone

And no man putteth new wine into old bottles; else the new wine will burst the bottles, and be spilled, and the bottles shall perish. But new wine must be put into new bottles; and both are preserved. No man also having drunk old wine straightway desireth new: for he saith, The old is better. (Luke 5:36–39)

1 Introduction and General Remarks[1]

With unprecedented enthusiasm, the justice system is currently embracing case management, but courtship has a long history. To reduce delays and costs depends on the development of case management skills by the judiciary and magistrates and has a direct impact on justice initiatives. An important component to take into account is that the judicial training to implement these reforms has traditionally been

[1] This report was presented at the Tianjin (International Association of Procedural Law Meeting) in November 2017. In preparing this report, I have been assisted by a team of distinguished colleagues. This is a collective effort. First, individuals provided direct transcriptions as contributions to the general report (main text and footnotes), without whose assistance this chapter would not be possible. I have opted, while referring to the national reports as direct 'copy-paste,' to summarize the main contents of each contribution. I would like to thank the national reporters and the coauthors of this general report: Prof. Ramón García (U. Santísima Concepción) and Prof. Claudio Fuentes (U. Diego Portales) (Chile); Prof. Giovanni Priori (Pontificia U. Catolica del Perú) (Perú); Prof. Jairo Parra Quijano (U. del Externado) (Colombia); Prof. Fernando Da fonseca Gajardoni (Universidad de Sao Paulo) (Brasil), Prof. Guillermo Ormazábal (Universidad de Girona) (Spain); Prof. Soraya Anrani-Mekki *Université* de Paris Ouest (France), Prof. Kinga Flaga-Gieruszynska and Klich, Aleksandra (University of Szczecin) (Poland); Prof. Richard Marcus (UC Hastings) (USA); Prof. Michael Stürner and Dr. Christoph Wendelstein (Universität Koblenz) (Germany); and Prof. Neil Andrews (U. of Cambridge) (England). I also thank Prof. Remo Caponi for his comments on the report. Finally, because English is not my native language, I would like to thank Prof. Richard Marcus for his review and correction of this manuscript. Of course, all the formal and content mistakes are mine.

Á. Pérez Ragone (✉)
Law Department, Pontificia Universidad Católica del Perú, Lima, Perú
e-mail: alvaro.perezr@pucp.edu.pe

L. Cadiet and Y. Fu (eds.), *On Judicial Management from Comparative Perspective*, Contemporary Chinese Civil and Commercial Law,
https://doi.org/10.1007/978-981-19-8673-4_5

jurisdiction-specific and knowledge-based rather than skills-based[2]; that is, court and case management depends on skills that are supported by knowledge. It is also worth noting the wide variations in judicial practice arising from local legal and cultural frameworks.

1. The reference to efficiency in judicial systems is really necessary because efficiency can be seen as a facet of the wider claim to the effectiveness of judicial protection of rights.[3] This is not to reduce the discussion to one of market ideology where the judicial protection of rights depends only on a profit-maximizing and cost-minimizing approach. As Prof. Caponi remarks, if one maintained that the judicial protection of rights and efficiency are incompatible, one would be bound to believe that individuals do not care about judicial protection of rights (except when they are parties to civil proceedings).[4]

Efficiency is different from effectiveness, as the first is connected with the purposes and arrangements of the whole civil justice system, while the procedural economy is rather linked to the purpose(s) of single proceedings (the most cost-efficient way).[5] The efficiency of civil procedure should be a link between the regulation and management of single civil proceedings and the systemic management of the mass of civil proceedings, that is, a connected micro and macro view of management for a better administration of justice.[6] The literature on the rule of law and economic growth has been one of the more dynamic areas of theoretical and empirical work in political science, economics, and law, joining interests in institutions and fundamental economic processes.[7] Access to the courts and the effective protection of rights should be provided in a fair process by the law in an efficient way. How? By taking into account the allocation to each case of an appropriate share of the court's resources in light of the need to allot resources to other cases.[8]

The real problem and challenge, as Prof. Caponi remarks, is finding a way to determine the degree to which individuals value the judicial protection of rights in comparison with other goods and services they want to obtain and, accordingly, how many resources they are willing to devote to the judicial system compared to other sectors of public administration. In this field, it is the political process and arena that are competent to decide.[9] The management of justice thus leads to a tension between market logic and the logic of human rights. In other words, it is necessary

---

[2] Benvenuti (2015, pp. 59–67).

[3] Tronson (2016, pp. 183–202), Uzelac (2014, pp. 21–23).

[4] Caponi (2016, p. 151); also in Althamer and Weller (2017, pp. 139–164).

[5] As Prof. Caponi explains, Caponi (2016, p. 151); also in Althamer and Weller (2017, pp. 139–164). See for the difference between efficiency and 'procedural economy' in Brändli (2013, pp. 46–62).

[6] Alt and Le Theule (2011, pp. 137–159), La Porta et al. (2004, pp. 445–470).

[7] Brändli (2013, pp. 62–70), Calabresi (2016), Stürner (2014, p. 271 ff).

[8] Caponi (2010, p. 389). As proposed by Prof. Caponi could be a good option to say 'The pursuit of efficiency shall not be detrimental to the right of access to courts and the effective protection of rights,' in Caponi (2016, p. 151).

[9] Caponi (2016, p. 141).

to manage the flow without reaching the guarantees of a fair trial.[10] The principle of case management is that the court, rather than the litigants, controls the pace of litigation. It is a modern approach to dispute resolution which seeks to move away from the bitter adversarial clashes of the past and encourage a greater start with a degree of judicial cooperation and partnership among all concerned.[11]

2. Judicial attention has come to be a scarce resource: (i) the rate of cases per judgeship has grown precipitously in lower, appellate, and supreme courts; (ii) there are reasons to discuss various proposals that scholars and judges have offered in response to the rising caseload, including ways to reduce the number of filings, increase the number of judges, and improve efficiency in the courts with an appropriate case and court management principles; (iii) there are frameworks to be taken into account to guarantee access to the courts and the effective protection of rights; and (iv) the demand for judicial attention will continue to exceed the supply of judicial time, thereby rendering judicial attention a scarce resource.[12] The adaptation of proceedings and court structures is prior to the public policies suited to local and temporal needs.[13]

Judicial 'managerial' theories must assure that proportionality will be considered on a case-by-case basis, according to constitutional standards, in the sense of weighing the harm to the parties against the benefit to the administration of justice. The subject is part of the connection between Constitutional and Procedural Law.[14] The constitutional theory recognizes positive and negative constitutional rights and stipulates a much wider judicial review of the law's constitutionality around the main issue: describing the scope and limitations of constitutional rights.[15] Constitutional limitations certainly apply also in the subconstitutional legal sphere (statutes or common law).[16] The enforcement proceedings impose limitations on fundamental rights and could be challenged if the limitations were centered on proportionality.[17] We could test the constitutionality of the entire case and the court managerial theory in the framework of the rule of law from the perspective of the limitation of fundamental rights. These constitutional discussions on the introduction of vigorous case management have prompted resistance, particularly among American academics.

---

[10] Amrani Mekki (2000), Stürner (2007, pp. 128, 140).

[11] Turner (1997).

[12] Prof. Andrews remarks that the following are problems with the English Civil Justice: lack of economic access to courts; delay during appeals; inefficiency within the system of enforcing judgments; slow movement toward superior forms of information technology within the court system; and disparities of judicial provision between London and the regions, the Capital being better served, in Andrews (2017). Briggs (2016).

[13] Chan and Van Rhee (2021, pp. 1–12), Da Fonseca Gajardoni (2017).

[14] See Petersen (2017, pp. 38–63); See Schwab and Gottwald (1984, p. 1 et seq).

[15] Ferreres Comella (2009, pp. 10–25); Cf. Zucca (2008, pp. 19–37); Cf. Baer (2009, pp. 417–468).

[16] See Petersen (2017, pp. 38–63). On the relationship of proportionality and constitutional rights as necessity or contingent connection, see Alexy (2014, pp. 51–65), Terhechte (2011, pp. 1–9, 54–59, limitation and proportionality).

[17] See in general constitutional theory with Emiliou (1998, pp. 25–50), Webber (2009, pp. 15–35), Barak (2012, pp. 1–12), Klatt and Meiste (2012, pp. 45–68), Tronson (2016, pp. 183–202).

Professor Resnik questioned its effectiveness 35 years ago.[18] Others worry that the managerial latitude of judges has given them too much unconstrained power.[19] As Prof. Wolff remarks, the explosion of interest in the role of judges over the last 30 years has produced valuable insights into the institutional responsibilities and limitations of the judiciary.[20]

According to Prof. Marcus, a significant part of that culture shift in the United States is related to enhanced judicial management by judges. Perhaps most importantly, the rule amendments emphasized proportionality in discovery. '*Actually, this concept had been in the rules since 1983, but in the 2015 amendments it was made more prominent and drew much attention. The idea is that the parties should scale their litigation efforts and expenditures to what is at stake. One hope was that the lawyers themselves would implement proportionality. But realism requires us to recognize that judges will have to play a role in achieving proportionality.*'[21] Most recently, the 2015 amendments to Rule 26(b)(1) of the Federal Rules of Civil Procedure (U.S.) stressed the need to limit discovery according to the proportionality principle, thus highlighting the courts' responsibility to ensure that litigation is cost-effective. Although the oral argument is not within the ambit of Rule 26, the concern is the same.[22]

Critical components within an efficient judicial system are court and case management. These deal with the court structure and the imperative arrangements within and between the courts both from a horizontal and vertical point of view. The structural design of one judicial system depends on multiple factors and the cultural aspect may be the main one.[23] As explained by Profs. Cappelletti and Garth 30 years ago, the images of courts and the system of civil justice derived largely from the characteristics of civil litigation in the first instance. These characteristics include horizontal arrangements within the courts (first instance and superior) beginning at the base of the pyramid, but also the vertical and adequate interplay between the superior and lower courts. These subjects connected with the court and case management shall be explained in this report.[24]

This report is divided into seven sections. After an introduction and general remarks, in Sect. 2, I discuss the complex connection between efficiency, effectiveness regulation, and judicial independence from the impact of case management and judicial performance requirements. In Sect. 3, I consider the key points of case and court management. In Sect. 4, I explore the relationship between procedural, cultural, and structural arrangements from the case management perspective and introduce the horizontal and vertical views to analyze those subjects. The next two sections examine the (Sect. 5) horizontal and (Sect. 6) vertical arrangements from

[18] Resnik (1982, p. 374); Comp. other view as replayed Flanders (1984, pp. 505, 519–20).

[19] Marcus (2017a, b, 2021a, b, pp. 109–122).

[20] Wolff (2013, pp. 1027, 1069), Turner (2004, pp. 73–88).

[21] Marcus (2017a, b, 2021a, b, pp. 109–122).

[22] *Idem.*

[23] Dondi et al. (2015, pp. 1–23).

[24] Damaška (1986) and after Damaška (2010, p. 3).

the case and courts managements. This contribution finishes with some concluding thoughts and reflections.

2 Efficiency, Effectiveness Regulation and Judicial Independence

1. Efficiency interplays with judicial independence. In this section, attention will be focused on the institutional and procedural devices designed to ensure judicial independence and the relationships and tensions between judicial independence and the use of tools for improving the performance of judicial systems.[25] Prof. Bovend remarks that the '*It is vitally important to have sufficient safeguards against outside pressures from executive branch authorities, to maintain the independence of the judiciary and respect separation of powers.*'[26] Providing effective judicial protection of rights includes guarding against the risk of unequal bargaining power between parties giving rise to unjust settlements due to the lack of a viable alternative before the courts. Also, in the dialogue between lower and appellate courts, it is important to keep in mind the tension between less, or more, appeal and efficiency. Taking account of key features for a judicial system such as independence (and specialization) of the courts, as well as overall performance, could help explain the real and effective role played by mediation bodies in that system.[27] For example, in Poland, indicators on the activities of common and military courts, grouped according to the fields of law, instance jurisdiction, departmental structure, and administrative division of the country, are collected by the Ministry of Justice's Statistical Management Information Department at the Department of Strategy and European Funds.[28] In Chile, official judicial statistics are produced by the judiciary.[29] It is important to note the following from Perú: '*In 2002, the National Competitiveness and Formalization Council was created, an organ assigned to the Ministry of Economy and Finance, in order to create projects that improve the climate of business competitiveness in the global market. However, the view of the justice system to that end has determined that the justice system only receives attention in those areas that reflect a result for statistics linked to the global economy. It is the one that reports for the ranking Doing Business, a reason why it is commercial justice that is the recipient of the most of reforms in (the) modernization of the justice system. Due to this, the position of Peru in the ranking of the Doing Business is not bad. Outside of those rankings, other indicators of the Judiciary do not exist or are not public.*'[30]

---

[25] See Caponi (2015a, b, pp. 117 ff), Shany (2012, pp. 251–267).

[26] Bovend'Eert (2016, pp. 333–353).

[27] Guinchard (2015, pp. 843–852).

[28] Flaga-Gieruszynska and Klich (2017).

[29] Odgers and Maureira (2017).

[30] Priori (2017).

Prof. Caponi remarks that one of the tasks for scholars is to recognize that the study of procedural law can only make sense if it is aware that every technical choice almost always fits into that broader context. This is linked with the additional ideological perspective that it is unnecessary to utilize indicators.[31] It is a complex task to find the right route to accurate information that contributes to, not impedes, the independence of the judiciary. It has become commonplace that some judicial systems of civil justice are inefficient because of the huge backlog of cases and delays in ordinary civil proceedings.[32] To assess the current state of affairs, one must use some indicators concerning the flow of proceedings, clearance rates, disposition time, the number of judges, the number of lawyers, the litigation rate, and so on.[33] Although the use of statistical indicators is important, it is risky in a comparative perspective unless the user of the statistics takes into account the methodological bases of their compilation.[34]

2. Worldwide judicial independence is a major and pivotal principle of civil procedure.[35] The Principles of Transnational Civil Procedure, as adopted by the American Law Institute and Unidroit in 2004, provide: 'The court and the judges should have judicial independence to decide the dispute according to the facts and the law, including freedom from improper internal and external influence.' As a principle, judicial independence has both institutional and procedural requirements that entail bodies and proceedings in charge of ensuring its realization and being able to react against violations and interference by other (public and private) entities. This independence requires a difficult interplay among different substantive elements[36]: recruitment, tenures, salaries, discipline, immunity, physical security, administrative autonomy, and training.[37] It generates an important paradox, in that the courts must manage the processes to avoid abuse, but this demand produces an immense amount of additional work that, given the current demand for justice, paralyzes the justice system.[38] It is also ruled the general case management as "Role of the Court" (Rule 4) within the ELI – UNIDROIT Model European Rules of Civil Procedure 2020: "The court is responsible for active and effective case management. The court must ensure

---

31 Caponi (2015a, b, p. 3).

32 Shany (2012, pp. 251–267).

33 *Idem.*

34 Kern (2007, *passim*), Davis et al. (2012, *passim*), Lindquist and Cross (2009, p. 9) (On results-oriented judging); Rottenburg (2015, *passim*). One mention is the EU Justice Scoreboard, published yearly by the European Commission: '*The EU Justice Scoreboard is an information tool aiming to assist the EU and Member States to achieve more effective justice by providing objective, reliable and comparable data on the quality, independence and efficiency of justice systems in all Member States.*'

35 Seibert-Fohr and Müller (2012, pp. 5–20), Burbank and Friedman (2002, *passim*).

36 Shetreet and Turenne (2013, pp. 4–20).

37 Guinchard (2015, pp. 843–852), Jackson (2012, pp. 19–25).

38 Lienhard and Kettiger (2017, pp. 7–19): '*The courts are the jewel of any state governed by the rule of law. Yet even the judicial system must modernise its methods of organisation and management if it is to guarantee sustainable jurisdiction. But how much management is itself sustainable within the judicial system?*'

that parties enjoy equal treatment. Throughout proceedings it shall monitor whether parties and their lawyers comply with their responsibilities under these Rules". It seeks, therefore, a way of judicially directing the processes where their social interventionist objectives are achieved and, at the same time, the cost and the time of its process are reduced. Is this possible? It would seem to require the articulation and coordination of the horizontal and vertical components of the courts to achieve the goals of reasonable time, low costs, and procedural and substantive justice.[39] All developed societies must respect the rule of law by ensuring an independent judiciary, an impartial court system, and a degree of separation consistent with efficient judicial administration.[40]

3. In 2011, the ENCJ adopted the Vilnius Declaration with recommendations for the judiciaries of Europe. The recommendations call for 'the development of long-term policies that include necessary reforms of the judiciary. Courts should improve their efficiency, ADR should be promoted, and the judiciary should develop stronger relations with civil society to reinforce public confidence and gain support for the necessary reforms. Councils for the judiciary should take the lead in the reform process involving judges and courts.' Judicial reform should have as its objective the improvement of the quality of justice and the efficiency and effectiveness of the judiciary, while also strengthening and protecting the independence of the judiciary, accompanied by measures to make its responsibility and accountability more effective.[41] Another aim should be to bring justice closer to the citizens. To this end, access to justice, including in cross-border judicial proceedings, must be facilitated.[42]

4. Justice is the cornerstone of the rule of law and, consequently, the independence of the judiciary is vital in any democratic society. Three major issues should be taken into account: judicial appointment, external judicial independence, and internal judicial independence. Many of the judicial reforms underway are efforts to improve the functioning of judiciaries. Other reforms are brought about by the economic crisis that affects most of the countries in Europe.[43] The impact of the economic crisis on the judiciary is significant in many European countries; the number of cases increases while budgets decrease. In some countries, the poor performance of the judiciary, for instance with respect to timeliness, is one factor that hinders economic development. Therefore, awareness of the importance of an effective functioning judiciary offers opportunities not only for reform but also to respond to the economic crisis.[44] The organization of the judiciary should balance different interests, including the power of the lower courts and superior courts, the confidence in the first instance and superior

[39] Resnik (1982, pp. 374, 380), Zuckerman (2004, pp. 127–149).

[40] Albers (2008, pp. 45–57), Van Rhee (2014, pp. 61–77).

[41] Fleck (2014, pp. 3–25).

[42] ENCJ (2012), '*The new landscape necessitates taking the opportunity to undertake measures aimed at improving the efficiency of the Courts, a situation not necessarily perceived and dealt with in better times to rethink the judicial map, to introduce and reform the procedures and the internal organization of the courts and the integration of the innovative information and communication technologies which are essential features to increase the efficiency of the court system.*'

[43] Comp. Dondi et al. (2015, pp. 23–26).

[44] Guinchard (2015, pp. 843–852).

courts according to agreed ends, respect for the internal independence of judges in their adjudication activities, and a clear limit between disciplinary measures to control judges respect for judicial independence, among others. As observed by Profs. García and Fuentes in Chile, the internal judicial independence has important problems: '*the Chilean constitution only regulates external judicial independence and says nothing about internal independence. On the contrary, the Chilean Constitution gave certain powers to the Supreme Court that seriously endangered the independence of the judges, as it will be explained.*'[45] In the same way, in Poland, based on Art. 178 of the Constitution of the Republic of Poland, judges are independent in the exercise of their office and subject only to the constitution and the acts. Judges shall be provided with working conditions and remuneration corresponding to the dignity of the office and the scope of their duties. At present, in Poland, changes are being made to the system of common courts and the status of judges, raising doubts about compliance with the constitution. Their effect may be to limit the independence of judges for political purposes.[46]

3 Courts and Case Management: A General Overview

The management of judicial administration takes two forms: case management and court management. Both are connected and interplayed. They are, among all the issues of procedural law and judicial practice, among those most related to 'legal culture.' This means, as we have just explained, that rules can have a 'primary design' of the judicial role. However, it is perfectly possible that the legal consecration of the 'primary design' does not transfer into its effective realization by the courts. This occurs, among other reasons, because the traditional role of the judge can be transferred from an old procedural system (which also has the weight of judicial traditions) to a new one that seeks to replace it. This, in turn, is because legislation alone cannot force cultural patterns on judges and because the rules are, in any case, always interpretable.[47]

Case management is a judicial process that provides effective, efficient, and purposeful treatment of a case so as to achieve a timely and qualitative resolution of

---

[45] Odgers and Maureira (2017) '*In the first place, and as a consequence of the pyramidal structure previously mentioned, the Supreme Court is the hierarchical superior of all other courts. Indeed, Rule 82 of the constitution assigns the Supreme Court the correctional superintendence over all the tribunals inside the judiciary, which is the power to supervise and sanction all other tribunals. This power is exercise more strongly over the appeals court and later, those courts exercise such power over first instance judges. But the point is that the roles of the Supreme court of having the final word with respect to the law and at the same time being the 'boss' of other members of the judiciary are sometimes conflicted, generating the risk that some judges could not be willing to solve matters in one way or the other, because the Supreme Court is there superior and eventually evaluate their decisions.*'

[46] Flaga-Gieruszynska and Klich (2017).

[47] Ervo (2017, pp. 77–89); for a comparative contribution Marcus (2017a, b, p. 55 et seq).

a dispute. The early identification of disputed issues of facts and law, establishment of a procedural calendar for the life of the case, and exploration of a possibility of a resolution of disputes through methods other than court trial are the progressive goals of case management.[48] This requires the early assignment of a case to a judge who then exercises judicial control over the case immediately and decides its adequate track at every stage. The judge applies judicial processes to secure active participation and joint communication among the parties and the lawyers.[49] The court assists the parties and lawyers in identifying the real controversies and seeking an early response from the other side on the questions of facts and law raised by the opponents, minimizing or narrowing down the controversies. It also may be to refer the case to ADR methods.[50]

However, it is necessary to offer good arguments to justify a change in the judicial role and in the horizontal and vertical arrangements for effective case and court management. These public policy reasons are not only of interest to the legislator but are also essential in the judicial phase within a legal and cultural context. The legislator adopts a norm to achieve a desirable social goal, behaving, in that sense, as a macro-generator of public policies. The judicial direction of the process responds to a basic idea—justice is in such demand that courts cannot be passive in the face of the phenomenon without risking, in time, the collapse of the system. To this end, therefore, it must carry out activities of 'direction', 'management', and 'control' that rationalize and optimize the use of judicial resources, which are always scarce. This function sounds very 'managerial', and therefore, incompatible with the traditional role of the judge within the liberal tradition. However, modern trends have sought to give these tools of the direction of the process to the courts.[51]

1. Let me begin with a brief summary of what has been discussed up to now. Since the end of the nineteenth century, discussions on the role of the judge within civil procedure have taken place in European law. That European debate has also moved to Latin America, where it has already developed over several decades. In general terms, it could be said that the judicial systems established in the codes, after the French Revolution and well into this century, were characterized by a privatistic and individualistic understanding of the ends of the process. To this understanding of the process, the authors began to call it the 'device principle.' Here, the word 'device' accentuated the primary capacity of litigants to initiate, promote (also often obstruct), and finally terminate the civil proceeding. Only the protection of private and individual rights was sought in the civil law tradition.[52]

---

48 Zuckerman (2009, p. 105).

49 Salas (1998, p. 119).

50 Dondi et al. (2015, pp. 77–82).

51 Posner (2006, pp. 1049, 1050).

52 Langbroek (2017, pp. 1–2). '*Napoleon's legacy is still holding European court administration and European judiciaries in a civil service position, including hierarchical disciplinary supervision of the judges on a national scale. Local court organizations therefore are not very autonomous. They may have their own budget, and their own management, but for most of the management they are bound to sometimes quite detailed national rules, especially for budgeting and accounting, security, personnel policies and so on. In this respect it does not make a lot of a difference whether*

2. The parties, but especially the plaintiff, could 'dispose' of their right and, therefore, directly control the purpose, nature, and speed of civil proceedings. Consequently, within the device principle, the direction of the process (its primary leadership, if desired) was conferred on the plaintiff. For these reasons, the civilian tradition has said that the claimant is the lord of the process. The defendant, on the other hand, responded (sometimes with enormous resistance, if not in open obstruction) to the direction. This characteristic of the device principle has been blamed for the extension of the average terms of resolution of a civil suit far beyond what is socially, politically, or economically acceptable.[53] The main contribution of this new doctrine consisted in making the civil process 'public', although it was true that individual private rights were also discussed and defined. It was also true that society had a general interest in achieving prompt solutions or civil outcomes that were egalitarian, true, and just.[54] One of the central strategies of this process was to prevent the parties from controlling civil procedure. Instead, the new approach emphasizes the need to establish the direction of the process in the hands of the courts.[55] Thus, the norms of civil procedure (both its principles and its rules of detail) were reconceived (though not without hesitation and setbacks throughout the twentieth century) as rules of public law. In a similar way, the role of the judge was gradually rethought, not as a passive spectator of the activity of the parties, but as a proactive actor who sought the direct realization of the public purposes of the process.[56] These were essentially of two types: on the one hand, the social objective was to match materially to the parties, controlling the social or economic superiority of one of them that could, without control, translate into procedural superiority; and at the same time, through the management of the process, it was sought to avoid delays or obstructive behavior of the parties.[57] As Prof. Andrews remarks, '*Case management has three main functions: to encourage the parties to pursue mediation, where this is practicable; secondly, to prevent the case from progressing too slowly and inefficiently; finally, to ensure that judicial resources are allocated proportionately, as required by 'the Overriding Objective' in CPR Part 1 (reformulated in 2013 to highlight the need for cases to be dealt with justly and 'at proportionate cost').*'[58]

3. The need for the 'conduction of proceedings' doctrine after 1930 developed in the Anglo-American world from the concept of 'case management.'[59] Between

---

the national court administration is headed by a ministry of justice or by an administrative council for the judiciary.'

[53] Andrews (2012, pp. 97–109), Dondi et al. (2015, pp. 97–102).

[54] Bettinger (2016, pp. 3–8).

[55] Tronson (2016, pp. 183–202).

[56] Turner (2004, pp. 73–88).

[57] Langbroek (2017, pp. 1–2).

[58] Andrews (2017), quoting the CPR 1.1(1): '*These Rules are a new procedural code with the overriding objective of enabling the court to deal with cases justly and at proportionate cost.*' Sorabji (2021a, b, pp. 137–152).

[59] Chayes (1976, p. 1281). In addition, Prof. Baldwin describes the birth of the early active judge in the United States justice: 'Rule 16 officially blessed the use of pre-trial judicial conferences, and they were widely used in several jurisdictions. These hearings were originally restricted to civil

civil and common law traditions, there are very striking similarities and differences that need to be emphasized. There is a first common characteristic that will be seen throughout the text and that may generate misunderstandings on the part of the reader: the rationalization techniques that constitute the contemporary process direction were originally deployed, both in Europe and the United States, within civil proceedings. Thus, for example, the European notion of 'process direction' developed fundamentally within the continental civil process. In the same way, the managerial judging of the United States was born in the civil process. This issue cannot be treated in isolation from the techniques of rationalization and optimization of the civil, labor or contentious-administrative process. In the latter, the German expression 'Prozessleitung des Richters' and its analogs in the Romance languages were preferred: 'dirección judicial del proceso' in Spanish, 'direzione del proceso' in Italian, and finally, 'direction (or maîtrise) du procès' in French and 'Gerenciamiento, conducao, direccao' in Portuguese. The new generation of judicial management of the civil process prefers the central metaphor of 'case management' or 'managerial judging.' As Prof. Marcus observes on another point is that some conceptions of the Continental system may overstate the extent to which it ever involved routine judicial control of the development of cases.[60] Prof. van Rhee[61] emphasizes that the influence of the French Code of 1806 was very much to support a laissez-faire approach to litigation, as when the litigants or the lawyers—not the judges—controlled the content and progress of cases. The Austrian Code of Franz Klein, introduced in the late nineteenth century, was more oriented toward the sort of judicial activism that characterizes American case management of the late twentieth century.[62]

4. The general trend toward increased and increasingly broad judicial management of litigation in the U.S. is ongoing. To illustrate, in January 2017, the federal court in San Francisco issued a Standing Order for Joint Case Management Statements in all their civil cases.[63] In Germany, as Stürner and Wendelstein remark, '*Case management is not a technical term used in German procedural law, nor is there a direct German translation. The closest would be the judicial power to direct the course of the proceedings. While it is up to the parties to initiate proceedings, to determine its scope and to state the material facts, the ultimate responsibility for the progress of the proceedings lies with the court.*'[64] These remarks could be applied to most continental civil procedure systems. The court is responsible for the direction of the proceedings. That extends to the formal aspects of the proceedings, namely the power to open the hearing and direct its course (sec. 136 (1) ZPO) and

disputes but expanded in some states, though with some caution, to also cover criminal disputes.' Baldwin (1985a, b, p. 6). In the same vein, Máximo Langer expresses himself when he asks what the civil procedure of the United States and the reforms to the procedural status of the International Criminal Tribunal for the former Yugoslavia may have in common. The common theme, as will be seen, is the existence of 'case management' techniques. See, Langer (2005).

60 Marcus (2017a, b).

61 See Van Rhee (2015, pp. 3–13).

62 Cappelletti and Garth (1984, p. 252), Ormazabal Sánchez (2017).

63 Marcus (2017a, b).

64 Stürner and Wendelstein (2017).

to close the hearing and deliver decisions of the court (sec. 136 (4) ZPO).[65] The court is to discuss with the parties the circumstances and facts, as well as the relationship of the parties to the dispute, regarding questions of substance and of the proceedings.[66] From the Chilean experience, it could be remarked that '*our case management had been a sort of spontaneous phenomenon, as we explain in the next question. In fact, case management is in our experience is so recent or embryonic, that there is no literature in the subject, nor on horizontal or vertical case management techniques.*'[67] Family and labor courts constitute the milestone for an incipient development of case management. Both recent reforms replaced the written procedures for hearings and the dynamic of the oral systems. The excessive caseload burden justified the administrative rules decreed by the '*Supreme Court with the goal that each courthouse establishes their own more elaborated criteria with respect to case scheduling, centering this responsibility in three figures: the judges' committee, the president judge and the Court administrator (all of them being designated as 'control and management entities').*'[68]

5. While the Europeans then spoke of 'judicial direction of the process', the Americans coined the term case management. In accordance with this new principle of moderation of the purely adversarial system, case management (in criminal or civil matters) is a process oriented toward ends in which the courts (and not the parties) control the impulse, progress, and disposition of the parts.[69] Just as the Europeans had built a critique of the excesses of the device principle (without turning the civil process into an inquisitive process), the Americans had discovered the limits of the adversarial principle.[70] The literature shows that, in fact, there may be excesses of 'adversariality.' The process remains a 'question of the parties' before a neutral arbitrator. However, as the Americans themselves have seen, the pure model of the neutral arbitrator does not allow judges to avoid the possible excesses of adversariality that appear in these systems.[71] As Prof. Marcus describes, '*The way in which case management can operate depends significantly on the structure and orientation of the court system in which it is to operate. The American system is, of course, a common law system. Iberoamerica, on the other hand, is mainly or entirely dominated by civil law systems modeled on Continental Europe. In a way, that means that judges may regularly be called upon to take a more active role in controlling the cases and lawyers.*'[72]

---

[65] *Idem.*

[66] *Idem.*

[67] Odgers and Maureira (2017).

[68] Odgers and Maureira (2017). '*In this management judicial acts it is possible to identify some case-tracks and certain space for judicial interventions in individual cases (managerial judging), both of them aim to simplify the judicial process and facilitate the termination of the cases.*'

[69] Ormazabal Sánchez (2017).

[70] Marcus (2017a, b).

[71] Jolowicz (1996 p. 198), Dondi et al. (2015, pp. 157–177).

[72] Marcus (2017a, b; 2021a, b, pp. 109–122).

6. These techniques of management also include a mechanism to coordinate and to allow collaboration between the courts with minimal standards of organization within the courts. The direction of the process, however, requires careful control of the case, the hearings and the record, as well as some political courage on the part of the judge, to 'direct' and 'control' the activity of the parties.[73] This direction is exercised, first, by persuasive methods and techniques, and second, by consensus and agreements among the parties as complementary and contemporary views.[74] Such direction is variously called 'process management', 'litigation management', or simply 'procedural control.' The 'management of the process' has been accompanied by parallel techniques of 'management of the office' (court management) and 'management of the judicial personnel' (personnel management). The assistance to the judge's adjudication activities is crucial. '*Although largely invisible to the public, behind the scenes, judicial assistants/law clerks frequently play a vital role in the process of adjudication. Yet, especially outside of the U.S., little is known about their role and duties in the judicial decision-making process.*'[75]

The Poland National Report describes a combination between the court's work and administrative requirements directly linked with optimal case management. There are three main areas of activity indicated in this regard that should contribute to the improvement of the work of the judges, which globally will have a positive effect on the management of court cases. A first point should be to increase the number of assistants of judges and organizational strengthening of the courts. Second, it is necessary to introduce changes aimed at reducing the scope of the cases recognized and resolved by the courts. In this respect, it seems necessary to introduce legal regulations and effective tools to eliminate (or significantly reduce) examples of the so-called judicial barratry (a framework of judicial proceedings to prevent the abuse of process). Finally, it is important to improve access to the justice system, especially for vulnerable groups (e.g., victims of crime, minors, minorities, people at risk of legal or social exclusion) linked with better social participation in the administration of justice and supported use of ADR methods.[76]

From the American perspective, the judges are becoming more and more active in controlling the lawyers in cases assigned to them. Prof. Marcus remarks: 'The American lawyer has long seemed unique in the world—almost a cowboy figure doing

---

[73] Turner (2004, pp. 73–88), Sorabji (2021a, b, pp. 137–152).

[74] In this sense see Cappelletti (1974, p. 104). '*But what matters most here is to emphasize that the contradiction which at times appears to be a true hypocrisy, of a code which proclaimed in the abstract principles which it had no further intention to make, such contradiction has been further accentuated by forensic practice. Even more than the 'private deeds of the parties', the Italian process has become, or rather has remained, private to the parties' lawyers, who too often regulate the course of the process according to their own interests and commitments (Not always coincident with those of their clients!) Their activity consisting almost exclusively in innumerable exchanges of defense writings with a large part of the hearing before the judge transformed into useless hearings of mere forwarding. Faced with this degeneration of Italian civil proceedings, the judge has to look passively and resignedly. Naturally, the results are disastrous [...]*' (The translations into English in mine).

[75] Holvast (2016, pp. 10–28).

[76] Flaga-Gieruszynska and Klich (2017).

justice against the odds.'[77] So what is left for U.S. judges to control is not the outcome but the manner in which the case is prepared for trial by the lawyers, mainly through the unique American discovery process.[78] Finally, the judge had to take control of that sort of 'institutional reform' litigation, or it would not work.[79] This was the beginning of American case management.[80] It was a way to supplant the laissez-faire approach and costly handling of litigation under the relatively unbounded pleading and discovery rules that applied in federal courts.[81] The most dramatic procedural innovation added to American court management in the late twentieth century strongly supported active case management.[82] This new trend of judging[83] was criticized and provoked opposition to what was considered dangerous 'judicial activism.'[84] Some interpreted this judicial behavior in political terms, seeing it as 'a shift to the right.'[85] Judges responded that this opposition reflected a wish 'to preserve the laissez-faire character of the adversarial system', which, from the judges' attitudes, had 'run amok.'[86] That debate remains ongoing today.

7. Within the case and court management development, it is important to mention the ADR. These can serve as important indicators for assessing the quality performance of the legal system taken as a whole. But these indicators must be carefully examined. It should be expected and ensured that dispute resolution methods are chosen by the parties in a truly free and informed (cultural) way.[87] Worth mentioning here is the case of *Livio Menini v. Banco Popolare Società Cooperativa*, decided by the Court of Justice of the European Union in 2017, about access to justice and mandatory mediation in Italy, in which it was explained that mandatory mediation procedures, required as a condition for the admissibility of proceedings before the courts, may prove compatible with the principle of effective judicial protection (also in consumer disputes). However, such procedures should not cause significant delay. They should not be required that the consumer as a party be represented by a lawyer, nor should they should be required to justify the consumer's withdrawal from the

[77] Marcus (2003, p. 3).

[78] Marcus (2017a, b).

[79] Chayes (1976, p. 1281).

[80] Marcus (2017a, b).

[81] See Elliott (1986, pp. 306, 308–309) (For historical backgrounds in American litigation).

[82] Marcus (2017a, b).

[83] *Idem.*

[84] Resnik (1982, p. 374) (Remarks that 'because managerial judging is less visible and usually unreviewable, it gives trial courts more authority and at the same time provides litigants with fewer procedural safeguards to protect them from abuse of that authority'); Resnik (2000, pp. 924, 938–940) (discussing case management); A contrary opinion in Zuckerman (2004, pp. 127–149), Andrews (2012, pp. 97–109).

[85] See Gavin (2006, p.196), Gensler (2010, 669–744) (Concludes that the choices we eventually make regarding how best to utilize case management must ultimately depend on the degree to which we continue to believe that the benefits of a system that relies on judicial case management outweigh the costs).

[86] Peckham (1985, pp. 253, 265).

[87] Fiss (1984, p. 1073), Resnik (1995, p. 211), Symposium (2009, p. 1117).

proceedings. Generally, participation in such mandatory proceedings should be available free of charge or at a very low cost for the consumer. The reduction of caseloads saves costs and/or, dependent on the budgetary system, may help to reduce court delays.[88]

The main disadvantage is that such measures could diminish access to justice; an increase in fees infringes on the fundamental right of access to an independent and impartial tribunal established by law (Art. 6 ECHR). Increased use of ADR may contribute to a reduction of caseloads, but it is not guaranteed that litigants are better off. The study of the active conduct of the civil process by the judge is an interesting prism through which to read the evolution of the place of the judge in civil society and, in doing so, to evaluate the choices made regarding procedural policy. The rules of civil procedure and, more fundamentally, the less visible rules governing the administration of justice, reflect important political choices. They define the place of justice in civil society and, more fundamentally, the relationship between law and justice and the development of ADR.[89]

'*In Germany as a general rule, a conciliation hearing precedes any oral hearing unless efforts to come to an agreement have already been made before an ADR mechanism, or the conciliation hearing obviously does not hold out any prospects of success. In the conciliation hearing, the court will discuss with the parties the circumstances and facts as well as the status of the dispute so far in a comprehensive manner* (sec. 278 (2) ZPO).' Should a party fail to appear at the conciliation hearing or should the conciliation hearing not meet with success, the formal court hearing is to be held immediately thereafter.[90] In Germany, the reform of 2012 rules an 'Internal-Court Mediation' possibility (sec. 278 a ZPO). Mediation within the court, also referred to as 'court proceedings', is a special form of court ruling. The judge may refer the parties to appear before a mediation judge. If this is the case, the classical litigation procedure is terminated, otherwise it will be continued after the failure of mediation within the referent court.[91] Usually, the mediation session with the mediation judge takes half a day or a maximum of one day. However, there are some regional courts in Germany where the lawyers are not themselves invited to the mediation. In jurisprudence, too, there are isolated voices supporting the position that the presence of lawyers is not necessary. However, it should be remarked that the involvement of attorneys in the freight-handling process is very useful in most cases.[92] In France also, the most recent reforms support and provide incentives for the use of ADR. It is a question of encouraging the amicable resolution of disputes, moving to an amicable form of justice, and the judge becoming 'the alternative mode of dispute resolution.' ADR methods are urged by the judge as part of the

---

[88] Cadiet (2017, pp. 83–95), Stürner (2017, pp. 128–140).

[89] Amrani Mekki (2000).

[90] Stürner and Wendelstein (2017).

[91] See as supporting for the reform Von Malte (2008, passim).

[92] Thole (2014, pp. 339–370), Roth (2016, pp. 3–21).

procedure by creating many tools. The judicial and the contractual are not excluded. The procedures must now contain an amicable face.[93]

In the UK, mediation is voluntary, but the court encourages parties to consider mediation, which takes place out-of-court. Mediation in the UK could be considered as popular.[94] In Poland, according to Art. 10 of the Code of Civil Procedure, in cases where a settlement is admissible, the court must urge settlement at every stage of the case, in particular by inducing the parties to mediate.[95] The Chilean legal system directs a judicial conciliation stage in its civil procedure as an essential stage of the proceeding.[96] '*Beyond the conciliation stage of the civil procedure code, the attention of the Chilean legislators to ADR mechanisms is quite recent*.'[97] There are no qualitative indicators about the popularity among the lawyers and the civil justice users about ADR.[98] The law in Europe, starting in November 2011, favors ADR in consumer matters to provide access to alternative methods to solve disputes in that field.[99]

8. The comparative contribution of this report can be summarized as follows, a conclusion: The 'inquisitor judge' does not turn out to be, despite all his powers, an efficient manager of the proceeding. It is important to note, at the same time, neither is the 'arbitrator' of the purely adversarial principle a good director of the process. The experience of many years in England and the United States has shown this, and for this reason, opportunities and procedural mechanisms have slowly been accommodated to allow for the judge, even though the trial is 'a matter of the parties.'

---

93 Amrani Mekki (2000).

94 Andrews (2017).

95 Flaga-Gieruszynska and Klich (2017): '*Mediation is voluntary. It is conducted on the basis of a mediation agreement or a court order leading the parties to mediation. The agreement may also be concluded by the party giving consent for mediation when the other party has filed a request in this case. Mediation is carried out before the initiation of proceedings, and with the consent of the parties also in the course of the case. The court may refer the parties to mediation at any stage of the proceedings. Mediation does not apply to cases identified in the payment-order proceedings or writ-of-payment proceedings, unless an effective filing of charges took place (at this stage the summary proceedings, deprived of adversarial character, change to ordinary proceedings). The chairman may invite the parties to attend an information meeting on amicable dispute resolution, in particular mediation. An informational meeting may be conducted by a judge, court referendary, court officer, judge's assistant or permanent mediator.*'

96 Odgers and Maureira (2017): '*Indeed, it is because of the procedural reform process that Chile has undergone since 2000, that the legislative world had contemplated ADR as a serious and useful mechanism to solve disputes. Today ADR is quite relevant in family, labor and health-related litigation. Regarding family law, today the mediation stage is mandatory and part of the legal procedure, in the sense that for a lawsuit to advance further the claimant must first proceed to a mediation stage in charge of a professional mediator and in which the judges play no role, and only when this mediation has failed the lawsuit is authorized to move forward.*'

97 *Idem.*

98 *Ibidem.*

99 See Stürner and Wendelstein (2017). Also to mention is the regulation for collective redress in the EU and the role of ADR. https://eurlex.europa.eu/legalcontent/ES/TXT/?uri=CELEX%3A52018PC0184&from=EN&lang3=ES&lang2=ES&lang1=EN. Accessed 1 Dec 2020; Cortés (2017, *passim*). Also the recent Directive June 30 2020 (9223/20).

There is an emergent vision of the role for a court as a combination and complementation of the director/referee/inquisitor views.[100] Each alternative requires a particular court structure, including arrangements in both horizontal and vertical views. As is remarked by Prof. Amrani,[101] justice today is under budgetary pressure but must not yield to it blindly. Rather than constructing the model of civil trial under duress, it is necessary to reflect on the budgetary independence of the judicial authority and on the capacity of the judiciary to guide developments rather than undergo them.[102]

4 Procedural, Cultural, and Structural Arrangements

Civil procedure in countries belonging to the Romance legal family (such as France, South American countries and, until the new Code of Civil Procedure of 2000, Spain) is structured from the Italian-canonical procedure in three different stages: the written introductory phase (made up of the statement of claim, the defendant's response, and the exchange of a number of briefs between the parties); the fact-finding phase (made up of the taking of evidence by the judge); and the final decision phase, in which the decision on the dispute is to be issued by the judge (or a judicial panel in certain cases), after the parties have been given the opportunity to exchange their final briefs. The fact-finding phase often requires several hearings or some written procedures after the evidence has been compiled. The model is decentralized. Alternative models include a central main hearing, such as in Germany and England.[103]

1. The different internal structure of procedure is important for the horizontal and vertical arrangements of courts and connects with case management. Even if the claims underlying the courts' case management practices can be supported, those practices are not beyond improvement. This proficiency, in turn, comes from training and experience, which can be attained either through specialization or extended tenure. In the continental system, the '*first instance judges are often new to the job, and appellate review allows more experienced appellate court judges to correct their errors and guide them into the profession of judging.*'[104] In the American tradition, '*the institution of the jury trial, and the constitutional and statutory provision created to preserve its continued validity, checked judicial authority by allowing public participation in the fact-finding process of the federal courts*'[105]; '*Trial court (first instance) judges are not young 'learners.' They are usually long-seasoned trial lawyers, often with much more legal experience than some of the younger appellate judges.*'[106]

100 Salas (1998, pp. 287–296).
101 Amrani Mekki (2000).
102 With the approach of Roth (2016, pp. 3–21).
103 See a comparative approach in Bettinger (2016, pp. 41–49, 69–71), Andrews (2012, pp. 97–109).
104 Marcus (2017a, b).
105 Peterson (1995, pp. 41, 59).
106 Marcus (2017a, b).

The court, not the lawyers or litigants, should control the pace of litigation to enable the just and efficient resolution of cases. In addition to reducing delays, maintaining a current docket is essential to increase the confidence in, and respect for, the judicial system. In the past 30 years, courts have changed; courts have taken on new roles, increased civil case filings have other dispute resolution methods, and finally, in some (especially small claim) courts, there has been a dramatic increase in self-represented litigants. As now is generally accepted in the court community, caseflow management denotes supervision or management of the time and events involved in the moving of a case through the court system from the point of initiation to disposition, regardless of the final outcome.[107] To make the sequence and timing of these events more predictable and timely is a goal of active case management. While caseflow management programs are constructed around the events themselves, including status conferences and discovery completion, the important focus involves time management. The management of the intervals between events clearly affects overall case disposition times. As remarkable as it is to acknowledge that just results are achieved by well-prepared attorneys, then effective caseflow management must encourage and facilitate attorney preparation.[108] Caseflow management is at the heart of high-performance courts. Individualized attention and proportional case treatment encompass the caseflow management principle of differentiated caseflow management. Caseflow management's due process and equal protection rights are within the procedures of high-performance courts. Throughout the process, judges need to ensure firm hearings and trial dates. To do so, they need to ensure the planned dates are realistic and that the parties agree to abide by them.[109]

2. According to Prof. Fleck, transparency in the division of authority and the separation of powers is a decisive factor concerning the operation of judicial administration as a whole.[110] The horizontal arrangement has two important components: (i) the specialization of the courts[111] and (ii) the flexibility to adapt to the composition to the importance and/or the complexity of the case (single judge, a panel of judges, etc.). One approach to the first point is distinguishing between ordinary and specialized courts, for example, family, labor, and social welfare disputes. With regard to the administrative courts, the situation is made more complex by the different systems. For these cases, the constitutional framework often includes a Council of State and other organs of administrative justice with the jurisdiction to protect subjective rights against public administration. There is no uniform existence of administrative courts. Some administrative cases are under the jurisdiction of the civil courts without specialization. The range of cases involving administrative disputes is vast: disputes about agreements between citizens and public administration amending or replacing administrative measures, the right of access to administrative documents, the breach of the duty of transparency, the granting of the use of public goods, public services,

---

[107] Guinchard (2015, pp. 789–800, 843–848).

[108] For a description and explanation of the legal profession Uzelac and Van Rhee (2011, *passim*).

[109] Steelman (2004).

[110] Fleck (2014, p. 11).

[111] Comoglio (2014, p. 16).

procurement, urban planning, and construction policy, challenging the rulings of independent agencies, and so on. Administrative judges may be selected from the merit or professional system, based on previous legal experience, or on internal or external affiliation criteria of the judicial organization. These are key points to make fair and legitimate appointments and to uphold confidence in the judicial system.[112]

3. In addition to horizontal arrangements, it is important to take account of vertical arrangements, that is, the interplay between superior and lower courts. The role and ends of appeal to the supreme courts, the filter to access, the caseload and scope of review and the organization, taking into account that the number of judges in superior courts is not the same as in the lower courts. The case and court management should be different. For example, regarding the German Reform, Prof. Stürner explains that the reform of 2001 is perhaps not the result of great comparative work. However, the explanatory memorandum of the draft reform bill referred to examples of 'good practice' from England, Austria, Switzerland (Zurich), France, and Italy to show that the envisaged changes had already implemented in other jurisdictions. The major development of the 2001 reform was the abolition of the full-blown first appeal where ordinarily a full rehearing of fact and of law was undertaken. References were made to Austrian and English law to demonstrate that the focus should instead be on the first instance proceedings.[113]

4. The crisis of the administration of justice must be attacked and treated on several fronts because the problem has several causes that can be traced back in time. The case management view should take into account alternative ways to judicialization, and in this case, ADR should also be an alternative under the conditions presented above regarding respect of the free option of parties and consistent with public policy. That is, the court is unlikely to assume exorbitant leadership when its workload is excessive and increasing. For this reason, judicial management of the process also has a context of dejudicialization.[114] Five key points should be mentioned here: (i) Rationalization and (re)organization of courts and public prosecutor offices; (ii) Reduction in the volume of court cases; (iii) Simplification of judicial proceedings, improvement in case management, and introduction of new technologies[115]; (iv) Financing of the judicial system (courts and public associated agencies); and (v) Court and case management (in first instances and superior courts) and allocation of cases within and between courts and within and between associated agencies, as a type of multiple-door justice through the interplay between adjudication and other forms of justice.[116]

---

112 Badó (2014, pp. 27–58).

113 Stürner (2021, pp. 75 ff).

114 Amrani Mekki (2000).

115 Wang (2021, pp. 195–198).

116 See Stürner (2021, pp. 75 ff).

5 Horizontal Arrangements

1. The number of courts and their geographical distribution have an important effect on justice quality and management tools. Multiple factors support the different options: (i) The introduction of IT into the courts creates a new, virtual space to complement the 'real' courts[117]; (ii) Opportunities exist for cost reductions through specialization, independent of judicial reorganization; (iii) Other reasons include cost reductions from closing underused or run-down courts shifting the cases to nearby courts: and (iv) Finally, consolidation could bring several small courts under one main major court's jurisdiction to reduce the costs of management and overhead.[118]

Insofar as these reorganizations all lead to longer travel distances for parties, they imply a deterioration of geographical access to justice. One point to make is that the physical presence of parties and other trial participants such as witnesses is becoming less important. It seems, however, that many judiciaries no longer attach much weight to this issue. For example, video conferencing is becoming normal in large countries, and participation in a hearing from a distance is not considered a serious obstacle. In other systems, however, the desirability of a visible presence of the judiciary in local communities (neighbor, community, or near justice) is an important consideration, especially in local cases, although this cannot be a decisive factor. The combination of new, virtual spaces and the proximity of citizen-centered, specialized and general courts is a central subject for the horizontal organization between courts.[119] An additional more radical and disruptive change and challenge is the introduction of artificial intelligence (AI) to justice system. Civil justice as a public and private framework for the protection of rights and especially in the exercise of jurisdiction through the judicial process is challenged in its traditional foundations. The replacement of lawyers and judges by digitalization and more by AI would have serious implications.[120] The challenges can be limited to: (i) the visibility and transparency of the judicial process and eliminating the physical presence of the court; (ii) the legitimacy of the courts of justice (or the privatized mechanisms that subroge them); (iii) the requirements of due and fair process in the state and arbitration justice system and process, as the right to a reasonable and transparent justification of automated decision making.[121]

The goal is to employ one option or mixed methods, such as concentration or decentralization, where the overall aim is to guarantee a fair trial within a reasonable time (Art. 6 ECHR). The criteria are population distribution, geographic distance and accessibility of public transportation, the existence and (digital) accessibility of

---

[117] A critical remark about the limits of IT in civil litigation could be found in Zeleznikow (2017, pp. 30–45). '*The growing rise in the number of self-represented litigants has negative implications for both the court system and access to justice. The expanding use of Artificial Intelligence and the World Wide Web has led to the development and use of Online Dispute Resolution.*'

[118] Stürner (2021, pp. 75 ff).

[119] Amrani Mekki (2000).

[120] Felzman et al. (2020, pp. 3333–3361), Ferrand et al. (2019, pp. 15–20).

[121] Huang (2019, pp. 102–107).

support services and/or infrastructure, a sufficient number of cases to allow efficient utilization of courts and assistance agencies, and an adequate number of judges and agencies. As the saying goes, 'Justice must be seen to be done;' concentration and IT transparency, visibility, accountability, and participation all matter.[122]

2. Optimization of the workloads of courts and judges is a priority matter for judicial reform in most of the responding countries. Proportionality is a key aspect of this subject. Resources are wasted when some courts and judges do not have enough cases, particularly while other courts and judges have an excess of cases. A good practice could be the computerized allocation of cases according to objective criteria and taking into account the specialization of judges. Objective criteria for case assignment are important, but some flexibility in the allocation of cases across courts is important to equalize workload. The parties will frequently have to travel further. In some countries, the choice is left to the parties; either they wait for their case to be heard in the competent court or have their case immediately heard in a court located at a distance.[123] Another good option is to have judges of other courts assigned to work temporarily at the courts that have too many cases. A random distribution system to ensure a balance in the distribution of cases among judges is also effective for judicial independence and transparency.[124] An example is a recent reform in Poland that introduced a systematic principle of random allocation of cases to individual judges starting on August 12, 2017. According to the promoters of this reform, a random allocation of cases, especially in the second instance, is intended to protect against fraud and to ensure that the case has not been assigned deliberately to the judge chosen for the case.[125]

3. When this approach is translated in specialized courts (according to the legal matter and/or without connection with the matter's complexity), distribution tends to be fairer and more efficient.[126] Flexible allocation of cases among courts and judges to optimize their deployment has clear advantages for the efficiency of the courts.[127] A potential drawback is the risk of undue influence of legal staff on judges. This risk is small for professional judges. From one comparative perspective, the specialization is organized in lower and superior courts. Let me describe as an example the cases of Poland and Germany. In Poland, '*The district court is divided into divisions: civil–for cases from the scope of civil law, family and caring law, cases considering demoralization and delinquency of juveniles, treatment of persons addicted to alcohol, narcotic and psychotropic substances and cases belonging to the guardianship court under separate acts; criminal–for criminal cases. The district court may have the following subdivisions: family and juvenile, labour, social security or work and social*

[122] Ervo (2017, pp. 77–89).

[123] With the recent French Reform, Cadiet (2017, pp. 83–95).

[124] Case distribution is an important element for the confidence and transparency of the Judiciary regarding independence and impartiality, see Badó and Szarvas (2014, pp. 59–73), Guinchard (2015, pp. 843–852).

[125] Flaga-Gieruszynska and Klich (2017).

[126] Badó and Szarvas (2014, pp. 59–73).

[127] Guinchard (2015, pp. 779–807).

security economic; land and mortgage registers–for keeping the land and mortgage registers. The regional court is divided into divisions: civil–for cases from the scope of civil law, family and caring law, criminal law. The regional court may have the following divisions: labour, social security or work and social security; economic; control of telecommunication, postal and internet data. The court of appeal is divided into following divisions: civil; criminal; labour and social security.'[128] In Germany, the arrangement in civil matters consists of four levels. In the first instance, Local Courts (Amtsgerichte) or Regional Courts (Landgerichte) are competent to hear civil cases, depending on the value of the claim: Local Courts hear cases with an amount in controversy of up to €5,000, whereas for all other cases the Regional Courts are competent. The latter are also competent to hear appeals against decisions of the Local Courts. Higher Regional Courts (Oberlandesgerichte) mainly have appellate jurisdiction over decisions by Regional Courts. Finally, the Bundesgerichtshof is the final court of appeal in civil (and criminal) matters.[129]

The organization of specialized courts could be considered an advantage, yet in other ways, the multiplication of the vision and enforcement of the law could lead to contradictory decisions. This last risk means that supreme courts should assume a directive of rule uniformity.

4. Lord Woolf recommended, instead, that civil case management be conducted by teams of judges and that a procedural judge should always be in charge of the case throughout the period during which it proceeds to trial. In his final report, Lord Woolf recommended the involvement of a procedural judge in the majority of cases.[130] Many factors beyond direct judicial control affect the success of case management initiatives. Effective case management relies on the quality of preparation for hearings by case participants and their willingness to comply with court orders and timetables. The nature of the relationship between the listing office and the judiciary is a vital aspect of case processing. It is an anomaly that judges have responsibility for listing but no management control of the court staff who carry it out. The court composition relies on cooperation between the courts and staff. Prior to the introduction of the English civil justice reforms, one judge described cooperation between court, staff, and judiciary as being on a knife's edge. Budget-driven staff and cost cuts have led to staff shortages, and those that remain are grossly underpaid.[131]

5. Distribution and redistribution of tasks depend on the court's organization and composition. The basic idea of redistributing tasks of courts (panel and individual judges) and support staff is to allow judges to concentrate on the core of their adjudication tasks. Redistribution has been put into practice by various countries as diverse as Poland and Spain, in which judges shift work to administrative and legal assistants.[132] There is room for improvement in this area in many countries; judges often

---

[128] Flaga-Gieruszynska and Klich (2017).

[129] Stürner (2021, p. 75 ff).

[130] Woolf (1996). Woolf emphasises that ëprocedural judgeí is a function, not a title for a new type of judge.

[131] Salas (1998, p. 122).

[132] Flaga-Gieruszynska and Klich (2017).

perform relatively simple, administrative tasks that can just as well be performed by staff. Also, depending on the legal system, legal staff can be utilized to prepare cases and/or drafts of verdicts and/or to conduct preliminary screenings of cases. For any management system to succeed, and this equally applies to court management, it is essential to identify the stakeholders. Any judicial system has only four players: judges, lawyers, litigants, and the court staff and registry (not necessarily in order of importance). The specific role played by each stakeholder is vital for ensuring the success of case management and court administration.[133]

Delegating simple judicial functions to legal staff goes against the independence of the judiciary; only appointed judicial office holders, including lay judges, should make judicial decisions. The delegation of simple judicial decision-making to judicial office holders with a brief confined to the task is a distinct possibility. An example of this is the use of *Rechtspfleger* in German and Austrian courts. The experience is that delegation leads to higher efficiency, but only if judges trust their legal staff and do not feel compelled to monitor their work intensively or redo much of their work.[134] There may be additional costs involved, but a highly qualified legal staff is needed; this also requires judges to adjust to working in teams instead of alone. Whether the use of legal staff in an advisory role opens the door to undue influence on judges and endangers their independence has not been an important issue in Germany and Austria, at least as far as the professional judges are concerned.

Another aspect of court reorganization is the centralization of supporting administrative tasks. Courts need staff to gather and analyze data. The deployment of IT and innovation also require staff to assume responsibilities outside the primary processes of dealing with cases. Employing IT for the administration of justice involves a change from organizations of people to organizations of people and information systems interacting.[135] How is the presiding judge to track events in the courthouse while handling his or her own docket? Judges are already pressed for time, and now the presiding judge must make the court's management decisions without the benefit of experience and/or training. The main problems include lack of training, funding issues, personnel problems, and a host of other issues that spotlight the need for someone to assist the presiding judge. Ideally, the court management partnership becomes a team that can manage the court and provide procedural due process and justice.[136] To manage a case effectively, a court must have the fundamental elements of effective caseflow management in place. Society entrusts courts with ensuring justice for individuals and organizations that seek resolution of their disputes.[137]

In Germany, the Regional Court is the role model for all other courts and divisions (cf. the explicit reference made in sec. 495 ZPO for the proceedings before Local Courts). A single judge will sit in Local Court proceedings. By the same token, cases heard by Regional Courts in the vast majority of cases are decided by a single judge

[133] Guinchard (2015, pp. 807–810).

[134] Kappl (2016, p. 1).

[135] CEPEJ (2016).

[136] Baum (2008, pp. 73–81).

[137] See Parkin (2012, pp. 1309, 1362).

(Einzelrichter, sec. 348 (1) ZPO). For petty cases with a value of the claim of up to 600 Euro, the Local Court may decide at its equitably exercised discretion on how to implement its proceedings (sec. 495a ZPO). On the contrary, large commercial cases will be heard by a three-judge panel of the commercial division of the Regional Court (sec. 348 (2) lit. f ZPO).[138] In England, the judge sits alone, with the exception of employment tribunals where appeal panels are made up of three judges, the appellate court, which nearly always has three judges, and the nearly always five judges on Supreme Court panels. An interesting variation between the lower and appellate courts is for simple appeals to go to a single judge while complex appeals go to the three-judge appellate court.[139] Poland provides another example, with a first instance with a court of one judge unless a special provision provides otherwise.[140] In the second instance, the case is heard by three professional judges. Decisions considering evidentiary proceedings are issued by a court of one judge at a closed session.[141] The Supreme Court recognizes the cassation appeal in the composition of three judges. In other cases, the Supreme Court decides in the composition of one judge.[142]

In Perú, each judicial district corresponds to a superior court. Specialized courts are single-member jurisdictions. In such courts, judges are assigned to the districts of smaller population centers. The procedural reforms of recent years have been in line with increasing the jurisdiction of these judges.[143] In Chile, the first instance criminal, labor, and family courts are integrated with a judges' pool, but when it comes to knowing cases, each of them works alone, except for the criminal trial courts that work on a three-judge panel.[144] '*Each civil court, not reformed yet, is integrated with a single judge, a secretary and a group of court staff in charge of handling the case-dossiers. In December 2016, the electronic filling law was published, according to which all lawsuits and other written communications must be filed digitally.*' '*Courts of appeal can get to know a matter divided in chambers or en banc. Each chamber is integrated by three judges and their decision represents*

138 Stürner and Wendelstein (2017).

139 Andrews (2017).

140 Flaga-Gieruszynska and Klich (2017). '*In the first instance, a court composed of one judge as a chairman and two lay judges shall hear the following cases: in the field of labour law considering: in the field of family relationships considering. Decisions outside the hearings and orders are issued by the chairman. The president of the court may order the case to be heard by three professional judges if he or she deems it appropriate because of the particular complexity or precedent character of the case.*'

141 Flaga-Gieruszynska and Klich (2017).

142 Flaga-Gieruszynska and Klich (2017): '*If during the recognition of cassation appeal a legal question that raises serious doubts emerges, the Supreme Court may postpone the judgment and refer the case to the enlarged panel of the judges of the court. The resolution the enlarged panel of the judges of the Supreme Court is binding in this case. The Supreme Court in the enlarged composition may take the case to its recognition.*'

143 Priori (2017).

144 Odgers and Maureira (2017). '*These reformed tribunals have a more modern internal administrative structure, in charge of a professional court administrator, who leads a team of units responsible for the courts' schedule, customer service,* etc.'

the whole court.'[145] The appellate court has a series of other staff in charge of many administrative tasks. Appellate courts are not specialized and they work in chambers of three judges, all of whom have general jurisdiction. The Supreme Court works in specialized chambers. '*However, this is not a specialization due to special knowledge or training by the Supreme Court judges, but an internal work distribution.*'[146]

6. Two important points are the simplification and digitalization of procedures for more effective case management. Procedural simplification could take place in three ways, as Prof. Gajardoni[147] remarks in the case of Brazil and that could be applied generally. The first simplification process involves three forms of procedural flexibility (adaptation) systems. The first of these is flexibility by virtue of the law. In fact, a legal provision may authorize the judge to adapt the procedure to the cause. A second system is judicial procedural relaxation. Although there is no legal provision on the subject, it would be for the judge—based on the variants of the specific case (objective and subjective) and on true control of the constitutionality/convention of the procedure—to model the procedure, choosing which procedural acts to perform in the series, as well as their form and mode. The third system would be to voluntarily relax the rules of procedure, in which the parties would elect, through procedural conventions, certain procedures or procedural acts of the series, albeit also in an exceptional and conditioned manner.

Another aspect is to facilitate the number of types of procedures as a step toward simplification of the procedures themselves and toward simplifying supporting IT systems. This can be effective in delivering better quality justice as well as reducing costs. Regarding the procedures themselves, one step could be the introduction of simple and fast procedures, which allows the judge control in limiting the repeated exchange of documents and the postponement of cases. Only in very complicated cases would further hearings be allowed. It is expected that this would increase the number of settlements. This kind of procedure is present in several countries in small claims courts/proceedings. These procedures offer simplicity, a strict format, and low cost and lend themselves to digitalization.[148]

Filing cases electronically and the digital exchange of documents with digital signatures are rapidly becoming common and serve to lower costs. In many countries, a written record has been replaced by audio and video recordings (regardless of the case complexity). Video conferencing is used in many countries, although the nature of its use differs. In all countries, video conferencing is used to hear parties and others such as witnesses abroad and to protect vulnerable or anonymous witnesses. In countries with large travel distances, video conferencing is used more intensively and leads to large efficiency gains for the parties. Over the last decade, technology

---

145 Odgers and Maureira (2017).

146 Odgers and Maureira (2017). '*Regarding its ordinary work schedule, the Supreme Court is divided in three main chambers: the first chamber or civil chamber, the second chamber or criminal chamber and the third chamber or constitutional and administrative chamber. When the Supreme Court works under an extraordinary schedule, the Court is divided in four chambers, the last one gets to know labor and work benefits issues.*'

147 Da Fonseca Gajardoni (2017).

148 Wallace (2017, p. 1).

has evolved in many countries to improve the work of judges and court staff. The implementation of electronic filing platforms, along with new electronic case and records management systems, have brought sweeping changes to the way many state courts conduct procedures.[149]

7. Judicial decision-making and management needs for trial court judges on the bench and in chambers. With the appropriate tools, technology can assist judges in performing their duties, as well as improve the operational efficiency of the court and the quality of service provided by the justice system.[150] Judicial tools could help make more flexible the functions and resources essential to accessing current and historic case information as an indicator of visibility. It is important to manage and prioritize the work of a judge in chambers and on the bench. Over time, judges have become more proficient at managing large numbers of cases and complex matters in the world of paper files and paper dockets. Some judges may struggle to translate the workflow and decision-making process into the electronic world. Workflow and a good decision-making environment must exist for judges both in the courtroom and in chambers to improve the quality of decision-making.[151]

The term 'case management' has traditionally been used to refer to the overall process of moving cases from the point of filing to disposition while ensuring procedural and substantive due process for litigants.[152] It is important for the administrative management processes to include collaborative actions on behalf of the judge, clerk, and court administrator within an electronic case records system. In addition to 'case management' are the concepts of 'judicial case flow management' (JCFM), which refers to the more isolated processes that relate specifically to the functions of a judge. JCFM relates to the process of managing formal and informal events as unstructured information, which is required to allow an effective adjudication in a reasonable time.[153] Introducing JCFM opens the discussion on the ability of the judge to utilize records to provide improved access to justice. This is not restricted to the formal indicators of the courts but also hinges on the development of configurable judicial tools that provide judges with more effective technological means of accessing case records, ruling on filed motions, electronically signing documents, and flagging case events, as well as scheduling and presiding over hearings and trials.[154]

These measures in themselves, but in particular in combination, reduce the duration of court procedures and increase the efficiency of proceedings. Digital access to justice is a necessity. As the access to services in society in general has already largely been redefined as digital access, judiciaries have to keep pace with this trend.

[149] Zeleznikow (2017, pp. 30–45).

[150] In CCJE (2011, pp. 13–14), *Justice and information technologies (IT)* could be consulted the development index of IT in each European Union Countries connecting the keypoints equipment-legal framework-governance applied for the judicial system; Alwidian et al. (2017, pp. 185–202).

[151] Langbroek (2010).

[152] Ng (2008, pp. 111–133).

[153] The reconstruction of the development of criminal case management is based on Scott (1995), Baldwin (1985a, b).

[154] See Caseflow Management Handbook (2016, pp. 13–20, 18–34).

A provisional evaluation could be that the simplified and digitalized procedures are fully consistent with the demands of a fair trial, although other questions could result from indicators that measure the quality of justice and that control judges. If judges have to constantly explain to management why a case took longer than the norm, judicial independence is compromised. Thus, great care must be taken when using such data to compare the performance of judges in the interest of internal administrative disciplinary control.[155]

6 Vertical Arrangements

In most cases, the move away from traditional appellate (second and highest instance) decision-making strikes many as troubling, and court scholars have raised concerns about the increased use of each individual case management technique. Here the term 'appeal' is used in its broadest, modern sense to designate any attempt to have a higher court review the factual or legal findings of a lower tribunal (*recursus, appellatio, revisio, cassatio*) to obtain the correction or elimination of a judicial decision. Countries with civil law traditionally have a wide range of options to seek remedies against a court's decision.[156] The method for challenging judicial decisions in superior courts determines the arrangements needed for efficient and qualified work by appellate courts. Prof. Jolowicz[157] has described a division of European Union countries into three categories: (i) countries such as England and Sweden where all proceedings after the first instance are considered an appeal; (ii) countries such as Germany and Austria where a distinction is made between a second level (appeal) and a third level (revision); and (iii) countries where the distinction is made between a second level (appeal) and a third level (cassation), as in Spain, Italy, and Poland.[158] The appellate and supreme court proceedings and administration are different from a lower court.[159] The heart of assessing judicial decision-making in the superior courts is a filter for access to appeal with correct selection criteria, the use of IT systems and oral or written presentations[160] to litigate, and additional case and court management techniques for superior courts.

Evaluating the appellate stage presents challenges in identifying what variables should be maximized. A second challenge is that, once identified, the potential variables defy easy measurement. It seems equally sensible that judges would spend

155 Bovend'Eert (2016, pp. 333–353).

156 Dondi et al. (2015, p. 291).

157 Jolowicz and Van Rhee (1999, pp. 2–3).

158 For France see Jeuland (2021, p. 19 ff); for Italy see Ferraris (p. 35 ff); for Spain see De Benito (p. 46 ff).

159 For a detailed examination between 'cassation' (in this case in France) and 'revision' (in Germany) see Ferrand (1993, *passim*); Bierschenk (2015, pp. 11–15).

160 For the oral argument in trial, see the American context in Langbein (2012, p. 522), Burbank and Subrin (2011, p. 399).

less of their own attention on cases that they thought could be corrected without full judicial treatment.[161] This assessment raises the question, then, of which cases are most likely to be decided correctly without receiving full judicial treatment. Based on how review takes place (vertical arrangements between lower and appellate courts), at least two categories of cases that do not need full treatments could be conceived of (i) those that are most likely to be reviewed effectively through a nonargument review process, and (ii) those that are least likely to have errors upon arrival at the appellate courts. Reducing the number of cases for the superior courts is an important issue. Appellate courts and the highest or supreme courts are struggling in many countries with large caseloads and budgets that have not adapted to ensure reduced waiting times. At the same time, too many unmeritorious cases are primarily motivated by delaying tactics while, simultaneously, meritorious and other public interest cases need prompt judicial attention.[162]

1. The appellate court management should focus on its responsibility to reach the correct or preferable decision. The court is an active participant in the review process, ensuring that each application is managed appropriately and proceeds in a timely manner, making necessary additional competences for the case management of appeals. From a vertical point of view, it is important to emphasize the main role played by an appeal and by a supreme court. A supreme court pursues additional ends to provide a guide for future decisions within the judiciary system. Because appellate and supreme courts serve different functions, selection criteria of cases may be necessary.[163] The superior courts, through the appeals, perform multiple and critical functions in our legal system to achieve different ends, including error correction, facilitating the uniform application of legal rules, general direction for the development of law, prospective interpretation, enforcement, and uniformity[164] for the accountability of the rule of law. In discharging their functions and seeking to reconcile the competing desires for finality and accuracy, appealed cases also form the foundation of what most observers know about the legal system.[165] Despite their importance, appellate decisions can too easily distort perceptions of the legal system.[166]

How could the courts reasonably maximize error correction and law development together? If error correction and law development could easily be measured and quantified, one could create a function that sought to maximize a combination of the two. Unfortunately, however, both error correction and law development defy precise

---

161 Reinhardt (1993, pp. 52, 53) ('*We seem to assume that judges can perform the same quality of work regardless of the number of cases they are assigned. That simply is not correct. Most of us are now working to maximum capacity. As a result, when our caseload increases, we inevitably pay less attention to the individual cases… Those who believe we are doing the same quality work that we did in the past are simply fooling themselves.*').

162 Kodek (2014, pp. 35–52).

163 Fiss (1983, pp. 1442, 1446), Bravo-Hurtado and Van Rhee (2021, pp. 5–7).

164 Frost (2008, p. 1567) (arguing that uniformity may not worth the cost of achieving it and that heterogeneity may, at times, be preferable).

165 Robertson (2013, p. 1219).

166 Eisenberg (2004, pp. 659–688).

measurement. If one attempted to find a measure for error correction, the appellate court's reversal rate—or the rate at which they reverse the lower court and agency decisions—would seem promising. Yet even without precise measures, it is still possible to consider how a court could reasonably attempt to maximize both goals by thinking through what maximization of these goals might look like in theory.[167] There is a tension between less appeal-more efficiency and more appeal-less efficiency. To simplify the task, one can disaggregate the two variables and consider maximizing them each in turn.[168] Starting with error correction, what would it mean for appellate courts to allocate judicial attention to as many cases as possible only to control that the lower decisions were free of material error? Or, put another way, what would it mean for courts to attempt to minimize the error rate when working with limited resources? An important mechanism is to develop adequate judicial selection criteria for case review that entails a combination of formal limitation with discretion to control its own docket.[169]

6.1 The Right to Appeal in Comparative Perspective

Prof. Marcus remarks that, in many legal systems, particularly of the continental model, frequent opportunities for review of first instance decisions are normal. In such a system, there would inevitably be limits on the ability of a judge managing litigation to control events because many decisions would be subject to frequent reconsideration by judges on a higher court.[170] The American system is very different.[171] *'There is no 'judicial course' in American law schools. Trial court (first instance) judges are not young 'learners', they are usually long-seasoned trial lawyers, often with much more legal experience than some of the younger appellate judges. Appellate review is not a learning experience for trial judges, and is not a normal thing.'*[172] Instead, most American cases *never* reach a point when an appeal is even possible. Under the 'final judgment rule', an appeal is normally not possible until all claims involving all parties are fully resolved by a final judgment.[173] The vast majority of cases never reach that point. For example, most cases are settled, and if there is a settlement, there is no appealable judgment.[174]

---

[167] Levy (2013, p. 401).

[168] Comp. Rehnquist (1993, pp. 1, 3) (*'Simply put, time and again the nation has looked to the federal courts to handle a larger and larger proportion of society's problems.... The point is that as a result of people looking to the federal courts those courts have become overburdened and the system has become clogged.'*).

[169] Herzog and Karlen (1982, p. 54).

[170] Marcus (2017a, b).

[171] See Marcus (2014, p. 105).

[172] Marcus (2017a, b).

[173] See 28 U.S.C.N 1291.

[174] Marcus (2017a, b).

As an opposing point of view that supports the right to appeal as part of a fair trial and promotes the values of institutional legitimacy, respect for individual dignity could be mentioned, among other positions.[175] The standard for reviewing a wide range of orders is an *abuse of discretion.* The result of the timing rule and the standard of review is that managerial judges in the U.S. have a very free hand. This does not mean that American judges ordinarily abuse their power. Giving the authority of a judicial officer to make sensible decisions about these matters is better than having multiple deciders making divergent choices.[176] An example is the case of California, although the California Constitution establishes appellate courts, where it does not explicitly recognize an appeal of right in civil or criminal cases. An appeal of right is established by statute in all cases, but this appeal is not necessarily to the California Court of Appeal.[177] Regardless of whether an appeal is to the appellate department of the superior court or to the California Court of Appeal, as in the federal courts, ordinarily an appeal must be taken only from the 'one final judgment' in an action (that is, the ultimate ruling that resolves all issues of all parties).[178] The one final judgment rule, which the California Supreme Court has characterized as 'a fundamental principle of appellate practice', is based on the theory 'that piecemeal disposition and multiple appeals in a single action would be oppressive and costly, and that a review of intermediate rulings should await the final disposition of the case.'[179] Neither is there a right to appeal in England; appellants must get permission from the court above or from the first instance judge. The Supreme Court hears each year only those cases selected by the court.[180]

In Italy, Prof. Lupoi describes appellate courts as courts of second instance, for appeals against the decisions of the lower court. They have functional territorial competence over the court of first instance (Tribunali) located within their circuit (on a regional or multi-provincial scale).[181] The Italian Constitution does not provide for a constitutional right to bring an appeal against a judgment of first instance. In other words, the Italian constitutional system does not grant a right to the so-called double tier of jurisdiction). Such double tier of adjudication on the merits, however, is recognized by the Code of Civil Procedure (Arts. 339 et seq.).[182]

As Prof. Stürner remarks, the German constitution does not guarantee a right of appeal.[183] This position is supported considering there is no explicit provision in the

---

[175] Robertson (2013, p. 1219): '*As a result, if appellate remedies are removed from the procedural framework, the system as a whole cannot provide adequate due process protection. Finally, recognizing constitutional protection for appellate rights would also express a normative policy choice, promoting the values of institutional legitimacy, respect for individual dignity.*'

[176] *Idem.*

[177] Saltzman (2014, pp. 95–104), Eisenberg and Heise (2015).

[178] *In re Baycol Cases I and II*, 51 Cal.4th 751, 756, 248 P.3d 681 (2011).

[179] *Morehart v. County of Santa Barbara*, 7 Cal.4th 725, 872 P.2d 143 (1994).

[180] Andrews (2017), Andrews (2014, pp. 73–94).

[181] Lupoi (2018, pp. 153 ff), Caponi (2012, pp. 1153–1178).

[182] *Idem.*

[183] Stürner (2021, p. 81). See e.g., the German Constitutional Court decision *BVerfGE* 1, 433, 437.

constitution conferring a right to a further instance, disregarding the existence of a general guarantee of judicial protection against any act of the public authority and that courts of law are part of the public authority. Some positions use this reasoning to support the idea that, in principle, an appeal must lie against any decision of a court.[184] '*However, as this would lead to an infinite chain of appeals, it is up to the legislator to set up limits, taking into account other constitutional values such as the principle of finality. Restrictions on access to the appellate court must be designed following the principle of proportionality.*'[185]

In Chile, there is no 'right to appeal' at the level of constitutional regulation. In addition, there have been some decisions made by the Chilean Constitutional Court that considered the right to appeal as part of the due process clause, but only in criminal cases. Formally, however, there is no filtering mechanism such as a 'leave to appeal' request or what is equivalent to a *certiorari,* only an examination of formal requirements.[186]

Based on Art. 46 of the Constitution of the Republic of Poland, everyone has the right to a fair and public consideration of a case without undue delay by a competent, independent, and impartial court. According to Art. 176 of the Constitution of the Republic of Poland, court proceedings are performed in at least two instances.[187] The system and characteristics of the courts and proceedings before the courts are defined by legislation. The judgment of the court of first instance is entitled to an appeal to the court of second instance. There is no closed list of appellate charges.[188]

6.2 Superior Courts Case Management and Cases Selection

Case management in appellate courts has often been overlooked. Appellate court decisions need special 'case management' to handle the following matters: (i) whether a case will receive oral argument or be decided solely on the briefs[189]; (ii) whether its disposition will be drafted by judges and their law clerks or by staff attorneys; (iii) whether it will be resolved by a published or an unpublished opinion[190]; and (iv) the dynamic generated by the interplay between dockets and court priorities. When dockets were small, courts did not have to make as many difficult choices about which practices to prioritize because practices were not in competition. Moreover, a thorough discussion of case management in the appellate and supreme courts requires not only a descriptive account but also an analytical account about why

[184] *Idem.*

[185] *Ibidem*; Stürner (2002, p. 79 et seq).

[186] *Idem.*

[187] Flaga-Gieruszynska and Klich (2017).

[188] Flaga-Gieruszynska and Klich (2017).

[189] Tidmarsh (2016, pp. 475–486).

[190] Wallace (2005, pp. 187, 192), Haworth (1973 p. 257), Martineu (1986, p. 1), Schiavoni (2002, p. 1859).

courts operate the way that they do, as well as a normative account of whether differences in operation can be justified.[191] An additional point is the use of mediation in appellate courts, which has received surprisingly little scholarly attention. While trial mediation has been the subject of a large and sustained literature focused on how mediation detracts from the public role of adjudication, the same is unaware that mediation programs also exist at the appellate level.[192] When the number of cases brought to the Supreme Courts exceeds the number that can be resolved we have two problems connected: (i) the undue delay, that means unjustice; and (ii) the obtacle for the public and private purposes served by the supreme courts.[193]

The courts' priorities are actually a combination of these and other values, including actual fairness, legitimacy, efficiency, and public interest, to name a few. The courts decide which practices to favor based on the values that they determine are most important; determining which practices will be most effective at maximizing those values is an ongoing problem.[194] Inevitably, cases in quality, type, and relevance produce asymmetric appellate reversal rates. Various factors affect appeal rates: incentive to litigation and settlement, the difference between the litigants, and the differential prognosis of an appeal's success.[195] The appropriate filter system has a qualitative and quantitative role and purpose. On the one hand, a qualitative approach allows the court to select those cases that are truly relevant and meritorious, thus avoiding frivolous cases. On the other hand, the filter has a quantitative approach in the application of the proportionality principle that takes into account the number of suitable and possible cases to be known by the court, human resources, and limited time. Proper filters tend to guarantee decisions of better quality.[196]

There are multiple ways to select the cases to be decided by the superior courts. The overload problem could be addressed by a combination of remedies such as reducing the quantity through court fees or access restrictions with an admissibility examination according to the instance goals. Usually, such decisions depend on public policy directives to be examined and decided upon with the cooperation of parliament by statutes. The increase is often intended to reduce the number of unmeritorious cases or applications that are chiefly designed to delay proceedings and even to get them shelved indeterminately.[197] If this proposal is adopted, the fees for civil cases will be higher than the actual cost of the proceedings. Nevertheless, increasing court fees can prevent access to justice and may, consequently, have adverse effects on the economy. In many countries, however, this will not be a big issue because even after

---

[191] See Cooper and Berman (1996, p. 685), Richman and Reynolds (1996, p. 273).

[192] Jordan (2007, p. 55).

[193] Bravo-Hurtado and Van Rhee (2021, pp. 5–7).

[194] Levy (2011, p. 315).

[195] Eisenberg and Farber (2013, pp. 73–109).

[196] Drago et al. (2015, pp. 1–20).

[197] Frydman (2008, pp. 18–29).

a substantial increase in court fees, these are still a small fraction of the actual costs of a case.[198]

Another way to reduce caseloads is to limit access by the law regulation of the appeal, for instance, by setting a financial minimum for civil cases, such as in Germany. This approach seems to focus primarily on reducing the number of appeals. The measure simplifies the appeal procedures and thereby reduces the number of appeal hearings. In the European Judiciaries, there appears to be a preference for various forms of leave arrangements, which allow judges to determine themselves which cases merit appeal instead of mechanically applying legal provisions. There are many cases in which it is immediately clear that the decision of the court of first instance will hold. The decision to leave the appeal depends on the probability of a meritorious case being accepted for a second instance.[199]

Prof. Stürner remarks that, in Germany, different approaches are taken in some jurisdictions to managing and tracking cases depending on their value, complexity, or other facts. One basic distinction is between cases of a claim value up to € 5,000 and values of claims superior to that. The first category is dealt with by the local courts (also with exclusive jurisdiction for certain types of cases as lease contracts and noncontentious matters) and the second by the regional courts.[200] This distinction between regional and local courts produces a different appellate regime. While the regional courts are competent to hear appeals against decisions of local courts, appeals from decisions of regional courts as first instance courts are decided by Higher Regional Courts. The proceedings in all of those cases, in principle, follow the general approach set out above, in which the regional court is the role model for all other courts and divisions. A single judge will sit in local court proceedings.[201] In general, almost every case will be suitable for appellate review. One admissibility requirement is that the value of the appeal subject matter should be greater than € 600. Even for cases below that threshold, the court of first instance may grant leave to appeal, namely if the legal matter is of fundamental significance or wherever the further development of the law or the interests in ensuring uniform adjudication require a decision to be handed down by the court of appeal.[202] Although the decision to leave the appeal is not discretionary, according to the mentioned statutory requirements, there is a considerable 'bulk of case law to clarify exactly what is a question of fundamental significance.[203] The allegation to support the appeal could

---

[198] See regarding the delay and the organization and administrative issues within the courts Bóka (2014, pp. 141–161).

[199] *Idem.*

[200] Stürner (2021, p. 81).

[201] Stürner (2021, p. 82). By the same token, cases heard by Regional Courts in the vast majority of cases are decided by a single judge. For petty cases with a value of the claim of up to 600 Euro, the Local Court may decide at its equitably exercised discretion on how to implement its proceedings. On the contrary, large commercial cases will be heard by a three-judge panel of the commercial division of the Regional Court. Usually there will be a fairly lengthy preliminary proceedings conducted in writing in order to prepare the case for the oral hearing.

[202] *Idem.*

[203] *Ibidem*; Bierschenk (2015, pp. 111–115), Dondi et al. (2015, p. 297).

be a wrong decision from a legal point of view or from a factual basis, but there is a limited scope of review of fact-finding.[204] Restrictions of access could be up for evaluation today since the 2001 Reform is a fairly efficient filter.[205]

Prof. Stürner remarks on three key points of case management in appellate courts. (i) The weeding out of unmeritorious cases is done in several stages.' The lower court, which probably knows the case best, decides on the admissibility of the appeal. 'That seems convincing with regard to the further development of the law or the interests in ensuring uniform adjudication, but maybe less so for the question of fundamental legal significance as this implies errors of law made by the appellate court itself.'[206] (ii) Inferior judges/law clerks. There are no inferior judges in the formal sense. But as every court, the Bundesgerichtshof is supported by a court registry. Each senate has its own registry with two or three clerks working there.' In addition, the Federal Supreme Court has around 50 academic staff.[207] (iii) The judgments: on appeal, the president of each senate allocates a file to one of the judges, the rapporteur. 'Each judgment, whether rendered after an oral hearing or not, is given in writing. However, in the case of a decision without oral hearing the rapporteur may give his account orally, while in all other cases he will do it in writing.'[208]

In addition to the mentioned restrictive appeal possibilities in American civil procedure, Saltzman explains that the appellate review in the California state courts is limited in scope in three basic ways.[209] First, as in the U.S. federal court system, the review is limited to reviewing the record in the trial court and determining if the court erred. '*In short, the trial court's role is that of fact finder and decision-maker and the parties to an appeal cannot retry their cases in appellate courts based on new evidence or new and different theories.*'[210] Second, the trial court's decision is the basis for the appellate court's review and decision. '*The trial court's decision is the starting point for the appellate court, and there is a presumption that the decision is correct, especially if a jury decided the case.*' Based on this presumption, there are three basic standards of review for civil cases: substantial evidence, abuse of discretion, or de novo review.[211] Finally and third, in addition to the deference to the trial court, the decision '*may not be reversed simply because the trial court erred; the error may be considered 'harmless' and harmless error is not a basis for setting aside a trial court decision.*'[212]

[204] *Ibidem.*

[205] Bierschenk (2015, pp. 1–5).

[206] *Ibidem.*

[207] *Ibidem.*

[208] *Ibidem.*

[209] Levy (2011, p. 315) (describing and analyzing the case management practices of five of the federal courts of appeals).

[210] Saltzman (2014, pp. 95–104).

[211] *Idem.*

[212] *Ibidem.*; for the USA Supreme Court see Marcus (2021a, b, pp. 183 ff); a good comparation would be with the UK, see Sorabji (2021a, b, pp. 155 ff).

In Italy, the ordinary appeal does not need meeting specific grounds and can be also be based on the general injustice suffered by the losing party. Apart from minor exceptions, every first instance decision may be appealed against before a superior judge. In 2012, however, access to the appeal level has been restricted through the introduction of the so-called filter to the appeal.[213] There are two admissibility examination stages (filters): first, the summons must contain the appealed part of the decision, should the proposed change and provide supporting evidence about the circumstances of why it is considered a violation of law; and second, according to the examination of the appeal summons, there should be a reasonable likelihood of success.[214] Moreover, the petition must state the circumstances from which the alleged violation of the law derives and their relevance in relation to the decision appealed against. The appeal judge should be in the position to decide the case by simply reading the petition (and the other party's reply) with no need to read any further materials. Many commentators have stated that the lawmaker has thus implemented the principle of self sufficiency of the appeal petition.[215]

6.3 *The Dilemmas of the Supreme Courts*

Among the issues listed at the end of the last paragraph, the heavy workload of the supreme court has been a serious problem for a number of decades. A right to review has dramatically increased the volume of appeal cases of supreme courts.[216] In the last decade, some procedural devices were introduced to reduce the workload of the court with modest results.[217] Filters on access to the Supreme or Cassational Court have been adopted to reduce the number of appeals only to those having 'great significance', relying on the discretionary decision powers of the Supreme or Cassational courts.[218] As Prof. Stürner explains in the case of Germany, these choices could present 'dilemmas.' From one perspective, the Supreme Court should emphasize litigants' interests; yet a case should also be relevant for its contribution

---

[213] Lupoi (2018), Ferraris (2014, pp. 259–272).

[214] Ferraris (2014, pp. 264–265).

[215] Lupoi (2018, pp. 153 ff); for a critical view see Caponi (2012, pp. 1153–1178), Ferraris (2021, pp. 35 ff).

[216] Dondi et al. (2015, pp. 307–318), CEPEJ (2014, p. 190) '*A clearance rate dose to 100% indicates the ability of the court or of a judicial System to resolve more or less as many cases as the number of incoming cases within the given time period. A clearance rate above 100% indicates the ability of the System to resolve more cases than received, thus reducing any potential backlog. Finally, if the number of incoming cases is higher than the number of resolved cases, the clearance rate will fall below 100%. When a clearance rate goes below 100%, the number of unresolved cases at the end of a reporting period (backlog) will rise.*'

[217] Stevens (2017, pp. 113–121).

[218] Hathaway (2001, pp. 601, 605), Perry (1987, pp. 215, 244) ('*[T]he state cannot justifiably permit the parties in one of its courtrooms to be treated in a manner that is at variance with how they (or any other set of litigants) would be treated in the courtroom next door.*').

to legal system values such as accountability, uniformity, and general directions for future cases as the result of a decision as the 'last word.' Maybe there are no 'dilemmas', but only complementary purposes.[219]

Let me provide one example to illustrate the courts' main goals of composition and articulation: the German Federal Court. According to Prof. Stürner, in the German judicial system (I extend this reasoning to supreme courts in general), '*When evaluating the role of supreme courts the main problem consists in finding the right balance between the goal of doing justice in the individual case and the overarching responsibility of every Supreme Court to clarify and develop the law.*' The permanent challenge through the history of reforms to the access to the German Federal Court of Justice seems to be an attempt to find a middle point. '*In Germany, traditionally, much weight has been placed on the goal of individual justice. However, in recent decades the collective aspects of Revision have been strengthened. The major reform of 2001 not only introduced restrictions to the Federal Court of Justice, but also reshaped the entire procedural system, giving more weight to the first instance. This has led to a significant reduction in the caseload of the Federal Court of Justice.*'[220] The role of the German Federal Court is not the focal point of the debate because fairly efficient filters of access have been successfully introduced in past years. At the same time as the 2001 reform, the German Federal Court recognized the priority of admitting cases with a relevant legal question useful for a future greater number of cases instead of those with only individual interest (independent of the amount).[221] The composition of the German Federal Court is interested in achieving the described priority goals of 129 judges (civil and criminal division). The civil division has 84 judges; it is divided into 12 Senates sitting in panels of five judges, each having predefined competences and specializations.[222] Prof. Stürner remarks that the degree of specialization also '*helps increase the quality of decisions and other sides to ensure uniformity within the 12 Senates a Grand Chamber will convene to decide on the request of one Senate wishing to deviate from the jurisprudence of other Senates.*' These are assisted by clerks with lower judicial tasks with no participation in case management or decisions.[223] Also worthy of mention are the academic staff of approximately 50 promising junior judges who prepare the legal work. It is important to mention that the parties to the dispute must be represented by an attorney admitted to practice before said court. There are currently only 43 such attorneys with a high reputation and sufficient experience.[224] This is an example of multiple public goals in a Supreme Court, from the filtering cases to be admitted, the guarantee of uniformity

[219] Van Rhee and Fu (2017, pp. 1–11), Genn (2010, pp. 10–23), Kornhauser (2012, pp. 19–41), Taruffo (2012, p. 341).

[220] Stürner (2021, p. 75); See also Kern (2016, p. 76).

[221] Stürner (2021, p. 100), Gross (2012, p. 27); Comp. Dondi et al. (2015, pp. 312–314).

[222] *Idem.*

[223] *Ibidem.*

[224] *Ibidem.*

in the quality of the court's decisions, and a pertinent and adequate court composition and articulation.[225] The goal of the German appellate proceedings before the German Federal Court is 'revision', not 'cassation.' '*This means that in the event of a successful appeal the judgment of the lower court will not just be quashed. The Bundesgerichtshof may hand down a decision on the merits, provided that 'the judgment is reversed only due to a violation of the law, in application of the law to the situation of fact as established, and if in light of said situation the matter is ready for the final decision to be taken.*''[226]

In Chile, with 21 judges in a Supreme Court with the appeal as 'cassation', the court has worked since 1995 under the notion of specialized chambers. '*Regarding its ordinary work schedule, the Supreme Court is divided in three main chambers: the first chamber or civil chamber, the second chamber or criminal chamber and the third chamber or constitutional and administrative chamber. When the Supreme Court works under an extraordinary schedule, the Court is divided in four chambers, the last one gets to know labor and work benefits issues. However, this is not a specialization due to special knowledge or training by the Supreme Court judges, but an internal work distribution.*'[227] Out of the formal admissibility requirements, there is no filtering mechanism such as a 'leave to appeal' regarding public goals or similar objectives. The individual interests of the litigants seem to be, formally, the key points.[228] '*According to the law on the books, if the legal requirements are met, every person has the right to go up to the Supreme Court. However, there is anecdotal and un-systematized information that presents a different scenario in which informally, in the context of the admissibility stage, the supreme courts filters the recourses presented by the parties to control their workload.*'[229]

In Poland, a cassation appeal submitted to the Supreme Court is inadmissible in some cases considering property rights, labor law and social security, and family law. A cassation appeal can be based on the following grounds: breach of substantive law by misinterpretation or misapplication or breach of the rules of proceedings if it could have a significant impact on the outcome of the case. The Supreme Court accepts a cassation appeal to be heard if there is a relevant legal issue in the case, if there is a need to interpret legal provisions that raise serious doubts or divergences in the jurisprudence of courts, or if the invalidity of proceedings occurs or the cassation appeal is clearly justified. The Supreme Court decides to accept or refuse a cassation appeal in a closed session. The decision does not require written justification.[230]

In Italy, a constitutional rule, such as Art. 111, para. 7o, guarantees the appeal by cassation; therefore, the rule could be considered obsolete.[231] The Court of Cassation

225 Comp. Schafft (2005, *passim*).

226 Stürner (2021, p. 84).

227 Odgers and Maureira (2017).

228 See the critics and description of the 'Cassation' and the Chilean Supreme Court role in Bravo-Hurtado (2017, pp. 149–173); other point of view in Tavolari (2006, pp. 471–500).

229 Odgers and Maureira (2017).

230 Flaga-Gieruszynska and Klich (2017).

231 Caponi (2012, pp. 1153–1178), Pisani (2009, p. 380), Ferraris (2021, pp. 35 ff).

adopted the German model in a recent reform, inserting a filter to the process of appeal admissibility.[232] The filter rules that the court should evaluate the complaint of violation when it involves a major issue of general concern or has been resolved in contradiction with the court's constant precedent. In this way, the admissibility of the appeal is made dependent on its consistency or not with a general clause, a general clause with an interpretation of the court excluding the use of its discretionary power.[233]

The highest court in Perú is the Supreme Court, which has jurisdiction for cassation appeals and for ordinary appeals from the regional superior courts. According to the Organic Law of the Judiciary, the Supreme Court is divided into three rooms: a civil hall, a criminal hall, and a constitutional and social hall. Although there are only three rooms according to the organic law because the caseload has increased with time, additional rooms have been created provisionally, but in practice, the work has become permanent. For example, there are two civil rooms (one permanent and one transitory), two criminal rooms (one permanent and one transitory), and four constitutional and social rooms (one permanent and three transitory). The Supreme Court itself has not been consistent in the self-determination of its own powers, preventing its proper functioning as the last stage and word without clear goals regarding uniformity, the development of law, or the consideration of predominantly individual interests. There is no special case selection filter to access, only formal admissibility requirements.[234]

The French Court of Cassation comprises six chambers. The presidents of the halls, of which there are seven in total, preside over the hearings of their formation. There are a total of 120 counselors, that is, judges of the court, to whom are added 35 planned for the appointment of the first presidents of appellate courts and the president of the Court of First Instance of Paris. Counselors are also called upon to attend different commissions and institutions, for which they are usually nominated by designation or proposed by the first president. The 70 legal advisors are chosen among the magistrates who have been active for a period that does not exceed ten years. An appeal in cassation tends to make the main function of the Court of Cassation to censure the nonconformity of decisions with the law.[235] The Court of Cassation controls the correct application of substantive and procedural law. Arts. 38 to 43 of Law No. 2016–1547 of November 18, 2016, on the modernization of justice in the twenty-first century are devoted to proceedings before the Court of Cassation, but a more detailed reform is still in discussion, i.e., about the admissibility filters.[236] The Court of Cassation must devote itself to appeals on the only questions of law that merit its intervention—new questions of law or those which present serious difficulties.[237] Almost all the Western democracies have sought to

[232] Dondi et al. (2015, pp. 312–314).

[233] See Caponi (2012, pp. 1153–1178).

[234] Priori (2017).

[235] See Jeuland (2021, pp. 19 ff).

[236] Guillaume and Bechillon (2014).

[237] Guinchard et al. (2015, p. 278), Dondi et al. (2015, p. 315).

refocus their supreme courts on these regulatory functions. To do the same, the Court of Cassation must strengthen its 'filters' system to make it effective. A case should be rejected that evidences an absence of a decision against fundamental principles, a lack of interest in the development of the law, or a lack of interest in the unification of case law.[238] The rationalization of litigation and the reduction of admissible appeals must be accompanied by better motivation and better dissemination of decisions. The aim of filtering here is to be able to select the most important cases for the Courts of Cassation to be able to fulfill their traditional functions of pronouncing the law, unifying the jurisprudence, and controlling the stoppages of appellate courts to fully assume their normative function.[239] Hence, the need for filtering and differentiated business processing depends on their level of importance.[240]

7 Conclusions

1. The reference to efficiency in a judicial system is vital because efficiency can be seen as a facet of the wider claim to the effectiveness of judicial protection of rights. This does not reduce the discussion to one of conforming with a market ideology where the judicial protection of rights depends only on a profit-maximizing and cost-minimizing approach.
2. The principle of case management is that the court, rather than the litigants, controls the pace of litigation. It is a modern approach to dispute resolution that seeks to move away from the bitter adversarial clashes of the past and encourage a greater degree of cooperation and partnership among all concerned.
3. Judicial attention has come to be a scarce resource for several reasons: (i) the rate of cases per judgeship has grown precipitously in lower, appellate, and supreme courts; (ii) there are reasons to discuss various proposals that scholars and judges have offered in response to the rising caseload, including ways to reduce the number of filings, increase the number of judges, and improve efficiency in the courts with an appropriated case and court management principles; (iii) there are frameworks to be taken into account regarding access to the courts and the effective protection of rights; and (iv) the demand for judicial attention will continue to exceed the supply of judicial time, thereby rendering judicial attention a scarce resource.
4. Critical components within an efficient judicial system are the court and case management. These depend on the court structure and arrangements within and between the courts from both a horizontal and from a vertical point of view. The structural design of a judicial system depends on multiple factors; one

---

[238] Jean (2017, pp. 42–43).

[239] Rapport de la Comission de Réflexion sur la Réforme de la court de Cassation (April 2017). https://www.courdecassation.fr/IMG///Rapport sur la réforme de la Cour de cassation.pdf. Accessed 1 Dec 2020.

[240] *Idem.*

major consideration is the legal, cultural context. Judicial reform should have as its objective the improvement of the quality of justice and the efficiency and effectiveness of the judiciary while strengthening and protecting the independence of the judiciary. Case management is a judicial process that provides effective, efficient, and purposeful treatment to a case so as to achieve a timely and qualitative resolution of a dispute.

5. However, it is necessary to offer good arguments to justify a change in the judicial role and the horizontal and vertical arrangements for effective case and court management. These reasons of public policy are not only of interest to the legislator but are also essential in the judicial phase within a legal, cultural context. The legislator designs a norm to achieve a desirable social goal and then behaves, in that sense, as a macro-generator of public policies.
6. The horizontal arrangement has two important components: (i) the specialization of the courts and (ii) the distribution in the court with the flexibility to adapt to the importance and/or the complexity of the case (single judge, a panel of judges, etc.). The first point could be described as distinguishing between ordinary and specialized courts, whether or not specialized courts are formally differentiated. That is, the court is unlikely to assert excessive control when its workload is excessive and tends to increase. That is why judicial management of the process also has an aspect of dejudicialization. Distribution and redistribution of tasks depend on the court's organization and composition. The basic idea of redistributing tasks of courts (panel and individual judges) and support staff is to allow judges to concentrate on the core of their adjudication tasks. Furthermore, horizontal arrangements should be taken with reference to vertical arrangements. They are related through the interplay between superior and lower courts. In superior courts, the role and ends of appeal, the filter to access, the caseload and scope of review, and the organization that takes into account that the number of judges is not the same as those of the lower courts. The case and court management should be different. The crisis in the administration of justice must be addressed and treated on several fronts, as the problems have several causes that are fed back to time.
7. Case management review should take into account alternative routes to resolution, including ADR under the conditions presented above regarding the free option of parties and public policy.
8. In general, the appellate stage must first identify what variables should be maximized, and second, confront the reality that the potential variables defy easy measurement. How can courts reasonably maximize error correction and pursue law development together? If error correction and law development could easily be measured and quantified, one could create a function that sought to maximize a combination of the two.
9. Among the topics listed at the end of the last section, the heavy workload of the supreme courts has been a serious problem for a number of decades. Recognizing a right to review has increased the caseload of supreme courts. Although some argue that supreme courts should decide every case to protect the interests of litigants interests, others posit that cases are relevant for supreme court review

only if they contribute to legal system values such as accountability, uniformity, and general directions for future cases because the decision is the 'last word.' Perhaps these are not really 'dilemmas' but rather complementary ends.

Finally and as the general contribution of this work, the aims of reform of justice systems and the judiciary must be predicated on sound principles that will improve the quality of justice for citizens and should include complex goals, including improving the quality of access to justice, increasing public confidence in the judicial system, improving the image of the judiciary, and providing an efficient system that does not compromise the quality of justice or access to justice.

References

Albers P (2008) Improvements of judicial systems: European experiences. Int J Court Adm 1:45–57

Alexy R (2014) Constitutional rights and proportionality. Revus: J Const Theory Phil Law 2:51–65

Alt E, Le Theule MA (2011) La justice aux prises avec l'éthique et la performance. Pyramide 22:137–159

Althamer C, Weller M (eds) (2017) Europäische Mindeststandards für Spruchkörper. Mohr, Tübingen, pp 139–164

Alwidian S, Amyot D, Babin G (2017) Evaluating the potential of technology in justice systems using goal modeling. In: Aïmeur E, Ruhi U, Weiss M (eds) E-technologies: embracing the internet of things. Springer, pp 185–202

Amrani Mekki S (2000) La conduite active des proces civils. France report. In: IAPL Conference 2017 (unpublished)

Andrews N (2012) A fresh start: the four pillars of civil justice judicial independence. In: Shetreet S, Forsyth CH (eds) The culture of judicial independence. Nijhoff, Leiden-Boston, pp 97–109

Andrews N (2014) Restriction on appeal in English law. In: Uzelac A, Van Rhee CH (eds) Nobody's perfect: comparative essays on appeals and other means of recourse. Intersentia, Cambridge, pp 73–94

Andrews N (2017) English case management system. England report. In: IAPL Conference 2017 (unpublished)

Badó A (2014) 'Fair' selection of judges in a modern democracy. In: Badó A (ed) Fair trial and judicial independence. Springer, Dordrecht, pp 27–58

Badó A, Szarvas K (2014) 'As luck would have it...': fairness in the distribution of cases and judicial independence. In: Badó A (ed) Fair trial and judicial independence. Springer, Dordrecht, pp 59–73

Baer S (2009) Dignity, liberty, equality: a fundamental rights triangle of constitutionalism. Univ Tor Law J 59:417–468

Baldwin J (1985a) Pre-trial justice. Blackwell, London

Baldwin J (1985b) Pre-trial justice: a study of case settlement in magistrates' courts. Blackwell, Oxford

Barak A (2012) Proportionality: constitutional rights and their limitations. Cambridge University Press, Cambridge

Baum L (2008) Judges and their audiences. Princeton University Press, Princeton

Benvenuti S (2015) The European judicial training network and its role in the strategy for the Europeanization of national judges. Int J Court Adm 7:59–67

Bettinger N (2016) Prozessmodelle im Zivilverfahrensrecht: Erfolg des Hauptverhandlungsmodells. Mohr Siebeck, Tübingen

Bierschenk L (2015) Die zweite Instanz im deutschen und französischen Zivilverfahren. Mohr Siebeck, Tübingen

Bóka J (2014) 'To delay justice is injustice': a comparative analysis of (un) reasonable delay. In: Badó A (ed) Fair trial and judicial independence. Springer, Dordrecht, pp 141–161
Bovend'Eert P (2016) Judicial independence and separation of powers: a case study in modern court management. Eur Public Law 22:333–353
Brändli B (2013) Prozessökonomie im schweizrischen Recht. Stämpfli, Bern
Bravo-Hurtado P (2017) The end of cassation in Chile? Recourse to the Chilean supreme court in civil matters. In: Van Rhee CH, Fu Y (eds) Supreme courts in transition in China and the west: adjudication at the service of public goals. Springer, Cham, pp 149–173
Bravo-Hurtado P, Van Rhee CH (eds) (2021) Supreme courts under pressure: controlling caseload in the administration of civil justice. Springer, Cham
Briggs Lord Justice (2016) Civil courts structure review: Final report. https://www.judiciary.gov.uk/wp-content/uploads/2016/07/civil-courts-structure-review-final-report-jul-16-final-1.pdf. Accessed 1 Dec 2020
Burbank S, Friedman B (eds) (2002) Judicial independence at the crossroads: an interdisciplinary approach. Sage Publications
Burbank S, Subrin S (2011) Litigation and democracy: restoring a realistic prospect of trial. Harv Cr-C L L Rev 46:399
Cadiet L (2017) La reforma de la justicia y el proceso civil en Francia: La cuestión del acceso a la justicia. In: Priori G (ed) Derecho material y proceso. Lima, Palestra, pp 83–95
Calabresi G (2016) The future of law and economics: essays in reform and recollection. Yale University Press, New Haven
Caponi R (2010) II principio di proporzíonalitá nella giustizia civile: Prime note sistematiche. Riv Trim Dir e Proc Civile 65:389–403
Caponi R (2012) La riforma dei mezzi di impugnazione. Riv Trim Dir e Proc Civile 66:1153–1178
Caponi R (2015a) 'Doing Business' come scopo della giustizia civile? Il Foro Italiano 5:3
Caponi R (2015b) 'Just settlement' or 'just about settlement?' Mediated agreements: a comparative overview of the basics. RabelsZ 79:117–141
Caponi R (2016) European minimum standards for courts. Independence, specialization, efficiency. A glance from Italy. Festschrift Professor Nikolaos K. Klamaris, vol 2, Sakkoulas Publications, Athens, pp 151–172
Cappelletti M (1974) Libertad individual y justicia social en el proceso civil italiano. In: Proceso, ideología, sociedad. Ediciones Legales Europa-America, Buenos Aires
Cappelletti M, Garth B (1984) A comparative conclusion. In: Cappelletti M (ed) Ordinary proceedings in first instance-international encyclopedia of comparative law. Mohr, Tübingen, pp 250, 252
Caseflow Management Handbook (2016) Guide for enhanced court administration in civil proceedings. Council EU, pp 13–34
CCJE (2011) Opinion No. (2011)14 of the CCJE on justice and information technologies (IT). https://www.coe.int/en/web/ccje/opinion-n-14-on-justice-and-information-technologies-it. Accessed 1 Dec 2020
CEPEJ (2014) Report on European judicial systems—edition 2014 (2012 data): efficiency and quality of justice. www.coe.int. Accessed 1 Dec 2020
CEPEJ (2016) Use of information technology in European courts. https://www.coe.int/t/dghl/cooperation/cepej/evaluation/2016/publication/REV1/2016_2-CEPEJStudy24-ITReport-EN.pdf. Accessed 1 Dec 2020
Chan P, Van Rhee CH (2021) Introduction. In: Chan P, Van Rhee CH (eds) Civil case management in the twenty-first century: court structures still matter. Springer, Singapore, pp 1–12
Chayes A (1976) The role of the judge in public law litigation. Harv L Rev 89:1281
Comoglio P (2014) II giudice specializzato in materia di impresa. Giappichelli, Torino
Cooper J, Berman D (1996) Passive virtues in the federal courts of appeals. Brook L Rev 66:685
Cortés P (ed) (2017) The new regulatory framework for consumer dispute resolution. Oxford University Press, Oxford

Da Fonseca Gajardoni F (2017) Procedimentos, déficit procedimental e condução ativa dos procedimentos civis pelo juiz no Brasil. Brazil report. In: IAPL Conference 2017 (unpublished)
Damaška M (1986) The faces of justice and state authority. Yale University Press, New Haven
Damaška M (2010) The common law/civil law divide: Residual truth of a misleading distinction. In: Walker J, Chase O (eds) Common law civil law and the future of categories. Lexis Nexis, p 3
Davis K, Fisher A, Kingsbury B (eds) (2012) Governance by indicators: global power through classification and rankings. Oxford
De Benito M (2021) Back in focus: case overload and case selection standards in the Spanish supreme court. In: Bravo-Hurtado P, Van Rhee CH (eds) Supreme courts under pressure: controlling caseload in the administration of civil justice. Springer, Cham, pp 49–74
Dondi A, Ansanelli V, Comoglio P (2015) Processsi civili in evoluzione: Una prospettiva comparata. Giuffre, Milano
Drago G, Fauvarque Cosson-Goré B (eds) (2015) L'accès au juge de cassation. Société de législation comparée, pp 1–20
Eisenberg T (2004) Appeal rates and outcomes in tried and nontried cases: further exploration of anti-plaintiff appellate outcomes. J Empir Legal Stud 1:659–688
Eisenberg T, Farber H (2013) Why do plaintiffs lose appeals? Biased trial courts, litigious losers, or low trial win rates? Am L Econ Rev 15:73–109
Eisenberg T, Heise M (2015) Plaintiphobia in state courts redux? An empirical study of state court trials on appeal. Cornell Law School research paper No. 14–02
Elliott E (1986) Managerial judging and the evolution of procedure. U Chi L Rev 53:306–309
Emiliou N (1998) The principle of proportionality in European law: a comparative study. Kluwer, London
ENCJ 2012, Vilnius Recommendation. https://www.encj.eu/images/stories/pdf/GA/Dublin/encj_report_judicial_reform_def.pdf. Accessed 1 Dec 2020
Ervo L (2017) Should fair trial rights be redefined? In: Uzelac A, Van Rhee CH (eds) Revisiting procedural human rights. Intersentia, Cambridge, pp 77–89
Ferrand F (1993) Cassation française et révision allemande: Essai sur le contrôle exercé en matière civile par la cour de cassation française et par la cour fédérale de justice de la république fédérale d'Allemagne. PUF
Felzmann H, Fosch-Villaronga E, Lutz C, Tamò-Larrieux A (2020) Towards transparency by design for artificial intelligence. Sci Eng Ethics 26:3333–3361
Ferrand F, Knetsch J, Zwickel M (2019) Introduction. In: Ferrand F, Knetsch J, Zwickel M (eds) Die Digitalisierung des Zivilrechts und der Ziviljustiz in Deutschland und Frankreich. FAU University Press, Erlangen, pp 15–20
Ferraris F (2014) The recent amendments to the Italian appeal system. In: Uzelac A, Van Rhee CH (eds) Nobody's perfect: comparative essays on appeals and other means of recourse. Intersentia, Cambridge, pp 259–272
Ferraris F (2021) Finding a cure or simply relieving symptoms? The case of the Italian supreme court. In: Bravo-Hurtado P, Van Rhee CH (eds) Supreme courts under pressure: controlling caseload in the administration of civil justice. Springer, Cham, pp 35–48
Ferreres Comella V (2009) Constitutional courts and democratic values: a European perspective. Yale University Press, New Haven, pp 10–25
Fiss O (1983) The bureaucratization of the judiciary. Yale L J 92:1442–1446
Fiss O (1984) Against settlement. Yale L J 93:1073
Flaga-Gieruszynska K, Klich A (2017) Poland report. In: IAPL Conference 2017 (unpublished)
Flanders S (1984) Blind umpires—a response to professor Resnik. Hastings L J 35:505–520
Fleck Z (2014) A comparative analysis of judicial power, organisational issues in judicial in judicature and the administration of courts. In: Badó A (ed) Fair trial and judicial independence. Springer, Dordrecht, pp 3–25
Frost A (2008) Overvaluing uniformity. Va L Rev 93:1567

Frydman B (2008) L'évolution des critères et des modes de contrôle de la qualité des décisions de justice. In: Mbongo P (ed) La qualité de la decision de justice. Conseil de l'Europe, Paris, pp 18–29
Gavin S (2006) Managerial justice in a post-daubert world. F R D 234:196
Genn H (2010) Judging civil justice. Cambridge University Press, Cambridge
Gensler S (2010) Judicial case management: caught in the crossfire. Duke Law J 60:669–744
Gross N (2012) Le juge de cassation en Europe: L'Allemagne. In: Le juge de cassation en Europe. Thèmes et commentaires, Dalloz, Paris, p 27
Guillaume M, Bechillon D (eds) (2014) La régulation des contentieux devant les cours suprêmes. Le Club des jurists, Paris
Guinchard S (2015) Les garanties institutionelles du droit à un bon judge. In: Guinchard S, Sinopoli L, Chainais C et al (eds) Droit processuel-droit fondamentaux du procès, 8th edn. Paris, pp 789–852
Guinchard S, Ferrand F, Moussa T (2015) Une chance pour la France et le droit continental: La technique de cassation, vecteur particulièrement approprié au contrôle de conventionnalité. Recueil Dalloz 5:278
Hathaway O (2001) Path dependence in the law: the course and pattern of legal change in a common law system. Iowa L Rev 86:601–605
Haworth C (1973) Screening and summary procedures in the United States courts of appeals. Wash U L Q 1973:257
Herzog P, Karlen D (1982) Attacks on judicial decisions. In: Cappelletti M (ed) Ordinary proceedings in first instance-international encyclopedia of comparative law. Mohr, Tübingen, p 54
Holvast N (2016) The power of the judicial assistant/law clerk: looking behind the scenes at courts in the United States, England and Wales, and the Netherlands. J Court Adm 7:10–28
Huang W (2019) The opportunities and challenges of judicial adjudication in the era of artificial intelligence. J Guangxi Inst Soc 30(4):102–107
Jackson V (2012) Judicial independence: structure, context, attitude. In: Seibert-Fohr A, Müller F (eds) Judicial independence in transition. Springer, pp 19–25
Jean JP (2017) Filtrage des recours en cassation: Adapter à chaque système judiciaire les principes directeurs communs d'une 'bonne justice'. In: Le filtrage des recours devant les cours suprêmes. Actes du colloque V, pp 42–43
Jeuland E (2021) Towards a reform of the French Court of cassation? In: Bravo-Hurtado P, Van Rhee CH (eds) Supreme courts under pressure: controlling caseload in the administration of civil justice. Springer, Cham, pp 19–34
Jolowicz A, Van Rhee R (1999) Recourse against judgement in the European Union. Kluwer Law International, The Hague, pp 2–3
Jolowicz JA (1996) The Woolf report and the adversary system. CJQ 15:198
Jordan S (2007) Early panel announcement, settlement and adjudication. B Y U L Rev 2007:55
Kappl T (2016) Guest editorial: strong justice for a strong Europe: a European Rechtspfleger. Int J Court Adm 8:1
Kern C (2007) Justice between simplification and formalism. Mohr Siebeck, Tübingen
Kern C (2016) El rol de la corte suprema. In: Taruffo M, Marinoni L, Mitidiero D (eds) La misión de los tribunales supremos. Marcial Pons, Madrid, p 76
Klatt M, Meiste M (2012) The constitutional structure of proportionality. Oxford University Press, Oxford, pp 45–68
Kodek G (2014) Appellate proceedings in civil cases: Traditional remedies in light of contemporary problems. In: Uzelac A, Van Rhee CH (eds) Nobody's perfect: comparative essays on appeals and other means of recourse. Intersentia, Cambridge, pp 35–52
Kornhauser L (2012) Appeal and supreme courts. In: Sanchirico C (ed) Procedural law and economics. Massachusetts, pp 19–41
La Porta R, Lopez-de-Silanes F, Pop-Eleches C, Shleifer A (2004) Judicial checks and balances. J Polit Econ 112:445–470

Langbein J (2012) The disappearance of civil trial in the United States. Yale L J 122:522
Langbroek P (2010) Quality management in courts and in judicial organisations in 8 council of Europe member states. CEPEJ Studies No. 13
Langbroek P (2017) From the managing editor: court administration in Europe—management in a different context. Int J Court Adm 8:1–2
Langer M (2005) The rise of managerial judging in international criminal law. Am J Comp Law 53
Levy M (2011) The mechanics of federal appeals: uniformity and case management in the circuit courts. Duke L J 61:315
Levy M (2013) Judicial attention as a scarce resource: a preliminary defense of how judges allocate time across cases in the federal courts of appeals. Geo Wash L Rev 81:401
Lienhard A, Kettiger D (2017) Between management and the rule of law: on the move towards a management model for the judiciary—results from the project 'basic research into court management in Switzerland.' Int J Court Adm 8:7–19
Lindquist S, Cross F (2009) Measuring judicial activism. Oxford University Press, Oxford, p 9
Lupois M A (2018) Civil procedure in Italy. Alphen aan den Rija, Wolters Kluwer
Marcus R (2003) Reining in the American lawyer: the new role of American judges. Hast Int'l Compar L Rev 27:3
Marcus R (2014) Appellate review in the reactive model: the example of the American federal courts. In Uzelac A, Van Rhee CH (eds) Nobody's perfect: comparative essays on appeals and other means of recourse. Intersentia, Cambridge, p 105
Marcus R (2017a) Controlling the cowboy lawyers: how American judges are managing American cases. USA report. In: IAPL Conference 2017a (unpublished)
Marcus R (2017b) Misgivings about American exceptionalism. In: Uzelac A, Van Rhee CH (eds) Revisiting procedural human rights. Intersentia, Cambridge
Marcus R (2021a) The litigation superpower's case management cure for adversarial ills. In: Chan P, Van Rhee CH (eds) Civil case management in the twenty-first century: court structures still matter. Springer, Singapore, pp 109–122
Marcus R (2021b) A happy-go-lucky story: the American supreme court and overload problems. In: Bravo-Hurtado P, Van Rhee CH (eds) Supreme courts under pressure: controlling caseload in the administration of civil justice. Springer, Cham, pp 183–210
Martineu R (1986) The value of appellate oral argument: a challenge to the conventional wisdom. Iowa L Rev 72:1
Ng G (2008) Case management: procedural law vs. best practices. In: Uzelac A, Van Rhee CH (eds) Judicial case management and efficiency in civil litigation. Intersentia, Antwerp, pp 111–133
Odgers R, Maureira C (2017) Chile report. In: IAPL Conference 2017 (unpublished)
Ormazabal Sánchez G (2017) Las facultades judiciales de dirección material de los procesos civiles en la legislación y experiencia españolas (unpublished)
Parkin J (2012) Adaptable due process. U Pa L Rev 160:1309–1362
Peckham RF (1985) A judicial response to the cost of litigation: two-stage discovery and alternative dispute resolution. Rutgers L Rev 37:253–265
Perry S (1987) Judicial obligation, precedent and the common law. Oxford J Legal Stud 7:215–244
Petersen N (2017) Proportionality and judicial activism: fundamental rights adjudication in Canada. Cambridge University Press, Cambridge, Germany and South Africa
Peterson T (1995) Restoring structural checks on judicial power in the era of managerial judging. U C Davis L Rev 29:41–59
Pisani P (2009) Sulla garanzia costituzionale del ricorso per cassazione sistematicamente interpretata. Foro Il 10:380
Posner R (2006) The role of the judge in the twenty-first century. B U L Rev 86:1049–1050
Priori G (2017) Peru report. In: IAPL Conference 2017 (unpublished)
Rehnquist W (1993) Seen in a glass darkly: the future of the federal courts. Wis L Rev 1993:1–3
Reinhardt S (1993) A plea to save the federal courts: too few judges, too many cases. A B A J 79:52–53
Resnik J (1982) Managerial judges. Harv L Rev 96:374

Resnik J (1995) Many doors? Closing doors? Alternative resolution and adjudication. O S J Dispute Res 10:211

Resnik J (2000) Trial as error, jurisdiction as injury: transforming the meaning of Article III. Harv L Rev 113:924–940

Richman W, Reynolds W (1996) Elitism, expediency, and the new certiorari: requiem for the learned hand tradition. Cornell L Rev 81:273

Robertson C (2013) The right to an appeal. N C L Rev 91:1219

Roth H (2016) Die Zukunft der Ziviljustiz. ZZP 129:3–21

Rottenburg R (2015) The world of indicators: the making of governmental knowledge through quantification. Cambridge University Press

Salas D (1998) Le tiers pouvoir. Hachette, Paris

Saltzman A (2014) Appellate review in California: limits on the right to recourse. In: Uzelac A, Van Rhee CH (eds) Nobody's perfect: comparative essays on appeals and other means of recourse. Intersentia, Cambrige, pp 95–104

Schafft T (2005) Selektion von Rechtsmittelverfahren durch gesetzliche Zugangsbeschränkungen. Tübingen

Schiavoni J (2002) Who's afraid of precedent? The debate over the precedential value of unpublished opinions. UCLA L Rev 49:1859

Schwab K-H, Gottwald P (1984) Verfassung und Zivilprozess. Gieseking, Bielefeld

Scott R (1995) Caseflow management in the trial court. In: Zuckerman A, Cranston R (eds) Reform of civil procedure. Whitened Press, Oxford

Seibert-Fohr A, Müller F (eds) (2012) Judicial independence in transition. Springer, pp 5–20

Shany Y (2012) Judicial independence as an indicator of international court effectiveness: a goal-based approach. In: Shetreet S, Forsyth CH (eds) The culture of judicial independence. Nijhoff, Leiden-Boston, pp 251–267

Shetreet S, Turenne S (2013) Judges on trial: the independence and accountability of the English judiciary, 2nd edn. Cambridge

Sorabji J (2021a) Structure of the court system and case management: lessons from England and Wales. In: Chan P, Van Rhee CH (eds) Civil case management in the twenty-first century: court structure still matter. Springer, Singapore, pp 137–152

Sorabji J (2021b) The supreme court of the United Kingdom and the court of appeal in England and Wales: sharing the appellate load. In: Bravo-Hurtado P, Van Rhee CH (eds) Supreme courts under pressure: Controlling caseload in the administration of civil justice. Springer, Cham, pp 155–182

Steelman D (2004) Caseflow management: the heart of court management in the new millennium. National Center for State Courts

Stevens J (2017) Deciding what to decide: the docket and the rule of four. In: O'Brian D (ed) Judges on judging: views from the bench. Sagge, California, pp 113–121

Stürner M (2002) Die Anfechtung von Zivilurteilen. C.H. Beck, München

Stürner M (2017) Wahrung oder Durchsetzung von Verbraucherrechten? Zur Rolle der Verbraucherstreitbeilegung im europäischen Justizraum. In: Hörnle T et al (eds) Courts and their equivalents. Nomos-Verlag, Baden-Baden

Stürner M (2021) Sharing responsibility: the German Federal Court of Justice and the Civil Appellate System. In: Bravo-Hurtado P, Van Rhee CH (eds) Supreme courts under pressure: controlling caseload in the administration of civil justice. Springer, Cham, pp 75–104

Stürner M, Wendelstein C (2017) Germany report. In: IAPL Conference 2017 (unpublished)

Stürner M, Gascón Inchausti F, Caponi R (2014) The role of consumer ADR in the administration of justice. European Law Publishers, Sellier

Stürner R (2007) Markt und Wettbewerb über alles? C.H. Beck, München, pp 128–140

Stürner R (2014) Die Rolle des dogmatischen Denkens im Zivilprozessrecht. Zeitschrift für Zivilprozess 127:271–332

Symposium (2009) Against settlement: twenty-five years later. Fordham L Rev 78:1117

Taruffo M (2012) Le funzioni delle corte supremi: Cenni generali. In: Mitidiero D, Rizzo G (eds) Processo civil. Atlas, São Paulo, p 341
Tavolari R (2006) Reflexiones sobre la corte suprema Chilena. In: Berizonce R, Hitters J, Oteiza E (eds) El papel de los tribunales superiores. Rubinzal, Buenos Aires, pp 471–500
Terhechte J (2011) Konstitutionalisierung und Normativität der europäischen Grundrechte. Mohr Siebeck, Tübingen, pp 1–59
Thole Ch (2014) Das neue Mediationsgesetz - Mediation im und an der Schnittstelle zum Zivilprozessrecht. ZZP 127:339–370
Tidmarsh J (2016) The future of oral argument. Loy U Chi L J 48:475–486
Tronson B (2016) Towards proportionality—the 'quick, cheap and just' balance in civil litigation. In: Picker C, Seidman G (eds) The dynamisme of civil procedure-global trends and developments. Springer, pp 183–202
Turner M (1997) Some thoughts on the multi-track inside track. Law Society Civil Litigation Newsletter
Turner R (2004) The proactive judge and the provision of a single transnational case management system and its associated procedures. In: Andenas M, Andrews N, Nazzini R (eds) The future of transnational civil litigation. The British Institute of International and Comparative Law, London, pp 73–88
Uzelac A (2014) Goals of civil justice and civil procedure in the contemporary world. In: Uzelac A (ed) Goals of civil justice and civil procedure in the contemporary judicial systems. Springer, Cham, pp 21–23
Uzelac A, Van Rhee CH (eds) (2011) The landscape of the legal professions in Europe and the USA: continuity and change. Intersentia, Antwerp
Van Rhee CH (2014) Civil justice in pursuit of efficiency. In: Uzelac A (ed) Goals of civil justice and civil procedure in the contemporary judicial systems. Springer, Cham, pp 61–77
Van Rhee CH (2015) Introduction. In: Van Rhee CH (ed) European traditions in civil procedure. Intersentia, pp 3–13
Van Rhee CH, Fu Y (eds) (2017) Supreme courts in transition in China and the west: adjudication at the service of public goals. Springer, Cham, pp 1–11
Von Malte J (2008) Gerichtsinterne Mediation. Mohr, Tübingen
Wallace A (2017) The impact of technology on courts. Int J Court Adm 8:1
Wallace J (2005) Improving the appellate process worldwide through maximizing judicial resources. Vand J Transnat'l L 38:187–192
Wang F (2021) A brief note on the application of information and communication technology in civil judicial case management. In: Chan P, Van Rhee CH (eds) Civil case management in the twenty-first century: court structure still matter. Springer, Singapore, pp 195–198
Webber G (2009) The negotiable constitution: on the limitations of rights. Cambridge University Press, Cambridge, pp 15–35
Wolff T (2013) Managerial judging and substantive law. Wash U L Rev 90(1027):1069
Woolf L (1996) Access to justice: final report to the Lord Chancellor on the civil justice system in England and Wales. London
Zeleznikow J (2017) Can artificial intelligence and online dispute resolution enhance efficiency and effectiveness in courts? Int J Court Adm 8:30–45
Zucca L (2008) Conflicts of fundamental rights as constitutional dilemmas. In: Brems E (ed) Conflicts between fundamental rights. Intersentia, Antwerp, pp 19–37
Zuckerman A (2004) Compliance with process obligations and fair trial. In: Andenas M, Andrews N, Nazzini R (eds) The future of transnational civil litigation. The British Institute of International and Comparative Law, London, pp 127–149
Zuckerman A (2009) Litigation management under the CPR: a poorly-used management infrastructure. In: Dwyer D (ed) The civil procedure rules ten years on. London, p 105

Court Management in Transformation

Yulin Fu

1 Overview

1.1 Concept of Judicial Management and Court Management

The concept of 'judicial management' in many Western countries is similar to 'case management', which is based on the idea/concept that the judge or tribunal that exercises judicial authority does so independently and integrally that it is a closed system of management to allocate procedural rights and responsibilities between the litigants and the tribunal.[1] In Mainland China, however, judicial management is much more complicated. Based on the idea/concept that the court exercises judicial authority independently and that the judge or tribunal is only a part of the court that manages a particular case, while the court managers (such as the Division Chief Judge, the President of the Court, and the judicial committee) actually manage the judge/tribunal by institutional reports, reviews, 'supervision', checks, and evaluations. It is an open system of management that allocates procedural rights and responsibilities among the litigants, the tribunal, and the court managers. Thus, judicial management in China includes not only management of judicature affairs that is something like 'case management', but also management of court staff including the judges and other adjudicatory personnel, and management of properties including the resources to support the operation of the courts and the property related to the cases from penalty and enforcement.[2]

[1] Cf. Van Rhee and Fu (2013).

Y. Fu (✉)
Law School, Peking University, Beijing, People's Republic of China
e-mail: fuyulin65@126.com

[2] The property management in the court includes two parts. One pare is the system of resource-obtaining and resource-distribution that sponsors the court. The other part is about the penalty,

L. Cadiet and Y. Fu (eds.), *On Judicial Management from Comparative Perspective*, Contemporary Chinese Civil and Commercial Law,
https://doi.org/10.1007/978-981-19-8673-4_6

The Chinese style of judicial management is criticized as judicial bureaucratization (judicatory with administrative characteristic) that hurts judicial independence of the tribunal for that these leaders and supervisors actually share partial judicial authority, obstructing the litigants' confidence in the judges and the court because of the non-transparency of the processes. Another criticism is the inefficiency of proceedings because a high level of bureaucratization waste human resources, especially when a head of the court act as a manager of the judges who are the real case managers but deal with cases by reporting their decisions to their managers/leaders for review. For all the above reasons, since 2013, the Party Central Committee proposed and the Supreme Court has implemented a series of reforms to change this 'trial mechanism' that is replaced by a new mechanism called the 'tribunal's responsibility.' By redefining the boundary of the authorities and responsibilities between the tribunal and the court managers and supervisors, Chinese courts are trying to establish a new mechanism of judicial management that is based on the judge or tribunal's exercising judicial authority independently through case management, which then become closer to the Western concept of 'case management.' Nevertheless, the 'management of judicial personnel' will still be a very important aspect of judicial management in the Chinese system, thus the court managers will still be the judges' managers by the evaluation of and supervision over 'case management', including quality management, efficiency management, process and progress management, and social effects management.[3]

To summarize, court management in China is an important part of judicial management, including case management, judiciary personnel management, and property management. This report will focus on judiciary personnel management for optimizing case management. Additionally, court management from outside, which includes political, financial, and personnel resources to support court operations, is also important to judicial management; but this topic is so broad and goes beyond the scope of this conference that I will only touch on some aspects which directly impact judiciary personnel.

1.2 The Four Districts of Judicial Jurisdiction

Based on special historical circumstances, China has four districts with dramatically different judicial traditions: Mainland China, Hong Kong, Macao, and Taiwan. Since New China was established in 1949, 'China's judicial system' generally means that of Mainland China. After 1997, Hong Kong returned to China from the United Kingdom's jurisdiction, yet the legal system and justice pattern still maintain the UK common law tradition with some traditional customs in local cases such as marriage litigation and land contracts. The situation in Macao is similar to that of Hong Kong,

---

confiscation, custody, turning over, and return by the court as the trial organ and enforcement organ. Both parts are important in the 2013 judicial reform.

[3] Cf. Van Rhee and Fu (2013).

while Macao applied Portugal's legal system and judicial pattern. Moreover, these two districts are still much influenced by the ongoing judicial reforms of their former metropolitan states; this is particularly the case in Hong Kong, where the 1998 civil justice reforms in the UK had a significant impact on civil justice in Hong Kong.

There is a relative connection between the legal sources and systems of Mainland China and Taiwan, although the political link here seems to be closer than that of the other two jurisdictions. The reason for this connection is that Mainland China became the new representative of China and the successor of the previous government ruled by the Guomingtang (Nationalist Party) that later governed Taiwan, where it established Nationalist Party laws. Although the New China abolished the Nationalist laws and set up a new legal system and court system based on public ownership, with obvious differences reflected in land, marriage, mediation, practice, and court systems, the legal history, culture, and customs are still shared and exercise influence in both territories. Moreover, since the 1980s, when Mainland China started its reform process and established a market economy, the legal system and trial pattern started learning from the Western systems, especially Germany, Japan, Taiwan, and the U.S., while Taiwan has been reforming and learning from the same 'teachers.'

Having different legal traditions in the same country provide opportunities for comparative studies, and scholars from the four jurisdictions frequently communicate on various legal issues; they not only contribute to law development, legal education, and legal practice in their own districts but also facilitate progress toward convergent evolution. Meanwhile, legal scholars from the mainland are able to learn about complex situations in their own society that may not be resolved by any other experiences. Researchers in this century are increasingly seeking to discover the 'Chinese way' to resolve 'Chinese problems', but still with an open view of global experiences, including those of the other three districts of China. Against this background, this report will focus on judicial reforms in Mainland China and partially introduce the basic system of the other three jurisdictions.

1.3 A General Introduction to the Judicial Reform in China[4]

New China was established in 1949. In 1954, the first communication and first court organic law were both enacted. But the first Civil Procedural Law was enacted late in 1982[5] (in 'test' version), and the first Judge Law was issued in 1995. This means that, in the first 30 years of the nation, there was no procedure law in civil justice, and being a 'judge' was not regarded as a separate profession until after the 1990s.[6]

[4] For more details and the comments, cf. Fu (2021).

[5] Criminal Procedural Law was issued in 1979.

[6] Judge Law 1995 was only a promise without implementation until the judicial reform after 2013. The test Civil Procedural Law of China was enacted in 1982.

Judicial reforms began in the early 1990s, first from trial patterns. Since the formal Civil Procedural Law of China was enacted in 1991,[7] civil justice reforms have been ongoing to establish a new system with transparent procedures, protections of the litigants' procedural rights, checks of judicial power, and rules of evidence. To this aim, the Civil Procedural Law was revised in 2012. Meanwhile, the Supreme Court issued more than 20 'judicial interpretations' and opinions to initiate a series of reforms in the areas of the organization and system of courts, involved litigation procedures, judicial management, and the enforcement system, etc.[8] Accordingly, specialization, professionalization, and independence of the judges have been promoted as another important goal of judicial reform.[9]

Since 2013, judicial reforms have focused on the court system and the mechanism of the judicial power's operation. The main goals are to promote the judges' independence from the court managers and the courts' independence from local governments, to improve impartiality, efficiency, and public credibility of the judiciary. The Supreme Court promulgated the Fourth Five-year (2014–2018) Reform Program for People's Courts. What is more important, the Court Organic Law was revised in 2018 and the Judge Law was revised in 2019, as a fruit of the reforms.[10] The 2018 amendment of the Court Organic Law readjusted the allocation of judicial authority and organizational relationship of the court by significantly enhancing the authority and responsibility of the single judge or the collegial panel to exercise judicial authority on behalf of the court. The Judges Law has been revised twice in succession in 2017 and 2019 that made important adjustments to the judges' rights, obligations and responsibilities, qualifications and appointment, evaluation and punishment, occupational security, so as to promote judicial professionalism and to enhance the professional goal of judges' qualifications by openness and fairness of the selection process, and accordingly push autonomy and self-discipline of the legal profession.

---

[7] For the history of civil procedure in China, cf. Fu (2013).

[8] The comprehensive guiding documents of judicial reforms issued by the Supreme Court are 'Five-year Reform Program for People's Courts' in 1999, 2005, 2009, and 2015.

[9] The function and form of 'Judicial Interpretation' is similar to a law issued by the Supreme Court with confirmation of the Congress after public participation and discussion with judges, scholars, and lawyers.

[10] The Court Organic Law was enacted in 1994 but replaced in 1979, which was amended in 1983, 1986, 2006 and 2018; the Judge Law was enacted in 1995 and amended in 2001, 2017, and 2019.

2 The Structure of China's Court System and Internal Departments

2.1 *The Constitutional Role of the Court and the External Relationship*

According to the constitution, 'The people's courts of the People's Republic of China are the judicial organs of the state' (Art. 123), and the people's courts shall exercise their adjudicative power independently and be free from any interference by any administrative organ, social organization or individual (Art. 126). The power of election of the president of the court and the appointment (at the recommendation of the president of the court) of the vice presidents, judges, and members of the judicial committee is exercised by the standing committee of the national and local congress (Art. 67). Therefore, the courts are responsible for and supervised by the congress that created them (Art. 128). Meanwhile, the People's Procuratorate, as the supervisory organ of law, is authorized to lodge a protest in accordance with the procedure of judicial supervision if it finds any definite error (listed under Art. 200 of Civil Procedural Law) in a legally effective judgment or order made by a people's court at any level or the court (under the procedure provided under Arts. 208–209 of CPL), and, accordingly, the court shall reopen the proceeding after receiving the protest from the procuratorate.

2.2 *The Four-Level and Two Instance Court System*

2.2.1 *Basic Structure of the Court System and Special Courts*[11]

China'S court system consists of ordinary courts/general jurisdiction courts, special courts, and military courts. As the core structure of the court system, ordinary courts are composed of four levels: the basic people's courts, the intermediate people's courts, the high people's courts and the Supreme People's Court. They are respectively placed in county-level administrative regions, municipal administrative regions, provincial administrative regions, and the capital city Beijing. Each level of courts has jurisdiction of criminal cases, civil cases, and administrative cases as the court of first instance. The 'jurisdiction by level of courts' indicates that the specific level of court has the original jurisdiction over a certain case depending on the claim amount and the influence of the case. The higher court next to the first instance court has appellate jurisdiction as the second instance. The decision made by the second instance court is final and effective, which marked the China's court system as 'two instance system' from perspective of judicial hierarchy. However, in addition to the two instance system, China has a special proceeding as a remedy for

[11] Cf. Chen and Chen (2017).

effective decisions which is called the judicial supervision procedure or reopening of proceedings.

The special courts include military courts and specialized courts, which are established not based on administrative region and authorized to exercise trans-regional jurisdiction over cases. Among the special courts, the specialized courts, including maritime courts, intellectual property courts, and financial courts, etc., are mainly intermediate courts under the supervision of the ordinary high courts in the province where they are located. Separately, the military courts have there own judicial hierarchy that consists of basic military courts, intermediate court (military court of a certain military region or armed service branch), and the high military court of PLA. In 2013, the organizational system of military courts was in the process of reform so that the basis of the setup of military courts changed from branches of services and systems into combat zones. The new military courts include the PLA Military Court (at the level of high court), the Military Court of the East, South, North, Central, and West Combat Zone of the PLA (there are two in the west combat zone), and 26 military courts of the PLA in Shanghai, Nanjing, Hangzhou, and other cities (at the level of primary court).

2.2.2 Some Important Reforms to the Court System

Circuit Courts (Divisions) of the Supreme People's Court

In January 2015, the Supreme People's Court established the No. 1 Circuit division in Shenzhen that covers the three southern provinces and the No. 2 Circuit division in Shenyang that covers the three northern provinces. These Circuit divisions are responsible for adjudicating major administrative cases and transregional civil and commercial cases. As the standing local judicial organs dispatched by the Supreme Court, the judgments, rulings, and decisions made by these Circuit divisions have the same effect as those made by the Supreme Court. The cases decided by the Circuit divisions have become 'experimental units' and 'pacesetters' of the judicial reform conducted by the Supreme People's Court, and have realized the original intention of delegating the adjudicative power, facilitating the initiation of lawsuits by the people, settling disputes locally, and safeguard the unification of the legal system. Four additional Circuit divisions were subsequently established in the east (No. 3, at Nanjing), central (No. 4, at Zhengzhou), southwest (No. 5, at Chongqing), and northwest (No. 6 at Xi'an) regions of China.

Establishing Transregional people's courts and Promoting Transregional Centralized Jurisdiction over Administrative Cases

The basic court system was established based on administrative jurisdiction, thus easily intervened in by local governments as so-called 'local protectionism' over justice. In order to ensure lawful and fair adjudication of transregional cases, especially those involving local interests, in December 2014, two of the intermediate courts were respectively established in Beijing and Shanghai as pilot transregional courts that are responsible for adjudicating major civil, commercial, administrative, environmental and resource protection, food and drug safety, and certain criminal cases involving different administrative regions. The Supreme People's Court will continue to explore and establish a new pattern of litigation system in which general cases are adjudicated in local courts and special cases are adjudicated in transregional courts.

Jurisdiction of administrative litigation cases has been limited to general judicial jurisdiction based on administrative jurisdiction. This means that the court is located in the geographic location of the local government that is the defendant of administrative litigation and thus subject to interference by local administrative organs. In June 2015, to integrate resources of administrative adjudication and improve the judicial environment for administrative adjudication, the Supreme Court promulgated 'The opinions on transregional centralized jurisdiction over administrative cases', instructing certain high courts to, according to their respective local conditions, designate some courts to exercise jurisdiction over transregional administrative cases. Then, the high courts in Fujian, Shandong, Henan, Guangdong, and other regions assigned the jurisdiction over certain administrative cases of first instance to some designated primary or intermediate courts other than the courts originally having jurisdiction over the cases, so as to eliminate the public's concern about officials shielding one other and to achieve a fair adjudication of all kinds of administrative cases according to the law.

Establishing Intellectual Property Rights (IP) Courts and International Commercial Court of the SPC

In order to further enhance the judicial protection of IP and unify the adjudicative criteria for IP cases, with the approval of the Standing Committee of the National People's Congress, IP courts were respectively established in Beijing, Shanghai, and Guangzhou at the end of 2014. Then in 2018 the Supreme Court established the Intellectual Property Division who accept the appeals against the courts at intermediate level only if the case fall in the types of 'the intellectual property appeal cases with strong expertise such as patents' under the rule.[12] Further more, the Supreme Court promulgated judicial interpretations to define the jurisdiction and provide guidelines on the appointment and participation of technological investigation officers, which is a new and unique role found only in IP courts.

In 2018, the Supreme Court set up the International Commercial Court of the SPC to adjudicate significant international commercial cases.[13] Since then the Supreme Court act as the first instance trial court and its judgments are final, though the special jurisdiction is limited under the rule (Art. 2) of the Provisions of the Supreme People's Court on Several Issues Regarding the Establishment of the International Commercial Court. Before than the Supreme Court has never tried a civil or commercial case as

---

[12] Provisions of the Supreme People's Court on Several Issues concerning Intellectual Property Courts, enacted in 2019. 〔2018〕 No. 22.

[13] Provisions of the Supreme People's Court on Several Issues Regarding the Establishment of the International Commercial Court. 〔2018〕 No. 11.

a first instance court, though it is abstractly authorized to do so under the Civil Procedural Law.

2.3 *Internal Structure/Departments of the Courts*

2.3.1 General Introduction to the Departments of the Courts

As mentioned above, the new Organic Law of the Courts was largely amended in 2018 and the sections related to 'internal structure' and personnel of the court were most dramatically changed.

Basically, a Chinese court includes the following departments: (1) specialized departments, including several judicature divisions, a docketing division, and an enforcement bureau, that deal with typical judicial affairs related to the cases; (2) the comprehensive judicial departments, including a judicial management office and a research office, that are influential or powerful in making judicial policies of the court and in evaluation of the judges' performance (especially from perspective of quality and quantity of their cases); (3) the personnel and administrative departments, including a political bureau or a personnel department, a general office, and a discipline inspection and supervision department (in most lower courts combined with the personnel office), that are powerful or even decisive in recruitment, evaluation, promotion, rewards and punishments of the judges.[14]

2.3.2 Judicature Divisions

The function of a judicature division is to deal with litigation cases.[15] Each court has several criminal divisions, several civil divisions, and an administrative division, but the number of judicature divisions varies from court to court, mainly depending on the grade and scale of a court. For example, the Supreme Court has 1 docketing division, 5 criminal divisions, 4 civil divisions, 1 environmental resources division, 1 intellectual division,[16] 1 administrative division, 1 state compensation office, 1

[14] Additionally, in the Supreme Court and some high courts, there are an information bureau, a bureau of international cooperation, a bureau of the judicial executive equipment, and/or a bureau of retired personnel, the Party committee of the Court, etc. Cf. https://english.court.gov.cn/organization.html, https://www.court.gov.cn/jigou-fayuanjigou.html (the later as Chinese website is updated more frequently than the English one, so the information is not unanimous). Last visit on May 2, 2022.

[15] In this paper, 'litigation cases' is in a broad sense to mention all the cases filed to the courts for judicial remedy under Civil Procedural Law, Criminal Procedural Law, and Administrative Procedural Law.

[16] The Civil Division 5th deal with the intellectual cases in the Supreme Court, but after 2018 its jurisdiction was taken over by the newly established Intellectual Property Division. So both of the divisions deal with intellectual property cases in their respectively legal jurisdictions.

judicature supervision division, 1 enforcement office, and 6 circuit divisions.[17] A large scale high court like Zhejiang Peoples' High Court has 2 docketing divisions, 3 criminal divisions and 1 commutation and parole division, 5 civil divisions, 1 environmental resources division, 1 administrative division including state compensation office, 2 judicature supervision division, 3 enforcement office. The intermediate courts usually have 2 docketing divisions, 2–3 criminal divisions, 3–7 civil divisions, and other divisions as above.

All the civil divisions deal with the cases fallen in Art. 2 of Civil Procedural Law, but the specific jurisdiction or functions of each civil division vary from court to court. In the Supreme Court, Civil Division No. 1 deals with cases involving marriage and family, labor disputes, unjust enrichment, negotiorum gestio, real estate, neighbor relations, easement, rural land contracts, contracts, and tort involving natural persons; setting aside revocation of arbitration and special procedures; and guides the work of the other divisions. Civil Division No. 2 tries cases involving contract and tort disputes between legal persons and other organizations, and cases of domestic security, future goods, bills, companies, and bankruptcy; applications for setting aside domestic arbitration awards; and applications for reconsideration. Civil Division No. 3 tries IP cases involving copyrights (including computer software), trademark rights, patents, technical contracts, unfair competition, the right of scientific and technological achievements, the right of new plant varieties, and re-considerations of IP application. Division No. 4 tries cases involving maritime litigation, affairs related to Hong Kong, Macao, and Taiwan that include contract and infringement disputes; reviews the application of setting aside, accepting, and enforcing international arbitration awards and judgments; and reviews the effect of arbitration clauses related to foreign affairs. The local courts generally follow but not copy the Supreme Court in that some courts establish a a Civil Division No. 5 or a separate financial division, etc., to take over some cases disposed by Civil Division No. 2 in the Supreme Court and the other courts. This also happens to the other types of the cases for the sake of the scale or/and local policy orientation.

Needless to say, a court's grade in judicial hierarchy is an important factor to decide the functions and jurisdictions of this court and therefore impact establishment of its judicature divisions. For example, the Supreme Court has none of first instance cases (except for the very rare international commercial cases), as contrast, the basic courts have no function of appeals at all; so the Supreme Court divide judicature with more consideration of specialization for judicial identification; while the basic courts establish their divisions, though based on basic specialization (such as family division, labour division or bankrupt division), may consider more classification of procedure (such as separate small claim division or non-contest division). However, since the local courts share first instance cases, the higher courts share second instance cases, and all the courts share the retrial cases, so the importance of the difference of the jurisdiction and functions to the courts in different level of the hierarchy are mainly

[17] There are 1 president and 9 vice presidents, 13 presiding judges, 41 vice presiding judges, and 179 ordinary judges (52 of them in the civil division). See 'Main personnel of the internal organs of the Supreme People's Court,' available at: http://www.court.gov.cn/jigou-fayuanbumen.html.

in the sense of theory. The actually important factor that impacts a court in setting up civil divisions in various ways, either to establish a separate division for some cases or to combine them to the other civil divisions, is the scale and importance of this type of cases in its own jurisdiction. Therefore, it's quite common that the courts even with same grade may have different numbers (amount) of civil judicature divisions and a specific division with same number (mark) may have different functions in different courts (Civil Division 3 in Court A may share functions with same Civil Division 5 in Court A).

2.3.3 Docketing Division

The docketing division is special and very important in China's court system because its functions are mixed and its judicial power get involved in merits but its decision making is flexible. Firstly, a docketing division take charge of 'checking in' all the cases filed in the court under various procedural rules, including filing of a lawsuits, appeals, reopening proceedings, revoking arbitration award, enforcement, state compensation, etc. For example, before docketing of a lawsuit, the docketing division shall decide whether an action to be instituted meet all of the following conditions: (1) The plaintiff is a citizen, legal person or any other organization with a direct interest in the case; (2) There is a clear defendant; (3) There are specific claims, facts and reasons; (4) The case is within the scope of civil actions accepted by the people's courts and under the jurisdiction of the people's court in which the action is instituted. It shall decide within seven days to docket a case which meets the conditions for instituting an action and notify the party, or to issue a ruling within seven days to refuse to accept an action which fails to meet the conditions for instituting an action (and the plaintiff may appeal against the ruling).

In the appellate courts, the docketing divisions shall also review appeals and appeal-involved petitions, deciding the cases involving the dispute of jurisdiction among the courts, reviewing all the application of judicial supervision against the legally effective judgments or orders and transferring them to the lower courts when the reopening of proceeding is needed, etc. Moreover, it take charge of serving all the case files that the court accepts, deciding judicial aid, conducting case management of all kinds of cases in the court (including set time for hearing), organizing the judicial police in official acts, and guiding the review of the reopening of proceeding in the lower courts.

2.3.4 Judicial Management Office

In the Supreme Court and some of the local courts, the judicial management office was established in the first decade of this century, while in the courts where there is no such office, its functions are exercised by the research office, the docketing division, or the administrative office.

The main function of the judicial management office is to establish an examination and evaluation system to assess the state of the judicature, which is very important for the court leader in the check and appraisal of the judges and the auxiliary judicial personnel, and for the higher courts in the check and appraisal of the lower courts. In the early years of this office being established, its functions were to those of the presidents' assistant to execute his/her power of case management and judge management. The role and importance of judicial management vary dramatically from district to district and from court to court; but the overall tendency is that, after a short energetic stage, its importance is weakening together with the president's power of case management, and its role is changing from that of 'manager' to an 'information provider.'[18]

2.3.5 Enforcement Bureau/Office

In China, enforcement bureaus exercise legal documents entered by the courts and other institutions. Since some disputes arising from the process of enforcement need to be judged and, as an institutional arrangement, most of these disputes are dealt with by the enforcement division in a judicature manner, the enforcement division is still considered to be a division with some judicature functions. This situation has been debated for more than 20 years and some steps toward reform have been attempted. However, the issue and problems related to the burden of enforcement in a society in transition are too complex; thus, there is still no consensus on the final arrangement.

3 Personnel Management of the Court[19]

3.1 Court Staff in Reform

The court staff are governed by the Court Organic Law, and according to Art. 47 of the Court Organic Law, the duties, management and safeguards of judges shall be governed by the Judge Law.

Under the amendment of Court Organic Law in 2018, court staff will include three classifications: (1) adjudicatory personnel, including only the president and associate presidents of the court, judicial committee members, judges, and people's assessors; (2) auxiliary judicial personnel, including assistants of judges, clerks, and judiciary technical experts (only in some specialized courts or divisions); and (3) judicial administrative personnel, including judicial policemen, personnel in the administrative or management offices, and researchers. The classified management

[18] Cf. Xinhuanet, 'The Supreme Court set up the Office of Judicial Management,' available at: http://news.xinhuanet.com/2010-11/23/c_13619132.htm, last visit on June 18th, 2014.
[19] Cf. Fu (2019).

of judicial personnel is an important reform, which aims to separate the judges from the civil servant system. From the outside perspective, the goal is to promote the judges to be separate and independent from administrative management. From the inside perspective, the allocation of human resources of the courts shall be optimized by classifying the judges from auxiliary judicial personnel and administrative staff, adjusting the proportion of judges to auxiliary judicial personnel, and saving the judges from routine and trivial procedural affairs. The device of the reform encourages the local courts to improve effective methods of recruitment and employment of auxiliary judicial personnel and to explore outsourcing of social services to optimize the structure of auxiliary judicial personnel.

3.2 *Judges*

The presidents of the courts at various levels are elected and removed by the congresses at corresponding levels; and the other judges are, with the president's proposal, appointed and removed by the standing committees of the congresses at corresponding levels. Persons to be appointed as judges for the first time are selected through examination and assessment from the personnel who have passed the national uniform legal profession qualification examination and have obtained the legal profession qualification, meeting the conditions for judges, and who are best qualified for the post. Presidents and vice presidents of the courts shall be selected among the judges or among other persons who are best qualified for the post.

3.2.1 Functions and Duties of the Judges

The functions and duties of judges are to take part in trials as a member of a Court Organic Law panel or to try a case alone according to law and to perform other functions and duties as provided for by law. Moreover, the judges, as the president or in other roles of management, shall perform additional functions and duties commensurate with their posts.

3.2.2 Qualifications of the Judges

Under the Judge Law, the qualifications of a judge are as following: (1) to be of the nationality of the People's Republic of China; (2) to have reached the age of 23; (3) to endorse the Constitution of the People's Republic of China; (4) to have fine political and professional quality and to be good in conduct; (5) to be in good health; and (6) to have engaged in legal work for at least two years in the case of Court Organic college or university graduates who majored in law or in the case of those who did not major in law but who possess professional knowledge of the law; those who assume the posts of judges of Superior people's courts and of the Supreme People's Court shall have engaged in legal work for at least three years or have engaged in legal work for at least one year in the case of those who have a Master's Degree of Law or a doctorate of Law, or those who have a Master's Degree or a doctorate in a field other than law but who possess professional knowledge of the law; and those who assume the posts of judges of Superior people's courts and of the Supreme People's Court shall have engaged in legal work for at least two years.[20]

The above qualification (6) was just added to Judge Law 2017. Before then, the Court Organic Law only provided that 'judicial personnel of people's courts must have an adequate knowledge of the law', and even this paragraph was only added in 1983. The qualification requirements of judges in legal specializations reflect the sustained efforts toward judicial professionalization in China since the 1980s.

As the result of the higher requirements of the legal qualification to be a judge, some of the former judges were at risk of losing their status as a judge. So the new Judge Law leaves some flexibility for them to speed up progress. The new Judge Law provided that, 'The judicial personnel who do not possess the qualifications as provided by item (6) of the preceding paragraph prior to the implementation of this law shall receive training, the specific measures shall be made by the Supreme People's Court.' Meanwhile, considering that some districts of China are too poor to attract and maintain qualified judges, the new Judge Law further provided that, 'For the places where it is really difficult to apply the academic qualification as provided by the sixth item of the first paragraph, after being examined and determined by the Supreme People's Court, the academic qualification for judges may be eased for a specific period as two-year graduates of law major of Colleges and universities.'

3.2.3 Evaluation, Protection and Punishment of the Judges

Appraisals of judges are conducted by the commission for examination and assessment of judges of the courts to which the judges belong. The commission shall consist of five to nine members and the president of the court shall be assumed to be the chairman. The appraisal of judges shall be carried out routinely and annually, with the emphasis laid on the achievements in judicial work and also including the judges' ideological level and moral character, competence in judicial work, mastery of law theories, and attitudes toward and style of work. The result of the appraisal shall be taken as the basis for awards, punishment, training, removal, or dismissal of a judge, and for readjustment of his or her grade and salary. A judge shall be informed of the result of the appraisal in written form. If the judge disagrees with the result, he or she may apply for reconsideration. If a judge is confirmed by annual appraisal as being incompetent for two successive years or unqualified for the present post and declines to accept other assignments, he/she shall be dismissed and be removed from the post of judge in accordance with the procedures as provided by law. If the judge

[20] Article 10 of Judge Law provides: The following persons shall not hold the post of a judge: those who have been (1) subjected to criminal punishment for the commission of a crime; or (2) discharged from public employment.

disagrees with the decision, he/she may apply for reconsideration to the organ that made the decision and appeal to an organ at a higher level.

3.2.4 People's Assessors

Citizens who have the right to vote and to stand for election and have reached the age of 23 are eligible to be elected people's assessors; persons who have been deprived of political rights are excluded. During the period of the exercise of their functions in the people's courts, the assessors are members of the divisions of the courts in which they participate and enjoy equal rights with the judges, but they continue to receive wages as usual from their regular place of employment and the court may give reasonable allowances.[21]

As a symbol of 'judicial democracy' and 'the people's right to participate in and supervise judicial work' in the socialist judicial system, the Central government and the Supreme Court keep reforming the system of people's assessors. Nevertheless, the result has never been as satisfactory as expected. In the renewed reform since 2015, with the authorization of the Standing Committee of the National People's Congress, the Supreme People's Court and the Ministry of Justice jointly promulgated a pilot program to reform the system of people's assessors and the measures for the implementation of the pilot program. The pilot program has been conducted at 50 courts in 10 provinces, autonomous regions, and municipalities directly under the Central government. The pilot program includes, among other things, reforming the requirements for the appointment of people's assessors, improving the mode of appointment of people's assessors, expanding the scope of participation in trials, defining the powers to participate in trials, enhancing job security, establishing the withdrawal mechanism, giving full play to the advantage of people's assessors in being familiar with the social situations and public opinions, and gradually realizing the goal that people's assessors no longer vote on issues relating to the application of law and only participate in fact-finding.

As of the end of April 2016, all the 50 pilot courts had finished the appointment of people's assessors, including 9,673 new people's assessors. These pilot courts had 13,322 people's assessors in total, 4.3 times their judge quota. There were over 220,000 people's assessors nationwide, reflecting a further enhancement of their extensiveness and representation. In 2016, the people's assessors nationwide took part in the trial of 3,063,000 cases, including 458,700 criminal cases, 2,481,300 civil cases, and 122,900 administrative cases. The people's assessors of the 50 pilot courts took part in the trial of 81,770 cases, including 1,624 cases involving mass interest or public interest or otherwise having great social influence that were tried using the mechanism of collegiate panel and assessors. The Supreme People's Court has developed the national people's assessor information management system, which is connected with the respective people's assessor information management systems of the pilot courts, to realize information analysis, random selection, and management

[21] Wang (2015).

of performance of the people's assessors. The Supreme People's Court has also conducted training courses for people's assessors and enhanced their knowledge in rights, obligations, litigation procedures, judicial etiquette, and other relevant issues to improve the capability of the people's assessors to perform their duties. The pilot courts in various districts also provided a diversity of experience based on the law.

3.3 Auxiliary Judicial Personnel

Under the current Court Organic Law 2006, the 'auxiliary judicial personnel' designation is unclear, except for clerks. The judges deal with almost all the procedural affairs personally, even in serving and delivering filing documents. On the other hand, associate judges, whose qualifications are much lower than judges, usually exercise judicial power similar to that of the judges. This situation is being changed in the judicial reform after 2013. After initial tests in some pilot courts appointed by the Supreme Court and the Party Central Committee, the experience of the samples has been amended into the Court Organic Law 2018. In the new mechanism, the auxiliary judicial personnel includes clerks and judge assistants (assistants of the judges), and there are some judiciary technical experts in some specialized courts or divisions (such as IP courts).

3.3.1 Clerks

Under Court Organic Law, 'people's courts at all levels have clerks to keep records of the court proceedings and to take charge of other matters concerning the trials.' But what the 'other matters concerning the trials' mean and what they include is not clear. The law authorized the Supreme Court to define that the 'Measures for the administration of the clerks of the people's courts shall be formulated by the Supreme People's Court.'

Then, under the 'measures for the administration of the courts', the Supreme Court defined clerks as 'auxiliary personnel of routine judicial work' whose duties include dealing with routine affairs in the processes of preparation for the hearing, checking the attendance of the litigants at the hearing, announcing disciplinary actions of the court, Court Organic Law lating and bookbinding the files of the case, assisting the court in serving the litigation documents, and other routine work assigned by the court. According to this provision, clerks would appear to be assistants of the judges.

However, since there is no assistant for any judge, and more and more of the clerks develop into associate judges and then judges with the growth in the number of cases, after the 1990s, clerks who have acted as assistants of a certain judge were shared by two or several judges in more and more courts. Moreover, since the 1990s, the functions of the pretrial work have been much expanded during the judicial reforms, so, based on the open provision of 'other routine work assigned by the court', the clerks' routine work has expanded to include, at the very least, establishing files of the case, receiving the documents of the proceedings, notifying the litigants, servicing documents, organizing evidence exchanges, arranging hearings, meeting the litigants for routine matters concerning the trials, taking notes of all the hearings and meetings with litigants presided by the judge(s), recording the deliberations of the tribunal, investigating the necessary evidence required under the law, collating and bookbinding the files of the case, sometimes drafting legal documents or orders, printing and stamping legal files, copying all kinds of documents in the files at the requirement of the litigants and other relative people, reporting the settlement of the case to the statistics department, entering the record of the case on the website, and archiving the case files.

3.3.2 From Assistant Judge to Judge Assistant

In the current judicial reform after 2013, as a part of the regularization, specialization, and professionalization of judicial personnel, national courts have carried out the reform of *the judge quota system*. The courts should scientifically establish the judge quotas for the courts according to the number of cases handled; the level of socioeconomic development, population, and other basic data of the places where the courts are located; the level of trial and functions of the courts; the workloads of the judges; and the current staffing of auxiliary judicial personnel. Mainly based on the number of cases, the proportion of judges in most courts was adjusted to around 30–40%, and the proportion of judges to clerks and judge assistants was aimed to be equal.[22]

Through the testing of the reform in pilot courts and then as provided under the Court Organic Law 2018, associate judges (assistant judges) have become judge assistants (assistants of judges), although this has not put an end to the debates. The main argument of the opponents is that there are no small claim courts or justices of the peace in China, yet small claim cases and simple cases take more than 80 cases in the basic courts that deal with more than 80 cases of the national courts. Associate judges may deal with these cases as authority-limited judges independently, while the assistants of the judges have to deal with the cases under the direction and supervision of the judges, meaning that the judges must be responsible for all the cases. Considering the drastic increase in the courts and judicial accountability, the situation in which fewer judges have a larger number of cases with insignificant salary increases will further reduce the competitiveness of the courts in the professional market, thus hurting the goal of judicial specialization.

Under the Court Organic Law 2018, the functions of the judge assistants are, under the guidance of the judge, to deal with the auxiliary affairs of the judicature, including reviewing documents/files of the litigation and drafting legal instruments

[22] Before the reform, the number of judges was 200,000. At the end of 2016, 27 provincial regions had completed the appointment of judges under the quota system, with 1044,442 judges appointed by 27 high courts, 340 intermediate courts, and 2,623 grass-roots courts (basic courts). The courts no longer set up posts for judges in their judicial administration departments and assigned more than 85% of their staff members to judicature work.

or orders, while clerks will only deal with auxiliary affairs such as taking notes in the hearings. Importantly, as a path of promotion, a judge assistant may be selected and appointed as a judge according to the qualifications and the procedures of judge appointments.

3.4 *Mediators and Legal Advisors*

3.4.1 Mediators

In Mainland China, mediation is the most important means of disposal of litigation cases, but it is mainly conducted by the judges as a part and a means of judicature, which is the so-called 'court mediation' or 'litigation mediation.' Under the Civil Procedural Law, 'the people's courts shall conduct mediation under the principles of the free will of the litigants and legality' is a principle (Art. 9); mediation shall be conducted first in an action instituted by a party in a court unless the litigants refuse mediation or mediation is not appropriate for the civil dispute involved (Art. 122); and the litigants must perform consent judgments based on the mediation agreement, just the same as effective judgments and rulings. Usually, judges and clerks affix their signatures and the court affixes its seal to a consent judgment, and as exceptions listed under the law, some mediation agreements shall become legally binding when it is signed by both litigants.

Court mediation is usually conducted by the same judge(s) who conducts the trial and enters the judgment. This type of mediation is mostly moved after the hearing; if mediation fails, then the judge shall enter a judgment. Sometimes, the mediation may be conducted before the hearing by the clerk or the judge assistant or by one of the judges of the tribunal who will be the trial judges.

Another type of court mediation is conducted by a judge other than the trial judge. This frequently happens in the docketing divisions; if mediation fails, then the case shall be forwarded to the judicature division for trial or further mediation. Many basic courts also have a fast-track division that conducts mediation and small claims trials; if mediation fails or the small claims case is too difficult to be entered as a simple judgment, then the case will be transferred to the judicature division for further disposal. In other courts, a separate mediation office or comprehensive office is still established that conducts mediation before the case is sent to the judicature division. In all these procedures, if the mediation agreement is entered, the court shall enter a consent judgment at the litigants' request or agreement.

In some basic courts, as a kind of local attempt at reform, there are mediators or mediation offices. These mediators are not employees of the courts but are rather invited to the court, as cooperators or experts, to conduct mediation for the cases filed in the court in different ways; for example, a case might be a filed lawsuit but is not yet docketed in the case file, the litigant might change his mind to request some advice from the documents in the court, from the public notice, or the recommendation of the docketing clerk, and move mediation by the mediator. In other courts, the mediators consist of retired judges. The mediation agreement entered by the presiding of all these mediators shall be binding and enforceable in two ways, depending on the court's institution: (1) by registration in the court files and being assigned docketing number, and the court will enter a 'consent judgment' after substantive review; and (2) by 'people's mediation' and applying for 'judicial confirmation', which is regulated by the People's Mediation Law and Civil Procedural Law.

3.4.2 Legal Advisors

In Mainland China, legal advice is offered by the docketing division. Under the Civil Procedural Law, the court, by their docketing clerk, is required to give the litigant advice, for example, about what is the right branch of the government to seek help if the case cannot be legally accepted by the court. Some courts have built up a 'litigation service center' and hire or invite lawyers or law school students to be volunteer advisors who can assume some tasks of the court clerk. Since such kinds of projects are combined with or related to complaints, petitions, mediation, and even negotiations with governmental or political branches, the functions and specific features of such legal advisors are various. For example, under an institutional device, the judge who disposes of a case has the duty to meet and explain to the litigants involved in complaining/petitioning about the settlement of the case. In such situations, the trial judge and even the president of the court is the 'advisor.'

3.5 Judicial Administrative Personnel

Under Art. 41 of the Court Organic Law, local courts at various levels have marshals to carry out the execution of judgments and orders in civil cases and the execution, in criminal cases, of the parts of judgments and orders concerned with property. People's courts at all levels have a certain number of judicial policemen. Local people's courts at various levels have forensic physicians, although they are rarely attached in the courts except in the case of some higher courts, so they will not be discussed here.[23]

4 Court Managers v. Case Managers

Just as introduced in the beginning, court management in Mainland China is conducted by the managers or 'leaders' of the court, via management of the judges

[23] Prosecutors (procuratorates) belong not to the courts, but to the Prosecution Courts, which are another 'judicial department' parallel to the courts but with functions of supervision over all the other government branches including the courts.

who manage the cases via management of the litigants, with the assistance of auxiliary personnel. In this administrative way, the court managers actually share some authority that the Civil Procedural Law reserves only for the judges for the sake of case management.

4.1 The President/Chief Judge of the Court

The president/chief judge of the court has various types of authorities/powers:

(1) Power of Judicature: trial cases as a judge, while he/she shall be the presiding judge of the tribunal;
(2) Power of Judicature of Procedural Issues: deciding the disqualification of a judge, granting a postponement of the deadline of a case settlement, issuing search warrants, deciding judicial sanction penalties, detentions, and issuing orders of coercive measures (with some risks);
(3) Power of Judicature Supervision: proposing and presiding the judicial committee to discuss important cases;
(4) Power of Personnel: proposing judges, members of the judicial committee, and associate presidents to be appointed and removed; appointing and removing the auxiliary personnel; and leading the training, assessing, and appraising of the judges as director of the Judge Evaluation Committee;
(5) Power of Discipline Monitor: deciding punishments of warnings, recording demerits, or recording serious demerits;
(6) Power of Administration: gaining and allocating resources and managing records, files, and documents.
(7) Power of Case Management: throughout the long history of justice in China, no judgment was issued before the president or the associate president in charge had signed. This entitled the president to intervene in cases that were to be handed to him for signature. Since the 1990s, with the pressure of improved efficiency and caseloads, this power was gradually delegated to the chief division judges, but the president still maintains the custom of 'investigating' cases. With the tendency of judicial independence and the regulations of the judicial reform attacking this custom as a type of 'judicial corruption', this power is dying out institutionally, but still takes place in practice and works through other legal authorities of the above, especially his/her power of personnel and power of judicature supervision.

4.2 Judicial Committee

The judicial committee is the maximum judicature organization of which the members are the heads of the court and the departments, including the president and associate presidents, the Chief division judges, usually the directors of the research department, and some full-time members who are mostly relieved from the above leadership or who were not promoted to leadership positions due to age or related reasons.

The judicial committee system was established under Court Organic Law 1954. The functions of the judicial committee are: summing up judicial experience, discussing hard, complicated and important cases, and other issues related to judicial work. Although its role as a judicature organization has been severely debated, especially for its manner of making decisions based on tribunal reports without its own personal hearing, thus hurting the independence of the tribunal and transparency of the judicial processes, the judicial committee has still been preserved after the amendments in 1979, 1983, 1986, and 2006, and even survived the Court Organic Law 2018 that focused on improving the independence of judges and the tribunals; thus, the post of the division chief judges was canceled, forbidding the presidents of the court to be involved in any case unless he/she acts as a judge of the tribunal and hears the case personally. The arguments of the proponents are from various perspectives. Politically, the judicial committee is the most important channel for the CCP to lead judicial work, and a very important manner for the court to collectively shoulder the risks of social reaction to sensitive cases; legally, the judicial committee is getting to be an important mechanism to maintain unification among the tribunals of the court, which will be more important after the cancellation of the division chief judges.

During the continual reforms since 1990, the functions, the component members, and the way decisions are made by the judicial committee have been changing. Its functions are increasingly limited, the boundary of its power is increasingly clear, and the frequency of committee meetings is steadily decreasing. Under *The Implementation Opinions on Reforming and Improving the Judicial Committee System of the People's Court* issued in January 2010 by the Supreme Court, the functions of the judicial committee of the court include: (1) To deliberate on hard, complicated, and important cases; (2) To sum up the experience of the judicial work; (3) To listen to the working reports of the judicature divisions; (4) To deliberate on and determine typical cases as models, examples, or guiding cases of this court so as to maintain judicial unification; and (5) To deliberate on other important issues concerning the judicial work of the court. The reform after 2013 further clarified the boundary of authority and responsibility between the judicial committee and the tribunals by requiring the tribunal to decide factual issues while the judicial committee, if necessary, decides the legal or policy issues based on the tribunal's fact-finding; both will be accountable for their respective decisions in their own scope.[24]

---

[24] See The Supreme People's Court of the Judicial Reform Group Office (2015, p. 89).

4.3 Assessment Indexes

Assessment indexes are quite localized and hardly ever met, as there might be more than a hundred indicators in some regions, such as Jiangsu province, which were criticized for fragmenting or weakening the legal standards set by the procedural law. Then, as an effort of unification case assessment of the national courts, the Supreme Court issued Instruction/Guideline of the Work of Quality Evaluation of Cases in 2011, which focused on quality assessment as follows:

4.3.1 Indexes of Justice (Fairness)

This includes the rate of changes of the case docketing, rate of the assessors' participation in the first instance, rate of the remanded and changed judgments (by the higher court), rate of the remanding and changing judgments (to the lower courts), rate of the reopened proceedings against effective judgments, rate of hearings in the second instance, rate of hearings in the reopened proceedings, the rate of judicial redress, and grade of judgment and other judicature documents.

4.3.2 Indexes of Efficiency

This includes the rate of docketing cases in the statutory period, rate of application of summary procedures, rate of pronouncing judgments in court (just at the time of the hearing finished), rate of settlements within the statutory period (three months for summary procedure and six for ordinary procedure), average time of enforcement, balance of the extent of settlements in the year (usually the cases at the end of the year are settled faster than those in the beginning, but this is assumed to be imbalanced), average number of the cases of the court staff annually, and average number of the cases of the judges annually.

4.3.3 Indexes of Effect

This includes the rate of reconciliation (no further complaint by appeals, petitions, or any other challenges against the result of the case settlement), rate of mediation settlement, rate of withdrawal, rate of actual settlement of enforcement, rate of the implementation of the subject matter, rate of implement on the debtors' self-motion, rate of application of enforcement of the judicial mediation cases, and rate of the complaint.

4.4 *Impact of the Evaluation Indexes*

These indexes and evaluations have deeply influenced the judges' practice, although its impacts may be decreasing. In 2014, the Supreme Court canceled the appraisal and ranking of the provincial courts, established the indexes and judicial statistics to be a reference of judicial dynamic analysis except for several necessary compulsory indexes required by procedure law, and required all the provincial courts to cancel the reasonable indexes so as to respect the judges' independence and autonomy. Some intermediate courts and even provincial courts still maintain the practice, however. Moreover, since the national courts assess and appraise judges and judge assistants based on this evaluation as a basis of promotions and other career changes, it is still very influential for both sides of the court managers and the case managers.

4.5 *From Executive Hierarchy to Tribunal's Responsibility*

In general, court management in Mainland China is changing from an administrative hierarchy to the tribunal's responsibility. The core of the tribunal's responsibility lies in restricting a new mechanism of judicial management that is based on the judge or tribunal's exercise of independent judicial authority to operate case management by replacing the division chief judges and the presidents of the courts, reassigning the judge managers as case managers, and redefining the boundary of the authorities and responsibilities between the tribunal and the court managers.

The above has made clear that the Chinese court system is actually a part of the administrative system. The internal operations of the court establish the rank of the department and the officers. Good judges can be leaders of the department and then go higher in the administrative rank. These ranks are similar to the ranks in the government, which means that judges earn the same salary and have the same political status while they transfer to different departments in government. This kind of system and its mechanisms are not only damaging the independence of judges externally from local government but also internally from the leaders of the court. The system erodes the efficiency and the utility of the court's human resources because the judges stop trying cases as soon as they become leaders. Furthermore, the boundary of the authorities and their responsibilities are becoming blurred. The two most important ideas of this phase of judicial reform are de-localization and de-bureaucratization. Attempts to delayer the structure, arrange the penal trial team in a random way, and exercise the power of case management by a presiding judge and vice presiding judge in the process of exercising judicial authority will ensure the goal of, 'Let the hearer decide, and let the decider be responsible.'

However, this circle of reform has to break the system's dilemmas and customs, in which the most difficult aspect is how to manage the conflict between exercising judicial authority equally and taking responsibility independently within a boss-political culture. On the one hand, judicial reform authorizes the judge to exercise judicial authority independently and forbids the president of the court to express an opinion on the case. At the same time, the system must keep reasonable room for presidents to intervene because of their political role and evaluation background when the press and public put pressure on some cases. Additionally, there are questions about judicial independence throughout society. Therefore, the reform shall seek to keep sharing judicial authority and judicial responsibility between judges; to maintain judicial management supervision; to make sure the transfer of judicial authority takes place step by step when the authority and responsibility are in the same space; to define the boundary between the panel and the judicial committee; and to change the power of case management and case supervision by the president and judge with the exercising of case management and supervision to the authority by themselves. In that case, the panel can exercise judicial authority independently, and the president can legally control difficult cases and social effects.

References

Chen H, Chen L (2017) The specialized courts in China: framework, history, and jurisdiction. In: IAPL Conference 2017 (unpublished)

Fu Y (2013) Social harmony at the cost of trust crisis: goals of civil justice in China. Peking Univ Law J 1:167–182

Fu Y (2019) Fully responsible judges and lost judicial assistants—loopholes and remedies in the revised judges law. China Law 4:112–119

Fu Y (2021) Dimensions and contradictions of judicial reforms in China. In: Bjorn Ahl (ed) Chinese courts and criminal procedure: post-2013 reforms. Cambridge University Press, Cambridge

The Supreme People's Court of the Judicial Reform Group Office (2015) The explanation on opinions of the Supreme People's Court on improving the judicial accountability system. People's Court Press, Beijing

Van Rhee CH, Fu Y (eds) (2013) Civil litigation in China and Europe: essays on the role of the judge and the litigants. Springer Press, Dordrecht

Wang P (2015) The discussion on the reform of people assessor system. J Law Appl 2:96–100

The History and Future of Civil Judicial Case Management in China

Fuhua Wang

1 Introduction

The Chinese judicial system, influenced by the interaction between socialist ideology and the Chinese legal tradition, is quite unique; hence the trial management or the case management as a microscopic judicial system has both a broad and a narrow definition in the contemporary Chinese legal context.[1] The broad definition is the internal administrative management of the court, including the management of court facilities and judges. It can be said that the success of the internal administrative management of the court is the key to determining whether the judiciary optimally utilizes available funding. The narrow definition of trial management is case management. This refers to the micromanagement of particular cases by judges and the courts. This kind of management mainly involves the categorization of cases, pretrial preparation, and cooperation between the court and the litigants during the litigation process. In addition, China's civil case management has made great progress in the use of modern information and communication technology (hereinafter referred to as "ICT"), electronic submission of litigation documents, and electronic service, while video conferencing and cyber courts have become specific methods of case management.

Although China belongs to the civil law system, its trial management system is closer to American caseflow management, focusing on the control of the litigation process and not merely on treating substantive rights as the core, while the civil law counterparts stress that judges manage the civil case, take substantive civil rights as the starting point, and construct the system of litigation command with the power of clarification as the core to serve the purpose of clarifying the relationship of litigation.

[1] Damaška (1986, p. 17).

F. Wang (✉)
Law School, Shanghai Jiaotong University, Shanghai, People's Republic of China
e-mail: wangfuhua021@126.com

L. Cadiet and Y. Fu (eds.), *On Judicial Management from Comparative Perspective*, Contemporary Chinese Civil and Commercial Law,
https://doi.org/10.1007/978-981-19-8673-4_7

As for trial management in China, all the courts are managed as a whole. Once the case has been accepted, the court is responsible for the management of the litigation process.

2 Judicial Management in the Context of Ideology

2.1 The Formation of New China's Legal Ideology

After the New China (People's Republic of China) was founded in 1949, the civil procedural law of the Republic of China was abolished, and the former Soviet Union civil litigation system became the reference. The civil procedure law was designed for the good of the masses; the quasi-judicial apparatus, and later on the courts, could not allow the propertied class to use the law to the detriment of the poor.[2] However, for a long time, China did not focus its attention on the civil litigation system but rather concentrated on criticizing the hypocrisy of bourgeois civil procedural law.[3]

With the deterioration of the relations of the former Soviet Union and China in the late 1950s, the influence of the Soviet legal system experience gradually weakened in New China, at the same time that China began to pay more attention to its own legal experience to develop a legal ideology based on the revolutionary experience (anti-government base) of the 1930s and 1940s. Mao Zedong advanced the theory of contradictions among the people, in which civil disputes are treated as nonconfrontational contradictions on the basis of consistent interests, emphasizing the use of democratic solutions (such as mediation). The principles that "rely on the masses, investigate and research, take mediation as the principal method, solve disputes where they arise" (依靠群众, 调查研究, 调解为主, 就地解决) were the procedural basis of regulations for resolving disputes instead of the Code of Civil Procedure.

2.2 Trial Management Under Contemporary Chinese Political Ideology

The Third Plenary Session of the Eleventh Central Committee of the Communist Party of China (hereinafter referred to as "CCCPC") was held in 1978, in which it was decided that the focus of the work should shift from class struggle to socialist modernization, marking the transformation of China's mainstream ideology to the construction of the material and spiritual socialist civilization. Since China embarked on legal reforms to promote law as the main method of dispute resolution, civil justice

[2] Chenoweth (1977, p. 9).

[3] Head (2009, p. 81).

began to pay more attention to traditional experience and international trends, and the country's civil litigation system began to normalize, despite that contemporary Chinese judicial management and case management in civil justice are developed in the context of ideology, a market economy, and legal technology, as well as other factors.

First of all, justice and politics are integrated in China. As is well-known, both Western and Chinese scholars share the common view that the civil litigation system is reflected by the specific social and historical conditions of social ideology; legal technology itself is not the purpose, nor is legal technology ideologically neutral. The first version of Civil Procedure Law was enacted in 1982 and has been modified five times, in 1991, 2007, 2012, 2017, and 2021, before the current civil trial system was established. The court or the judge must play an active role in civil justice; they are both responsible for resolving civil disputes and are defenders of the social order; thus, they must keep in close contact with the masses, practicing the idea that the law serves the people.

Second, social management and the market economy also have had a very important impact on China's civil justice system. The civil litigation system is the mixed product of the country, the market, and society. The contemporary civil justice system is embedded in politics, society, and the market. Who can control the proceedings and initiate legal proceedings? These issues depend on the comprehensive role of the nation, the market, and society. At the end of the last century, China's planned economic system ended up proclaiming that the traditional inquisitorial system in civil justice had lost its social basis. In the context of the market economy, the introduction of the adversarial system model will undoubtedly improve the level of due process and the efficiency of dispute resolution. The market economy favors the adversary system model, but the Chinese social management has adopted the inquisitorial system because of China's national conditions. The former takes the contest or fight factor as its archetype, encouraging both parties to compete before a neutral judge, who complies with the law of competition, while the latter is a type of litigation that requires intervention from judges. In contrast, the Chinese civil justice reform led by the Supreme People's Court of the People's Republic of China (hereinafter referred to as "SPC") in the 1990s tended to the former (adversary system), while the judicial reform after the new era turned to the latter (inquisitorial system).

Third, the demands of social justice have intensified during the transition period. Over the past three decades, China's economy and society have been dramatically transformed, which has required the strengthening rather than weakening of the judge's authority in civil justice. The traditional feudal society in old China has long been scattered and the social structure was atomized, but after the reform and opening up (改革开放), which led to increasing social stratification, socially vulnerable groups lack the ability of self-protection. On the other hand, in terms of the external environment, China's legal profession has not developed much; the roles of legal aid and judicial aid are extremely limited in the protection of vulnerable groups, and the low bargaining power of poor parties cannot be made up for effectively; thus, adverse financial, intellectual, and human factors contribute to substantial disadvantages in litigation for vulnerable members of society. For example, it is not easy for poor parties to obtain legal aid in civil cases; at least, the probability is less than in criminal proceedings; resolving disputes through small claim proceedings or accessing justice through contingent fees is difficult to accomplish. Those who benefit the least in society (*Rawls*) has become a problem of the case management.

In summary, China's judicial administration presents the following characteristics: it is the judge nor the case that forms the object of management.[4] The most striking feature of China's judicial management is the management of judges,[5] which ignores the judge's management of cases. Administrative means are used to urge the manager (the judge) to achieve the objectives of the organization, showing the intervention, initiative, and unilateral will of managers, among other basic characteristics.[6] It is sufficient to illustrate the importance of the court and its administrative division that the judge's management of cases and trial management are assigned the functions of appraisal and punishment, so the result of the judge's performance is the main basis of the judge's assessment and promotion. The model that focuses on the performance of judges, ignoring the management of the case itself, is also called "managing the person (judge) regardless of the case".[7]

The advantage of the above-mentioned management model is that it can improve the efficiency of the trial, but its shortcomings are obvious—ignoring the technical requirements of the substantive case and not attaching importance to the judge's case management in substantive and procedural matters. In particular, in the context of China's tradition of civil law, a case trial requires everything from legal concepts and legal terms stipulated in the substantive law (civil law) to be measured; if the court is not able to interpret the substantive law, it cannot achieve the purpose of litigation.

Due to factors such as the litigation models, judicial types, and the Chinese legal system, trial management in China is totally different from Western case management in various respects. First, case management in Western countries originates in the adversarial system, whereas trial management in China is connected to the administrative functions of the judiciary. Although case management and trial management appear to be similar to each other at first sight, they are quite different. Since the beginning of the twenty-first century, the Chinese court system has developed a trial process management system with the following three characteristics: first, the trial process management is, by its nature, procedural management for the case process, not the substantive problem; second, the trial process management conducted by specialized agencies that exercise functional management, separates the trial function and management functions; and third, the trial process management is full and dynamic, including clear responsibilities, follow-up supervision, and post-accountability in three stages. As stated, case management in Western countries originates in the adversarial system in which the parties must establish the facts and bear the burden

[4] The reform of the staff member system and the strengthening of judicial accountability since 2015 can be incorporated into the trial management system.

[5] The reform of the post of judges and the strengthening of the judges' trial responsibilities since 2015 are part of trial management.

[6] Liang (2017).

[7] Huang (2010).

of proof. In terms of procedure, the parties have the power to start, continue, and withdraw their cases as they see fit. It can be said that, originally, the Western lawsuit was similar to a game of chess in which only the two players control the game. The referee (i.e., the judge) was not entitled to assist either side. This adversarial system, however, could not bring about substantive equality between the parties. Quite to the contrary, it could lead to undue delays and a waste of resources. Case management is a significant tool introduced to eliminate such defects.

The SPC promulgated the Opinions on Strengthening the Trial Management of the People's Courts (《关于加强人民法院审判管理工作的若干意见》, No. 2 [2011], hereinafter referred to as "the Opinions on Trial Management") in January 2011, which set the following goals for trial management: to strengthen the management of the people's court trial, to standardize judicial practices, to improve the quality and efficiency of judicial work, and to achieve judicial fairness and honesty for the people (司法公正, 廉洁, 为民). It is obvious that trial management in China integrates the court's overall administrative management and case management activities. The integration focuses on the appraisal of the judicial work of judges, and the management of the caseflow and the control of case quality, which are summarized as the comprehensive effect that, "through the administrative judge, promote case handling and management combined with that of the management judge" (以管人促管案, 管案与管人相结合).

A judiciary that is capable of proactively managing cases and resolving disputes by way of mediation is better than the traditional adversarial system. From the perspective of judicial activism, case management extends the power of judges instead of restricting their power. Assessing the judge is never the central issue of case management. In trial management, however, judges are the main focus.

It can be said that trial management in China and case management in other jurisdictions share the same goal—minimizing the backlog of cases. In fact, the revision of the Civil Procedure Law of the People's Republic of China (hereinafter referred to as "Civil Procedure Law") in 2012 is a good example of implementing the proportionality principle of litigation, which strives to match the dispute resolution procedure with the value, importance, and complexity of the case. In view of this, the court should give full consideration to the trial of the case resources and possible benefits and help the parties reasonably choose the proper proceedings, such as the trial proceeding/ADR, and the ordinary/summary/small claims proceedings.

Trial management in China has its unique characteristics. In the mid-1990s, the judiciary needed to respond to societal needs regarding adjudication, such as shortening the period of trial while guaranteeing judicial quality. The model of trial management has since been further developed to meet societal needs. The legislative authority of Civil Procedure Law belongs to the National People's Congress Standing Committee; the SPC can formulate the judicial interpretation, both of which constitute the basis of case management procedures. In this context, the SPC issued several judicial interpretations, such as the Opinions on Further Promoting the Split-Flow of Complex and Simple Cases and Optimizing the Allocation of Judicial Resources (《关于进一步推进案件繁简分流优化司法资源配置的若干意见》, No. 21 [2016], hereinafter referred to as "the Opinions on the Case Split-Flow"), the Opinions on

Trial Management in 2011, and the Guiding Opinions on Carrying out the Case Quality Evaluation Work (for Trial Implementation) (《关于开展案件质量评估工作的指导意见(试行)》, No. 6 [2008]), together with the Provisions on the Strict Observance of the Case Trial Period (《关于严格执行案件审理期限制度的若干规定》, No. 29 [2000], revised by No. 18 [2008]). These above interpretations have further reinforced the trial management system in China.

The latter interpretation expressly confirmed the assessment mechanism for the quality of adjudication. The interpretation provided indices of judicial fairness, efficiency, and effectiveness. The assessment system measures the performance of the judiciary. It operates in such a way that finalizing a higher number of cases provides a higher grade in the assessment. However, from the perspective of justice, the assessment mechanism is problematic. First of all, trial management is pure procedural management, which does not involve substantive justice. The goal of trial management is to enhance efficiency via case categorization, scheduling, etc.

Secondly, the indices can be described as a reflection of the *status quo* of civil trials in China made by the superior courts. In order to achieve better grades in the assessment, the lower courts tend to accept all the orders from the superior courts. Although most of these indicators have been abandoned, under the administrative pattern of the court, the assessment power as well as supervision and review still come from the superior. This has led to some cases that are not suitable for mediation being referred to the mediation track, because the ratio of cases settled through mediation is one of the indices in the trial management assessment model. This kind of assessment did not take into consideration the opinion of the litigants, who had no way to express their opinions or to influence the outcome of the assessment.

Again, these assessment indicators are for the judge, which has the goal of ensuring justice, improving efficiency through the rational allocation of cases to enable cases to obtain reasonable trial resources, taking into account the needs of other cases, and retaining reasonable trial resources for them. The problem, however, is that these indicators lack a fundamental guide to the litigant parties and their representatives, so it is difficult to use them to assess the status of case management; because they cannot be involved in the administration of the trial, the trial management itself is closed and lacks meaning. In short, although this kind of trial management is important, it is still far from what the courts think is important or effective. It should be recognized that this type of evaluation system has some rationality, yet the problem is that it should not be linked with specific cases; the management of the case is the judge's responsibility because each case has its own particularities. Therefore, the purpose of trial management should be limited to improving the trial skills of judges and helping them to continue their training needs, allocate tasks reasonably, and get better career development opportunities. As for how to speed up and improve the quality of trials, the case management system can assume these functions.

In modern society, performance evaluation exists in many different areas. It is, therefore, also reasonable to evaluate the performance of judges. Trials are associated with the inspection rewards and punishment management system; performance appraisal results are the main determinant of promotions and the selection of those who will be advanced. The SPC emphasized that, "through the administrative judge, promote case handling and management combined with the management of judge" (以管人促管案,管案与管人相结合). The purpose of the evaluation is to promote the improvement of justice.[8] It should be carried out by a comprehensive committee comprised of judges, lawyers, and nonlegal professionals. The evaluation standards should target issues such as impartiality, legal knowledge and understanding of the law, communication skills, trial preparation, the accuracy of judgments, and monitoring of procedures. Management should be based on full reliance on and respect for the judges. However, the trial management assessment system in China is usually controlled by nonlegal professionals. In such a situation, the autonomy of the courts and the judges cannot be guaranteed.

The various digital assessments of the courts and judges have proven to be highly inconsistent with the rules of justice. In December 2016, the SPC decided to abandon the ranking system, holding that the quality assessment and the trial performance appraisal played an active role in analyzing the overall quality of the case and the running of the trial work. However, to respect the judicial work and the status of the judges, as well as to further mobilize the judges' enthusiasm, they decided to cancel the assessment rankings for the high courts; other indicators shall be set in a statistical analysis of reference indexes to conduct the assessment of all courts, in addition to the trial period index, and for analyzing the status of the trial run data reference. This shows that the Chinese court system is gradually diluting administrative trial management and turning its attention to case management.

3 Judges as Project Managers

In the Decision on Major Issues concerning Comprehensively Deepening the Reform (《中共中央关于全面深化改革若干重大问题的决定》) issued by the CCCPC, some new ideas were put forward, such as improving the responsibility system of the presiding judge and the collegial panel. "The judge who hears the case is the referee, and the referee is responsible for the case" (让审理者裁判, 由裁判者负责), marks the start of China taking a big step forward to the goal of judge independence, as well as providing an opportunity for the emergence of administrative judges.

Professor Resnik published her standard-setting article, "Managerial judges" in the Harvard Law Journal, according to the case flow management principles. This has meant that courts should have greater control over the progress of cases. This control requires that the court promote cooperation litigation before the trial stage for effective supervision. As you can imagine, if there is no judge in charge of litigation, allowing the parties to carry out any litigation behavior with no restraint not only fails to achieve litigation justice and litigation efficiency, but due to the court's aimlessness, the purpose and principle of litigation are also unable to be carried out. Therefore, the civil judicial branch needs integral management, to which the role of the parties and lawyers is indispensable. The U.S. civil case management

[8] Huai (2006, p. 239).

test has shown that lawyers endorse and promote increased judicial case management oversight of docket. Fair and efficient resolution of complex litigation requires at least that (1) the court exercise early and effective supervision (and, where necessary, control); (2) counsel act cooperatively and professionally; and (3) the judge and counsel collaborate to develop and carry out a comprehensive plan for the conduct of pretrial and trial proceedings.[9]

Case management by Chinese judges also includes the mission of achieving substantive justice. The more the judge injects himself into procedural matters, the more the usual contest style and its accompanying structure of incentives are weakened.[10] Over the past two decades, the transformation of the civil litigation model from an inquisitorial system to an adversary system has resulted in problems in the parties' equality of litigation rights. There is a difference in the litigation capacity between the parties, providing them with equal litigation weapons and failing to ensure their actual equality. The measures to change this situation should include, first, to provide legal services through the legal aid system for the disadvantaged party, to realize substantive equality, and second, to allow the judge to take positive action, in case the power of the parties is not balanced, to intervene to help the weaker side. In contrast, the two strategies have their own advantages and disadvantages: the first corrective mechanism (activating the judge) may make the parties doubt the decision-maker's neutrality, while the second strategy (subsidizing the weaker contestant) may end up impoverishing the arsenal of adversarial techniques.[11] Nevertheless, the latter is still worthy of the strategy's attention. Having judges engaged in case management has at least two benefits. First, the judge can predict the substantive and procedural issues in the case through case management, rather than wait for the parties or lawyers to raise them. Second, the judge can formulate a reasonable trial plan to keep the parties and lawyers from getting into a dead end when considering the case, or going astray in the details of the case, thus their train of litigation thought can be guided to the real legal issues.

Due to specific characteristics of the courts in China, administrative management should not be used for managing the courts. Rather, the trial judges should control and be in charge of managing litigation and its pace. Equality of arms between the parties can be guaranteed in two manners. One is to provide legal aid to the weaker party by using public funds. Another manner is to request that the trial judge assist the weaker party. However, both approaches have disadvantages. After all, public funding cannot be unlimited and assistance by the judge may endanger neutrality.

Case management as a breakthrough to enhance the efficiency of litigation, its necessity lies in the reality of China's nearly-depleted judicial resources. Up to now, although the "staff reform" of the judges is nearly completed, the number of national judges has been reduced from the previous 210,000 to 120,000. Still, the proportion of Chinese judges of the total population is still high, with an average of 120,000 citizens per judge, far higher than Japan (46,928) and the Hong Kong Special Administrative

[9] Federal Judicial Center (2004, p. 7).

[10] Damaška (1986, p. 107).

[11] Ibid., p. 108.

Region (37,937). Thus, even though increasing the number of judges may be beneficial for increasing efficiency, this is not an option in China given the country's already large number of judges. Instead, case management in place of trial management must have priority.

Like any system, the case management system is important in terms of content, but its operating conditions are equally important. The transition from trial management to case management in the field of civil judicature in China must take into consideration the environmental factors, and the negative factors of the system should be minimized. One of the most dangerous problems is that an increase in the judge's authority means an increase in the possibility of abuses of power. Because of the wide power and the weak supervision of the administrative hierarchy, judges often show greater initiative than traditionally in determining the nature of cases and arranging the results of cases.

On the other hand, this means that case management is likely to foster the judge's personal prejudices. The close relationship of the judge with the parties and their lawyers can lead to strong emotions, including admiration, friendship, or hate in the process of case management. Meanwhile, case management can become the origin of subjective bias. On account of a lack of clear standards or rules in the process of case management and that management of quality relies on the intuitive judgment of the judge, the individual's idea of justice has become the most important factor. As a result, there is great importance attached to the judge's neutrality to prevent understanding the case in the court and mastering too much to lose neutrality. For legal purposes, the activities of the private contact with lawyers must be limited to the premise of not violating neutrality.

It should be highlighted that the principles of equality and fairness may be betrayed if a judge is excessively active during the affirmation of law cases. Hence, judges should execute the duty of program management under the principles of equality and fairness, avoiding, for example, clarifying specific facts to help one party while not allowing facts that might help the other party. In short, while establishing the system of judge management, how to protect and pay attention to the interest of the parties and how to prevent the interest of the parties from constantly interfering with the judge's power should be considered. Although case management aimed at guaranteeing the performance of judgments is important, the justice of the procedure is more important.

American scholars generally agree that the role of the judge (especially, perhaps, the federal judge) has become more bureaucratic or administrative in recent decades, which is obvious. They are responsible not only for deciding motions and overseeing trials and other traditional "judicial" roles but also are increasingly responsible for managing the court's caseload.[12] As in the United States, Chinese judges have a tendency to engage in administrative matters, and as the trial business has increased, a need to use the judges' assistants has also grown.

In recent years, the division of responsibilities between judges and assistant judges constitutes a key part of the judge's classification reform. Because of the shortage

[12] Freer (2009, p. 408).

of judges, the courts are complex and the cases are growing, and the judges need staff assistants. Inside the court, the original "assistant judges" (助理审判员) role has gradually faded out, and the court clerk role has been reordered, caused by the absence of judge assistants and providing an opportunity for the emergence of judge assistants. In this context, the SPC plans to allocate the personnel proportion of trial staff between judges, assistant judges, and court clerks, according to the court trial and the difficulty of the case, to properly determine the position and relationship of responsibilities to maximize the effectiveness of the trial staff.

The revision of Civil Procedure Law in 2012 led the composition of the judiciary to be more scientific; the process was streamlined into two distinct phases: the pretrial stage and the formal trial stage. The purpose of the pretrial stage is to facilitate the trial proceeding, in other words, the formal trial. The formal trial should be held in one continuous oral hearing, in which all the evidence should be presented immediately to the judge or a panel that gives the verdict based on the material presented in the formal trial. The assistant judges have no judicial power; his main job is to prepare business and manage cases. According to the idea of the SPC, the assistant judges are responsible for service, scheduling trials, preservation, appraisal, uploading judgments on the internet, and other auxiliary affairs.

4 From Confrontation to Cooperation: From the Perspective of the Litigation Subject

In China, there is a consensus on the theoretical division of the adversary and inquisitorial systems, with the legislation and practice of civil litigation having clearly turned to the adversary system model. Under the framework of such a model, civil litigation is a matter of the parties—the commencement of the proceedings, the process of proceedings, and the evidence on which the court is dependent may only be made by the parties. This raises the need for case management at the technical level. In contrast, China's traditional practice of the inquisitorial system model, in which the process of the end of the proceedings, the litigation, and other litigation initiatives by the court to master case management, belongs to the terms of reference of the judge.[13] In the context of the conversion to the civil litigation model, case management is also put on the agenda as an auxiliary question. Moreover, after several years of practice, China's civil case management presents two types: the traditional management model of extrinsic command and control by judges, and the autonomous or intrinsic model of management rules. The former model uses the threat of sanctions to urge the

[13] From the beginning of the 1990s to the beginning of the 2000s was the key period when the Chinese civil litigation model changed from an adversary system to an inquisitorial system. The transformation began with 'strengthening the trial mechanism, strengthening the power of collegial bench and strengthening the burden of proof'. See Hu and Zeng (2016, p. 65).

parties to promote litigation, while the latter emphasizes that the parties are actively engaged in litigation with the assistance of the courts.[14]

In the first type, the authority of the court is the core, and the authority of the court is significantly enhanced both at the start and the end of the proceedings. The litigation responsibilities of the judges and the parties are also activated; the parties have to advance in the proceedings in a prudent manner, and the judge must also take on "substantive leadership" and form a resolving dispute group with the parties (Arbeitsgemeinschaft). In the second type, the role of the court is to help the parties to the correct claims for litigation and produce the appropriate materials; this will eliminate the risk that the parties may manipulate the litigation process and manage the material evidence in the traditional litigation context, expressing the right (the duty of clarification) of the court and the parties to the main form of litigation cooperation. To avoid the above danger, judges should enjoy the power to lead the parties and be required to dispose of the case properly. Although *clarification* has different terms in different jurisdictions,[15] all of them aim toward the same goal of achieving substantial justice.[16]

4.1 Cooperation Between the Litigants and Judges

In modern civil litigation, cooperation between the judge and the parties can benefit the resolution of disputes. This implies that not only the role of the judges but also that of the parties should be considered in trial management. The parties are the center of any litigation, so they must also be the center of trial management. There should be full participation of the parties in the trial management, and their evaluation should be an important basis for trial management.

A civil case management system should achieve greater efficiency, participant cooperation, and participant satisfaction. The discussions between the judges and the parties are, therefore, essential, being an opportunity for each participant to refine and understand their dispute issue.

At the political level, the justice of China has been emphasized as satisfying the people's right to know, to participate, and to express, and the right of supervision on this work; these have great significance to judicial authority and the protection of the parties' rights. However, if the people are not put in the process of litigation and court management, those rights will disappear into thin air. In this sense, the participation of the parties involved in case management activities is indispensable.

---

[14] Prince (2014, p. 175).

[15] In Germany, the judge's duty of clarification, *richterliche Hinweispflichtung* finds its constitutional root in the principle of equality before the law, and is an important implication of the principle of 'equality in weapons' (Waffengleichheit) in the procedural law.

[16] Huang (2003, p. 29).

4.1.1 Participation of the Litigants

The experience with case management abroad has shown that strengthening the judges' powers and reducing the autonomy of the litigants are not central issues in a modern system of case management. Instead, encouraging cooperation between the litigants and the court is used to increase the efficiency of litigation and public confidence. Cooperation between the litigants and the court should be the objective of modern litigation and this implies that relevant information is sufficiently disclosed.

Litigants are more concerned about whether their substantive civil rights can be properly remedied and their procedural rights can be safeguarded. It is conceivable that the excellent judicial statistics of the court are not particularly related to them; they are rather concerned with whether they can win their lawsuit and whether they can collect evidence that is beneficial to them. They are also concerned with the total time needed for completing the action. An annual assessment of the court, as what takes place in China, that does not take these issues into consideration is meaningless to them. Moreover, the trial management performance statistics reflect the court's work status and results, not that of the parties or lawyers; neither are they done by neutral third parties. It is difficult to consider a self-test as comprehensive and objective or as reflecting the actual operation of the civil justice situation. Based on these considerations, it is necessary to consider the shift from the traditional evaluation management to the management of cases, which strengthens the authority of the judge and encourages cooperation between judges and parties. There are two successful models of litigation in today's world we can learn from. First, there is the model of the American federal courts, which emphasizes that the judge as case manager should become involved in the lawsuit at an early stage and cooperate with the litigants in terms of setting a litigation schedule. Second, there are civil law countries that emphasize that the procedural calendar should be determined by the judge, the parties, and their lawyers.

In terms of case management in China, there are some obstacles that prevent cooperation between the litigants and the court. First, the parties do not have sufficient powers to negotiate and determine the procedure even though the right to select the procedure and to switch between procedures is a basic right of the parties in China. This right enhances the litigants' confidence in the procedure and resolves disputes. Although the right to switch between proceedings was incorporated in the Civil Procedure Law since 2012,[17] in theory, the procedure option should be a basic right of the parties; the more communication and debate between the parties and the more evidence they put forward, the more their understanding of the whole picture of the dispute. They may realize that the proceedings that they used at the beginning perhaps are not the most suitable for reaching a solution, so they should have the right to request the court to change from unsuitable proceedings to suitable proceedings, e.g., turn the referee into reconciliation, convert the referee into mediation, or convert the

[17] The latest revision of China's Civil Procedure Law was in 2021. Article 125 provides that civil disputes that are brought before the people's court and that are suitable for mediation should first be mediated, except if the parties refuse mediation.

reconciliation and referee; convert the settlement to arbitration, convert the mediation to referee, or convert the mediation to arbitration, etc. Articles 125 and 136 of the Civil Procedure Law stipulate that the court has the power to transfer procedures *ex officio*,[18] which is also a distinct feature of China's case management. Practice shows that investing time in the early stages of the litigation, however, will lead to earlier dispositions, less wasteful activity, a shorter trial period, and, in the long run, economies of judicial time and fewer judicial burdens.[19]

Second, the Civil Procedure Law in the past did not set a litigation promotion obligation for the parties, which means the litigants have no obligation or duty to promote litigation. In order to encourage the participation of the parties in the action and shorten the length of the procedure, legislation encouraging the participation of the parties in the action is needed. According to the author's research, nearly all key players were of the opinion that legislation should be put in place. In addition, 90.4% of the judges, 86.7% of the legal scholars, 95.4% of the lawyers, and 96.4% of the parties interviewed believed that the period of time for introducing evidence should be limited by statute. Our research also shows that 20% of the delays were actually caused intentionally. When introducing the amendments to the 2012 Civil Procedure Law, the legislature suggested punishing the parties that caused undue delays in submitting evidence. However, the introduction of a ban on the submission of late evidence seemed to be too harsh in practice. Even the courts have expressed doubts on this issue. Sanctions in the form of monetary fines are more suitable if parties deliberately and unduly prolong the hearing of a case.

Some research confirms that the elements of procedural justice can be boiled down to the simple idea that the parties' feelings about justice are not just related to the judgment itself but also to whether they are treated fairly in the proceedings. Therefore, the future Chinese civil case management system should strengthen the procedures for the protection of the parties, the following key dimensions of procedural justice should be incorporated: (1) voice: the participant must feel heard in the proceedings; (2) neutrality: decision-making must appear unbiased and principled; (3) respect: the participant must believe he or she was treated with dignity; and (4) trust: the participant must believe the decision-maker is taking into account the participant's needs and sincerely trying to address the litigants' needs.

4.1.2 The Assistance of Lawyers

It is well known that China adheres to the civil law system, the judicial logic of which is that almost all litigation activities are based on substantive law, and disputes must

[18] As prescribed in Article 136 of the Civil Procedure Law, 'the cases people's court accepted should be dealt with respectively as following: (1) the parties can apply to payment order proceeding for those cases without dispute; (2) for those cases that are not controversial, they may be resolved by mediation so as to be disposed of timely; (3) determine the summary procedure or ordinary procedure according to the nature of the case; (4) the cases need to trial request the parties to exchange evidence and clarify issues.'

[19] Federal Judicial Center (2004, p. 5).

be re-expressed in accordance with applicable legal norms; thus, lawyers play an important role in preventing unreasonable submissions by their clients.[20] The lawyer is the judge's ally with the crew, not an opponent. Therefore, lawyers should play an important role in the initial stages of litigation. Cooperation between the court and the litigants alone is not enough; the lawyer's control of the pace and scope of most cases can be a major impediment to the litigation process. Lawyers must also be involved in cooperation, although this may appear unrealistic at first sight. After all, their income will be affected if the length of the action is shortened as a result of cooperation. Yet, if the litigants' interests are their first priority, lawyers should be willing to cooperate with the court. In this regard, lawyers should better prepare their cases to avoid undue delay.

During the trial, lawyers should cooperate actively with the court to promote the centralization of the case trial, so as to improve the efficiency of litigation on the whole. In the Anglo-American legal system, the judge is a negative arbiter; judges' passive and neutral roles are often described as "hostage under the lawyer's strategy", and even lawsuits controlled by lawyers become an obstacle to case management. Although the authority is more important in our civil judicature and there is no danger of the lawyer "kidnapping" the judge, how to deal with the relationship between the judge and the lawyer is also a subject that trial management must pay attention to. If the judges and lawyers can form a professional community by forming a good relationship characterized by identification, communication, trust, and cooperation, this will help the parties exercise their rights of litigation rationally and correctly, which will ease the atmosphere of confrontation between parties, increase the possibility of negotiation and reconciliation, and improve the efficiency of litigation objectively. Furthermore, the experience of case management also shows that the effective cooperation between courts or lawyers in pretrial procedures, especially in complex cases, through the formulation and implementation of a wide range of trial plans will also play a role in improving the quality and efficiency of litigation.

All in all, in various ways of court administration in recent years, the importance of managing judges has been repeatedly highlighted and emphasized, while judges in case management are powerless and weak. The implementation of the former (to manage judges) is in conformity with the current national management system, not contributing to the formation of the legal profession or enhancing the efficiency of lawsuits. In contrast, the latter (case management by judges), on the premise of respect for the judge's subjectivity, is in line with the judicial rules of technical management and puts emphasis on the necessity of substantive rights for the parties involved in case management. The latter is more conducive to promoting trial quality and efficiency, so it should become a key element of civil judicial reform. Of course, the transition from trial management to case management should be implemented through gradual, phased reform. Meanwhile, according to actual needs and urgency, to changes in the degree of difficulty, and to the consensus of all parties, the extent of the reform can be modified. We should first strengthen the cooperation between the judge and the parties, enrich the power to clarify, and then slowly fade out the

[20] Ibid.

administrative management as we eventually move toward the case management system with Chinese characteristics.

4.2 Case Management Under Litigation Cost Control

In recent decades, both developed and developing countries have felt overwhelmed with regard to judicial resources; most are unable to solve the tension between the number of judges and the caseload burden, which, with the increasing number of cases, has become the nightmare of civil judicial systems. In this context, academic and judicial circles are seeking help with the costs of litigation to remedy the shortage of judicial resources. As a tool of justice, litigation costs have the ability to allocate litigation resources and guide the parties to choose the implementation of lawsuit behavior; it is also an aspect of case management. Litigation costs can influence, adjust, and control the application of the parties to choose and to help promote achieving the goal of litigation justice and litigation efficiency.

Litigation cost mechanisms affect the parties through the following two options: (1) to use litigation/nonlitigation procedures, as litigation costs can encourage or dissuade the parties from choosing mediation, arbitration, or litigation for dispute resolution, so the split-flow is implemented; and (2) within the litigation proceedings, the cost mechanism can motivate or eliminate the options of withdrawal, appeal, mediation, and reconciliation. In conclusion, the ultimate goal of cost instrumental value lies in the pursuit of more justice with the least amount of judicial resources to improve the marginal benefit of the law. The Measures on the Payment of Litigation Costs (《诉讼费用交纳办法》, State Council Order No. 481 [2006], hereinafter referred to as "the Measures on the Costs") significantly reduced the standard cost of labor dispute cases, mediation cases, summary procedures cases, and counterclaim cases, which was the external performance value tool of litigation cost mechanisms.

4.2.1 Discouraging Abuse of the Process

In China's Civil Procedure Law and relevant judicial interpretations, the instrumental function of litigation costs mainly reflects its ability to regulate abuses of the process. Specifically, in the case of unnecessary litigation (frivolous litigation), the litigants will not be able to recoup their costs, according to Article 34 of the Measures on the Costs, even if they win the case. In the case of plaintiffs who apply to withdraw the suit or appellants who withdraw the appellate, the people's court may make an order determining that the fees shall be borne by the plaintiff or the appellant. Additionally, Article 35 of the Measures on the Costs provides that "the parties who reduce the amount of the request after the end of the investigation should change the burden of the cost for the reducing part." Second, the court may make an order for fees to be repaid when the parties have intentionally, or due to gross negligence, caused undue litigation costs. Article 409 of the Interpretation of the SPC on the Application of the Civil Procedure Law of the People's Republic of China (《最高人民法院关于适用 < 中华人民共和国民事诉讼法 > 的解释》, No. 5 [2015], revised by No. 11 [2022], hereinafter referred to as "the Judicial Interpretation of the Civil Procedure Law") stipulates that "where the new evidence submitted by a party overturns the retrial, the people's court shall support the claim by the party against whom the retrial application is made and other parties to be compensated for their increase of necessary expenses, such as transport, accommodation, meals and lost working time as a result of failure to submit evidence in the original trial due to the fault of the applicant for a retrial or the party requesting procuratorial supervision". The above provisions express the spirit of prohibiting parties from abusing their litigation rights and impairing the interests of other parties. At the same time, these provisions raise the predictability of the litigation costs. The parties can clear possible expenses during the litigation and be prompted to submit their evidence in time.

4.2.2 Encouragement to Use Mediation (Reconciliation)

If the litigation costs are too high and uncertain, the ADR may become the parties' realistic choice. China's civil judicial practice attaches great importance to litigation costs as a means of encouraging mediation (reconciliation). Article 15 of the Measures on the Costs provides that if the case is settled by mediation or the party concerned applies for withdrawal, they only need to pay half of the cost of litigation (the court fee). The clause expresses the guidance that, since the win is not assured, it is better to reduce costs by resorting to mediation or reconciliation rather than to continue to invest resources in litigation.

4.2.3 Motivate the Parties to Use Small Claims Litigation

The 2012 Civil Procedure Law provides small claims procedure; an auxiliary system is now needed to guide the parties to use it. In accordance with Article 16 of the Measures on the Costs, the fee for accepting cases is less than half of the cases for summary proceedings. The litigation fee for the small claims procedure as one of the summary procedures should only be lower than this fee (in accordance with the summary fee of one-fourth charged, for example). Lower fees are also offered in exchange for the legislative reduction of the right of appeal or if they lost the trial level interests and, thus, must be afforded some compensation or redistribution.

5 The Judicial Management of Each Litigation Stage: From the Functional Perspective

Although some scholars may believe that only court management, not case management, exists in China's civil justice field, this argument is not exact. Although the case management in China's civil justice system has not been raised separately, the contents of some aspects of case management are implicit in the practice of legislation and judicial reform, such as ADR and the split-flow of cases.

The most practical motive for the development of case management system in Chinese courts is to solve the problem of "more cases with fewer judges" (案多人少). Over the past few years, most Chinese scholars attributed the causes of "more cases with fewer judges" in the civil justice system to the following factors: the limited trial track, the too low threshold of filing a lawsuit, and an excess of cases crowded in the ordinary procedure track of the first instance, all leading to a high degree of tension between the trial and the power of the trial.[21] In order to relieve such stress, the caseflow management system is one of the focuses of Chinese trial management, as in Western countries, through caseflow monitoring and implementing whole process management, including case registering, case allocation, trial, judgment execution, and archiving. In 1999, in the first Five-Year Reform Plan of the People's Court (《人民法院五年改革纲要》, No. 28 [1999]), Article 8 provides for establishing the scientific case trial process management system and the specialized agencies to manage the caseflow on different cases of filing, service, trial, closing, and other stages, to ensure that the case trial is fair and efficient. The first application of the case management process was undoubtedly the Shanghai First Intermediate People's Court; the introduction of this type of management was influenced by the Anglo-American practice of caseflow management. The concept of trial management was then widened to include the management and control of different facets of civil procedure, such as trial procedure, trial quality, and efficiency. Multiple assessment mechanisms have been developed to evaluate judicial work. The assessments cover the length of the trial and the annual case clearance rate.

5.1 Case Split-Flow at the Filing Stage

One premise to be tested in China is that early and active judicial case management will result in decreased time to disposition and reduced litigation costs. If litigation becomes more efficient and less costly while still achieving just outcomes, the hope is that litigants, lawyers, and judges will have greater satisfaction with the judicial process. In all early management methods, in addition to ADR, a traditional dispute resolution method in China, the Chinese government also emphasized to develop administrative mediation, civil mediation (人民调解), commercial mediation, and

[21] Cai (2013, p. 131).

the role of arbitration in dispute resolution. With entering the twenty-first century, the court began to attach importance to the connection mechanism of litigation and mediation to promote the dispute triage before litigation.

The SPC deems that trial resources should be rationally distributed through trial management, and that simple and complicated cases should be classified into split-flow according to some sorting standards for the purpose of improving trial efficiency. Simple civil cases should be trialed quickly, while complex cases should be trialed more carefully (简案快审, 繁案精审). First, professional trials should be promoted according to the different types of cases and their status to choose judges who are responsible for simple or complex cases. Second, split-flow of judgment documents of structure or reasoning according to the levels of trials, types of cases, and the situation of court hearings, among others, should be implemented. The judgment document of complex cases should be targeted based on the reasoning around the focus of dispute. The simple cases in new types and with insightful significance can be reasoned strongly; other simple cases can be simplified reasoned by using the judgment documents of the order type (summary judgment), element type, table format, and other simple judgment documents. The judgment document may be appropriately simplified when the court announces a judgment or a sentence. Instant fulfillment of civil cases in court may record relevant circumstances on court transcripts, with judgment documents no longer issued after the consent of all parties.

According to the provisions of the Civil Procedure Law, the term "case management" mainly refers to the involvement of a judge assistant in the pretrial in preparing business. Even without developing rules of formal case management, some judges still have the judicial discretion to intervene in cases and have pushed the parties to take certain steps.

The Civil Procedure Law confirms the legitimacy of mediation in advance. Mediation in advance includes mediation before litigation and mediation after case acceptance. The preregister mediation system in Article 125 of the Civil Procedure Law is a way of case management. "If an action is brought on civil disputes that are suitable to mediation, the people's court shall conduct the mediation first unless the parties refuse to do so." The preregister mediation is that the court mediates between the plaintiff and the defendant when the plaintiff issues a case after the court reviewed the prosecution that conforms with accepted conditions and is suitable for mediation, as that has the consent of all parties. For the mediation after register, Article 136 of the Civil Procedure Law provides for the split-flow of cases, that is, "the cases people's court accepted should be dealt with respectively as following: (1) the parties can apply to payment order proceedings for those cases with no dispute; (2) for those cases that are not controversial, they may be resolved by mediation so as to be disposed of timely; (3) determine the summary procedure or ordinary procedure according to the nature of the case; (4) the cases need to trial request the parties to exchange evidence, and clarifying issues." The above provisions show that the involvement of judges from the early stages of the action, whether called case management or otherwise, is likely to increase as well. In short, early and active judicial case management is key to efficient litigation, particularly in complex cases, which is consistent with the experience of Western countries.

The provisions of the Civil Procedure Law and the Judicial Interpretation of the Civil Procedure Law actively guide both parties to agree to the application of summary procedures in civil cases. In simple civil cases where the subject matter exceeds the prescribed standard or where the provisions of the first section of Article 160 of the Civil Procedure Law cannot be applied but the amount of the dispute is below the prescribed standard, the parties can agree to apply small claims procedures. According to special procedures for cases on security interests, parties will be actively guided to transfer the cases of creditor requests to the debtor to pay the money and urged to use electronic payment orders.

5.2 The Pretrial Conference

The purpose of case management in China is to move cases to trial quickly, and the conference is to focus the litigation on the issues that are truly in dispute and to understand what is required to resolve the litigation efficiently and fairly. The SPC of China has put forward the ideals of giving full use to the functions of the pretrial conference after the 2012 Civil Procedure Law stipulates the pretrial conference system. Specific programs include the judge or judge assistant who is guided by the judge presides over the pretrial conference to resolve matters, such as the identity of parties, organize the exchange of evidence directory, and initiate illegal evidence exclusion. In the case of suitable mediation, it actively contributes to the pretrial to facilitate the settlement of parties or to reach a mediation agreement. Confirming the undisputed facts and evidence at the pretrial conference can simplify the trial's introduction of evidence or cross-examination. For the controversial facts and evidence, the pretrial conference can be used to summarize the issue after seeking input from parties.

The court will consider the possibility of settlement or ADR in the pretrial conference, and it will endeavor to gain the parties' consent if it believes that the course of action is appropriate. The court may consider other perspectives, such as the mode of trial and the exchange of documents between the parties.

The widespread use of the pretrial conference also requires judge assistants to play their role as much as possible in pretrial proceedings. Through their specialized assistance work, judge assistants can prompt the parties to submit proper claims and requests related to facts and evidence as soon as possible, and help the parties and the court as soon as possible organize, identify, and simplify the facts and evidence on the issue so that the parties can attack or defend in the trial through oral debate proceedings, as well as enhance the correctness of the facts in court trials in direction and save costs. Among them, the fixing of issues is the central task of the judge assistant. They can assist parties to sort out the subject matter (*der Streitgegenstand*), the facts of the cases, and the legal issues of evidence according to a particular order and manner, so that the rights and obligations between the parties or the distribution of rights and obligations between the parties are clear, which will help centralize the follow-up trial and improve litigation efficiency.

5.3 The Reform of the Trial Mode

The SPC put forward the Opinions on the Case Split-Flow in September 2016. For those small claims, the court may hear directly by the claims and not be subject to restrictions on the segmentation of investigation proceedings and debate proceedings. For civil cases in which the elements of the case and the issues are relatively concentrated, the court can determine trial order according to the relevant elements and claims. The court investigation and court debate can be carried out simultaneously with the disputed elements.

The reform of the trial record is also an integral part of trial reform. Chinese courts have developed the use of intelligent voice recognition technology to convert trial voices into text and generate court records simultaneously. The SPC also implements trial activities throughout the recording video requirements, and explores ways to use the trial recording video to simplify or replace the clerk court records.

Our court implements the practice of concentrating on time trial cases. Those civil cases that are appropriate for summary procedures should be centralized to register, deliver, schedule trials, open a court session, and pronounce judgments. The same trial organization should hear several cases in the same period.

5.4 The Loss of Rights

The civil case management of China was proven successful—as opposed to just sounding good—as shown by the effort to the loss of the right of evidence, meaning that the loss of rights is a necessary means of case management. China adopted a strict system of loss of rights at the beginning of this century, Article 68 of the Civil Procedure Law stipulates the loss of rights of evidence: "the parties shall provide timely evidence to support the opinions put forward by themselves. The people's court shall determine the evidence that the parties should provide and the time limit thereof, in accordance with the claims of the parties and the situations of the trial. If the parties have genuine difficulty in providing evidence within the time limit, they may apply to the people's court for a prolongation; the people's court may prolong the time limit properly according to the application of the parties. Where a party provides evidence beyond the time limit, the people's court shall order him to explain the reasons; if he refuses to do so or the reasons are untenable, the people's court may, according to different situations, not accept the evidence, or accept the evidence but impose an admonition (训诫) or fine upon him."

The article provides that if the parties did not submit evidence on time due to their fault, while the judgment has a significant impact on them, and if the judge did not perform duties to promote litigation, which includes clarifying or publicly evaluating evidence promptly so that the parties will lose their opportunity to express or add statements and the parties only find and make evidence after the proceedings (oral debate period). On the basis of the principle of the best treatment, adverse consequences should not be accepted by the parties, but should belong to the situation that may lead to a wrong decision. In this case, the court should not dismiss or allow their evidence to be produced.

5.5 *Sanctions on Abuse of the Process*

The SPC recently emphasized that courts should guide parties to litigate honestly and take some measures to fight against false litigation, malicious litigation, and other unethical actions; they should also play an important role in leveraging litigation costs and the cost of lawyers so that the parties modify their actions by choosing the appropriate way to resolve disputes. Where the parties abuse the process and delay meeting their litigation obligations, which cause a direct loss to the other person involved or the third party, the people's court could support no-fault parties who require compensation for counsel fees and other reasonable claims according to the specific situation.[22]

5.6 *Case Management in Class Action*

As with the problems faced by Western countries, the case management of class action in China is inevitably difficult; it not only tests the court's case management ability but also determines the necessary conditions for the effectiveness of class action. The trials of complex cases require the judge to be given full power to prevent litigation from the controlling party, and was controlled by the representative. The judge's case management rights should include the following elements. (1) Public notice and register: where the subject matters of an action are under the same category and one of the parties has numerous litigants but the exact number of the litigants is uncertain when the lawsuit is filed, the people's court may issue a public notice to explain the nature of the case and the claims of the litigation and informing those interested persons who are entitled to the claim to register their rights with the people's court within a fixed period of time. (2) Select the representatives: Those who have registered their rights with the people's court may elect representatives from among themselves to proceed with the litigation; if the election fails its purpose, such representatives may be determined by the people's court through consultation with those who have registered their rights with the court. Sometimes subclasses must be created when differences in the positions of class members require separate representatives and separate counsel. (3) Judicial review: in order to protect the interests of a large number of parties, the judge must also have full supervision to review the fairness, reasonableness, and adequacy of proposed settlements in class actions. In addition, for the acts taken by these representatives, the results shall

---

[22] See Article 22 of the Opinions on the Case Split-Flow.

bind all litigants of the party whom they represent. However, any substitution of representatives, relinquishing claims, acceptance of claims of the opposing party, or negotiating settlements shall be approved by the litigants of the party. In this way, the court must supervise the representative; if the representative does not perform their duties or abuses their representation, the court can replace them at the parties' request.

It is unquestioned that Chinese judges and lawyers lack experience in class actions. China is also still developing its experience with test litigation (model litigation, 示范诉讼) before being considered to have mature experience. For some mass tort cases, the court may select individual or a few cases through precedent litigation as test cases; the results of its referees will be used to deal with other similar cases and the test cases will promote the efficient settlement of batch cases. Although China's substantive law and procedural law do not stipulate the test litigation system, environmental disputes, labor disputes, securities disputes, real estate disputes, and other types of cases have applied this kind of case management in China's judicial practice.

6 The Application of ICT in Judicial Management: The Technical Perspective

Most trends in civil justice reform in recent decades have been increasingly dependent on technology, most paradigm reformers assume the combination will be more efficient, and applying technology to case management has become a global trend. As electronic court systems continue to increase their online presence, many countries now have more requirements to dispose of case filings electronically. Many legal software vendors intend to develop products that can take advantage of electronic communication by pulling data from the case management product and pushing it into court filing systems.

In the age of the Internet, instant electronic contacts such as WeChat and email have taken the place of traditional face-to-face contacts and transactions. Inevitably, this trend has permeated the field of civil justice. In China, for example, synchronizing with e-commerce, since 2000, the construction of electronic court and electronic litigation began. As can be seen in the implementation of the 2012 Civil Procedure Law and the Five-Year Plan for Information Construction at People's Courts (2016–2020) (《人民法院信息化建设五年发展规划》) released by the SPC in 2015, the application of ICT in litigation has been legalized.[23] Article 90 of the Civil Procedure Law, Article 135 and Article 136 of the Judicial Interpretation of the Civil Procedure Law

[23] According to the Five-Year Plan for Information Construction at People's Courts (2016–2020), 'Stage 1' is the internal foundation construction stage, 'Stage 2' is to promote the construction of website construction and construction of 'smart court', and 'Stage 3' is for 'digital management' and 'embedded Internet plus'. See Wei (2015).

establish the electronic service system, and Article 259 of the Judicial Interpretation of the Civil Procedure Law provides a video trial system.

The SPC recently proposed the establishment of a platform for online mediation, online register, online judicial confirmation, online trial, electronic supervisory proceedings, and other electronic service, which will carry out the functions of dispute resolution involving prejudgment, information sharing, resource integration, and data analysis, among others. This proposal promotes the development of informatization for the diversification of dispute resolution and achieves split-flow in litigation through the use of electronic service and remote video technology.[24] This indicates that China has embarked on a transition from the construction of an electronic litigation system to its practical application.

On February 28, 2017, the national court's new unified electronic service platform (http://songda.court.gov.cn) did its test run in Fengman Primary People's Court, Jilin, Jilin Province; Huadian Primary People's Court, Jilin Province; Hangzhou Railway Transportation Court, Zhejiang Province; and Yuhuan Primary People's Court, Zhejiang Province. The platform will support the service litigation documents by Sina microblog, Sina Email, Alipay, and other platforms.

6.1 Internet E-Court: Electronic Case Management

In January 2011, the SPC issued the Opinions on Trial Management, which proposed establishing a case information management system and a trial management network, and building a national court case information database and case information query system. These will then promote the application of information technology in scheduling the trial, trial quality assessment, trial flow, file management, performance appraisal, judicial statistics, and human resources allocation, among other aspects. This will help achieve the trial management of information technology and transition from extensive trial management to intensive management, fine management. Trial management should be based on information technology, actively use internet thinking, follow the requirements of the age of big data, and strengthen legal intelligent data development and application. We should also merge the trial management and information technology together and build the "wisdom of the court", as proposed in December 2016 by Shen Deyong, the vice president of the SPC at that time. The Central Leading Group for Comprehensively Deepening Reforms (中央全面深化改革领导小组) decided to set up the Hangzhou Internet Court (杭州互联网法院) on June 26, 2017, to meet the needs of the masses, improve trial mechanisms to enhance the trial effectiveness, resolve network disputes, and promote the deep integration of the internet and economic society to enhance judicial protection.

---

[24] The Supreme People's Court issued the Opinions on People's Court Further Deepen the Reform of Diversified Dispute Resolution Mechanism (《关于人民法院进一步深化多元化纠纷解决机制改革的意见》, No. 14 [2016]) on June 28, 2016, and released the Opinions on the Case Split-Flow on September 12.

In accordance with the Trial Procedure of the Litigation Platform of Hangzhou Internet Court (《杭州互联网法院诉讼平台审理规程》, August 18, 2017), the court uses internet technology to carry out most of its litigation activities online, including filing and accepting lawsuits, services, mediation, the electronic filing and cross-examination of evidence, pretrial preparation, adjudication, and execution of cases. The jurisdiction of the Hangzhou Internet Court covers cases that arise online, including internet shopping, services, and microfinance loans and other contract disputes; internet copyright ownership and infringement disputes; the use of the internet infringement of personal right disputes; internet shopping product liability infringement disputes; internet domain name disputes; and internet administrative disputes caused by administrative disputes. The above practice reflects that China attaches great importance to ICT in trial management, while the construction of electronic litigation aimed at judicial public services is in need of further development.

Both in China and other countries, there has been a debate between "management theory" and "service theory" in the construction of electronic courts and electronic litigation systems. The focus is on whether the system ends with internal management or extends to judicial public service. The "management theory" bases its target on the development of an internal e-Court and equates the electronic court with the court's construction of information, which tends to focus its application on the trial quality assessment, letters and visits (信访), information management, and case management tools. Internal e-Court does not change the traditional organizational structure of the court, the principle of judicial management, or other leadership styles, and has already been achieved in China.

In contrast, external e-Court aims the functions of the electronic court in the context of party-centered judicial services, and seeks to establish a virtual court that can provide judicial information or services for parties and the legal professional community in a timely manner and a convenient place. It will promote the communication between court and parties, such as through electronic filing of a lawsuit, and will facilitate submitting electronic documentary evidence, electronic service, and even establish a virtual court corresponding to the substantive court. This kind of external e-Court has a number of applications in China, such as Jilin Electronic Court and the electronic courts in Hangzhou Yuhang, West Lake, and Binjiang District.

The scope of the internal e-Court is infrastructure, while the ultimate goal of the external e-Court is the electronic court system. The e-Court expansion from the internal management of court functions is a way to provide public service. In the construction of electronic litigation and e-Court, the core issue is the legitimacy of the electronic legal communication between the electronic submissions and the electronic service. So the legislation should make the following rules. (1) Limiting the subject of electronic litigation. The legal professional community has the duty to develop electronic litigation. In Jilin Province, China, the electronic court made such a design: lawyers use e-Court in any case in which their agents have opened an electronic litigation account and no longer need to identify themselves. (2) Online-Offline conversion and procedure options. The e-Court communication between the court and the parties is a legal effect that is two-way. How to apply e-Court communication in different situations depends on what way is most conducive to protecting the party's substantive interests and providing procedural benefits. For example, China's current judicial interpretation stipulates that parties and their lawyers can log in to the platform to further query and download electronic documents while the court continues to use traditional service methods. The court respects the parties' right to choose whether they prefer to conduct the procedures through the online and offline options. (3) The cases of electronic litigation centralized jurisdiction. The professionalization of the electronic courts is more secure under the centralized jurisdiction system, such as the Yuhang and West Lake District e-Courts in Hangzhou, Zhejiang Province.

The SPC in the Opinions on the Case Split-Flow put forward that, first, to use electronic service positively, if the parties agree to use electronic service, we should provide and confirm the fax number, email, WeChat, and other electronic addresses. We can establish the unified national court electronic service platform and complete the nationwide court-specific post services. Second, the court also established that if the parties agree to use summary proceedings, a court session can be opened by remote video, and witnesses, appraisers, and victims can use audiovisual transmission technology or a synchronized video test room to testify.

6.2 *Internet E-Court: Electronic Trial Management*

The purpose of the informatization construction of court is to serve the community. If the information construction still lies in strengthening judicial power, or even using ICT as a means of strengthening social control and judicial means, as well as simply digitizing the paper proceedings; then it has deviated from the original intention of the electronic court and electronic litigation system.

Chinese courts use this technology to achieve node management and process connection and enhance trial efficiency. First, this gives expression to the automation concept. Judges complete case management on the internet. Collegiate panels, judges (or assistants), and other trial groups collaborate to complete the trial work and reduce human intervention in the judiciary with the help of computer and network techniques, which is conducive to fair litigation and improving judicial authority. Second, this also gives expression to the informatization concept. As the platform of network information, the e-Court permits the parties and courts to keep in touch with and interact with each other. "Virtual litigation through the internet" can have "surreal" consequences, improving the quality of legal protection. A third impact is in flattening the trial organization concept. The electronic court also changed the organizational principles of the court. In the past, the court emphasized the organization of bureaucracy and the administration, and the communication between the judge, the superior leadership, and the superior court; owing to the sharing of resources, the trial organization takes on the tendency of flattening. The independence of the trial organization has increased, and a quick feedback loop has been formed between members of the collegial panel, judges, and litigants, thus lowering the handicap in time and space and saving trial resources.

The functions of the internal e-Court include various elements. (1) The function of case management: the traditional judicial management system is built around the "court-centered" closed system to achieve real information, so the information of litigation flows and is widely shared. This will promote the process, optimization, and adjustment of the organizational structure. (2) The function of electronic files: the transition of files from paper to digital is also the basis for the construction of e-courts. The electronic files broke through the geographical limitations of the paper record, with the characteristic that multiple people could use them at the same time, with non-exclusivity in the use of information. (3) The sharing and exchange function of electronic litigation information: the internal e-Court should have the function of information release and data flow, and the judicial data should be widely shared and used to achieve an increase in marginal revenue, which will promote legal research and the parties rationally choosing suit litigation strategies. The court system of various cases in an open court session also relies on judicial big data, including scheduling, hearing, appeal registration, case inquiries, report processing on judicial statistics, archive registration, and the registration of complaint letters and visits (信访), and other data, as well as decisions involving the evaluation of judicial performance and the rational configuration of judicial resources, policies, and judicial planning.

References

Cai Y (2013) An analysis on the mechanism of civil judicial cases management in China. China Legal Sci 1:131–143 (in Chinese)

Chenoweth DW (1977) Soviet civil procedure: history and analysis. Trans Am Philos Soc 67(6):1–55

Damaška MR (1986) The faces of justice and state authority: a comparative approach to the legal process. Yale University Press, New Haven

Federal Judicial Center (2004) Manual for complex litigation, 4th edn. https://www.uscourts.gov/sites/default/files/mcl4.pdf. Accessed 9 April 2022

Freer RD (2009) Civil procedure, 2nd edn. Aspen Publishers, New York

Head JW (2009) The China's legal soul, the modern Chinese legal identity in historical context. Carolina Academic Press, Durham

Hu J, Zeng Y (2016) The optimization of civil trial. People's Judicature 19:65–69 (in Chinese)

Huai X (2006) Court and judge. Law Press, Beijing (in Chinese)

Huang KC (2003) Introducing discovery into civil law. Carolina Academic Press, Durham

Huang X (2010) People-oriented, service trial. China Trial 53:86–88 (in Chinese)

Liang P (2017) Research on the internal institutions and power operation in court under the dual structure of management. Legal Forum 32(3):152–160 (in Chinese)

Prince D (2014) A new model for civil case management: efficacy through intrinsic engagement. Ct Rev 50(4):174–195

Wei J (2015) Run the informatization engine. People's Court Newspaper, 2 Nov 2015 (in Chinese)

The Specialized Courts in China: Framework, History, and Jurisdiction

Hangping Chen and Liubing Chen

1 Introduction

The court system in China has a division of ordinary courts and specialized courts. Among the ordinary courts, there are four levels from top to bottom: the Supreme People's Court of P.R.C. located in Beijing (which also sends six Circuit Courts of the SPC separately seated in Shenzhen, Shenyang, Chongqing, Nanjing, Zhengzhou, and Xi'an), 31 High People's Courts established in each capital city of all provinces, municipalities, or autonomous regions (excluding Hong Kong, Macao, and Taiwan), over 400 Intermediate People's Courts established in each prefecture-level city, autonomous prefecture, or municipality, and over 3,000 Primary People's Courts established in each county, district, and autonomous county.[1] Beyond the ordinary courts, there are also several kinds of specialized courts established in China, including 34 military courts, 11 maritime courts, 4 intellectual property courts, and 3 financial courts.[2] From 1949, the country has also established other specialized courts, including railway transport courts, water transport courts, forest courts, cultivated land courts, oilfield courts, and mining courts. However, as China developed, these specialized courts, which had been attached to respective administrative departments, either were absorbed by the formal national judiciary system or were abolished.

[1] https://xw.qq.com/cmsid/20211008A0027K00. Accessed May 2022.

[2] https://xw.qq.com/cmsid/20211008A0027K00. Accessed May 2022. In February 2022, the Thirty-three Meeting of the Thirteenth NPC Standing Committee passed the 'Decision on the Establishment of Cheng Yu Financial Court' and established the third financial court.

H. Chen (✉) · L. Chen
School of Law, Tsinghua University, Beijing, People's Republic of China
e-mail: chenhp@mail.tsinghua.edu.cn

L. Chen
e-mail: clb19@mails.tsinghua.edu.cn

L. Cadiet and Y. Fu (eds.), *On Judicial Management from Comparative Perspective*, Contemporary Chinese Civil and Commercial Law,
https://doi.org/10.1007/978-981-19-8673-4_8

For many years, the specialized courts in China did not receive the attention they deserved. In Chinese law journals, the number of essays analyzing the specialized courts is too few to be counted, not to mention the lack of foreign language resources on this theme. This situation is understandable. Compared with the ordinary courts that accept and dispose of all kinds of first instance cases amounting to over 10 million each year, all the specialized courts together receive fewer than 100,000 yearly, less than 1% of all cases.[3]

However, with the development of the Chinese economy and its increasing significance in the global political and economic landscape, new types of specialized courts have acquired national and international significance. For example, the president of the SPC, Mr. Zhou Qiang, pointed out in his speech 'Explanation on the Decision (Draft) on the Establishment of IP courts in Beijing, Shanghai and Guangzhou' made during the Tenth Session of the Standing Committee of the Twelfth National People's Congress on 25 August 2014, the three rationales for establishing IP courts: first, the need to promote the implementation of the national innovation-driven development strategy; second, the need to strengthen the judicial protection of IP rights; and third, the need to improve the quality of IP adjudication. On 25 April 2018, at the second meeting of the Standing Committee of the 13th National People's Congress, President Zhou Qiang pointed out in the Note on the Decision (Draft) on the Establishment of the Shanghai Financial Court that the Establishment of the Shanghai Financial Court has the following significance: first, it is conducive to enhancing the international influence of China's financial justice; second, it is conducive to the in-depth implementation of the national financial strategy; and third, it is conducive to the development and construction of Shanghai international financial center.

In view of this, this paper will focus on the organizational framework, historical evolution, and jurisdiction of China's specialized courts. The purpose of this paper is to provide an overview of the specialized courts in China and to provide a basis for further observation and analysis by interested researchers.

2 Framework and History of Specialized Courts

Conceptually, the specialized court is composed of two elements: 'specialized' and 'court.' From the perspective of jurisprudence, the so-called 'specialized' mainly refers to the particularity of the area where certain cases occur (such as 'military battalion areas' or 'sea or sea waters'), the particularity of the parties of the case (such as soldiers or military units), and the specialization or technicality of the case (such

[3] For example, in 2018, all the courts accepted 139,209,640,000 first instance cases, among which the maritime and maritime trade cases accepted by the maritime courts were 15,784. See the National Bureau of Statistics of China. http://data.stats.gov.cn/easyquery.htm?cn=C01 (Accessed August 2020). Also, the author synthesized all types of news reports and judicial statistics, determining that the military courts accepted hundreds of civil and commercial cases, the IP courts accepted 40–50 thousand intellectual property cases, and the Shanghai Financial Court accepted less than 10 thousand financial cases per year.

as patents or new plant varieties).[4] Such cases are different from ordinary civil cases and need to be handled by judges with specialized judicial knowledge and experience to ensure the quality and effectiveness of the adjudication.[5] The so-called 'courts' are national judicial organs established by the People's Congress and its Standing Committee and authorized by the Constitution of P.R.C. and statutes according to actual needs. The courts in China have a unified system of adjudication divisions and judicial administration departments. The leadership of the Chinese Communist Party provides for the establishment of adjudication divisions and administration affairs offices, trial management offices, political departments (personnel departments), and other administrative agencies divided by function.[6] The establishment of the court is not only a legal issue but also subject to the restriction of the 'Institutional Establishment Committee Office', which is an administrative unit unique to China that reviews and decides the court's internal departments, staffing, leadership, positions structure, and total organizational size. For this reason, the number of specialized courts is limited.

Meanwhile, in practice, many local courts concentrate their judicial resources and set up specialized trial divisions, such as environment and resources divisions, juvenile divisions, small claims divisions, medical disputes divisions, and traffic accident divisions. Such trial divisions are either established with the approval of the SPC or the provincial High People's Court or established by the courts where they belong. Such specialized divisions neither have the organizational structure of the court nor possess independent jurisdiction, but they concentrate on disposing of specific types of cases accepted by the court to which they are attached. In addition to the specialized divisions, some special tribunals between the courts and the trial divisions have been established in recent years by the SPC, such as the IP Court of the SPC and the International Commercial Court of the SPC. These courts have independent offices locations (different from the SPC location) and relatively independent case handling procedures (where cases can be individually accepted, served, scheduled for court sessions, etc.),[7] yet are restricted by institutional requirements and, thus, do not constitute a court in the full sense. To be specific, they are branch divisions of the SPC with more independence than ordinary trial divisions.

---

[4] Liu (2017, p. 6).

[5] More typically, after the establishment of the IP courts in 2014, the Guiding Opinions of the SPC on the Selection of Judges of the IP Court (Trial Implementation) requires that the judicial personnel must be selected from personnel working on intellectual property and relevant judicial work, or experts practicing intellectual property law, doing legal research, and performing legal teaching with equivalent qualifications and conditions. The judges must have more than six years of relevant career experience in judging intellectual property cases. This threshold is high for specialized judicial knowledge and experience.

[6] Chen (2021, pp. 53–65).

[7] See Provisions of the SPC on Several Issues Concerning the Establishment of the International Commercial Court, No. 11 [2018]; Notice of the General Office of the SPC on Issuing the Rules of Procedure of the International Commercial Court of the SPC (Trial Implementation), No. 13 [2018]; Provisions of the SPC on Several Issues Concerning the IP Court, No. 22 [2018]; Guidelines for the Litigation of the IP Court of the SPC.

The legal text Article 26 of the 1954 Organic Law of the People's Courts stipulates that specialized courts include military courts, railway transport courts, and water transport courts, and Article 27 stipulates that the organization of specialized courts shall be separately prescribed by the Standing Committee of the National People's Congress. In 1957, the State Council revoked the railway transport courts and water transport courts and their dispatched divisions based on the domestic political situation at that time and the recommendation of the Ministry of Justice. During the Cultural Revolution, military courts and local courts were destroyed, and the national judicial system was severely damaged. The 1979 Organic Law of the People's Courts reinstated the provisions of specialized courts. Among them, the specialized courts listed in Article 2, paragraph 3 include military courts, railway transport courts, water transport courts, forest courts, and 'other specialized courts.' The so-called 'other specialized courts' mainly refer to those established in the areas of cultivated lands, oilfields, mining areas, and so on, to hear cases involving relevant administrative departments and their competent areas based on economic development needs at the time.[8] Article 29 of the law stipulates that the organization and powers of the specialized courts shall be separately prescribed by the Standing Committee of the National People's Congress. However, there was intense controversy over what types of specialized courts should be established and the organization and jurisdiction of the specialized courts. Therefore, the enumerated clauses were deleted when the Organic Law of the People's Courts was amended in 1983, retaining only the vague expression of 'specialized people's courts such as military courts.'[9] Since then, despite two revisions in 1986 and 2006, the relevant articles have not been modified. It was not until 2018 that the new Organic Law of the People's Courts made more detailed provisions in Article 15: 'Specialized people's courts include military courts and maritime courts, IP courts, financial courts, etc. The establishment, organization, functions and powers of specialized people's courts, the appointment and removal of judges thereof shall be prescribed by the Standing Committee of the National People's Congress.'

Judging from the history of the establishment of specialized courts, in 1955, the Ministry of National Defense transformed the military law offices at all levels into military courts based on the provisions of the 1954 Constitution and the 1954 Organic Law of the People's Courts and incorporated them into the national judicial system. After that, according to the 1982 Constitution and the 1983 Organic Law of the People's Courts, the military courts were set up on three levels.

In addition to military courts, public sector-run specialized courts were once popular in China. For example, the six maritime courts in Shanghai, Tianjin, Qingdao, Dalian, Guangzhou, and Wuhan, which were established in the 1980s, were initially organized by the Ministry of Communications and managed by the Port and Shipping Bureau and Maritime Bureau of the same ministry.[10] The staffing, funding, building, and facilities of such specialized courts were run by the administrative departments of

[8] Yang (2019, p. 109).

[9] Wang (1983, A7).

[10] Zeng et al. (2017, p. 88).

the particular sector or related state-owned enterprises. The problems inherent in the 'no separation between government and enterprise' model that mixed the executive and the judiciary and related to departmental protectionism have seriously affected judicial credibility. The latter four maritime courts in Haikou, Xiamen, Ningbo, and Beihai, which have been established since 1989, have been administered by the high courts of the provinces they are located in from the beginning. Since the mid-1990s, the Central Committee of the CPC and the SPC have successively decided to change the status of the railway, farming, forestry, oilfield, and other specialized courts that were under the management and supervision of administrative departments or state-owned enterprises, and incorporate their staffing into the unified management of the national judicial system.[11] At present, China has basically realized the transformation of the oilfield courts, forest courts, railway transport courts, and cultivated land courts into local governments and high courts, incorporating them into the country's formal judicial system.

Take the railway transport court as an example. Until 2012, the two-tier railway transport court system was transferred from the railway system to the local high courts to be integrated into the national judicial system; but since 2014, without increasing its organizational size—just through the reorganization of the courts of the 'replace cages for birds' type—the 'railway court' identity was removed and changed to the cross-administrative regional courts. This means that these courts can handle administrative cases from other municipal districts or counties in the same municipality. With the approval of the SPC, the two-tier railway transport courts in Xi'an, Lanzhou, Nanchang, Guangzhou, Shanghai, and some other places currently have begun to govern cross-administrative regional cases, the Hangzhou Railway Transport Court became the Hangzhou Internet Court, and the Beijing Railway Transport Court was revoked and converted into the Beijing Internet Court.[12]

At present, there are only four categories of specialized courts specifically established in China: military courts, maritime courts, IP courts, and financial courts. According to Article 15 of the Organic Law of the People's Courts, a specialized court must be established by the Standing Committee of the National People's Congress. Any court not established in this way is not a specialized court. For example, the three Internet Courts in Hangzhou, Beijing, and Guangzhou were established based on the 'plan' that had been reviewed and approved by the Deep Reforming of the CPC Central Committee rather than the NPC Standing Committee. Even if the Internet Courts are responsible for first instance civil cases involving the internet that should be accepted by the Primary People's Courts of the city where the Internet Courts sit, by having a cross-district jurisdiction and issue specialization, they still belong to a normal court with the centralized jurisdiction rather than a specialized court.[13]

---

[11] See Outline of Five-Year People's Court Reform by the SPC, No. 28 [1999]; Notice of Opinion by the General Office of the Central Committee of the Communist Party of China Regarding the Issuing of Opinions on the Reform of Local People's Court Organizations at All Levels and Institutional Reform of Local People's Procuratorates at All Levels, No. 9 [2001]; etc.

[12] Li (2019).

[13] Article 2 of the Provisions of the SPC on Several Issues Concerning the Trial of Cases by Internet Tribunals No. 16 [2018].

Despite this, the existing specialized courts in China are still a complex and irregular system. Among them, the military court system is the most complete, having 34 courts at three levels from top to bottom subject to the judicial supervision of the SPC[14]; 10 maritime courts and two financial courts have only one level, which is equivalent to the intermediate people's court. If the parties are dissatisfied with the case being tried, they can appeal to the high people's court in the province where the specialized court is located. Likewise, the four IP courts are equivalent to the intermediate people's court, but their first trial cases are reviewed by the IP Court of the SPC. From the perspective of the jurisdiction of the trial level, the maritime court is a court of first instance; the financial courts and the IP courts accept both first instance cases and financial and IP appellate cases heard by ordinary primary courts; and the military courts have their own relatively independent judicial system, covering first and second instances.

3 The Jurisdiction of Specialized Courts

3.1 Military Court

Until the early 1980s, the military court was still a court of specialized jurisdiction for military-related criminal cases and did not accept civil cases.[15] Since the mid-1980s, to make up for the shortage of military funds, the military began to engage in large-scale economic activities. Various military-related economic disputes have occurred since then. To handle such economic disputes concerning the military, in 1988, the Military Court of the People's Liberation Army reported to the SPC the Request for Authorization of the Military Court to Receive Economic, Civil, and Administrative Cases, which was approved to carry out pilot trials of economic disputes in which both involved parties were within the military. In 1992, the SPC issued the Response Letter to Military Courts on Trial of Military Economic Disputes in Military Affairs (No. 130 [1992]), agreeing that the military court could continue to resolve economic disputes when both parties were involved in the military. Since then, with a substantial increase in the number of disputes related to servicemen's marriage and family affairs, torts, servicemen's disappearance or death, military procurement, and socialization of military support, the SPC in 2001 issued the Response Letter to Military Court to Pilot Trial on Civil Cases (No. 33 [2001]) permitting the military court to accept civil cases where both parties are active-duty soldiers, retired cadres managed by the army, staff members of the military, or legal persons within the military, and

[14] After the military reform in 2016, there are in total 25 military courts named after the capital cities in which they are located, 1 military court directly under Beijing, 6 theater command military courts, 1 general military court directly under Beijing, and 1 military court of the People's Liberation Army.

[15] Shi and Ding (1986, p. 73).

nonlitigation cases that apply for the declaration of the disappearance or death of soldiers based on the voluntary participation principle.[16]

Due to doubts about the effectiveness of the 'Response Letter'[17] and the tendency of military cases under the jurisdiction of the local courts to suffer obstacles during the investigation, evidence collection, service of process, and enforcement, as well as the narrow jurisdiction of the military courts and the inadequate use of the trial resources of military courts, in 2012, the SPC issued the Regulations on Several Issues Concerning the Jurisdiction of Civil Cases by Military Courts (No. 11 [2012]) and has once again expanded the scope of the civil jurisdiction of military courts.[18] Article 1 of the 'Regulations' prescribes four types of exclusive jurisdictional matters. Among them, the third type of 'election eligibility for the establishment of an electoral committee by the military' is strictly a citizen's constitutional right litigation and the fourth type of 'unowned property in the camp' is a nonlitigation case. Only the first type, in which 'the parties are both soldiers or military units' and 'cases involving military secrets above the confidential level', is within the scope of the specialized jurisdiction. However, according to Article 4, paragraph 2, if the first type of case does not have a first instance military court within the provincial administrative division where the party is domiciled or the party is domiciled in a remote area where transportation is inconvenient, and the parties agree to submit their case to the local court, the local court may then have jurisdiction over the case. In other words, there is an exception made for 'inconvenience in litigation' to this kind of specialized jurisdiction.

Article 2 of the 'Regulations' grants local parties the right to choose in cases where one party is a serviceman or an army unit and the other party is a local one, that is, a 'military-related' case on the subject. Specifically, based on the complaint of the local party, the military court could accept and dispose of the following 'military-related' civil cases: military service tort cases; military-related tort cases that occurred in the barracks; servicemen's marriage and family cases; real estate cases that happened within the military camp; and military-related cases to which nonlitigation procedures apply. Certainly, local parties can also choose to sue in a local court with jurisdiction. In addition, Article 3 of the 'Regulations' allows the parties to agree to choose the jurisdiction of the military court for military-related contract disputes where the contract is executed or the subject matter is located within the military base.[19]

---

16 Pan (2002, p. 49). However, this provision has caused great controversy. The opposing opinion, see Ren (2003, pp. 62–63).

17 According to Article 6 of the 'Regulations on Judicial Interpretation' in 2007, the 'reply' is applicable to requests for specific legal application issues, whereas regarding how to apply the law to a certain rule or a certain type of case or issue during the judicial work, the 'interpretation' should be adopted.

18 Sun et al. (2012, pp. 15–16).

19 The scope of cases governed by the agreement (contract disputes only) and connection points (only the place where the contract is performed or the location of the subject matter) are narrower than the provisions of Article 25 of the 2012 Civil Procedure Law. About its background, see Sun et al. (2012, p. 17).

In summary, as a specialized court, the military court has the following two main characteristics in its jurisdiction over civil cases. First, due to the economic disputes caused by the military's economic activities during the 1980s and 1990s, and the practical need to facilitate the trial of military-related civil cases, the SPC had no choice but made judicial interpretations allowing military courts to accept civil cases. Historically, such jurisdictional matters were not considered specialized. Second, from the perspective of the particularity of jurisdictional matters and the compulsory and exclusive nature of the jurisdiction, strictly speaking, only civil cases involving military secrets above the confidential level are exclusively under the jurisdiction of military courts; the rest are either subject to exceptions or constitute joint jurisdiction with local courts, which are up to the parties.

3.2 Maritime Court

In 1984, the Eighth Session of the Sixth National People's Congress Standing Committee made the 'Decision on the Establishment of Maritime Courts in Coastal Port Cities', authorizing the SPC to set up maritime courts and clarifying that the maritime courts are specialized courts that only accept and hear first instance maritime cases, maritime trade cases without criminal cases, and other civil cases. Subsequently, the SPC made the 'Decision on Several Issues concerning the Establishment of a Maritime Court', provisionally stipulating that maritime courts shall have jurisdiction over 17 specific maritime and maritime trade cases, with the bottom clause of 'other maritime and maritime trade cases delivered by the high court or provided by law.' The jurisdiction of the 11 maritime courts covers all waters and ports in the country, including the Heilongjiang River in the north, the islands in the South China Sea, and the Yangtze River waterway that crosses from east to west.[20]

Articles 31–33 of the civil procedure law in 1991, for the first time, prescribed territorial jurisdiction of the maritime court for cases arising from ship collisions or other maritime accidents for damages, shipwreck salvage expenses, and common average damages. In 2000, the Standing Committee of the National People's Congress adopted the Maritime Special Procedures Law based on the actual needs of the disposal of maritime cases, maritime trade cases, and other litigation out of maritime disputes provided by law. Articles 6–8 of the law, respectively, stipulated the territorial jurisdiction, the exclusive jurisdiction of maritime litigation, and agreement jurisdiction of foreign-related maritime disputes. It further clarified the division of jurisdiction among the 10 maritime courts.

However, the maritime court faced problems such as narrow jurisdiction, the small number of cases received, and the small number of subject matters, failing to fully realize its judicial potential.[21] Considering this, in 2011, the SPC issued Several Provisions on the Scope of Acceptance of Cases by the Maritime Court

[20] Zhang et al. (2016, p. 43).

[21] See Fu (2009), Zeng et al. (2017); etc.

(No. 27 [2001]) which refined the specialized jurisdiction of the maritime court into four categories (maritime tort dispute cases, maritime commercial contract dispute cases, other maritime trade dispute cases, and maritime enforcement cases), with a total of 63 types. In 2016, the Regulations on the Scope of Cases Accepted by the Maritime Court (No. 4 [2016]) expanded the specialized jurisdiction to six categories (adding development and utilization of ocean and navigable waters and environmental protection-related cases, maritime administrative cases, and maritime special procedures cases that included maritime enforcement cases), for a total of 108 types.

In summary, the maritime court is a specialized court that was gradually established and perfected through the development of maritime trade and shipping after the reform and opening up. Its jurisdiction was first limited to cases of maritime tort and maritime contract disputes. In 2016, it was expanded to include maritime administrative cases. In 2017, it began to conduct partial pilot maritime criminal cases.[22] As far as civil litigation is concerned, the maritime court most clearly reflects the approach that 'specialized jurisdiction equals specialized court jurisdiction.' Ordinary local courts have no jurisdiction to hear maritime cases and maritime trade cases.[23]

3.3 IP Court

Since the mid-1980s, the country has focused on the centralization and specialization of the adjudication of IP cases such as patents, forming a judicial structure of which the intermediate court located in the provincial capital and the intermediate court designated by the SPC shall have jurisdiction over first instance IP cases. From the establishment of the IP divisions in Beijing's high and intermediate courts in 1993 to the end of 2016, there are today 224 intermediate courts either designated by the SPC or provided by law that have jurisdiction over patents, new plant varieties, integrated circuit layout designs, monopolies, and civil disputes involving the recognition of well-known trademarks.[24]

According to the 2014 Decision on the Establishment of IP Courts in Beijing, Shanghai, and Guangzhou, the three IP courts have jurisdiction over first instance cases of highly technical IP rights related to patents, new plant varieties, integrated circuit layout designs, and technical secrets, as well as appeals from civil judgments and rulings of the first instance by the city's primary courts involving IP rights such

[22] Wu and Liu (2019, p. 46).

[23] Because the maritime court implements jurisdiction over maritime cases across administrative divisions, it is sometimes inconvenient for parties to litigate. In practice, the local court accepts cases that should be under the jurisdiction of the maritime court either explicitly or implicitly. See Fu (2009, p. 143).

[24] Supreme People's Court (2017, A2).

as copyrights and trademarks.[25] Subsequently, the SPC in the Provisions on the Jurisdiction of IP Courts in Beijing, Shanghai, and Guangzhou (No. 12 [2014]) extended the scope of specialized civil jurisdiction to computer software civil cases and civil cases involving the recognition of well-known trademarks (Art. 1). The 'Provisions' also stipulate that if the subject matter of the case contains both the specialized jurisdictional content of the IP court and other content, the case shall be accepted by the IP court (Art. 4). Immediately afterward, the SPC issued the Notice on Issues Related to the Jurisdiction of IP Courts (No. 338 [2014]), stipulating in Article 3 that the IP courts shall have jurisdiction over the first instance cases of monopoly civil disputes in the scope of municipal jurisdictions (Guangzhou IP Court shall govern Guangdong Province). Therefore, the jurisdiction of the first instance civil cases of IP courts includes 'patents, new plant varieties, integrated circuit layout designs, technical secrets, computer software, well-known trademarks, monopolies' and other technical IP cases. This decision unlocked the door to specialized adjudication for special types of IP cases and the specialization of judicial institutions, judicial personnel, and judicial work.[26] On 31 December 2020, the fourth IP Court, Hainan Free Trade Port Intellectual Property Court was formally inaugurated in Hainan province.

In order to promote the professionalization of IP trials, the SPC has established 20 IP tribunals in 18 provinces across the country since 2017. These IP tribunals are attached to intermediate courts in the cities where they are located and are listed separately to handle cases independently. However, subject to the establishment of the organization, they do not have the size or organizational structure of a court, only that of a relatively pure judicial organ. In terms of jurisdiction of specialized matters, it is basically the same as that of the IP court.[27] In terms of territorial jurisdiction, some tribunals govern a province's technical IP cases (such as the Wuhan IP Tribunal of Hubei province and the Changchun IP Tribunal of Jilin province), and some jointly govern a province by region (such as the Hangzhou IP Tribunal and the Ningbo IP Tribunal of Zhejiang province, the Nanjing IP Tribunal and the Suzhou IP Tribunal of Jiangsu province).

[25] The IP Court implements a civil and administrative 'two in one' trial mode. Article 2(2) of the 'Regulations' stipulates that the first-instance intellectual property rights authorization and confirmation of an administrative case initiated by or decided by the State Council administrative department shall be exclusively under the jurisdiction of the Beijing IP Court.

[26] Wu (2018, pp. 6–9).

[27] Reply of the SPC on the approval of Nanjing, Suzhou, Wuhan, and Chengdu Intermediate People's Courts to set up specialized adjudication agencies and to cross-regional jurisdiction over some intellectual property cases; Reply of the SPC on the consent of Hangzhou, Ningbo, Hefei, Fuzhou, Jinan, and Qingdao Intermediate People's Courts to set up specialized adjudication bodies and to cross-regional jurisdiction over some intellectual property cases; Reply of the SPC on the approval of the Third Intermediate People's Court of Tianjin and the Intermediate People's Courts of Zhengzhou, Changsha, and Xi'an to set up specialized adjudication agencies and cross-regional jurisdiction over some intellectual property cases; etc. In addition to specialized jurisdiction matters, these specialized intellectual property adjudication agencies also have jurisdiction over non-technical intellectual property cases by forum level.

More importantly, in 2018, the Standing Committee of the National People's Congress passed the Decisions on Several Issues Concerning Litigation Procedures in Patents and Other Cases submitted by the SPC. This document stipulated that the jurisdiction of the second instance of IP civil cases with strong technical expertise (such as invention patents, utility model patents, new plant varieties, integrated circuit layout designs, technical secrets, computer software, and monopolies) shall be exercised uniformly by the SPC. On 1 January 2019, the IP Court of the SPC was inaugurated in Beijing as a permanent judicial institution by the SPC. According to Article 2 of the Provisions on Certain Issues Concerning the Intellectual Property Court of SPC (No. 22 [2018]) mentioned earlier, the IP Court of the SPC is responsible for the second instance trial of technical IP cases. For the parties involved in first instance judgments of the IP Court and the IP Tribunal of intermediate courts, it is equivalent to overstepping the high court and directly filing a 'Leap Appeal' to the SPC's IP Court. So far, the '1 + 4 + 20' specialized judicial institutional model for technical IP cases has been formed. In the near future, with the maturity of the relevant conditions in various provinces and cities, a system of specialized judicial institutions for technical IP cases covering all regions of the country may be expected to be formed.

In summary, the system of specialized judicial institutions for technical IP cases has gradually improved. Strictly equating a specialized jurisdiction with a specialized court's jurisdiction, at present, only the three IP courts that have jurisdiction over technical IP cases can be deemed as specialized jurisdictions, while other high courts, intermediate courts, and IP tribunals attached to the intermediate courts only have centralized jurisdiction over technical IP cases in administrative regions or cross-administrative regions. In this way, the same technical IP case will be heard by the Guangzhou IP Court under the jurisdiction of the specialized jurisdiction, but when it is heard by the IP tribunal of the Wuhan Intermediate Court, it will not fall under the specialized jurisdiction. This arrangement is not only difficult to accept logically, but it also causes inherent tension and conflict in the jurisdiction system and unnecessarily increases the complexity of jurisdictional disputes. Therefore, the authors advocate for the application of specialized jurisdiction in civil cases of technical IP rights, regardless of whether they are tried by IP courts or by specialized IP tribunals in normal courts.

3.4 Financial Court

In July 2018, the SPC adopted the Regulations on the Jurisdiction of the Shanghai Financial Court (No. 14 [2018]) which stipulates that the Shanghai Financial Court shall accept certain types of first-instance civil financial and commercial matters that should be received by the intermediate court within the Shanghai metropolis as well as appellate cases from the first instance civil financial and commercial cases adjudicated by Shanghai's primary courts.[28] As the first specialized court for financial cases in the country, subject to the lack of particularity in the parties of litigation, the location of disputes, and technical legal issues, the financial court indeed exercises centralized jurisdiction within Shanghai. That is, financial cases under the jurisdiction of the three intermediate courts in Shanghai are to be adjudicated by the financial court. As a result, this specialized court does not enjoy specialized jurisdiction. The judges who drafted the Regulations on the Jurisdiction of the Shanghai Financial Court declared that the cases accepted by the financial court should be those where a party is a financial institution holding a financial license, an internet lending platform, a private equity fund, or other financial organizations, rather than involving loan disputes between natural persons.[29] This is the essential characteristic of the financial court's jurisdiction. In January 2021, the Standing Committee of the National People's Congress passed the Decisions on Setting up the Beijing Financial Court. In March 2021, the SPC issued the Regulations on the Jurisdiction of the Beijing Financial Court (No. 7 [2021]) which stipulates that the Beijing Financial Court has the similar jurisdiction with the Shanghai Financial Court. At the same time, the Beijing Financial Court was formally inaugurated. In February 2022, the Standing Committee of the National People's Congress passed the Decisions on Setting up the Cheng Yu Financial Court.

To summarize, there are roughly four types of relationships between the jurisdiction of specialized courts and civil jurisdiction in China: (1) specialized courts only exercise specialized jurisdiction, such as maritime courts; (2) specialized courts partly exercise specialized jurisdiction, with military courts as the typical model; (3) specialized jurisdictions are jointly exercised by specialized courts and tribunals, with IP courts and IP tribunals as typical examples; and (4) specialized courts mainly exercise centralized jurisdiction, without specialized jurisdiction, with financial courts as the typical model. Therefore, that 'specialized jurisdiction equals specialized court's jurisdiction' is not established in most scenarios. At present, the jurisdictional matters that meet the mandatory and exclusive features mainly include maritime and maritime trade disputes, patents and other technical IP disputes, disputes where both parties are soldiers or military units (with exceptions), and disputes involving military secrets above the confidential level. Specialized jurisdiction matters in a narrow sense are limited to the aforesaid.

---

[28] These include (1) securities, futures trading, trust, insurance, bills, letters of credit, financial loan contracts, bank cards, financial leasing contracts, entrusted financial management contracts, pawns, and other disputes; (2) independent guarantees, factoring, private equity funds, non-bank payment institutions such as online payment, online lending, internet equity crowdfunding and other new types of financial civil and commercial disputes; (3) bankruptcy disputes involving financial institutions as debtors; (4) judicial review cases of arbitration of financial civil and commercial disputes; and (5) application for recognition and enforcement of judgments and ruling cases in financial civil and commercial disputes in foreign courts.

[29] Zheng et al. (2018, pp. 29–30).

4 Conclusion

Specialized courts are an important component of China's judicial system. Despite the limited number of cases accepted and handled, the IP court, the financial court, and other new types of prospective specialized courts aim to implement national strategic goals by means of professional and specialized adjudication, to show China's judicial justice and judicial efficiency to foreign counterparts and to contribute Chinese judicial wisdom on governance and development in related fields to the world. Maritime courts also play an important role in foreign-related maritime cases. Of course, China still has a long way to go before it can achieve its goal of setting up the specialized courts system; challenges in this regard include whether specialized courts can have an organizational framework different from ordinary courts, whether they will weaken the bureaucratic management within the court, how to further safeguard judicial independence, how to summarize the expert experience of the specialized court, how to enhance the guidance or binding effect of typical judgments in the specialized court system, and how to achieve similar treatment of similar cases. China is on the way.

References

Chen H (2021) The unified system of adjudication and administration of chinese courts. In: Chan Peter CH, van Rhee CH (eds) Civil case management in the twenty-first century: court structures still matter. Springer, pp 53–65

Fu R (2009) Chinese maritime court: problems and solutions concurred on other specialized courts. Hebei Law Sci 5:142–147 (in Chinese)

Li L (2019) Retrospect and prospect of the reform of the railway transportation court in the past 40 years: written on the 40th anniversary of the restoration and reconstruction of the railway transportation court. China Court. https://www.chinacourt.org/article/detail/2019/06/id/4052550.shtml. Accessed June 2020 (in Chinese)

Liu S (2017) Some thoughts on the establishment of specialized courts in the organization law of the people's courts-based on the background of the internet power strategy in the internet age. Res Rule Law 5:3–14 (in Chinese)

Pan J (2002) Evolution and system forms of military courts trying civil cases. Leg Sci 3:48–51+58 (in Chinese)

Ren H (2003) Military courts are not suitable for hearing civil cases. Law Sci Mag 4:62–63 (in Chinese)

Shi C, Ding R (1986) Jurisdiction of Chinese current military courts. Mod Law Sci 2:73–74 (in Chinese)

Sun Y, Wu Z, Sun Q (2012) Understanding and application of the regulations on several issues concerning civil cases under miltary courts' jurisdiction. People's Judic (Appl) 3:15–18 (in Chinese)

Supreme People's Court (2017) Outline of China's judicial protection of intellectual property (2016–2020). People's Court News, 25 April 2017 (in Chinese)

The National Bureau of Statistics of China. http://data.stats.gov.cn/easyquery.htm?cn=C01. Accessed Aug 2020 (in Chinese)

Wang H (1983) Notes on amending the organizational law of the people's court and the organizational law of the people's procuratorate. People's Diary, 3 September 1983 (in Chinese)

Wu H (2018) Theory and practice of the construction of Chinese IP court. Intellect Prop 3:2–13 (in Chinese)

Wu Y, Liu X (2019) The specialized jurisdiction of maritime criminal litigation: taking the maritime criminal case trialed by ningbo maritime court as the starting point. People's Judic (Appl) 25:46–50 (in Chinese)

Yang W (ed) (2019) Understanding and application of the articles of the organizational law of the people's court of the People's Republic of China. People's Court Press (in Chinese)

Zeng Y, Liu Q, Zhang K (2017) Thoughts on the reform and improvement of China's maritime court system and mechanism. J Law Appl 1:88–91 (in Chinese)

Zhang Y, Wang S, Fu X (2016) Understanding and application of the regulations on jurisdiction of maritime litigation. People's Judic (Appl) 10:42–45 (in Chinese)

Zheng X, Bao J, Li S, Guo M (2018) Understanding and application of the regulations on the jurisdiction of the shanghai financial court. People's Judic (Appl) 34:26–30 (in Chinese)

The Civil Case Management in Chinese Court: Focusing on the Time Limit for Adjudication and Adducing Evidence

Hao Li

1 Introduction

Although case management exists in all kinds of procedures, including civil procedures, it can show great variation in different countries and regions due to the diversity of jurisdiction, procedure law, legal traditions, and historical culture. Countries may define the object of case management differently. For instance, in the U.S., class action cases highlight the importance of case management by the judge, while in China, representative actions likely need no special case management.

Moreover, even in the same country, case management may show different forms and conditions due to judicial reforms implemented in different historical moments. For example, before the reform and implementation of the "tribunal responsibility system" (主审法官负责制) and the "judge quota system" (员额制), the court in Mainland China managed case quality by asking the president of the court and the leader of the tribunal to review and sign the judgment. After the reform, under the new concept of "Let the trial judge make judgments; let the judicator be responsible for the referee," new methods for controlling case quality were established, replacing the original approach of leaders' reviewing and signing judgments.

Case management, of course, refers to the essential purpose of the judicial system, which is to provide a fair and efficient judiciary for citizens. But for case management pro se, under the premise of admitting judicial independence and although it may enhance judicial fairness to some degree, the primary purpose of case management should be to increase litigation efficiency through necessary and proper management.

Note: The original text is written in Chinese. MENG Xing (Law School, Liaoning University, People's Republic of China) translates it into English.

H. Li (✉)
Institute for Chinese Legal Modernization Studies, Nanjing Normal University, Nanjing, People's Republic of China
e-mail: nsdlihao@sina.com

L. Cadiet and Y. Fu (eds.), *On Judicial Management from Comparative Perspective*, Contemporary Chinese Civil and Commercial Law,
https://doi.org/10.1007/978-981-19-8673-4_9

Therefore, I would like to introduce two systems of civil procedure law of Mainland China that are highly relevant for case management: the time limit system for adjudication and the time limit system for adducing evidence.

2 The Time Limit System for Adjudication

The time limit for adjudication is a statutory time limit for the court to adjudicate cases. In other words, the law establishes a time period for the judge, requiring him to finish the adjudication task within this time period. For the civil procedure, this system was established through the amendment of the civil procedure law in 1991.[1] The 1991 Civil Procedure Law regulates time limits for both first instance cases and second instance cases. It also classifies first instance cases into two types—simple civil cases and major and complicated civil cases—to which it applies different proceedings and time limits. Cases that apply the ordinary proceeding shall be adjudicated in six months, while cases that apply the simplified proceeding shall be adjudicated in three months. The time limits for second instance cases vary with the nature of the appeal. For appeals of court orders, the time limit is 30 days, while for appeals of court judgments, the time limit is three months. Considering the complexity of some cases, the civil procedure law provides that, under special circumstances, the adjudication of cases applying ordinary proceedings can be extended by another six months upon the president's approval. For cases applying simplified proceedings, if the judge finds it does not belong to the "simple civil case" during the trial, the civil procedure law allows the proceeding to be transferred to an ordinary proceeding. After the transfer, the time limit will thereupon abide by the regulations for ordinary proceedings. Due to the fact that the law does not stipulate different time limit rules for different levels of the court, the provisions mentioned above are applicable for all four levels of court, from the basic people's court to the Supreme People's Court.

It is worth noting that the conditions of individual cases can be very different. Some cases need authentication while others do not, and different cases may require different lengths of time for authentication. Some cases, such as cases on construction engineering, may need an audit, which can take a lot of time. Such time-consuming requirements are beyond the judge's control, and hence, the time limit system must be flexible enough to take these circumstances into consideration. On account of these specific practical problems during the application of the time limit system for adjudication, the Supreme People's Court issued *Some Rules Set Forth by the Supreme People's Court for Strictly Abiding by the Time Limits for Case Hearing and Execution* in September 2000, providing more specific and detailed rules. For example, it regulates the time period for the bulletin and authentication in civil and administrative cases; it also clarifies that the time required for audits, evaluations,

[1] In the Civil Procedure Law of the People's Republic of China (For Trial Implementation), the first Civil Procedure Law of New China enacted in 1982, there were no regulations on the time limit for adjudication.

and asset liquidations made by professional agencies will not be included in the time period for adjudication.

The time limit system for adjudication has a great influence on the court's adjudication management and the arrangement of the judge's procedure schedule. To the court, ensuring that most, if not all, of the cases adjudicated by its judges are completed within the stipulated time period is not only an important task in terms of adjudication quality and efficiency, but also is an important working content of adjudication management. To practically implement the work on adjudication management, the court in Mainland China generally has a division called the adjudication management office,[2] and one of the regular jobs for this office is to manage the time period for adjudication. With the support of modern technologies, every case docketed in the court will be recorded into the case handling computer system; as the case procedure progresses, the system will remind the judge of the remaining time within the time limit for adjudication.[3] Once the case is finished, the judge should immediately report to the adjudication management office through the system, while the office should review the report immediately upon receiving it.

Although most cases can be closed within the time limit for adjudication, there are also cases that cannot be closed for extended periods of time (more than one year since docketing). All courts pay great attention to this type of case and take the appropriate measures for its supervision. For example, in Suzhou of Jiangsu Province, the Wujiang District Court issued the *Regulation on strictly Managing Time Periods for Adjudication* to finish all cases that have been open for a long time and to avoid such situations. The regulation establishes six mechanisms, including screening the case log to identify cases that have exceeded the time limit for adjudication, supervising the adjudication of these cases, making special reports on these cases, carrying out special evaluations of these cases, and making special bulletins about these cases.[4]

Aside from the inner management from the court, some courts also supervise the time for adjudication by asking the parties whether the judge has abided by the time limit for adjudication. After the case docketing, the court will send text messages to the parties, informing them of the time limit for adjudication (such as the length of time for adjudication, the issues that may not be calculated into the time period for adjudication and why, and extensions of time and why). On the one hand, this can help the parties understand the progress of the adjudication; on the other hand, it can help the parties supervise the judge's abiding by the time limit. If the judge violates the time limit and delays the litigation, the parties can file a complaint against him.

The court's management of the time limit for adjudication naturally influences the judge, making him focus more on the requirements for closing the case within

---

2 In the basic people's court, although there is no special office for adjudication management, there will be certain specialized people responsible for the management of the time period for adjudication.

3 The system will remind the judge by using different colors to show the different time progress. For example, in ordinary proceedings, the color will be green in the beginning and will turn orange when 10 days are left. The color will become red if the time limit is overpassed.

4 See Ren (2015).

the established time limit. This will cause the judge to enhance his control of the management of the proceedings, doing his best to finish the case within the time limit. Whether the judge is able to finish the case within the time limit also provides evidence of the judge's judicial capability. Under the mechanism of random case allocation, if a judge has a large number of cases that cannot be finished in time, while all other judges are able to finish cases within the time limits, the judicial capability of this judge will, naturally, be questioned.[5]

3 The Time Limit System for Adducing Evidence

The time limit for adducing evidence is established by the court for the submission of evidential materials based on the parties' claims and the condition of the adjudication. The time limit for adducing evidence can be set in two ways: by the court's assignment during pretrial and by the parties' agreement and the court's approval after review. In practice, the time limit for adducing evidence in most cases is established through the first way.

The time limit system for adducing evidence was first established by the Supreme People's Court through its judicial interpretation. It then became a stipulated system through legislation. The 1991 Civil Procedure Law did not contain this system, and the first regulation that mentions it is *Some Provisions of the Supreme People's Court on Evidence in Civil Procedures* issued by the Supreme People's Court in December 2000. The regulation includes the time limit for adducing evidence in first instance and second instance proceedings, the definition and disposition of "new evidence," and the consequences of late submission of evidence.

Regulating the time limit for adducing evidence can greatly influence the efficiency of civil procedures and the judge's management of proceedings. In civil procedure, most cases originate in factual disputes. Under the contemporary litigation system, whether a party can submit evidential materials to court in time will have a great effect on the speed and progress of adjudication, and is highly relevant to whether the judge can close the case within the time limit for adjudication or not.[6] In contrast, delaying the submission of evidence can cause delays in litigation and harm the opposing party's procedural interests. Therefore, it is necessary to establish the time limit for adducing evidence.

Because submitting evidence is an essential and important right of the parties, after establishing the time period for adducing evidence, the parties can still apply for an extension, and the court will agree as long as they have justified reasons. In

[5] During the judge quota reform, many judges failed to obtain the quota because of many unfinished cases.

[6] This is the main reason why the Supreme People's Court establishes the time limit system for adducing evidence. The Supreme People's Court thinks that it is not balanced to have a time limit for the court on adjudication while having no time limit for the parties on adducing evidence. This flaw is observed in the legal system and is one of the main reasons why the judge cannot close the case within the time limit.

the case of late submission of evidence, the court shall order the party to provide an explanation. According to the civil procedure law, if the party refuses to explain or the party's explanation is not acceptable, the court may, depending on the circumstances, deem the evidence inadmissible or adopt the evidence but impose an admonition or a fine on the party.[7]

Article 65 of the Civil Procedure Law provides two options for the court on the disposition of the late submission of evidence without acceptable reasons. These two options provide opposite answers toward the admissibility of the late evidence, due to the fact that the law only authorizes the court to choose different options based on different circumstances, but fails to specify under what circumstances the first option or second option should be chosen. To help the judge correctly understand the law and unify the application of the law, the Supreme People's Court provides in the judicial interpretation that "Evidence provided by a party beyond the time limit deliberately or due to gross negligence shall be deemed inadmissible by a people's court. But the evidence related to the basic facts of the case shall be deemed admissible by the people's court, which shall impose an admonition or a fine in accordance with the provisions of Article 65 and paragraph 1, Article 115 of the civil procedure law."[8] Based on this regulation, even if the party submits the evidence beyond the time limit and even if such a late submission is made deliberately or due to gross negligence, as long as the evidence is related to the basic facts of the case, the court shall choose the second option.

The reason why the Supreme People's Court of China makes such regulation in judicial interpretation is that, on the one hand, the basic principle of the civil procedure law clearly provides that, "When trying civil cases, the people's courts must regard facts as the basis and regard law as the yardstick" (Article 7). Furthermore, judicial reform in Mainland China also requires the court to "push forward restrict judiciary, to insist on regarding facts as the basis and regard law as the yardstick, to ensure the fact-finding consistent with objective truth, to fit the case result with substantive fairness, and to fit the case handling process with procedural fairness."[9]

In practice, because of the court's assignment of the time limit for adducing evidence, the parties are restricted in the time of adducing evidence. Most parties are able to submit the evidential materials within the established time limit, which basically is for the purpose of accelerating litigation and avoiding litigation delays. There are also parties who may make late submissions without reasonable causes or even deliberately or due to gross negligence; in these cases, the parties will be subject to a monetary sanction by the court. Based on the different conditions of cases and

[7] See Article 65 of the Civil Procedure Law of the People's Republic of China.

[8] Paragraph 1, Article 102 of the Interpretation of the Supreme People's Court on the Application of the Civil Procedure Law of the People's Republic of China.

[9] See the Fourth Part, 'Ensuring Judicial Fairness and Enhancing Judicial Credibility' in the Decision of the Central Committee of the Communist Party of China on Major Issues Pertaining to Comprehensively Promoting the Rule of Law.

parties, some courts set the fine up to 1000 or 2000 yuan, while other courts may set the fine up to 50,000, 80,000, or even 100,000 yuan.[10]

The late submission of evidence can also cause unnecessary damages for the opposing party, forcing it to pay extra costs for transportation, accommodation, and lawyers. For the party bearing the extra costs, Chinese law allows him to make a claim for compensation. The implementation of such compensation rights not only protects the damaged party's interests, but also increases the costs of adducing evidence beyond the time limit and thus provides an incentive to avoid the late submission of evidence. In the case of expenses arising from the overdue provision of evidence, a people's court may be supportive.

If time limits for adjudication can be considered as a regulation for civil case management from the perspective of the court and judge, then time limits for adducing evidence can be considered as case management regulation from the perspective of the parties. Both systems complement and bring out the best in each other, together increasing litigation efficiency. These litigation systems make Mainland China's civil procedure highly efficient and quite successful in managing litigation delays.

Reference

Ren H (2017) Imposing inhibition onto the time period for adjudication. People's Court Newspaper, 30 July 2017 (in Chinese)

[10] In China, fine payment is a compulsory measure of civil procedure. According to Article 115 of the Civil Procedure Law, the amount of a fine on an individual shall not be more than RMB 100,000, and the amount of a fine on an entity shall not be less than RMB 50,000 but not be more than RMB 1 million. Therefore, for the parties who deliberately delay the proceeding through late submission of evidence, the court can fulfill the procedural fairness through heavy fee sanction.

Appendix A
Agenda of the Conference

On Judicial Management from Comparative Perspective

(8–10 November, 2017, Tianjin)

November 8, 2017 (Wednesday)

10:00–13:30 **Registration**

Opening Ceremony (14:00–15:00)

L. Cadiet and Y. Fu (eds.), *On Judicial Management from Comparative Perspective*, Contemporary Chinese Civil and Commercial Law,
https://doi.org/10.1007/978-981-19-8673-4

14:00–15:00	**Moderator**: Prof. Zhang Weiping, Chairman of China Civil Procedural Law Society, Distinguished Professor of Tianjin University **Speakers:** 1. Executive Vice-President Chen Jiping, China Law Society; Deputy Director-General, the Committee for Social and Legal Affairs of CPPCC 2. Prof. Loïc Cadiet, Chairman of International Association of Procedural Law, University Paris 1 Panthéon-Sorbonne, France 3. Prof. Shu Gequn, Executive Vice President of Tianjin University and Prof. Sun Youhai, Dean at Law School, Tianjin University 4. Head of Division Cheng Xinwen, No.1 Civil Adjudication Tribunal of the Supreme People's Court
15:00–15:30	**Tea Break**

Session 1: Introductory Reports (15:30–17:30)

15:30–15:35	**Moderator**: Prof. Eduardo Oteiza, Universidad Nacional de La Plata, Argentina
15:35–15:50	Prof. Li Hao, Nanjing Normal University, China, representing China
15:50–16:05	Prof. Hanki Sohn, Yonsei University, Korea, representing Asia
16:05–16:20	Prof. Margaret Woo, Northeastern University, USA, representing North America
16:20–16:35	Prof. Remco van Rhee, Maastricht University, Holland, representing Europe
16:35–16:50	Prof. Antonio do Passo Cabral, University of Rio de Janeiro State, Brazil, representing Latin America
16:50–17:30	**Discussion**

Gala Dinner (18:00–)

November 9, 2017 (Thursday)

Session 2: Case Management (9:00–11:30)

9:00–9:05	**Moderator**: Prof. Chen Gang, East China University of Political Science and Law & Guangzhou University, China
9:05–9:35	**Chinese Reporter**: Prof. Wang Fuhua, Shanghai University of Finance & Economics, China
9:35–10:10	**Discussion**
10:10–10:25	**Tea Break**
10:25–10:55	**Foreign Reporter**: Prof. John Sorabji, University College London, England
10:55–11:30	**Discussion**

Session 3: Court Management (14:00–17:00)

14:00–14:05	**Moderator**: Prof. Masahisa Deguchi, Ritsumeikan University, Japan
14:05–14:35	**Chinese Reporter**: Prof. Fu Yulin, Peking University, China
14:35–15:25	**Discussion**
15:25–15:40	**Tea Break**
15:40–16:10	**Foreign Reporter**: Prof. Emmanuel Jeuland, University Paris 1 Panthéon-Sorbonne, France
16:10–17:00	**Discussion**

18:30–21:00 **Meeting of IAPL Presidium and Council**

November 10, 2017 (Friday)

Session 4: Structure of Court System (9:00–11:30)

9:00–9:05	**Moderator**: Prof. Wu Yingzi, Nanjing University, China
9:05–9:35	**Chinese Reporter**: Assi. Prof. Peter Chan, City University of Hong Kong, China
9:35–10:10	**Discussion**
10:10–10:25	**Tea Break**
10:25–10:55	**Foreign Reporter**: Prof. Álvaro PÉREZ-RAGONE, North Catholic University, Antofagasta, Chile, sharing with Prof. Ramon García, Catholic University of Concepcion, Chile
10:55–11:30	**Discussion**

Session 5: Fact-Finding And Legal Reasoning (14:00–16:30)

14:00–14:05	**Moderator**: Prof. Margaret Woo, Northeastern University, USA
14:05–14:35	**Chinese Reporter:** Prof. Zhang Baosheng, China University of Political Science & Law, China
14:35–15:10	**Discussion**
15:10–15:25	**Tea Break**
15:25–15:55	**Foreign Reporter**: Prof. Dmitry Maleshin, Lomonosov Moscow State University, Russia (absent; alternated by Prof. Alan Uzelac, Zagreb University, Croatia)
15:55–16:30	**Discussion**

Closing Ceremony (16:30–17:00)

Moderator: Prof. Zhang Weiping, Chairman of China Civil Procedural Law Society

Speakers:

1. Prof. Sun Youhai, Dean at Law School, Tianjin University
2. Prof. Loïc Cadiet, Chairman of International Association of Procedural Law

Appendix B
Biography of National Reporters

Dr. Pablo Bravo Hurtado

He is Ph.D. Researcher at Maastricht University (The Netherlands). He did his LL.B. at University of Chile and the research sufficiency (Research master equivalent) at the Catholic University of Valparaíso, Chile. He also worked in the Chilean Ministry of Justice, in the consultant team for the reform of civil justice. From an academic point of view, he is interested in comparative civil procedure, sociology of law, and legal history.

Prof. Ramon Alexis Garcia Odgers

He is Professor of procedural law and Director of the post graduate programs in the Catholic University of Concepcion School of Law. His research areas are the judicial reforms, case management, civil procedure and evidence. He is a lawyer from the Pontificia Universidad Católica de Chile (1996), LLM from de Universidad del Desarrollo, and Doctorate at Pontificia Universidad Catolica de Valparáiso. He has been appointed as a visiting scholar in the Washington University in Saint Louis, Law School, Missouri, USA. 2005, and later in Leicester School Law, UK (2013).

Prof. Alan Uzelac

He is Professor of Civil Procedural Law at the Zagreb University, Faculty of Law, where he teaches Civil Procedure, Arbitration, ADR, Organization of Judiciary, and Protection of Human Rights in Europe. He holds degrees in law (LL.B., LL.M., LL.D.) and social sciences (M.A. (phil.), M.A. (literature)) from Zagreb University. He was Visiting Researcher and Scholar at a number of universities, including Harvard Law School (Fulbright grant), and universities of Vienna (Austria), Maastricht (the Netherlands), Oslo (Norway), Kazan (Russia), Uppsala (Sweden) and Pavia (Italy). His professional experience includes work in various Croatian courts, Croatian State Bar Exam, and internship at the Secretariat of the ICC International Court of Arbitration in Paris. As an international expert, he worked in the region

L. Cadiet and Y. Fu (eds.), *On Judicial Management from Comparative Perspective*, Contemporary Chinese Civil and Commercial Law,
https://doi.org/10.1007/978-981-19-8673-4

and Europe, assisting legal reforms and legal collaboration in Serbia, Bosnia and Herzegovina, Montenegro, Russia and Kosovo.

Dr. Wei Wang

She is Assistant Professor at the University of Macau, Faculty of Law. She received her law degree at the University of Macau and Ph.D. in Law at the China University of Political Science and Law. Prior to joining the University of Macau, Dr. Wang was a lawyer/corporate legal counsel, and currently teaches comparative civil procedure in Master of Law Program.

Prof. Leandro J. Giannini

He is Ph.D. and Chair Professor (Profesor Titular) of Procedural Law at the University of La Plata and full Professor and Lecturer on several post-graduate courses and conferences on Civil Procedure. Member of the Argentinean Association of Procedural Law, the Ibero-American Institute of Procedural Law and the International Association of Procedural Law. He is the author of many books, papers and articles regarding different aspects of civil justice and civil procedure.

Prof. Kinga Flaga-Gieruszyńska

She is Doctor Habilitatus of Juridical Science, Professor of the University of Szczecin, Head of the Department of Civil Procedure, President of the Presidium of the Court of Arbitration of West Pomerania in Szczecin, of counsel in Legal Office Mazurkiewicz Cieszynski Mazuro Attorneys and Legal Advisors Partnership Company, guardian of legal projects in the Consumer Federation, arbitrator in the Permanent Arbitrary Consumer Court of West Pomeranian Voivodship Inspectorate of Trade Inspection in Szczecin. Her main field of interest is civil proceedings, arbitration and mediation, bankruptcy law, and computerization of the system of justice.

Dr. Aleksandra Klich

She is Doctor of Juridical Science, Assistant Professor in the Department of Civil Procedure of the Faculty of Law and Administration at the University of Szczecin, attorney in Legal Office Mazurkiewicz Cieszynski Mazuro Attorneys and Legal Advisors Partnership Company, legal expert in the Consumer Federation, graduate of l'Université d'été du droit continental, Paris—Sorbonne, arbitrator in the Permanent Arbitrary Consumer Court of West Pomeranian Voivodship Inspectorate of Trade Inspection in Szczecin. Her main field of interest is civil proceedings, medical law, and computerization of the system of justice.

Prof. Yashomati Ghosh

She is an Associate Professor at the National Law School of India University, Bangalore from 2006. Her teaching area and specialization include Administrative Law, Legal Ethics, Law Poverty and Development, Law of Torts, Consumer Protection Laws and Digital Copyright Law. She was awarded the Shastri Indo–Canadian Fellowship for the year 2016–17 and the Fulbright-Nehru Doctoral and Professional

Research Fellowship for the year 2010–2011. She was also awarded doctoral fellowship at the Berkman Center for Internet and Society, Harvard University, Boston, as a Berkman Fellow. She was also an awardee of the SUN Scholarship by the Central European University and was invited to attend the program on Teaching Human Rights and Legal Ethics, Budapest (2009).

Prof. Marco de Benito

He is a full professor of law at IE University in Madrid. His areas of interest include international arbitration, comparative private and procedural law and legal history. He earned his Dr. iur. from Comillas Pontifical University in 2010. He spent the 2008–2009 academic year at Yale Law School. During his doctoral studies, he also spent several funded researches staying at the Max Planck Institute for Comparative and International Private Law in Hamburg. Since then, he has taught or spoken at universities such as Harvard, Bologna, Maastricht and other universities in Mexico, Guatemala, Peru, Argentina and China. He has practised international arbitration for over 15 years.

And since 2015, he is an appointed member of the Procedural Law Board of the Spanish Royal Academy of Jurisprudence and Legislation.

Prof. Michael Stürner

He (Dr. iur, Munich; M. Juris, Oxford) is Professor of Civil Law, Private International Law and Comparative Law at the University of Konstanz, Germany, since 2012. He also serves as a judge at the Higher Regional Court of Appeals (Oberlandesgericht) in Karlsruhe, Germany. From 2009 to 2012 he has held a chair of Civil Law, Private International Law and Comparative Law at Europa-Universität Viadrina Frankfurt (Oder), Germany. He has been appointed as a member of the Council of the International Association of Procedural Law (IAPL) and as a Fellow of the European Law Institute. In 2013, he has been a Visiting Scholar at the University of California at Berkeley, Boalt Hall School of Law. In 2016/17, he is a Fellow at the Institute for Advanced Study Konstanz. His main research interests lie in the fields of cross-border dispute resolution, comparative law, conflict of laws, and European private law.

Prof. Zagaynova Svetlana

She is Doctor of Law, professor of the Department of Civil Procedure of Ural State Law University (Yekaterinburg, Russia), Director of the Center for Mediation of Ural State Law University. She is a member of IAPL. She is also a member of Scientific Advisory Council of the Supreme Court of the Russian Federation. Her sphere of scientific interests is civil procedure and ADR (arbitration, mediation, negotiation and so on).

Ms. Vera Kudryavtseva

She is Researcher at the Department of Civil Procedure of the Ural State Law University. Her sphere of scientific interests is civil procedure and enforcement proceedings.

Mr. Jesús Ezurmendia

He has been faculty member, procedural law Lecturer and legal Researcher at University of Chile from 2014. He is Bachelor in Law University of Chile (2012, Summa cum Laude), and LLM in Litigation and Dispute Resolution at University College of London (2016, Distinction).

Prof. Mostefa Maouene

He is Professor of private law and criminal sciences, Professor-researcher, Chairman of the Scientific Committee of the Department of Law in Algeria. He is responsible for the LMD field of law and political science of the faculty of law and political sciences of the University Djilali Liabès–Sidi bel abbes–Algeria. He is also corresponding member in Algeria of the International Association of Procedural Law (IAPL).

Mr. Hugo Miguel da Luz dos Santos

He got his law degree at Coimbra Faculty of Law, branch legal-forensic science. He is post-graduate in Urbanism Law. And he had specialization course in legal-forensic science for the devoted to the exercise of the Public Prosecutors Office by the Centre for the Judicial Studies for 3 years and 6 months. He has been the Magistrate of the Public Prosecutor for ten years, having served in the courts in Beja, Portalegre, Seixal, Vila Franca do Campo, Praia da Vitória, Horta and Funchal (Madeira). His current court is Funchal, Madeira, Portugal. He is currently in sabbatical leave, conceded by the Portuguese Government. And he is focusing on academic research in Gaming Law, Criminal Law, and Civil Procedure Law of Macau.

Prof. Giovanni Priori

He received his law degree at Pontificia Universidad Católica del Perú, and his Master degree at Università degli Studi di Roma Tor Vergata. He is Principal Professor at Law Department of Pontificia Universidad Católica del Perú. He is also Director of Procedural Law Master at Pontificia Universidad Católica del Perú. In addition, he is President of Group to reform Procedural Civil Code in Perú.

Prof. Claudio Fuentes Maureira

He received his LLB and LLM at Diego Portales University, Chile. He is Master of the Science of Law (JSM), Stanford University and Doctor of the Science of Law Candidate, Stanford University. From 2006 to 2009, he is researcher at the OAS entity Justice Studies Center of the Americas (JSCA). From 2009 up to day, he has been Law Professor at the procedural law department at Diego Portales University, Santiago city, Chile. Currently he teaches Introduction to civil procedure, criminal procedure and trial skills. His main areas of research include procedural reforms in Chile (mainly criminal and family courts reform and the failed civil procedure reform), evidence law, class action and legal culture in these contexts.

Prof. Walter H. Rechberger

He is Professor emeritus at the Vienna University Faculty of Law and Head of the Research Institute of Legal Development. He held the position of Dean, of the Head of the Department of Civil Procedure Law (Institut für Zivilverfahrensrecht) and member of the Council of the International Association of Procedural Law (IAPL) for many years. He received his J.D. from Vienna University and holds degrees of an Honorary Doctor of the University of Pècs, Hungary and of the University of Athens, Greece. In 1989, he was a Visiting Professor at the Kansas University School of Law, Lawrence, US. From 1992 to 2007, he was a member of the Faculty of European Studies, Department of European Integration, at Danube University Krems. He is also a member of several boards, such as the Vienna International Arbitral Center (VIAC) and the Institute for Danube Region and Central Europe (IDM).

Dr. Bartosz Karolczyk

He is a legal scholar and a practicing attorney at the law firm Domanski Zakrzewski Palinka in Warsaw, Poland. He is a graduate of the George Washington University Law School and has been a Visiting Scholar at the UC Berkeley School of Law. He specializes in civil litigation, representing clients in a wide range of civil and commercial disputes before common and arbitration courts. In addition, he teaches civil procedure at the Kozmiński University.

Mr. Ubaid-Ur Rehman

He is a practising barrister in Hong Kong. He has degrees from Duke University, University of London and the University of Hong Kong. He commenced his practice at Alexandra Chambers and has been a tenant there since 2004. He has a mixed practice with particular focus on personal injury litigation, professional negligence, contract and commercial law, insurance law and probate matters. He qualified as a CEDR Accredited Mediator in 2013. He is also a Teaching Consultant at the School of Law of the City University of Hong Kong and has been teaching there since 2010. He is the course leader of the LLB Civil Procedure course and the co-course leader of the Personal Injuries elective on the PCLL programme. He also teaches Equity and Trusts, Civil Litigation, Criminal Litigation and Advocacy.

Prof. Elisabetta Silvestri

She is Associate Professor of Italian Civil Procedure and Comparative Civil Procedure; Scientific Director of the postgraduate program on Mediation and ADR, Department of Law, University of Pavia. She graduated from the University of Pavia and received a LL.M. degree from Cornell Law School. She is co-director of the annual seminar 'Public and Private Justice', Inter-University Centre, Dubrovnik, Croatia, and member of the Scientific Advisory Board of Almo Collegio Borromeo, Pavia. She is also a member of the European Law Institute and the International Association of Procedural Law. Currently she is a member of one of the Working Groups established by the European Law Institute and UNIDROIT for the development of the project 'From Transnational Principles to European Rules of Civil Procedure'.

Prof. Masood Ahmed

He is Associate Professor in Civil Dispute Resolution at the University of Leicester. His research and teaching interests focus on civil justice/procedure and alternative dispute resolution. He is the Alternative Dispute Resolution Editor for the Civil Justice Quarterly and the founder and convenor of the Civil Procedure and ADR stream for the Socio-Legal Studies Association Conference. He is also a member of the Civil Procedure Rule Committee.

Prof. Magne Strandberg

He is Professor at the Faculty of Law, University of Bergen. His main field of interests is civil procedure law and tort law. Currently, he is the leader of the research group for civil procedure at the faculty, and he is a member of the ELI/UNIDROIT working group on the obligations of parties and lawyers.